An Introduction to Cognitive Psychology

An Introduction to Cognitive Psychology: Processes and disorders is a comprehensive textbook for undergraduate students. Uniquely, it provides in a single volume chapters on both normal cognitive function and related clinical disorders. Especially written to cover all levels of ability, it has sufficient depth and recent research to appeal to the most able students while the clear and accessible text, written by experienced teachers, will help students who find the material difficult. It will appeal to any student on an undergraduate psychology degree course as well as to medical students and those studying in related clinical professions such as nursing.

Key features:

- Chapters on all the major areas of normal cognitive psychology (perception, memory, language and thinking) are paired with their corresponding disorders of cognition (agnosia, amnesia, aphasia and thought disorder)
- Clearly signposted: chapter topics are clearly separated and easily located
- Specially designed textbook features include chapter summaries, annotated further ~~reading and a glossary of key terms~~
- Autho   st
  up-to-

David Groo

Hazel Dewa
Lecturers i   r
Lecturer in   a

An Introduction to Cognitive Psychology

■ Processes and disorders

David Groome

with Hazel Dewart, Anthony Esgate,
Kevin Gurney, Richard Kemp and
Nicola Towell

London and New York

First published 1999
Psychology Press Ltd, Publishers
A member of the Taylor & Francis group
27 Church Road
Hove
East Sussex, BN3 2FA
UK

Reprinted 1999

Typeset in Century Old Style by Keystroke,
Jacandra Lodge, Wolverhampton
Printed and bound in Great Britain by
TJ International Ltd, Padstow, Cornwall

British Library Cataloguing in Publication Data
A catalogue record for this book is available
from the British Library

*Library of Congress Cataloging in Publication
Data*
Groome, David, 1946–
    An introduction to cognitive psychology :
    processes and disorders / David Groome ;
    with Hazel Dewart
    ... [et al.].
    Includes bibliographic references and
    index.
    1.   Cognitive psychology.
    2.   Cognitive disorders. I. Dewart, Hazel.
    II. Title.
    BF201.G76 1999
    153–dc21   98–31146

ISBN 0–86377–639-6 (hbk)
ISBN 0–86377–640-X (pbk)

Contents

6 Thinking

7 Disorders of thinking

CONTENTS

Figures

FIGURES

Sources for figures are given below the captions on the pages where they appear in the book. All reasonable efforts have been made to contact copyright holders but in some cases this was not possible. Any omissions brought to the attention of Routledge will be remedied in future editions.

About the authors

The authors who have contributed to this book are all lecturers in the Psychology Department of the University of Westminster, except for Kevin Gurney who lectures at the University of Sheffield. The authorship of individual chapters was as follows:

Chapter 1 : David Groome
Chapter 2 : Anthony Esgate
Chapter 3 : Richard Kemp
Chapter 4 : David Groome
Chapter 5 : David Groome
Chapter 6 : Nicola Towell
Chapter 7 : Nicola Towell
Chapter 8 : Hazel Dewart
Chapter 9 : Hazel Dewart
Chapter 10 : Kevin Gurney

Preface

This book is aimed primarily at undergraduate students of psychology and other related disciplines, who should find sufficient depth and range of content to carry them right through to the completion of their degree courses. Whilst this inevitably means that much of the content is pitched at a fairly advanced level, the opening chapter has been deliberately written for the absolute beginner, offering a very simple introduction to the principles, methods and terminology referred to in the subsequent chapters.

We wrote this book because we felt that it filled an important gap. As far as we know it is the first textbook to cover all of the main aspects of cognitive psychology and all of their associated disorders too. Although there are plenty of books about normal cognition, and a few books about cognitive disorders, nobody seems to have incorporated a full account of both areas in a single text. We feel that this combined approach offers a number of advantages over previous texts. In the first place, combining normal and abnormal cognition in one book makes it possible to take an integrated approach to these two related fields. References can be made directly between the normal and abnormal chapters, and theories which are introduced in the normal chapters can be reconsidered later from a clinical perspective. Another advantage of a combined textbook is that students can use the same text for several different courses of study, offering the benefits of continuity as well as saving the cost of buying extra books.

In order to keep the layout of the book as clear and logical as possible, we decided to put the chapters into pairs, so that for example the chapter on 'Memory' is followed by a chapter on 'Disorders of Memory', and so on. We have deliberately chosen to use very simple chapter titles, such as 'Memory' and 'Language', which clearly indicate what each chapter contains. This may seem an obvious strategy, but if you glance through a few other cognitive texts you will find some remarkably complicated and obscure chapter titles, which make little sense to the beginner.

Previous textbooks about cognitive disorders (or 'cognitive neuropsychology' as it is also known) have usually included a great deal of detail about the biology of the brain and nervous system, often making up more than half of the book. However, a detailed knowledge of brain anatomy is not needed by most psychology students, so we decided to concentrate instead on the psychological aspects of cognitive disorders rather than the anatomical details.

Writing a textbook is a daunting task, and there are many problems and pitfalls along the way. To give but one example, in an earlier draft of our manuscript page 19 read as follows:

5lb potatoes
6 eggs
jar of coffee
teabags

Whilst some of you may feel that this makes for a more interesting read than the version of page 19 which replaced it, I mention it here as a warning to the unwary. The moral is that you should never allow your shopping list to get into the print queue. I hope that all such errors and intrusions have now been eliminated, though my doubts are raised by the fact that my food cupboard at home is looking suspiciously empty.

We would like to thank the following people for their helpful advice and comments on earlier drafts of this book: Philip Seymour (University of Dundee); David Jones (Cheltenham and Gloucester College of Higher Education); Colin Hamilton (University of Northumbria at Newcastle); Thomas Heffernan (University of Northumbria at Newcastle); Alan Richardson-Klavehn (University of Westminster).

I would like to conclude by offering my sincere thanks to my co-authors, and to the people at Routledge (especially Moira Taylor, Viv Ward and Fintan Power), who have worked miracles to turn our rough manuscript into a textbook. We hope that you enjoy reading it.

David Groome

Chapter 1

Introduction to cognitive psychology

1.1 Cognitive processes

A definition of cognitive psychology

Cognitive psychology has been defined as the psychology of understanding and knowing. It has also been described as the study of mental processes. However, these are rather vague terms, and whilst they do provide an indication of what cognition involves, they leave us asking exactly what is meant by 'knowing', 'understanding', and 'mental processes'. A more precise definition of cognitive psychology is that it is the study of the way in which the brain processes information. It concerns the way we take in information from the outside world, how we make sense of that information, and what use we make of it. Cognition is thus a rather broad umbrella term which includes many component processes, which partly explains why psychologists have found it difficult to come up with a simple and unified definition of cognitive psychology. Clearly, cognition involves various different kinds of information processing which occur at different stages.

Stages of cognitive processing

The main stages of cognitive processing are shown in Figure 1.1, where they are presented in the sequential order in which they would typically be applied to a new piece of sensory input.

Information taken in by the sense organs goes through an initial stage of perception, which involves the analysis of its content. Even at this early stage of processing, the brain is already extracting meaning from the input in an effort to make sense of the information it contains. The process of perception will often lead to the making of some kind of record of the input received, and this is the process we call learning and memory storage. Once a memory has been created for some item of information it can be retained for later use, to assist the individual in some other setting. This will normally require the retrieval of the information. Retrieval is sometimes carried out for its own sake, merely to access some information stored in the past. For example, if you were asked what you did this morning, you might simply attempt to retrieve that information without making any more use of it. On the other hand, we sometimes retrieve information to provide the basis for further mental activities. Retrieval is often used as a part of the thought process, to assist in dealing with some new situation or problem. Sometimes this involves the rearrangement and manipulation of stored information, in order to make it fit in

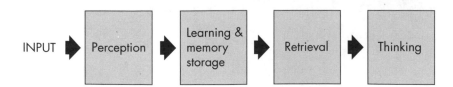

Figure 1.1 The main sequential stages of cognitive processing

with some new perceptual input. Thought is thus rather more than just retrieval of old memories. Indeed, all the cognitive processes shown in Figure 1.1 are in reality a good deal more complex and interactive than this simple diagram implies.

One major limitation of Figure 1.1 is that it suggests that the various stages of cognitive processing are clearly distinct from one another, each one in its own box. This is a drastic oversimplification, and it would be more accurate to show the different stages as merging and overlapping with one another. For example, it is impossible to establish in a clear way the exact point at which perception ceases and memory storage begins, because the process of perception develops into learning and memory storage. A memory is probably best regarded as the trace left behind by the perceptual analysis of the sensory input, and thus in a sense is continuous with the perceptual process. In fact all the stages of cognition shown in the diagram extensively overlap one another, but a diagram which attempted to do full justice to these complex interactions would be far too confusing, and in any case many of the interactions would be speculative.

Figure 1.1 should therefore be regarded as a much simplified representation of the general sequential order of the cognitive processes which typically occur, but it might be better to see the diagram as representing a continuous flow of information from the input stage through to the output stage, undergoing different forms of processing along the way.

Approaches to the study of cognition

There have been three main approaches to the study of cognitive psychology (see Figure 1.2), each of which has made a valuable contribution. In the first place there is the approach known as **experimental psychology**, which involves the use of psychological experiments on human subjects to investigate the ways in which they perceive, learn, remember or think. Usually these experiments test hypotheses and predictions deriving from particular theories and models of information processing.

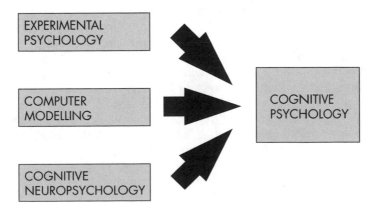

Figure 1.2 The three main methods of studying cognitive psychology

A second approach to cognitive psychology is the use of **computer modelling** of cognitive processes. Typically this approach involves the simulation of certain aspects of human cognitive function by writing computer programs, in order to test out models of possible brain function. This approach is sometimes referred to as cognitive science.

The third approach is known as **cognitive neuropsychology**, which is concerned with the activities of the human brain during cognitive processing. Sometimes this approach has involved the use of brain scanning equipment and recordings of neural activity. However, the most instructive method of studying brain function has been the observation and testing of brain-damaged patients. We can discover a great deal about the working of the normal brain by studying the types of cognitive impairment which result from lesions (i.e. damage) in certain regions of the brain. Brain damage can impair information processing by disrupting one or more stages of cognition, or perhaps by breaking the links between stages.

These three approaches to the information processing activities of the brain began as separate disciplines, but in recent years they have gradually begun to merge, as their supporters have discovered an increasing degree of overlap which has generated a new level of understanding.

However, the approaches of experimental psychology, cognitive neuro-psychology and computer modelling continue to comprise the three main strands of cognitive psychology, and they therefore provide the main subject matter of this book.

The remaining sections of this chapter will examine these three main approaches to cognitive psychology, starting with experimental psychology (Section 1.2), then computer modelling (Section 1.3), and finally cognitive neuro-psychology (Section 1.4). Subsequent chapters of the book will continue to apply the same three approaches in a more detailed study of each of the main areas of cognitive psychology.

1.2 Experimental psychology

The first cognitive psychologists

The scientific study of psychology began towards the end of the nineteenth century. In 1879 the first psychology laboratory was set up by Wilhelm Wundt at Leipzig. Wundt's research was mainly concerned with perception, including some of the earliest studies of visual illusions. In 1885 Hermann Ebbinghaus published the first experimental research on memory, and many subsequent researchers were to adopt his methods over the years that followed. Perhaps the most lasting work of this early period was a remarkable book written by William James in 1890, entitled *Principles of Psychology*. In this book James proposed a number of theories which still remain acceptable to modern cognitive psychologists, including (to give just one example) a theory distinguishing between short-term working memory and long-term storage memory.

The rise and fall of behaviourism

There was little progress in cognitive psychology in the early years due to the growing influence of **behaviourism**, an approach which constrained psychologists to the investigation of externally observable behaviour. The behaviourist position was clearly stated by Watson (1913), who maintained that psychologists should consider only observable variables such as the stimulus presented to the organism and any consequent response to that stimulus. He argued that they should not concern themselves with processes that they could not observe in a scientific manner, such as thought and conscious experience. The behaviourists were essentially trying to establish psychology as a true science, comparable in status with other sciences such as physics or chemistry. This was perhaps a worthy aim, but it had unfortunate consequences for the study of psychology for the next fifty years, as it had the effect of restricting experimental psychology mainly to the recording of externally observable responses, often of a rather trivial nature. Indeed, some behaviourists were so keen to eliminate inner mental processes from their studies that they actually preferred to work on rats rather than on human subjects. A human being brings a whole lifetime of personal experience to the laboratory, which cannot be controlled or observed by the experimenter. A rat presents rather fewer of these unknown and uncontrolled variables, especially if it has spent its whole life in the laboratory living in standardised conditions. A good example of the behaviourist approach is the classic work carried out on learning by B.F. Skinner (1938), who trained rats to press a lever in order to obtain a food pellet as a reward (or 'reinforcement').

Despite these restrictions on mainstream psychological research, some psychologists began to realise that a proper understanding of human cognition could only be achieved by investigating the inner mental processes which the behaviourists were so determined to eliminate from their studies. Among the first of these pioneers were the **Gestalt psychologists** in Germany, and the British psychologist Frederick Bartlett, and they helped to lay the foundations of modern cognitive psychology.

Gestalt and schema theories

It is very easy to demonstrate the importance of inner mental processes in human cognition. For example, a glance at Figure 1.3 will evoke the same clear response in almost any observer. It is a human face. However, a more objective analysis of the components of the figure reveals that it actually consists of a circle and two straight lines. There is really no 'face' as such in the figure itself. If you see a face in this simple figure, then it was you, the observer, who ADDED the face from your own store of knowledge.

The idea that we contribute something to our perceptual input from our own knowledge store was actually proposed by a number of early theorists, notably the Gestalt group (Gestalt is German for 'shape' or 'form'). They suggested that we add something to what we perceive, so that the perception of a whole object will therefore be something more than just the sum of its component parts

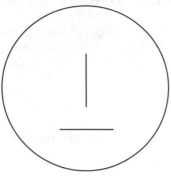

Figure 1.3 A shape recognised by most observers

(Wertheimer, 1912, Kohler, 1925). They argued that the perception of a figure depended on its 'pragnanz', which favoured the selection of the simplest and best interpretation available (Koffka, 1935). These theories were perhaps rather vague, but they did at least represent an attempt to explain the perception of complex figures such as faces. The behaviourist approach, which refused to consider any influence other than the stimulus itself, could not offer any explanation at all for such phenomena.

The **schema** theory proposed by Bartlett (1932) was another early attempt to provide a plausible explanation for our ability to make sense of perceptual input. The schema theory proposes that all new perceptual input is analysed by comparing it with items which are already in our memory store, such as shapes and sounds which are familiar from past experience. These items are referred to as 'schemas', and they include a huge variety of sensory patterns and concepts. Figure 1.4 illustrates the process of selection of an appropriate schema to match the incoming stimulus (NB: This is purely diagrammatic. In reality there are probably millions of schemas available, but there was not enough space to draw the rest of them).

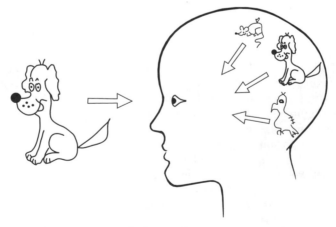

Figure 1.4 The generation of schemas for comparison with new input

The schema theory has some interesting implications, because it suggests that our perception and subsequent memory of an input may be changed and distorted to fit our existing schemas. It also suggests that we make sense of our perceptual input in terms of our knowledge and past experience, which will differ from person to person. Different people will therefore perceive the same input in different ways, depending on their own unique backlog of experience. Both of these phenomena were demonstrated by Bartlett's experiments (see Chapter 4 for more details), so the schema theory can be seen to have considerable explanatory value.

The schema approach has much in common with the old saying that 'beauty lies in the eye of the beholder'. Perhaps we could adapt that saying to fit the more general requirements of schema theory by suggesting that 'perception lies in the eye (and brain) of the perceiver'. As a summary of schema theory this is probably an improvement, but I would concede that it possibly lacks the poetry of the original.

Schema and Gestalt theory had a major influence on the development of cognitive psychology, by emphasising the role played in cognition by inner mental processes and stored knowledge, rather than considering only the stimulus.

1.3 Computer models of information processing

The computer analogy

A major shift towards the cognitive approach began in the 1950s, when the introduction of the electronic computer provided a new source of inspiration for cognitive psychologists. Computer systems offered some completely new ideas about information processing, providing an instructive analogy of possible brain mechanisms. Furthermore, computers could be used as a 'test-bed' for modelling possible human brain functions, not necessarily duplicating the exact neural mechanisms involved, but none the less providing a means of testing the feasibility of the processing system.

It was Neisser (1967) who first gathered together these computer-derived concepts and applied them to human cognition, using the computer metaphor to bring a new legitimacy to the cognitive approach.

Computer modelling of brain function

Selfridge and Neisser (1960) devised a computer program which could identify simple visual patterns and shapes, by applying a series of **feature detectors** which were tuned to distinguish certain specific components of the stimulus such as vertical or horizontal lines. This raised the possibility that human perception could conceivably involve similar feature-detecting systems. This approach paved the way towards further theories of perception and pattern recognition based on computer models, notably those of Marr (1982) and McClelland and Rumelhart (1986).

Newell *et al.* (1958) developed computer programs which were able to solve simple problems, suggesting a possible comparison with human problem-solving and thought. More recently, programs have been developed which can tackle far more complex problems, such as playing a game of chess.

In recent years the computer has not only provided a source of ideas and inspiration for theories which attempt to explain information processing in the human brain, but computers have also provided a means of testing the feasibility of such theories in a direct way. By separating out the various component stages of a cognitive process, it is possible to devise a sequential flow chart which can be written as a computer program and actually put to the test, to see whether it can process information as the brain would. Of course such experiments cannot prove that the programs and mechanisms operating within the computer are similar to the actual mechanisms which occur in the brain, but they can at least establish the basic feasibility of a processing sequence.

The limited-capacity processor model

Broadbent (1958) carried out experiments on divided attention, which showed that people have difficulty in attending to two separate inputs at the same time. Broadbent analysed his findings in terms of a sequence of processing stages which could be represented as a series of stages in a flow chart. Certain crucial stages were identified which acted as a 'bottleneck' to information flow, because of their limited processing capacity (see Figure 1.5). This was an approach to information processing which owed its inspiration to computing and telecommunications technology. There is a clear parallel between the human brain faced with a large array of incoming information and a telephone exchange dealing with a large number of incoming calls, or alternatively a computer whose input has exceeded its processing capacity. In each case many inputs are competing with one another for limited processing resources, and the inputs must be prioritised and selectively processed if an information overload is to be avoided. Broadbent referred to this process as 'selective attention', and his theoretical model of the 'limited capacity processor' provided cognitive psychology with an important new concept.

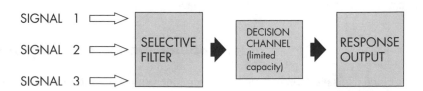

Figure 1.5 A flow chart based on the selective attention model of Broadbent (1958)

These studies will be considered in more detail later in the book (Chapter 2), but for the moment they are of interest for their role in the early development of cognitive psychology.

1.4 Cognitive neuropsychology

The structure and function of the brain

Neuropsychology is concerned with the relationship between brain function and cognition. It is now accepted as an important component of cognitive psychology, since it has become clear that we can learn a great deal about cognitive processes by studying the neural processes underlying them.

This is not a textbook of neurology, so it would not be appropriate here to deal with brain anatomy and function in depth. However, there will be references throughout this book to various regions of the brain, so there is a need for a very basic working map of the brain. Figure 1.6 presents a side view of the human brain, showing the position of its main structures.

The outer shell of the brain is known as the cerebral cortex, and it is responsible for most of the higher cognitive processes. The various lobes of the cortex are extensively interconnected, so that a single cognitive process may involve many different cortical areas. However, the brain is to some extent 'modular' in that certain brain areas do perform specific functions. We know this largely from the study of brain lesions, since damage to a certain part of the brain can often cause quite specific impairments. In recent years the introduction of brain scanning equipment has provided an additional source of knowledge to supplement the findings of brain lesion studies.

Taking a general overview of the whole brain, it has been established that the left and right hemispheres have particular specialisations. In right-handed people the left hemisphere of the brain is normally dominant (the nerves from the brain cross over to control the opposite side of the body), and the left hemisphere also tends to be particularly involved with language and speech. The right hemisphere seems to be more concerned with the processing of non-verbal input, such as the

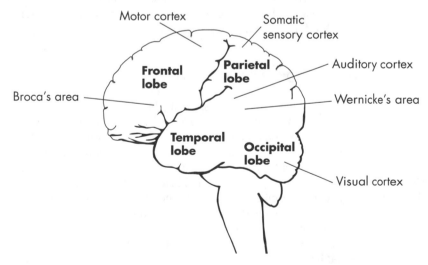

Figure 1.6 A side view of the human brain

perception of patterns or faces. These functions may be reversed in left-handed people, though most have left hemisphere specialisation for language. In some left-handed people, however, the cerebral hemispheres may be relatively un-specialised.

The frontal lobes include the motor region of the cortex, which controls movement. Associated with the motor region is **Broca's area**, which controls speech production and is normally in the left hemisphere of the brain (Broca, 1861). Other parts of the frontal lobes seem to have less specific functions, but the frontal cortex does seem to be involved in the **central executive** system which controls the making of conscious decisions and which may control the override of **automatic processing** (Parkin, 1997). Automatic and conscious processing will be discussed further in Section 1.5.

The temporal lobes are so called because they lie beneath the temples, and they are known to be particularly concerned with memory. Temporal lobe lesions are often associated with severe amnesia (Milner, 1966). The temporal lobes also include the main auditory area of the cortex, and a language centre known as **Wernicke's area** (again usually in the left hemisphere), which is particularly concerned with interpreting the meaningful content of speech (Wernicke, 1874).

The parietal lobes contain the somatic sensory cortex, which receives tactile input from the skin as well as feedback from the muscles and internal organs. This region is also important in the perception of pain, and other parts of the parietal lobes may be involved in some aspects of short-term memory.

The occipital lobes are mainly concerned with the processing of visual input. Damage to the occipital lobes may severely impair visual perception, though even in cases of functional blindness there often remains some underlying ability to detect visual input at an unconscious level. For example, the individual may be able to avoid an object such as a tree, despite having no conscious awareness of seeing a tree. This phenomenon is known as **blindsight** (Weiskrantz, 1986), and it suggests that processing of input may begin at a sub-cortical level, but may not reach conscious awareness until cortical processing has taken place. Blindsight is discussed further in Chapters 2 and 3.

The effects of brain damage on cognition

In practice, the most effective way of investigating brain function has been the study of cognitive impairment in those who have suffered brain damage of some kind. Brain lesions (i.e. areas of damage) may originate from a variety of different causes, such as accidental injuries, strokes and tumours. Studying the effects of brain damage is not a particularly new idea. As long ago as 1861, Paul Broca described a patient who had suffered damage to his left frontal cortex, and who had lost the power of speech as a consequence. The condition Broca described has come to be known as Broca's aphasia (aphasia means an impairment of speech), and unlike some other aphasias it is characterised by an impairment in speech production rather than speech perception. Broca's observations provided the first clear evidence that (at least for most right-handed people) speech production was controlled by the left hemisphere of the brain, and more specifically the left frontal cortex. Brain lesion studies of this kind provided valuable information about the location of certain functions in the brain, but not a great deal about the cognitive processes involved. Over the years many lesion studies have been reported, and more sophisticated techniques have been developed which have made it possible to investigate specific components of cognitive function, so that neuropsychology has now begun to make a vital contribution to cognitive research. For example, Milner (1966) reported the results of a series of memory tests on a patient called HM, who had suffered extensive lesions to the temporal lobes of both brain hemispheres as a result of brain surgery. Tragically, the surgeon's knife had robbed HM of his memory. However, certain memory functions remained intact, for HM was able to retain information for a few seconds despite the fact that he had virtually no ability to hold anything in his memory for longer than that. From these observations it was deduced that HM's lesion had caused severe impairment in his ability to store items in **long-term memory (LTM)**, but had caused no apparent impairment of **short-term memory (STM)**. This finding suggests a degree of independence or a 'dissociation' between STM and LTM. An interesting observation was made in a later study by Warrington and Shallice (1969), whose patient KF suffered an impairment of STM but with an intact LTM. This is an exact reversal of the pattern of impairment found in HM. It has thus been shown that either STM or LTM can be separately impaired while the other remains intact. This is known as a **double dissociation**, and it provides particularly convincing evidence for the view that short-term and long-term memory probably involve separate storage mechanisms. Later in this book there will be many references to dissociations of various kinds, but where a double dissociation can be demonstrated this is regarded as a particularly convincing argument for the independence of two functions.

By studying the effects of brain lesions on cognition it has been possible to find out a great deal about the way in which the normal brain works. At the same time, clinical neuropsychologists have drawn heavily on the findings of normal cognitive psychology, so there is a valuable two-way interaction between the normal and clinical fields of study.

The study of brain and cognition obviously overlap and interface with one another, and the relationship between the two fields is growing stronger as our knowledge of them both increases. A deliberate attempt has been made in this book to bring normal cognitive psychology and neuropsychology together, to take full advantage of this relationship.

Information storage in the brain

In order to operate as an information processing system, the brain must obviously have some way of representing information for both processing and storage purposes. Information clearly must be encoded in some representational or symbolic form, which may bear no direct resemblance to the material being encoded. Consider, for example, how music may be encoded and stored as electro-magnetic fields on a tape, as grooves on a vinyl disc, or even as notes written on a piece of paper. It does not matter what form of storage is used, so long as you have the equipment to encode and decode the information. There have been many

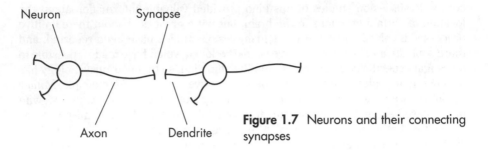

Neuron   Synapse

Axon   Dendrite

Figure 1.7 Neurons and their connecting synapses

theories about the way this might be done by the brain, including some early suggestions that information could be stored in some chemical form (Ungar *et al.*, 1968). However, the most plausible explanation currently available for the neural basis of information storage is the **cell assembly** theory proposed by Donald Hebb (1949). Hebb's theory is based on the assumption that if two adjacent neurons (i.e. nerve cells) are fired off simultaneously, they will tend to become connected to one another (see Figure 1.7).

The entire nervous system, including the brain, is composed of millions of neurons, which can activate one another by transmitting chemical substances called **neurotransmitters** across the gap separating them, which is known as the **synapse**. All forms of neural activity, including perception, speech, or even thought, work by transmitting a signal along a series of neurons. These cognitive processes are therefore dependent on getting a signal across the synapse to the next neuron. The basis of Hebb's theory is that a synapse which has been frequently crossed in the past will be more easily crossed by future signals. Put another way, the synaptic resistance decreases as a result of frequent synaptic activation. The end result is that a path is worn through the nervous system, much as you would wear a path through a field of corn by repeatedly walking through it. In both cases, a path is left behind which can be more easily crossed in future. Hebb suggested that in this way it was possible to build up a network of interconnected neurons which he called a 'cell assembly', which could represent a

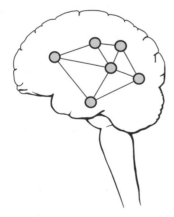

Figure 1.8 A cell assembly

particular pattern of input. Figure 1.8 shows a diagrammatic representation of such a cell assembly, though in practice there would probably be thousands of neurons making up a single cell assembly.

Hebb argued that a cell assembly such as this could come to represent a particular stimulus, such as an object or a face. If the stimulus had caused this particular group of neurons to fire simultaneously, then the neurons would become connected to one another more and more strongly with repeated exposure to the stimulus. Eventually the cell assembly would become a permanent structure, readily activated by any similar stimulation in the future.

Hebb's theory has considerable explanatory value. In the first place it can explain how thoughts and memories may come to be associated with one another in memory. If two cell assemblies are activated simultaneously then some of the neurons in one assembly are likely to become connected to neurons in the other assembly, so that in future the activation of either one will activate the other.

Hebb's theory can also explain the different types of memory storage which are thought to occur. Hebb speculated that the temporary activation of a cell assembly by active neural firing could be the mechanism of short-term memory, which is known to be transient and fragile. However, after repeated firing the synaptic connections between the neurons in the assembly eventually become permanent, and this provides the basis of long-term memory storage. The creation of a lasting memory is thus seen as depending upon permanent changes to the synapse.

When Donald Hebb first proposed this theory in 1949, it was still largely speculative. However, since that time a great deal of evidence has been gathered to confirm that the synapse does indeed change as a result of frequent firing of the neuron. Perhaps the most convincing evidence is the discovery that when electrical stimulation is applied to living tissue taken from the brain of a rat, the neurons do actually change in a lasting way, with their threshold of firing becoming much lower so they can be more easily activated by subsequent stimuli (Bliss and Lomo, 1973; Lynch, 1986). This phenomenon is known as **long-term potentiation (LTP)**. It has also been found that rats reared in a stimulating and enriched environment, with plenty of sensory input, develop more synaptic connections in their brains than rats reared in an impoverished environment where there is little to stimulate them (Greenough, 1987; Lisman and Harris, 1993).

In view of the growing amount of evidence that the synapse is changed by repeated firing, there is now widespread agreement that memory storage almost certainly depends upon synaptic change and the consequent formation of cell assemblies of some kind, possibly corresponding to the feature-detecting hierarchies suggested by Neisser (1967) and the more recent PDP models of Mclelland and Rumelhart (1986).

1.5 Minds, brains and computers

The brain as an information processing device

The modern approach to cognitive psychology has developed from the interaction between experimental psychology, computer modelling and neuropsychology, and these three strands were first brought together in Ulric Neisser's (1967) book *Cognitive Psychology*. This book was a major turning point in psychology, and its title was to become synonymous with the entire field of study. Subsequent cognitive psychologists have tended to regard the brain as a form of information processing device, and theories of brain function have borrowed heavily from concepts derived from the processing of information by computer. This has led to a number of concepts and dichotomies which are frequently utilised in models of brain function, the most important of which are explained below.

Top-down and bottom-up processing

Cognitive psychologists have come to distinguish between two main types of input processing, known as **top-down** and **bottom-up** processing. They differ most obviously in that the flow of information through the nervous system travels in opposite directions, as shown in Figure 1.9.

Bottom-up theories of cognition make the assumption that the stimuli impinging on the sense organs are primarily responsible for setting off some appropriate form of processing. It is referred to as 'bottom-up' processing because it is initiated by stimulation at the 'bottom end' of the nervous system (i.e. the sense organs) which then progresses up towards the higher cortical areas. Bottom-up processing is also referred to as 'stimulus-driven' or 'data-driven' processing, since the type of processing carried out is largely determined by the nature of the incoming stimulus. Such theories have been popular for a long time, and they continue to hold considerable explanatory value (Gibson, 1979). However, bottom-up theories have difficulty explaining the perception of complex stimuli, since they

Figure 1.9 Top-down and bottom-up processing

assume that the stimulus strikes an entirely passive nervous system. Most modern theorists therefore assume that there is a second type of processing based on the generation of schemas acquired from past experience, which are sent down the nervous system for comparison with the incoming stimulus, as proposed by Bartlett (1932). This type of processing is referred to as 'top-down', 'schema-driven' or 'concept-driven' processing.

Although there have been disputes in the past about the relative importance of 'top-down' and 'bottom-up' processing, Neisser (1967, 1976) suggests that both types of processing probably play a part in the analysis of perceptual input and that in most cases information processing will involve a combination of the two. We can thus think of input processing in terms of stimulus information coming up the system, where it meets and interacts with schemas coming down in the opposite direction.

Automatic and controlled processing

Schneider and Shiffrin (1977) made a distinction between **controlled** cognitive processes, which are carried out consciously and intentionally, and **automatic** cognitive processes, which are not under conscious control. They suggested that because controlled processes require conscious attention they are subject to limitations in processing capacity, whereas automatic processes do not require attention and are not subject to such processing limits. Automatic processing will therefore take place far more rapidly than controlled processing, and will be relatively unaffected by the distraction of a second task taking up the attention. Schneider and Shiffrin suggested that cognitive processes become automatic as a result of frequent practice, as, for example, the skills involved in driving a car, playing the piano, or reading words from a page. However, we have the ability to override these automatic sequences when we need to, for example, when we come across an unusual traffic situation while driving. For a simple demonstration of automatic processing in a cognitive task, try looking at the words in Figure 1.10, taking care *not* to read them.

You will undoubtedly have found it impossible to obey the instruction not to read the message in Figure 1.10. Reading is a largely automatic process (at least for practised readers) and you will therefore find that if you attend to the message you cannot prevent yourself from reading it. The automatic processing of words was

DO NOT READ THIS MESSAGE

Figure 1.10   A demonstration of automatic processing

first demonstrated by Stroop (1935), who presented his subjects with colour words (e.g. red, blue, green) which were printed in different coloured inks. Subjects were instructed to name the ink colours as rapidly as possible, but they were not required to read the words. Stroop found that subjects could name the ink colour far more rapidly if it matched the word itself (e.g. the word 'red' printed in red ink) than if it did not (e.g. the word 'red' printed in blue ink). Since the words had a marked interfering effect on the colour naming task despite the fact that subjects were not required to read them, it was assumed that they must have been read automatically. More recent theories about the stroop effect are discussed in MacLeod (1998).

The distinction between controlled and automatic processing has been useful in many areas of cognitive psychology. One example is recognition memory. If you meet a friend in the street you recognise the **familiarity** of their face automatically, without any apparent effort, and without needing to devote conscious attention to the task (Mandler, 1980). The role played by automatic processing in familiarity judgements will be considered in more detail in Chapter 4.

Automatic processing has also been used to explain the occurrence of everyday 'action slips', which are basically examples of absentmindedness. For example, I found during a recent car journey that instead of driving to my present house as I had intended, I had in fact driven to my previous address by force of habit. Another of my recent action slips involved absentmindedly adding instant coffee to a mug which already contained a teabag, thus creating a hybrid beverage of a highly unpalatable nature. Action slips of this kind have been extensively documented and in most cases can be explained by the activation or perseveration of automatic processes which are not appropriate (Reason, 1979). Such studies add an interesting perspective to our view of automatic processing. Automatic processes are obviously of great value to us, as they allow us to carry out routine tasks rapidly and without using up our attentional capacity. However, automatic processes lack flexibility, and when they fail to provide appropriate behaviour they need to be overridden by consciously controlled processing. There is some evidence that this override system which allows controlled processes to take over may be located in the frontal lobes of the brain, since patients with frontal lesions are often found to exhibit perseveration of automatic behaviour and a lack of flexibility of response (Shallice and Burgess, 1991a; Parkin, 1997). Frontal lobe functions will be examined further in Chapters 6 and 7.

Conscious awareness

We all have conscious awareness. This means that we are aware of our perceptions, our thoughts, our memories and our actions. We can all therefore understand what is meant by the term consciousness as a subjective experience, yet no one has yet been able to provide an explanation of what conscious awareness actually is, or how it might arise from neural activity. Consciousness remains the last unexplored frontier of psychology, and arguably one of the greatest mysteries of life itself. Sutherland (1989) summed up the situation when he remarked of consciousness that 'nothing worth reading has ever been written on it'. Indeed, the very assumption that conscious awareness must somehow arise from the mere firing of neural circuits has been described by Crick (1994) as 'the astonishing hypothesis', yet this remains the only plausible hypothesis. However, although we do not understand what consciousness is or how it arises, we are beginning to learn something about what consciousness does, and the part it plays in cognitive processes.

As explained in the previous section, psychologists have recently devised methods of distinguishing between processes which are consciously controlled and those which are unconscious and automatic. Although this research has focused mainly on the nature of automatic processes, it has also shed a certain amount of light on the conscious processes which sometimes replace them. For example, judging whether a person's face is familiar may be done automatically and unconsciously, but if we need to remember the actual situation in which we have previously met them then a conscious recollection process is required (Mandler, 1980). Tests of **explicit memory** and **implicit memory** have also been used to distinguish between conscious and unconscious memory retrieval (Schacter *et al.*, 1984), as explained in Chapter 4.

The study of patients with certain types of brain lesion has provided particularly valuable insights into the nature of conscious and unconscious cognitive processes. For example, the occurrence of blindsight in patients with occipital lobe lesions (Weiskrantz, 1986) has demonstrated that some patients can detect visual stimuli at an unconscious level, despite having no conscious awareness of seeing them. Blindsight will be examined in more detail in Chapters 2 and 3. A similar phenomenon has been observed in amnesic patients, who often reveal evidence of previous learning of which they have no conscious recollection whatsoever. Mandler (1989) has argued that it is usually not the memory trace which is lost, but the patient's ability to bring it into consciousness. These studies of amnesia will be discussed further in Chapter 5.

Autism is another type of disorder which has shed light on the nature of consciousness, because autistic individuals appear to lack some of the characteristics of conscious processing. Their behaviour tends to be highly inflexible and repetitious, and they usually lack the ability to form plans or generate new ideas spontaneously. They also tend to lack the ability to develop a rapport with others and to disregard other people, treating them as though they were merely objects. Observations of such symptoms have led Baron-Cohen (1992) to suggest that autistic people may lack a 'theory of mind', meaning that they are unable to understand the existence of mental processes in others. This may provide a clue about some of the possible benefits of having consciousness. An awareness of other people's thoughts and feelings is crucial if we are to understand their behaviour, and it is also an essential requirement for normal social interaction.

Other theories of consciousness have tended to emphasise the distinction between controlled and automatic processing. It is argued that consciousness provides us with some extra level of flexibility and control over our cognitive processes, whereas unconscious automatic processes tend to be rigid and stereotyped. Norman and Shallice (1986) suggest that automatic processes can provide adequate control of our neural functions in most routine situations without needing to use up our attention, but they must be overridden when more complex tasks require the flexibility of conscious control. Crick and Koch (1990) argue that the flexibility of this conscious control system stems largely from its capacity for binding together many different mental activities, such as thoughts and perceptions. Baddeley (1997) suggests that conscious control may reside in the central executive component of the working memory (see Chapter 4), which is largely associated with frontal lobe function. Johnson-Laird (1983) compares consciousness with the operating system which controls a computer. He suggests that consciousness is essentially a system which monitors a large number of hierarchically organised parallel processors. On occasion these processors may reach a state of deadlock, either because the instructions they generate conflict with one another, or possibly because they are mutually dependent on output from one another. Such 'pathological configurations' need to be overridden by some form of control system, and this may be the role of consciousness.

Our understanding of consciousness is still very limited. However, the little knowledge we do have about consciousness provides an excellent example of the integration of ideas from all three of the main approaches to cognitive psychology.

Integrating the main approaches to cognition

The three main approaches to cognition are experimental psychology, computer modelling and cognitive neuropsychology. However, it is the integration of these three approaches that has led to the emergence of the modern science of cognitive psychology. The combination of these three related approaches provides the subject matter of the rest of this book, and will be applied to each of the main areas of cognitive processing in turn. These areas are perception, memory, thinking and language, and there will be a separate chapter on each of these processes. A unique feature of this book is that each chapter on a particular cognitive process will be followed by a chapter dealing with disorders of that process. In this way it is intended that the relationship between normal cognition and cognitive disorders can be fully explored.

Summary

- Cognitive psychology is the study of how information is processed by the brain. It includes the study of perception, learning, memory, thinking and language.
- Historically there have been three main strands of research which have all contributed to our present understanding of cognitive psychology. They are experimental cognitive psychology, computer modelling of cognitive processes, and cognitive neuropsychology.
- Experimental cognitive psychology has provided theories which can explain how the brain interprets incoming information, beginning with the schema theory which postulates that past experience is used to analyse new perceptual input.
- Computer modelling has provided models of human cognition based on

information processing principles, and introducing important new concepts such as feature detector systems and processors of limited channel capacity.

- Cognitive neuropsychology has provided knowledge about human brain function, based on observations of people who have suffered cognitive impairment as a result of brain lesions.
- Combining the approaches of experimental psychology, computer modelling and cognitive neuropsychology has led to the emergence of cognitive psychology.
- The new science of cognitive psychology has generated new concepts and theories, such as the distinctions between top-down/bottom-up processing, and between automatic/controlled processing.

Further reading

Neisser, U. (1967). *Cognitive Psychology*. New York: Appleton-Century-Crofts. This book provided the main starting point for modern cognitive psychology. Obviously well out of date now, but still of historical interest.

Payne, D.G. and Wenger, M.J. (1998). *Cognitive Psychology*. Boston, MA: Houghton Mifflin. A book on normal cognition, but rather unusual in that it includes several mathematical approaches to cognition, such as signal detection theory.

Parkin, A.J. (1996). *Explorations in Cognitive Neuropsychology*. Oxford: Blackwell. A detailed yet readable account of the main forms of cognitive disorder, with chapters on aphasia, agnosia and amnesia. Gives fairly thorough coverage of recent research in these areas.

Crick, F. (1994) *The Astonishing Hypothesis*. Simon & Schuster. London: Francis Crick embarks on a scientific search for the soul. He doesn't actually find it, but it's an interesting journey. Despite the whimsical title this is a very scientific account of the study of consciousness, and it is by no means an easy read.

Chapter 2

Perception and attention

2.1 The biological bases of perception

The process of perception

Perception is the process by which we make sense of our surroundings by interpreting the information from our sense organs. Perception progresses from sensation (i.e. the intake of information by the sense organs) to the higher-level cognitive processes that are performed on that information. In addition, the perceptual system needs to be directed in some way towards those stimuli in the external world which need to be selected for further processing. The inherent limitations on our cognitive processing abilities, coupled with the great richness of the environment in which we live, makes it impossible for us to fully process all of the objects that may impinge on our sense organs. This selection process is referred to within psychology as attention, and this topic is considered in this chapter alongside perceptual processing.

For the purposes of the present discussion, visual processing is emphasised. To some extent this reflects the inherent bias of the human brain which devotes far more capacity to vision than it does to any of the other senses. However, clear analogies exist between visual perception and perception in those other sensory modalities.

The visual system

The general structure of the visual system is illustrated in Figure 2.1. The starting point for the visual system is the eye which, in principle, is very similar to a camera. The photographic film of the eye is the layer of photosensitive receptor cells on the retina at the back of the eye. The receptor cells are far too numerous to each send their own axon to the brain. Instead, groups of receptor cells are gathered together to form overlapping, differently sized receptive fields.

All retinal cells project to the optic disk at the back of the eye where they join with other axons to form the optic nerve. The optic nerves of each eye converge at a point called the optic chiasm. The optic chiasm organises the flow of information from the left and right halves of the visual world, referred to as the left visual field (LVF) and the right visual field (RVF) respectively. Fibres then project along the optic tracts to the lateral geniculate nucleus (LGN) of the thalamus. From here axons are sent along the optic radiations to the visual cortex.

All the sensory systems, with the exception of olfaction (smell), synapse initially in the thalamus. This large brain structure is thought to have, amongst other functions, a key role in causing the organism to orient, or attend, to a particular stimulus. The LGN of the thalamus has two types of cells in layers called the parvocellular layers and the magnocellular layers because they contain small and large cells respectively. Receptive fields that connect to the parvocellular layers are called the P pathway, whilst receptive fields that connect to the magnocellular layers are called the M pathway. These two pathways have functional as well as structural differences. M pathway neurons are mainly sensitive to movement and direction, whereas P pathway neurons are mainly sensitive to colour. Each type of

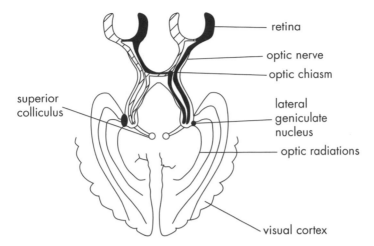

Figure 2.1 The visual system
Source: From Humphreys and Riddoch (1987) with permission

cell responds to a particular stimulus so that **parallel processing** of multiple attributes of stimuli, such as movement, detail and colour, starts to occur very early on in visual processing.

Damage to the visual pathway

Damage can occur at any level in the visual system. Referring to Figure 2.2, damage to either optic nerve will impair visual input from that eye, but damage to the fibres crossing the optic chiasm will result in loss of vision in parts of both visual

Damage to the different sites shown produces the following visual field defects (in all cases, lesions of the same sites on the left side of the brain will produce equivalent field defects, but in the right rather than the left visual field):

	Left eye	Right eye
Lesion of the right optice nerve (a):	○	●
Lesion of the optic chiasm (b):	◐	◑
Complete lesion of the optic radiations projecting to the right hemisphere (c):	◐	◐
Lesion to the upper radiations projecting to the right hemisphere (d):	◓	◓
Lesion to the lower radiations projecting to the right hemisphere (e):	◒	◒

Figure 2.2 Effects of damage to the visual system
Source: From Humphreys and Riddoch (1987) with permission

fields (termed bilateral hemianopia). Sometimes, individuals develop 'blindspots' (scotomas) which result from isolated lesions of the primary visual cortex. Individuals with visual field impairments may be aware of what they see because involuntary eye movements (nystagmus) occur and these cover for the blindspots. Cortical blindness results from damage to the primary visual cortex of the brain. It can result in the inability to distinguish forms and patterns but the patient may still have awareness of light.

Primary visual processing

Primary visual processing occurs in the primary visual cortex which is in the occipital lobe of the brain. It is also referred to as striate cortex. Hubel and Wiesel (1962, 1968) discovered cells of the visual cortex that respond preferentially to stimuli with linear properties (lines and bars). These cells are often referred to as 'feature detectors', and they were classified by Hubel and Wiesel as simple, complex or hypercomplex cells. Simple cells are smaller than the other types of cells and are excited by lines in a particular orientation, the images of which fall on a particular part of the retina. The larger, complex cells respond to the position and movement of a stimulus as well as to lines of particular orientations, in this case anywhere on the retina. Most complex cells are binocularly driven. Hypercomplex cells respond to more complex features such as corners and junctions. Columns of cells in the primary visual cortex respond best to lines of a similar orientation so, for obvious reasons, are referred to collectively as **orientation columns**. However, orientation of lines is not the only feature of a stimulus that is analysed in early visual processing; we have seen that processing of colour and movement also starts early on.

Evidence for two separate systems

Whilst some 90 per cent of the fibres in the optic tract project from the retina to the LGN and primary visual cortex, many of the remaining 10 per cent connect with the superior colliculus (see Figure 2.1). Schneider (1969) identified a double dissociation between collicular and cortical functions in studies of the visual system of hamsters. Cortical lesions disrupted visual acuity and pattern discrimination, whilst collicular lesions damaged the animals' ability to locate a stimulus. This finding provided persuasive early evidence for two separate subsystems within the visual system, sometimes referred to as the 'what' and 'where' systems. The former is mediated by the lateral geniculate pathway whilst the latter is mediated by the collicular pathway. This dissociation is supported by the clinical phenomenon of blindsight (see Chapter 3) in which cortically blind patients may be able to correctly guess the position of a target in a blind part of their visual field even though they are quite unable to identify that target and may, in the extreme case, have no conscious awareness of the target at all.

Ungerleider and Mishkin (1982) provided further evidence to support the view that separate systems exist for object location and object identification.

They argue that the system underlying the perception of an object's identity is located in the inferotemporal cortex, whilst perception of spatial location takes place in the posterior parietal cortex. On the basis of animal studies, they further propose that these systems receive independent projections from the primary visual cortex. These are termed the **ventral** and **dorsal** streams. The ventral stream is projected to the inferotemporal cortex whilst the dorsal stream is projected to the posterior parietal cortex. Ungerleider and Mishkin found, in animal studies, that damage to the ventral or dorsal streams resulted in difficulties with object identification or object location respectively. Damage to the dorsal and ventral systems in man also has predictable effects, and these are often observed in disorders of visual processing. In the case of blindsight, the role of the retino-collicular pathway may reflect residual function in the 'where' pathway following disruption of the dorsal stream by cortical damage. However, interpretation of this condition is not straightforward, and it will be examined further in Chapter 3.

Spatial frequency analysis

As well as colour, motion, position and form (as orientations of lines and combinations of such lines), the visual system appears to possess another channel for the initial analysis of stimulus material. This channel is concerned with spatial frequencies. **Spatial frequency** refers to the alternation of patterns of light and dark in a visual stimulus. This has been investigated by making use of grating stimuli (see Figure 2.3). For example, if you fixate the left-hand grating in Figure 2.3 for a minute or so, you will probably notice an after-effect when you switch your attention to the right-hand grating, causing an apparent distortion of the orientation of the lines.

These gratings may be regarded as a generalisation of the bar-like stimuli used by Hubel and Wiesel (1962, 1968) to stimulate feature detectors. However, whilst bars have abrupt divisions between areas of light and dark, the alternations used in experimental gratings instead move gradually from areas of light to areas of dark. Complex gratings can then be made up by the addition of components whose luminance profiles (patterns of light and dark) are known.

Measures of spatial frequency are formally defined in terms of changes in the luminance profile as a function of the size of the pattern on the retina (i.e. number of alternations of light and dark per unit of visual angle). Bearing in mind that this takes account of the distance of the grating from the viewer, spatial frequency is, roughly speaking, low in gratings made up of broad stripes and high in stimuli made up of narrow stripes. Studies of spatial frequency have measured the effects of adaptation, after prolonged exposure to stimuli, on apparent contrasts or contrast thresholds of patterns. Apparent contrast refers to the perceived luminance differences between the light and dark components of gratings, and contrast threshold refers to the lowest contrast level at which a grating pattern can be distinguished rather than merely appearing grey. Adaptation effects have been found that were both orientation specific and spatial frequency specific (Campbell and Robson, 1968; Blakemore and Nachmias, 1971) and which could not be explained solely

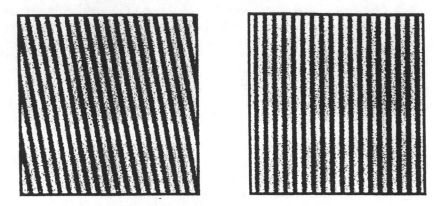

Figure 2.3 Examples of gratings used in studies of spatial frequency analysis

in terms of orientation columns. It is necessary, then, to postulate that visual processing involves the summation of outputs from a range of fairly independent detector groups, or channels, coded for spatial frequency as well as for orientation. Just as orientation columns depend upon activity in simple, complex and hyper-complex cells, so particular sorts of cells have been identified that are sensitive to high or low spatial frequencies. These are termed sustained and transient cells respectively.

The importance of spatial frequency analysis is that any real scene can be decomposed into components at varying spatial frequencies by the application of spatial frequency filters. The crucial point here is that the fine detail of a stimulus, referred to as **local** information, tends to be contained in the high spatial frequency components, whilst the overall gross outline, referred to as **global** information, is contained in the low spatial frequency components. The difference in the time course of activity in the corresponding cells creates the interesting possibility that global information may be extracted from a stimulus before processing of the constituent fine detail is complete. This is a specific prediction of the spatial frequency approach and some evidence has been found to support it (Navon, 1977). In broad terms, this is also consistent with the much earlier Gestalt view (see below).

2.2 Psychological approaches to visual perception

The Gestalt approach

If the output of preliminary visual processing is a set of data resulting from the parallel processing of colour, position, form, motion, orientation and spatial frequency attributes of stimuli, it is necessary to consider how this may be converted into a stable picture of the world in our heads.

One attempt to understand how the perceptual system produces a coherent picture was made by the Gestalt psychologists, whose approach was developed in

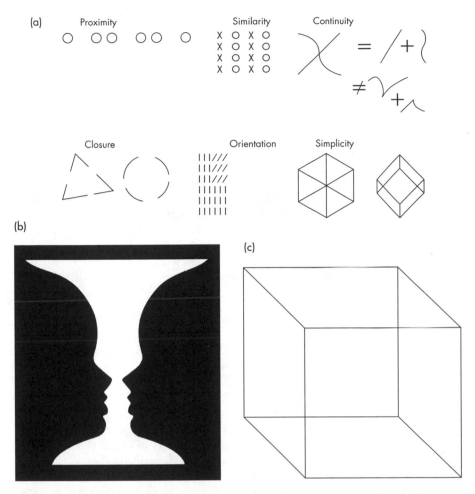

Figure 2.4 Gestalt principles: (a) illustrates general grouping principles; (b) illustrates reversible figure; (c) illustrates Necker cube

the first half of the twentieth century (Rubin, 1915; Wertheimer, 1923). The Gestalt researchers identified certain tendencies to group perceptual stimuli together. These tendencies were presented as the Gestalt 'laws' of perception, which were thought to represent natural human tendencies to perceptual organisation. Some of these laws are illustrated in Figure 2.4(a), in particular those of proximity, similarity, continuity, closure, orientation and simplicity. All of these laws were regarded by the Gestalt psychologists as being special cases of a general law known as the law of 'pragnanz', which states that the subject's interpretation of a stimulus will be that which offers the simplest and best structure available. Unfortunately, the Gestaltists did not specify very clearly what 'best' or 'simplest' would mean in this context, though attempts have subsequently been made to do so (e.g. Chater, 1997).

Perceptual groupings are involved in figure–ground relations, such as the extraction of an object from its background. This may be accomplished in different ways within the same figure, as demonstrated in a reversing figure such as the 'Peter/Paul goblet' (Figure 2.4(b)). This figure can be seen as either two faces or as a vase and it is not difficult to make it alternate rapidly and at will between the two interpretations. Although the interpretations may be seen to alternate, we can never see the two simultaneously. The property of reversibility is not limited to two-dimensional figures. Figure 2.4(c) illustrates the Necker cube which the observer can make alternate between two possible interpretations. A physical model of this cube, made as a framework of its outer edges, can also be made to alternate, and produces some surprising effects when the cube is made to rotate. These effects will be discussed further when we consider visual illusions in a later section.

The best-known slogan of the Gestalt school is that 'the whole is greater than the sum of the parts'. This implies that some vital extra ingredient, not present in the stimulus, is added by the observer in order to produce the best possible interpretation. An example was given in Figure 1.3, a simple line drawing to which most observers appear to add their own concept of a 'face'. This is an example of top-down processing, which will be considered below.

Top-down and bottom-up processing

As mentioned in Chapter 1, top-down processing, or conceptually driven processing, is processing which makes use of stored knowledge and expectations in order to guide the interpretation of a visual stimulus. Bottom-up, or data-driven, processing on the other hand is processing based on the applications of processing rules to the data present within the stimulus in a way that does not depend upon such previous experience. Schema theory (see Chapter 1) is a good example of 'top-down' processing, whereas most physiological accounts of visual processing, as well as Marr's (1982a) information processing model (described in Section 2.4), are examples of bottom-up approaches to perception. In general, bottom-up models are fairly amenable to implementation as computer models. Top-down models, however, are much less amenable to such implementation.

Perceptual constancy

Perceptual **constancy** refers to the fact that our perceptions of the world remain reasonably stable despite a continuously changing stimulus environment in which an object is rarely ever seen twice under precisely the same viewing conditions.

For example, a person walking towards you presents an increasingly large retinal image, yet you do not conclude that the person is growing in size. You are able to maintain a constant perception of their size by making a correction for their increasing proximity. Similarly, a simple visual object such as a rectangular table continues to be perceived as a rectangular table even though we may never have actually seen it as a rectangle (which would involve looking at it from directly above) and typically see it as a variety of rhomboidal shapes, depending upon the viewing angle. As well as seeing the table as being of a constant shape and size, we also see its colour and brightness as constant even when viewing it under a variety of different ambient lighting conditions. Even more distortions are overcome when we perceive a friend's face as being that of the same person, despite the extremes of emotional expression or the effects of ageing. These examples illustrate the visual constancies of shape, size, colour and brightness. These are all components of the general tendency of the cognitive system to assume constant objects.

An explanation for constancies emphasises the fact that objects are usually seen against a background context which provides much additional information. In the case of size constancy, registration of an object is always accompanied by registration of depth cues giving an indication of the distance of that object from the observer. If distance information is available, it is possible to propose a simple algorithm (or rule) enabling an accurate perception of size to be achieved. The further away an object is, the smaller will be the image of that object on the observer's retina. In order to correct for distance, then, the size of that image must be multiplied up by the perceived distance of the object. Using simple proportionality relationships, this multiplication will yield a reasonable approximation to the actual object size.

In certain conditions the environmental cues triggering a constancy correction are inadequate, and this may give rise to visual illusions. Examples of this type of misperception include the Muller–Lyer illusion and the Ames room illusion, and these will be considered in Section 2.3.

Depth perception

What then are the environmental cues to depth that underlie depth perception? These are referred to as depth cues and may be divided into two classes. Monocular depth cues are those which are available to one eye and which may be used by artists to create an impression of depth in painting. Binocular depth cues, on the other hand, are only available to the two eyes working together.

Monocular depth cues include relative size, occlusion or overlap, linear perspective, shadowing, texture gradient and motion parallax. Relative size refers to the tendency of distant objects to give rise to a smaller retinal image than would nearer objects. A small object in a painting will therefore be seen as more distant than a similar large object in the same painting. Occlusion refers to the partial overlap of one visual object by another. The overlapping object is seen as nearer than the object partially covered. Linear perspective refers to the apparent convergence of parallel lines at infinity, as when we look at a railway track receding into the distance. Shadowing can give rise to a variety of depth information. This often depends on some assumptions about the source of illumination, usually that it comes from above. Thus, given overhead illumination, shadows provide cues to concavity and convexity since concavities are illuminated at the top and in shadow underneath, whilst convexities have the opposite pattern of illumination and shadow. Texture gradient refers to the tendency of a textured surface, such as paving slabs, to appear more closely packed together in the distance. Motion parallax is a sort of moving equivalent of texture gradient. As we ourselves move, objects close to us appear to rush by quite fast whilst objects at greater distances appear to be moving more slowly. This is easy to observe when travelling on a train – compare the perceived rate of movement of mile-posts with that of trees in the distance.

Binocular depth cues include accommodation, convergence and binocular disparity. Accommodation refers to the focusing of the lens of the eye. Feedback is generated which helps the brain to estimate the distance of the object focused upon, since the more focusing that is required, the nearer the object must be. Convergence refers to the requirement for both eyes to fixate an object foveally which necessitates some degree of convergence or 'cross-eyedness'. Again, feedback from the muscles controlling these eye movements ensures the provision of information concerning depth since the more convergence that is required, the nearer the object must be.

Julesz (1960) showed that binocular disparity is crucially important for the perception of depth. Binocular disparity refers to the fact that, as the two eyes are separated in space, they cannot have identical retinal images. The computation of

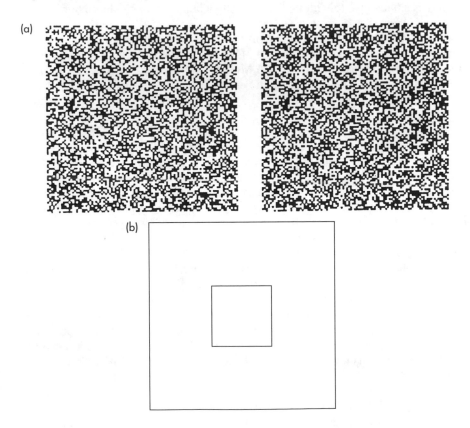

Figure 2.5 Random dot stereograms: (a) stereograms presented to each eye (a small centred square differs); (b) appearance following stereoscopic presentation of the two figures – the smaller square appears to float above the larger

depth information from the two different retinal images is called stereopsis and can take place in the absence of meaningful visual objects. Julesz devised stereograms made up of random dots in which the image seen by the right eye is identical to that seen by the left eye in all but, for example, a central square area which has been cut out and shifted a little to one side (see Figure 2.5). The resulting empty section is filled in with more random dots. If the two figures are viewed through a stereoscope, such that they are seen by one eye each, the square appears to 'float' in front of the background which is therefore seen as being at a greater depth. These figures can also be made up in two different colours and viewed through glasses with different coloured lenses as an alternative to stereoscope presentation (Frisby, 1979). The disparity between the two figures appears, therefore, to be processed automatically by the visual system in order to compute depth.

2.3 Visual illusions

Theoretical explanations of illusions

Whilst visual processing is normally reliable, there are occasions when it does not lead to accurate perception. These are termed visual illusions, and they can provide us with valuable clues about the way visual perception processing occurs. Some well-known examples are given in Figure 2.6. A persuasive case was been made by Gregory (1970) that certain illusions such as the Muller–Lyer and Ponzo illusions arise from the misapplication of perceptual mechanisms, especially those concerned with constancy scaling. In the case of the Muller–Lyer illusion, subjects presented with this figure typically overestimate the length of the vertical line in (ii) and see it as longer than that in (i). Gregory argues that this is a consequence of the use of depth information in the figure and consequent constancy scaling. He suggests that (i) appears to represent the outside corner of a building jutting out towards the viewer, whilst (ii) represents the inside corner of a room receding away from the viewer. On that interpretation, the vertical line in (i) is perceived as being nearer to the viewer than that in (ii), and it is therefore assumed to be shorter since it produces the same retinal image size.

(a)

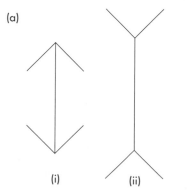

(b)

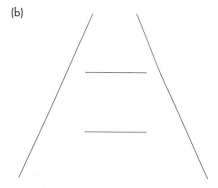

(i)   (ii)

Figure 2.6 (a) Muller–Lyer illusion;   (b) Ponzo illusion

Similar explanations can be applied to a number of related illusions, such as the Ponzo illusion. Once again there is thought to be a misperception of three-dimensional depth (possibly through the figure's similarity to a railway track receding into the distance), leading the subject to make an inappropriate constancy correction so that the lower horizontal line appears to be smaller than the upper one.

The misapplied constancy scaling approach is not limited to simple, two-dimensional stimuli since it appears to account for real-life examples such as the moon illusion. This refers to the tendency of subjects to overestimate the size of the moon when it is low in the sky, and hence close to the horizon which acts as a cue to distance, as compared to when it is high in the sky and seen against a black background.

Misapplied constancy scaling cannot, however, be the whole explanation for these types of illusion, since minor modifications to the stimuli used in the Muller–Lyer illusion, for example replacing the arrowheads by distance-neutral features such as circles or squares, does not abolish (but does reduce) the tendency to overestimate the vertical line in (ii).

Top-down, bottom-up, side-ways rules or physiological fatigue?

Gregory (1996) suggests that visual illusions usually fall into one of four main categories. Firstly there are illusions based on top-down processing, and secondly there are those based on bottom-up processing. A third category of illusions reflects the use (or misuse) of mechanisms which are neither top-down nor bottom-up, which Gregory terms 'side-ways rules'. Gregory uses this term to refer to operations such as grouping, depth perception and constancy scaling. A fourth category of illusions depends on physiological mechanisms such as fatigue in orientation-specific cells.

The illusions most studied by psychologists are those based on side-ways rules and physiological mechanisms. As outlined above, side-ways rules such as constancy scaling have been used to explain illusions like the Muller–Lyer illusion and the Ponzo illusion. Illusions based on physiological mechanisms include adaptation effects such as illusory complementary colours and the tilt after-effect.

The Ames room (Figure 2.7) is an example of an illusion in which top-down information and side-ways rules corrections are in conflict with one another. When viewed through a small peep-hole, a person walking across the room appears convincingly to grow or shrink, despite the fact that top-down knowledge is telling us that real people neither grow nor shrink. The reason for this perceptual error is that the person is in fact walking a considerable distance either towards or away from the observer but the cues that would normally provide this information to the viewer are concealed as a result of the unusual geometry of the Ames room. The viewer is thus prevented from making the appropriate constancy correction by the lack of accurate distance information. The changes in the size of the retinal image of the person formed in the observer's eyes are interpreted, under such circumstances, as changes in physical size of that person. In this case, top-down information appears to have been overridden by side-ways rules.

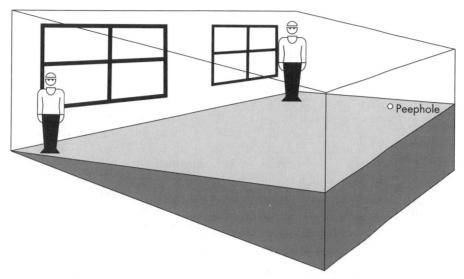

Figure 2.7 The Ames room

What is the relationship between top-down knowledge, bottom-up data and side-ways rules? We have seen that top-down knowledge concerning sizes of people can be overridden by side-ways rules in the Ames room. We also know from the Muller–Lyer illusion that constancy scaling can be set by bottom-up signals from the eyes. Gregory (1998) argues that a key point is that bottom-up scaling can be set by depth cues even though depth is not actually seen. He also points out, however, that a rotating, wire-frame Necker cube appears to rotate in the wrong direction when depth reversed because motion parallax is wrongly attributed to front and back and it changes shape. Gregory argues that the distortion when the cube is reversed shows that size constancy, at least in the case of the cue-free Necker cube, can be set by the prevailing top-down perceptual hypotheses based on knowledge or assumptions. Moreover, unlike the cube, a hollow face refuses to look hollow when rotated. This does not, however, apply to depth-neutral objects such as egg boxes. Gregory (1996) argues that this phenomenon may separate top-down knowledge from side-ways rules rather neatly.

2.4 Marr's theory

The primal sketch

Marr's model represents the best worked out attempt to model human vision to be made to date. Though elaborated since Marr's untimely death in 1980, the basic details remain in place and these are presented in summary form here. Marr's (1982) approach draws upon research into receptive fields (Kuffler, 1953), work in spatial frequency analysis (Campbell and Robson, 1968), and work on feature analysis (Hubel and Wiesel, 1962, 1968), as well as the earlier work of the Gestalt psychologists (Rubin, 1915; Wertheimer, 1923) and Julesz's (1960) work on random-dot stereograms. It is perhaps surprising that all these disparate lines of work had to be 'incubated' for so long before Marr was able to draw the strands together into a unified, computational model of vision.

The starting point of the model is the two retinal images, which are of course two-dimensional. The retinae only register levels of light intensity (brightness) and light wavelength (colour) via temporal and spatial encoding (i.e. in terms of the rate of firing by receptor cells and the nature of the receptor activated). In Marr's model, a complex mathematical algorithm translates these intensity changes into a contour pattern indicating sudden alterations in intensity. The output of this first stage of processing is the '**primal sketch**', in which edge and boundary information is included as contours. In order to compute the primal sketch from the array of brightness fluctuations on the retina, Marr holds that certain 'primitives' or place tokens are derived from the retinal image. These are edges, bars, blobs, terminations, edge segments, virtual lines, groups, curvilinear organisations, zero-crossings and boundaries.

The two-and-a-half-dimensional representation and the three-dimensional model

The second stage of the model leads to what Marr termed the '**two-and-a-half-dimensional sketch** (or representation)' which maps the orientation and depth of visible surfaces around the viewer by making use of information provided by, for example, depth cues such as shading and motion. In addition, patterns of movement may be important. Johansson (1973), in a celebrated experiment, attached point sources of light to an actor in a darkened room. Subjects were quite unable to identify the result as a human being. When, however, he got up and moved about, the pattern of movement of the lights enabled subjects to immediately group those lights in a way that suggested the presence of a human being. The two-and-a-half-dimensional sketch has been constructed around the viewer and is therefore viewer centred and contains perspective and other distortions. In particular, object constancy has not been achieved and perceptual classification (the identification of the object) had not occurred. The last stage of processing ultimately delivers a three-dimensional, viewer-independent, mental representation. Although the processing leading from the two-and-a-half-dimensional sketch to the **three-dimensional representation** (or model) are the least explicit aspects of the theory, Marr argued that the perceiver makes use of the component axes of a shape in the construction of the three-dimensional model of that shape. The normal perceiver finds it relatively easy to identify the principal axes of elongation of a shape and this ability probably underlies our ability to rapidly comprehend 'matchstick' or pipe-cleaner figures. Marr suggests that representations of objects may be constructed from cylinder-like elements aligned along such axes.

Evaluation of Marr's approach

Marr's (1982) approach has found much favour amongst workers endeavouring to model aspects of vision on computers (see Chapter 10). As well as its importance in computational work, however, Marr's theory has acquired particular importance as a result of the identification of a number of neuropsychological disorders of perception and attention (see Chapter 3) that appear to be usefully discussed in terms of the terminology of the model. Ellis and Young (1996) suggest that Marr's scheme offers a way of classifying some of those disorders and their scheme is presented in Figure 2.8. The figure represents stages that are involved in

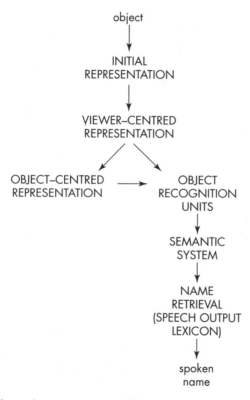

Figure 2.8 Ellis and Young's (1996) adaptation of the stages in Marr's model for application to disorders of perception or attention
Source: From Ellis and Young (1996) with permission

perceiving and naming an object in the world. Correspondences to Marr's model are readily identifiable. Firstly, the viewer establishes an initial representation (or primal sketch) based on the retinal image of the object. Disorders of the early stages of perception may intervene to prevent this formation as a result of blind areas of the visual fields (e.g. scotomas, blindsight) or improperly directed visual attention (e.g. unilateral visual neglect). The viewer's task is next to establish a viewer-centred, pre-categorical representation (or 2.5-dimensional representation). Recognition of the object may be achieved by linking the viewer-dependent representation to stored recognition units (templates etc.: see Section 2.5) in memory or may occur via the formation of a viewer-independent representation (three-dimensional model) having perceptual constancy.

2.5 Object recognition processes

Templates and prototypes

In general, the recognition of an object involves the matching of a pattern of stimulation to a stored representation of that object. Thus the song or visual appearance of a bird will lead to recognition by an expert ornithologist, whilst almost any literate human being should be able to recognise words of their native language based on their sound when spoken or their appearance when written. An account based on this simple 'matching' approach may be termed a **template** model. The stored representation is a template to which patterns of stimulation must be matched for recognition to occur. Whilst woefully simplistic, template models form a clear starting point for attempts to model recognition processes, especially for situations in which the variety of objects to be recognised is not large. Before considering alternatives to the template view, however, a preliminary note of caution must be sounded concerning the boundaries between 'objects' in our perceptual world. This is the figure–ground issue first studied by the Gestalt psychologists. Unfortunately, boundaries between objects are themselves a result of perceptual processing itself and rarely exist in the external world. The point is illustrated by the experience of listening to a language which we have never studied. What are the words? The impression is of a continuous sequence of sound with no obvious breaks – word separation effects themselves are a result of early stages in language processing.

Whilst template models fit easily with the sort of recognition processes taking place when a bar-code is read automatically at a supermarket checkout, their application to biological systems are fraught with problems. Logically, they are an extension of the recognition processes that take place in lower creatures such as frogs or sticklebacks for whom most perceptual processing takes place in the retina (the receptive field structure being much more complicated than in the mammalian eye) and strong links exist between visual stimuli and motor responses – an example is the 'bug-detector' (Kuffler, 1953) identified among the retinal ganglion cells of the frog, stimulation of which is linked to predatory behaviour. The models have little place in higher organisms in which so much more cognitive processing of sensory input is possible in the brain. The main problem is lack of cognitive economy. It is rather like storing the answers to all known arithmetic problems rather than learning a procedure for working out the answer. The memory load is massive and it is unlikely that evolution would equip us for such a high level of redundancy as would be required to store templates of stimuli which we may never encounter again. Even for stimuli that we do encounter, the template view would require a separate template for each possible size, shape and orientation of that stimulus. Where the stimulus has alternative forms, such as, for example, capital, lower case or italicised letter 'A's, the number of templates required becomes astronomical.

An alternative to the template view is one based on **prototypes**. These represent a sort of averaging over the family of instances of the object that has been actually encountered and from which a certain amount of deviation is possible. However, the issue of prototypicality is not straightforward and begs the question of cognitive categorisation. This is a major area of research in its own right but a few summary points can be made here. A lengthy theoretical controversy has occurred between accounts of categorisation based on defining features and accounts based on family resemblances (Rosch and Mervis, 1975). Attempts to confer category membership on the basis of a defining list of features is actually quite tricky since it is easy to construct artificial examples of objects that have few, if any of those features but would still be admitted as members of the category. Instead of using a defining feature or list of features, the family resemblances approach suggests that members of a category should have at least some features in common with other members of that category. On this account the most 'typical' members of a category are thus those which have most features in common with other members of the category and fewest with members of other categories. Moreover, those features that are possessed should probably exist in certain relations to one another.

Feature analysis

A more compelling version takes account of the fact that a large measure of pre-processing is carried out in early visual processing. As we have seen, information about colour, form, motion, position, orientation and spatial frequency is all encoded early in visual processing. It is possible that Gestalt-type grouping mechanisms are also employed at an early stage. These operations may be referred to as feature analysis and will occur prior to any process of matching input against prototypes. However, distinguishing two objects is not solely a matter of listing their constituent features. This would not, for example, distinguish 'K' from 'Y' since both consist of a vertical bar, and two oblique, oppositely slanted bars. The prototype to which the feature list must be matched must also take account of the relations, for example spatial relations, between features. This type of prototype may be called a 'structural description' (Sutherland, 1973) and encodes family resemblances in terms of patterns of featural relations between members of the constituent feature set.

Some of the most persuasive evidence in favour of the feature analysis view comes from **visual search** experiments. These were first employed by Neisser (1964, 1967), who wished to investigate the considerable variation in the ease with which we can identify a given object amongst a field of distractors. One case, quoted by Neisser, in which it is comparatively easy is the identification of a familiar face in a crowd. Neisser found that (American) subjects could identify the face of the late President Kennedy from amongst many thousands in a photograph of a crowd at a baseball match extremely easily. This contrasts with other visual search situations, such as identifying objects on the ground or sea from the air, which can be extremely difficult.

Search time in milliseconds:

		Background	
		Angular	Round
Target	Q	80	580
	Z	240	110

Figure 2.9 Results of Neisser's (1967) visual search study

Neisser modelled the visual search task by asking subjects to search amongst a collection of letters for a specified letter. In one experiment (Neisser 1967), subjects tried to locate a letter defined by angular or round features ('Z' or 'Q' respectively) amongst a group of predominantly angular or round distractors. He found a very considerable advantage for identification of targets against a dissimilar background (see Figure 2.9).

The advantage of a dissimilar background may be readily explained in terms of feature analysis. Here we are using the term 'feature' to refer to constituent components of letters. These correspond in a ready way to orientations of lines and combinations of such lines and it is not unreasonable to assume that the feature detectors that are active in processing these features are the simple, complex and hypercomplex cells (Hubel and Wiesel, 1962, 1968). Since there are no features in common between the target and distractors when the background is dissimilar to the target, distractors may be rejected on the basis of the most preliminary analysis of one such discrepant feature. This is called a 'pop-out' effect. Further experiments (e.g. Treisman and Gelade, 1980) suggest that feature analysis is a **parallel process**. If a single target is to be located against a background of distractors that are dissimilar to the target, then the total number of distractors present has little or no effect on the response time and the set size function is flat, indicating that all the elements of the display are processed in parallel (see Figure 2.10(a)). Treisman (1988) suggests that parallel processing and the ability to generate such pop-out effects may be taken as evidence that the feature in question may be considered to be an elementary visual feature.

Where many features are common to target and distractors, however, much more processing is required in order to reject distractors. Such a situation is provided by the conjoint search in which a target is defined by a combination of features, for example, a white circle against a background that includes circles that are not white and white items that are not circles. Stimuli of this sort are illustrated in Figure 2.11. The set size function in this case shows a linear increase indicative of **serial processing** (see Figure 2.10(b)). This issue will be returned to when the role of attention in perception is discussed.

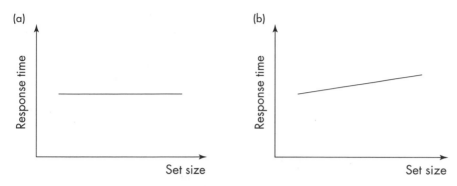

Figure 2.10 Set size effects: (a) simple search; (b) conjoint search

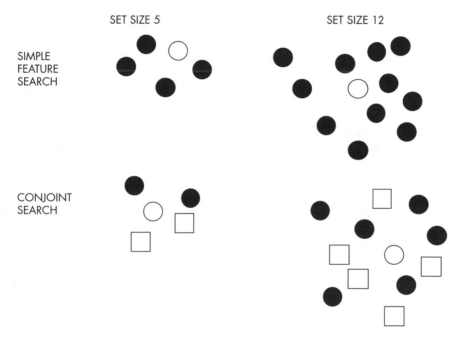

Figure 2.11 Simple and conjoint searches
Note: Target is white circle in all cases.

Pandemonium

An early, computational model of letter recognition that made use of feature analysis was called 'Pandemonium', for reasons that will become apparent below. This was described by Selfridge (1959) and devised for such tasks as automatic letter sorting but never fully implemented. Its importance in this context is that it represents a fully articulated, bottom-up, parallel-processing, template-matching model of object recognition. In essence, Pandemonium consisted of a four-layer hierarchy of detector units which Selfridge termed 'demons' (partly explaining the name). All demons at one level were connected to all demons at the next level up. Activation of demons resulted in shrieks (fully explaining the name) up to the next level. The demons were tuned for the detection of specific items or the performance of particular computations. At the lowest level, the data (or image) demons acted as feature detectors looking out for constituent features of letters such as vertical or oblique lines. At the next level the computational demons looked out for key combinations of features. When, for example, two oblique lines and one horizontal bar were detected by a computational demon, the cognitive demon (or template) for the letter 'A' received enough input from that demon to be activated itself. It then shrieked to the decision demon which was able to decide whether or not a given letter had actually been detected.

Although Pandemonium was never intended to be a model of human perception, we may ask what sort of assumptions about human perception would need to be made if it were to be modelled in such terms. These assumptions could then be tested against human data. The assumptions would include (1) that top-down effects, other than to the minimal extent of recognition based on stored templates, would be absent, (2) that context would have minimal effects on recognition, (3) that local features would be processed before the complete stimulus could be recognised, and (4) that there would be no significant role of learning in perception. Empirical studies have been conducted to examine all these predictions and the findings of studies pertaining to the first three of these predictions will now be discussed. Consideration of learning effects will be deferred until Section 2.9, where we consider automaticity.

Top-down influences

Gregory (1980) suggested that the task of the perceiver is the same as that of an intuitive scientist – it is one of making and testing inferences about the world. Clearly such perceptual hypotheses and inferences may be wrong, and tests of them may be flawed, so that perception may be inaccurate. An example of a situation in which erroneous hypotheses may be induced by stimulus characteristics is that of the visual illusions. The process of hypothesis and test may be seen at work in the interpretation (assuming that it has not been seen before by the reader) of a degraded picture such as that in Figure 2.12. After some examination the viewer will probably agree that this represents a dog, probably a dalmatian, sniffing at some leaves on the ground. If the viewer introspects on how this interpretation is arrived at it will probably be agreed that, on the basis of the minimal information provided in the picture, some feature such as the dog's ear or collar may be identified and the scene reconstructed by making and testing informed guesses and using these as a basis for further inference. This type of processing requires the perceiver's active use of prior knowledge and of problem-solving and inferential strategies.

Figure 2.12 The degraded dog

Source: Photo by R.C. James, from Thurston, J. and Carraher, R.G. (1966). *Optical Illusions and the Visual Arts*. Litton Educational Publishing. Copyright © Van Nostrand Reinhold & Co.

Top-down processes in perception are especially evident when stimuli are ambiguous or incomplete (as in Figure 2.13), when they are presented for a very short period of time, or when they are distorted or interfered with or their processing interrupted. A very simple example is given in Figure 2.13(a). Here, two well-known sequences are given – A, B, C and 12, 13, 14. However, the middle item in each case is drawn identically as a vertical line with two semi-circles, one above the other, in close proximity. However, the semi-circles are close enough for the item to be either 'B' or '13' and is seen as either, depending upon whether one reads along or down. This example makes some important points. Firstly, even when an object is defined both by its constituent features and their spatial relations, this may still be inadequate for its unequivocal identification. Where such conflicts arise, context must be invoked in order to resolve the possible interpretations.

Top-down processes enable us to read poor handwriting and recognise upside-down or obscured objects. Consider the examples in Figure 2.13(b and c) of two equally badly handwritten sentences which are, however, very different in the ease with which they can be read. The reason for this difference is that one sentence makes sense and the other does not. Expectations are generated by the context so that hypotheses can be generated. It would appear that even poor-quality stimuli and incomplete contextual information is sufficient to generate these hypotheses and enable reading of the meaningful sentence. Neisser (1967)

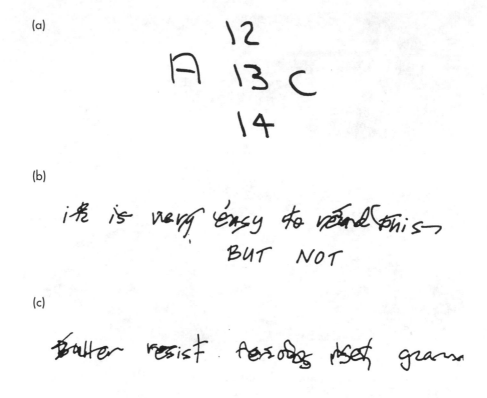

Figure 2.13 Top-down influences
Source: (b) and (c) reproduced from Norman (1988)

proposed the analysis-by-synthesis model or 'perceptual cycle' as a framework for interacting top-down and bottom-up processes. On this account the relative contribution of each type of processing is flexibly determined by the quality of stimulus information and the availability of contextual information. Repeated processes of information extraction and hypothesis generation are then initiated until a satisfactory interpretation is achieved.

Context effects

Context effects have been examined in a variety of experiments employing very brief (tachistoscopic) presentations with **visual masking** and manipulations of context. Visual masking involves presentation of an unrelated, usually meaningless stimulus immediately after and in the same location as a briefly presented stimulus, usually on a computer screen. This causes interference with, or interruption of, processing of the first stimulus. An experiment involving visual masking is the word-superiority effect (Reicher, 1969; Wheeler, 1970). In this paradigm, subjects fixate a point on a tachistoscope display. They then receive a rapidly presented test stimulus followed immediately by a visual mask which interferes with processing of the stimulus and makes recall of that stimulus difficult. Stimuli were of three kinds: words (e.g. 'WORD'), control combinations of letters or non-words (e.g. 'ORWD'), and single letters (e.g. 'D'). In all cases subjects were cued visually to recall the letter from a particular position in the word or non-word or just the single letter. In order to remove response bias, subjects were given a two-alternative forced choice task which offered two answers, each of which would make a word if the original stimulus was a word (e.g. 'D' or 'K' to make 'WORD' or 'WORK'). A 10 per cent improvement in performance accuracy was found if the letter was part of a word as compared to when it was a non-word or a single letter. Performance was about the same in the latter two cases. Subsequent experiments have also indicated an object superiority effect (Biedermann, 1977) for objects that form part of a coherent scene as compared with ones forming part of a jumbled scene.

Local and global relationships

Experiments by Navon (1977) suggest that it may actually be the norm to process the global attributes of a stimulus before the local detail, in direct contradiction to the bottom-up view. Navon presented stimuli to subjects in which large letters were made up of many smaller ones (see Figure 2.14). Subjects were asked to report either the large or small letters (global or local features). It was found that conflicting information at the global level impaired report of local features but not vice versa. Thus global level processing appears to take priority over processing of local features. This, it will be recalled, was an explicit prediction of the spatial frequency approach to object recognition processes. Moreover, there is another echo of the Gestaltist view here, in particular their slogan that the 'whole is greater than the sum of the parts'. This certainly seems to be true to the extent that the whole may be apprehended before all of its parts have been processed.

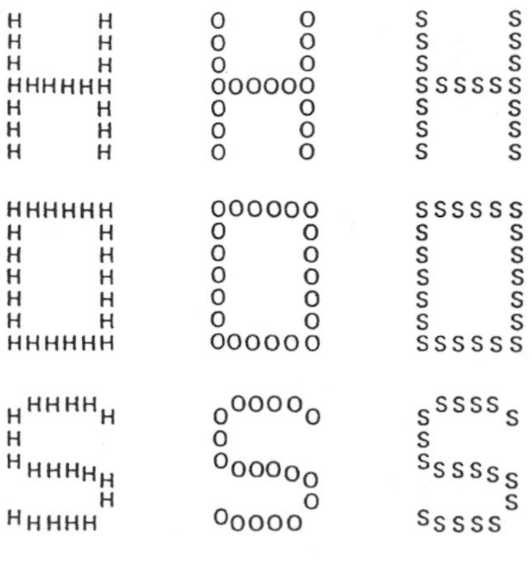

Figure 2.14 Stimuli of the type used by Navon (1977)

2.6 Perception: a summary

General conclusions

In sum, experiments have shown that a bottom-up view of perception based on such processes as feature analysis and matching with templates or prototypes is inadequate for a complete account of all perceptual phenomena. It is clear from studies of the effects of context, of local/global manipulations and of responses to ambiguous figures that a wealth of top-down processing must be invoked in addition to the hierarchy of processing initiated by incoming sensory data, possibly in the manner indicated by Neisser's perceptual cycle. Two further points can be made. Firstly, part of the role of top-down processing may be to engage the correct set of feature analysers in response to the context in which the object to be perceived is embedded. Thus, if printed language is expected, certain analysers may be employed but not others more suited to face or spoken language recognition. The physiological substrates of the letter analysers may be less well understood, however, than are the simple, complex and hypercomplex cells of the visual cortex or the sustained and transient cells tuned to particular spatial frequency ranges. Furthermore, part of what we call top-down processing may be the guidance of current processing by the complete or partial output of recently processed material in what has become known as 'cascade' processing (McClelland, 1979). Marr (1982) argued that bottom-up processing is sufficient in natural environments for the production of a 3-dimensional representation of objects but, significantly, he did not explicitly deny the reality of top-down influences. Wilding (1994) attempts to summarise the situation by suggesting that top-down processes are particularly likely when artificial, human-created patterns such as spoken or written language are to be recognised.

A good illustration of top-down influences at work in the perception of written language is provided by the interactive activation model of letter and word

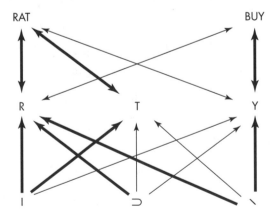

Figure 2.15 Interactive activation model of letter and word recognition
Note: Bold lines indicate excitation, others inhibition. Arrowheads indicate whether excitation/inhibition is unidirectional or bidirectional.
Source: Wilding 1994

recognition described by McClelland and Rumelhart (1981) and illustrated by Figure 2.15. Input excites feature detectors which are in turn connected to letter detectors. These can be excited or inhibited according to whether or not the feature forms part of the letter. Similar connections exist between letter and word detectors. Moreover, feedback occurs in the reverse direction so that activation of a word detector may in turn activate letter and feature detectors. Feedback from letters to words explains how letters can be more easily identified when presented in words than when presented on their own, as was the case in the word superiority effect studies (Reicher, 1969; Wheeler, 1970). The model also enjoyed the rare privilege of generating new predictions that were borne out by human experimentation. For example, it predicts that word units will respond correctly to partly obscured words because the correct word receives excitation from all the letters. As a result, an advantage for a letter forming part of a word may be detected in the word superiority effect paradigm, even if that letter was not previously seen as part of the word.

2.7 Attention

The cocktail party phenomenon

We will turn now to the issue of the maintenance of attention to a particular source of sensory input in preference to the very large number of competing sources to which the perceiver is subject. This is a classic issue within experimental psychology and one of the first topics to be addressed from within the cognitive perspective (Cherry, 1953; Broadbent, 1958; Moray, 1959). Whilst much of the discussion of issues in perception has relied on examples and experiments from visual perception, most early studies of attention involved hearing, largely because of the ease with which the two ears can be provided with separate inputs via headphones.

One of the first attentional phenomena to be studied by Cherry (1953) was the 'cocktail party phenomenon'; that is, the ability of normal people to attend to a single conversation against a background of numerous conversations taking place in parallel, whilst retaining the ability to switch attention to another person upon hearing one's own name spoken. Thus, as well as being able to maintain attention to a single source of stimulation, a complete account must also explain the ability to switch attention to something else.

The cocktail party situation can be modelled experimentally by means of the technique of dichotic listening, which entails asking subjects to listen to two competing sources of auditory stimulation, each coming simultaneously via headphones to different ears. This enables both the study of focused attention (i.e. maintaining attention to one particular source), and divided attention (i.e. processing two or more competing inputs). In order to study focused attention, the technique of shadowing has been widely used. This involves the subject attending to one input (termed a channel) and repeating the material presented on that channel (termed a message) back aloud. The task is actually surprisingly difficult to accomplish and requires much effort on the part of the subject.

Early or late selection?

When the subject is required to shadow the input to one ear in the dichotic situation, how much of the input to the other ear is perceived? Early experiments (Broadbent, 1958) suggested that virtually nothing is registered from the non-attended ear. Only the most simple physical aspects of the stimulus are noticed, such as whether it is speech or music, or the sex of the speaker in the case of spoken input. This finding is consistent with Broadbent's (1958) filter concept of attention, which was represented diagrammatically in Chapter 1 (see Figure 1.5). In this model, selection takes place at an early stage on the basis of physical characteristics, the most obvious of which is channel. Where the Broadbent model is less successful, however, is in trying to account for switching of attention. For switching to take place in a way that is dependent upon the content of the stimulus to which attention is to be switched, then at least some processing of that input must occur. Further problems with the model include the finding that the amount of material registered on the unattended channel greatly increases with practice of shadowing (Underwood, 1974). In addition, if a message alternates between the two ears, subjects follow it back and forth rather than continuing to shadow the ear receiving only part of the whole message. This can also be shown in the divided attention situation when subjects recall messages in coherent forms, for example, 'A B C' and '1 2 3' rather than chunking by ear which, in the case of the example, might be '1 B 3' and 'A 2 C'.

Another difficulty for the filter model is the phenomenon of subliminal perception, in which a subject's behaviour is found to be influenced by an input, despite their lack of any conscious awareness of that input. The occurrence of subliminal perception questions the view that the role of attention is to control entry into consciousness in order to prevent cognitive overload by irrelevant material. A typical subliminal perception paradigm involves conditioning subjects to produce galvanic skin responses (GSRs) in response to certain stimuli. This can be readily accomplished by, for example, associating the stimuli with mild electric shocks. Subjects will continue to exhibit a GSR indicative of anticipation of the shock for some time after the conditioning session. Experiments by Von Wright *et al.* (1985) and others have clearly demonstrated the occurrence of GSR responses to words presented on the unattended channel and which the subjects were not consciously aware of.

In addition, Govier and Pitts (1982) found that subjects were capable of discriminating between alternative meanings of an unattended, shock-conditioned word. They presented 'polysemous' words (that is, words having multiple mean-ings, such as 'bank', which could refer either to a money bank or a river bank), and conditioned subjects to expect shocks in response to the presentation of one of the two meanings. In a subsequent dichotic shadowing task subjects displayed the same pattern of selective GSRs to particular meanings of the polysemous word on the unattended channel, where this meaning was determined by the context provided by the message on that channel.

Demonstrations such as the above clearly indicate that there is far more processing of unattended material than the filter model would predict. Broadbent's filter model is an 'early selection' model, in which filtering takes place at the earliest opportunity in perception, usually on the basis of physical attributes and before any significant amount of processing can occur. In contrast, experiments such as that by Govier and Pitts (1982) suggest that processing of the unattended message may reach the very highest levels of semantic processing, involving the extraction of specific meanings of ambiguous words, without conscious awareness and therefore before any filtering operation controlling entry to consciousness.

One way out of this dilemma is to propose a 'late selection' model in which all stimuli are processed to the highest level possible, usually the semantic level, before any filtering operations take place. This view is associated with the work of Deutsch and Deutsch (1967), who postulated that selection actually takes place at the level of response. Stimuli which are not responded to in some way are therefore less likely to enter consciousness, or to be forgotten if they do. The main objection to this view concerns the issue of cognitive economy. It is intuitively very unlikely that evolution would equip us to process all stimuli to the highest level possible when virtually all those stimuli are quite irrelevant to our survival.

Probably the most satisfactory model of attention is the 'attenuation' model proposed by Treisman (1964), which contends that the non-attended channel is not completely shut down but merely attenuated (i.e. adjusted), much as one might turn down the volume knob on a radio. On this account, incoming stimuli undergo three different types of analysis. The first is concerned with physical properties, the second is concerned with determining whether or not stimuli are linguistic and, if so, grouping them into syllables and words. The final stage is concerned with the allocation of meanings. This is the highest level of processing and is referred to as semantic processing. The approach has much in common with the influential levels-of-processing model of memory described in Chapter 4. Disentangling two competing stimuli, then, becomes difficult if both require the same level of processing. The cocktail party situation is readily accounted for by simply rejecting competing input on the basis of physical characteristics (e.g. sex and position of speaker). To that extent the model is similar to Broadbent's but, unlike Broadbent, the attenuation account does not require that the unattended message is completely ignored. Instead it is merely attenuated to a lower level. Processing of the unattended message may therefore be much more complex and may occur at any level up to and including the semantic level. The model assumes that inputs are attenuated differently and flexibly, so the setting for a personally relevant item, such as one's name, reflects much greater sensitivity for such material. Moreover, the flexibility of settings allows for attention to be paid to other aspects of the environment under conditions which require this. The model therefore deals with the switching of attention much more readily than did Broadbent's.

Experimental evidence has tended to favour Treisman's view (Broadbent, 1982). In one such study the effects of response were compared. It will be recalled that on the late selection view a response is predicted to result in a greater likelihood of that item entering consciousness. Using tapping in response to word stimuli presented under dichotic shadowing conditions, many more taps were generated in response to occurrences on the attended ear as compared to the unattended ear. In order to eliminate the possibility that shadowing itself may be increasing the likelihood of recognition, as it could be regarded as a second response to the stimulus on the attended channel, the experiment was repeated with subjects instructed to stop shadowing when the target occurred on either ear. Although this reduced the difference between the number of detections on either ear, the difference was still large (Treisman and Geffen, 1967).

Visual studies

In vision research, comparatively few studies have addressed the issue of whether subjects can attend to physical dimensions and filter out high-level information. Studies of selective attention in vision have required attention to a physical property such as colour, as in the Stroop task, or spatial location, as in the Eriksen interference paradigm. The Stroop effect (explained briefly in Chapter 1) depends upon subjects trying to do something other than read a word that they are presented with. In the classic study, colour words are written in variously coloured inks, for example the word 'green' in blue ink. Subjects are instructed to call out the colour of the ink rather than the word written in that ink. Most subjects show a considerable interference effect (that is, slower responding and more errors) when there is an inconsistency between the colour word and the colour of the ink. Under such conditions semantic or identity information from unattended elements affects performance. However, early studies did not assess whether access to high-level information could be prevented when the task only requires the processing of a physical property. This was investigated by Boucart and Humphreys (1992) and Boucart *et al.* (1995), who found that semantic properties affect performance even though the tasks required attention to a physical property of the stimulus only. This held when subjects attended to the global shape of the stimulus but not when they attended to other physical features such as colour or luminance. Boucart and Humphreys offered three possible explanations for these findings. Firstly, there may be separate processing channels for form and for colour or luminance information. Secondly, form and surface information may have different roles in object recognition. Thirdly, differences may have arisen from the different modes of processing required in the various form-matching tasks that they used. These were based on global shape, orientation or size.

Semantic interference may have occurred in the form-based tasks because subjects had to compute the global shape of the object in order to extract the required attributes. Analysis of global form was not necessary, however, for matching on colour or luminance, because stimuli were not made of parts having different colours or different levels of luminance. Attention to a single local part was therefore sufficient to perform the task under those conditions. Boucart *et al.* (1995) suggested that locally directed attention may be sufficient to prevent semantic processing. They examined this by investigating whether, by attending to physical properties of stimuli, subjects can prevent the activation of semantic information. Subjects received a reference object followed by a display containing both a matching target and a distractor and were required to attend to motion and to surface texture. Some evidence for semantic processing occurred, in contrast with Boucart and Humphreys (1992, 1994). These results suggest that what is crucial in activating stored object representations is whether or not the global shape of the stimulus is processed; it does not appear to depend upon activity in particular physiological channels.

Inhibitory mechanisms

Driver (1989) used a task devised by Francolini and Egeth (1980), in which subjects were presented with a circular array of red and black letters or numerals and the task was to count the number of red items whilst ignoring the black items. Performance speed in the original experiment was reduced when the display included red numerals which conflicted with the answer but there was no distraction from the black items. In Driver's version, the question was whether conflicting numerals presented on the previous trial would affect performance times. He found that there was an interference effect and that it was comparable regardless of the colours of the numerals. The fact that such interference occurs from a previous trial clearly implies that those items must have been processed on that previous trial. This phenomenon is termed **negative priming**. In another experiment, Driver and Tipper (1989) found that having a picture as the unattended stimulus on one trial slowed the processing of the corresponding word on the next trial. Whilst the interpretation of this finding is not clear, it does imply semantic-level processing of unattended material.

From the work on negative priming, Tipper *et al.* (1994) has developed a theory of inhibitory processes in attention where these complement the excitatory processes applied to representations of desired information. Excitatory processing enhances and maintains representations of selected objects whereas other representations merely decay passively. A mechanism which actively inhibits unwanted representations will increase the rate and level of this differentiation. Tipper argues that these inhibitory mechanisms may be flexible enough to operate at the level of individual features, as well as whole objects, and that their role is to facilitate action. This led Tipper *et al.* (1994) to conclude that the main reason for the existence of selective attention is to link perception to action. This approach has echoes in the emphasis on response found in the late-selection theory of Deutsch and Deutsch, as well as in the much more recent work of Goodale and Milner (1992).

2.8 The role of attention in perception

Attentional glue

The visual search paradigm has been described above (see Figure 2.10), and it was observed that the set size function for a simple single-feature search is flat, indicating that the features are processed in parallel. This is, of course, averaged over a set of trials in which the position of the target in the array is systematically altered. In contrast, the search time associated with a conjoint or other complex search, in which a target is defined as a combination of features which do not always co-occur, has a positive gradient suggesting that each item in the distractor array is receiving a certain amount of processing. The type of strategy that subjects adopt appears to be one of serial search in which each item receives inspection.

These findings may be taken as evidence of attention-dependent serial processing in the conjunctive search task. Given the clear limitations of short-term working memory (see Chapter 4), it is doubtful whether more than one item can be evaluated at a time. This provides a clue to the role of attention in visual perception.

On one level, stimuli are presented to the visual system as sets of features, on another level they are perceived as coherent objects in the world. What processes intervene between the input and output levels of the perceptual system? One possible view (Treisman and Schmidt, 1982) is that the role of attention is to act as perceptual **glue** which binds the sets of features that we process together into coherent percepts of objects. This is termed the feature integration theory, or FIT. The FIT suggests that features are assembled in appropriate relationships to form percepts of objects as we attend to those objects. In keeping with Marr's (1982) account, it may be hypothesised that feature integration depends upon use of spatial relationships, depth cues and principal axes.

One observation that is consistent with the FIT is that subjects can be induced to experience illusory conjunctions of features. That is, unattended features could be glued together to create a percept of a stimulus that was not initially presented. For example, subjects might report seeing blue 'B's in a display that included blue stimuli and 'B' stimuli, though not blue 'B's, when they were required to attend neither to blue items nor to 'B's. In a more recent version of the FIT, Treisman (1988) postulates a mechanism for the gluing process. Feature maps are suggested as representational structures that indicate the presence or absence of features. These feature maps correspond to visual dimensions such as colour or shape. Conjoint searches cannot be performed by simply checking the activation of detectors on feature maps. Instead, they require activation on two different maps not only to be checked but also linked to a specific location. Treisman (1993) suggests that generation of feature and location maps may take place in parallel as a result of activity in the 'what' and 'where' systems.

Duncan and Humphreys (1989, 1992) have modified the FIT to produce an attentional engagement theory (AET) of visual attention. They argue that the time taken to detect a target depends upon two factors. These are the similarity between targets and non-targets, and the similarity amongst the non-targets themselves. They suggest that search times will increase with increased similarity between targets and non-targets and with decreased similarity amongst the set of non-targets. Thus, the longest search times will occur when non-targets are dissimilar to each other but similar to the target. The term 'similarity' is used here in a fairly informal way but can be subject to much more rigorous definition (Tversky, 1977). Humphreys *et al.* (1985) have demonstrated that search times could be very rapid even in conjoint searches if non-targets were all the same and dissimilar to the target. In this case targets were inverted Ts whilst the distractors were upright Ts.

2.9 Automaticity

Shiffrin and Schneider's theory

This section will consider evidence that some forms of perceptual processing, following extensive practice, become effectively 'automatic'. This issue was introduced in Chapter 1. The possibility of automatic processing was investigated by Shiffrin and Schneider (1977), who defined automatic processing as processing which is not capacity limited; that is, not affected by the limitations of short-term or working memory, and not dependent upon attention. As a result of this lack of capacity limitation, automatic processing of a number of stimuli may occur in parallel. They also argued that automatic processes are difficult to change once learned. They defined controlled processing as being exactly the opposite. That is, processing which is capacity limited, attention dependent and therefore almost inevitably serial. The main advantage of controlled processing is that it is under much more conscious control than automatic processing, enabling it to be used flexibly and adaptively.

An adequate definition of 'automatic' would also include that automatic processing is inevitable, that it will always occur when an appropriate stimulus is presented and that, once activated, it will run to its completion. For most adult readers, reading a word is an example of an automatic process. It is virtually impossible to not read a word of one's native language. Here, 'reading' may be defined as accessing the phonology (sound), semantics (meaning) and orthography (spelling) when the perceived word is (automatically) matched to an internal representation of that word in our memory store of word knowledge (referred to as the internal lexicon). The effect is readily demonstrated in the classic Stroop effect (Stroop, 1935), in which an automatic task (reading the word) is interfering with an attention-dependent one (identifying the ink colour). The definitions of automatic and controlled processing would not allow for interference in the reverse direction.

Shiffrin and Schneider (1977) made use of the visual search paradigm to investigate automaticity. Subjects memorised a memory set comprising one, two, three or four letters and had to decide as quickly but also as accurately as possible whether any of those targets were present in a visual display comprising a sequence of arrays of letters and numbers. Two experimental conditions will be considered. In one, called 'consistent mapping', only consonants were used as memory set elements and numbers as distractors (or vice versa). In the 'varied mapping' condition a mixture of consonants and numbers were used as elements of both the memory and distractor sets. Two main effects were found. Firstly, negative trials, in which the targets did not occur in any of the arrays examined, took longer than positive trials in which targets did occur. This is not surprising and readily explainable since, on average, targets will occur half-way through arrays and, once the target has been located, no further processing is required. In contrast, on a negative trial, processing can only stop when all the array has been processed. Secondly, Shiffrin and Schnieder (1977) found no set size effects under consistent mapping conditions for positive or negative trials but found linearly increasing functions for both under varied mapping conditions. They interpreted this as implying that subjects in the consistent mapping condition employed automatic, parallel processing based upon many years of discriminating letters from numbers. Since there does not appear to be any hard-wired basis in the brain for such discrimination, this ability therefore represents a clear example of the acquisition of perceptual skills by learning from experience.

2.10 The spotlight model of visual attention

Visual orienting

Posner (1978) and his colleagues have developed an approach to visual attention that has been very influential. He offers an account of visual attention, or 'orienting', that is fairly independent of the FIT and AET and which has been very useful in understanding failures of perceptual and attentional processes following brain injury or disease. Posner (1978) proposed a two-stage model of attention in which presentation of a stimulus initially makes contact with its internal representation. This is seen as an automatic process which is fast and involuntary and results in activation of representations associated with that stimulus. This activation may then produce facilitation, that is, more rapid and less error-prone processing of subsequent, related stimuli. The second stage of attention is both conscious and slower. This may result in the generation of expectancies based on the information contained in priming stimuli. These may produce a facilitative effect if expectations are confirmed but otherwise inhibition, that is, slower, more error-prone processing, if they are not. This differential pattern of costs and benefits was demonstrated by Neely (1977), who showed a rapid, facilitative effect of naturally related priming words (such as 'bird' – 'robin') and a slower-emerging pattern of facilitation and inhibition to arbitrary associations at intervals between prime and target long enough for conscious expectancies to build up.

A similar technique has been applied to visual **orienting**. This may be defined as the shifting of visual attention to various spatial locations. If such orienting is in response to visual stimuli, then it may again be either automatic or voluntary. Posner (1978) used the technique of priming spatial locations using cues that varied in their reliability as predictors of the spatial location of a subsequent target stimulus that had to be processed. For example, an arrow stimulus may correctly cue the subsequent position of the target on 40 per cent of trials and incorrectly cue its position on 10 per cent of trials. A neutral cue (e.g. a cross) would be presented on 50 per cent of trials. Relative to the neutral cue, the correct cue produced a facilitation of detection of the target and the invalid cue produced an inhibition of the detection of the target. This effect was independent of eye movements since the result still emerged even if the intervals between cue and stimulus were too short for eye movements to occur. On the basis of findings of this kind, Posner and his colleagues produced the spotlight model for covert (that is, unrelated to eye movements) visual orienting such that the spotlight enhances efficiency of detection of events within its beam. The size of this beam has been estimated at one degree of visual angle (Humphreys, 1981). In addition, a number of distinct process in visual orienting have been identified. These include general alerting, disengaging attention from the currently attended stimulus, shifting attention to a new target, and engaging attention to that new target.

Neurological impairments of orienting

Neurological impairments of perception and attention have been found in which some of the processing elements (alerting, disengaging, shifting or engaging) appear to have been disturbed. One such condition, unilateral visual neglect (UVN), is described more fully in Chapter 3. Posner *et al.* (1984) found that patients performed very poorly on the standard Posner task when the cue was presented to the unimpaired visual field and the target to the impaired field. UVN is characterised by the tendency to ignore objects on one side of space, usually the left side following right-hemispheric brain damage, usually to the parietal region. Posner *et al.* (1984) suggests that some UVN patients have difficulty in disengaging attention from the unimpaired side of space. Similar studies of patients with mid-brain damage, such as supranuclear palsy or Balint's syndrome (Posner *et al.*, 1985) have shown that these patients experience problems with the shifting of attention. Finally, studies of patients with damage to the pulvinar nucleus of the thalamus (Rafal and Posner, 1987) have shown that these patients have difficulty in engaging attention to a new target. Posner and Petersen (1990) conclude that the parietal lobe is responsible for disengaging attention from its present focus, mid-brain areas act to shift attention to a new focus, whilst the pulvinar nucleus is involved in reading out information from the newly selected location.

Central and peripheral cueing: two systems?

Central and peripheral cueing exert differential effects. Peripheral cues produce rapid cuing effects which are the same, regardless of whether or not the cues are informative. Moreover, they cannot be ignored even when subjects are instructed to do so, and they are unaffected by asking subjects to carry out a concurrent task (see Humphreys and Bruce, 1989). Peripheral cues therefore have all the characteristics of automatic shifting of attention. Central cueing, on the other hand, appears to have the characteristics of controlled processing, to the extent that they have slower effects, are affected by informativeness, can be ignored and are affected by a concurrent load. Posner (1980) distinguishes two visual orienting systems. One is an automatic, or exogenous, attentional system driven by external stimuli. The other is a voluntary, or endogenous, system. Properties of visual attention, such as the costs involved in attending to attributes of two objects simultaneously, may not apply to both of these systems equally.

The zoom-lens modification

Eriksen (1990) proposed a 'zoom-lens' modification of the original spotlight metaphor. This has the advantage of being more flexible, since the size of the beam is alterable depending upon task demands. The zoom-lens may be regarded as simply a variable beam spotlight. Laberge (1983) produced some supporting data. He asked subjects to judge either an entire word (global attention condition) or the central letter within the word (directed attention condition). When subjects had to recall a particular letter when presented with a surprise probe, no effect of letter position was found for the subjects in the global condition, whilst subjects in the letter condition were as fast as the global attention group on the central letter only but slower for all other letters. Clearly, letters falling outside the main focus of attention received less processing than did the central letter in the directed attention condition, indicating that the size of the spotlight is indeed modifiable by task requirements.

Subsequent studies, however, indicate that visual attention can be oriented towards arbitrary shapes (such as an annulus, banana-shape or other shape) that appear prima facie to have little to do with the spotlight or zoom-lens (Juola *et al.*, 1991). Equally, attention may be cued on the basis of non-spatial cues such as relative motion (Neisser and Becklin, 1975). More recent work by Driver and his colleagues (summarised in Driver, 1996) has shown that visual attention is cued as readily by attributes of objects as it is by spatial location or relative motion. This work will be considered in more detail in a later section.

Inhibition of return

Efficient attention-directed search for an object requires that attention be prevented from returning to recently examined environmental locations. This is termed 'inhibition of return' (IOR). Posner and Cohen (1984) proposed that IOR is a search mechanism that prevents attentional perseveration (i.e. wasteful re-examination of empty or previously checked locations). The internal representations upon which IOR operates were examined by Tipper *et al.* (1994). They found that IOR mechanisms have access to both object-based and environment-based representations. Environment-based inhibition can be associated with a featureless environment whereas the object-based mechanism requires that attention be oriented to a visible object. Once a target has been engaged in an environment, the object-based system ensures that attention moves with that target rather than becoming fixed to locations in space previously occupied by that object.

2.11 Visual attention

What or where?

Until recently the spotlight was on the prevailing view of visual attention. An alternative view holds that covert attention performs functions that eye movements cannot (Duncan, 1984). Whereas eye movements can only enhance a fovea-shaped region of space at any one time, covert attention may flexibly adopt various configurations in order to enhance the object that is the focus of attention. This object may not necessarily be fovea-shaped but may be contained within any shape. On this view (Kanwisher and Driver, 1992) covert attention gets directed to grouped objects rather than regions of space illuminated by the spotlight.

An initial problem for the visual system is to isolate those parts of the complex image that belong together from those that belong to separate objects. The

Gestaltist approach identified several basic principles for doing this. Objects so grouped are then likely to be part of the same object in the real world. Influential models of vision, such as that of Marr, suggest that early visual processing must first segment the visual image of an object into candidate objects by such grouping processes. Later attentional processes (Treisman, 1988, 1993) then go on to identify each segmented object more fully. On this view, then, grouping precedes the allocation of attention, with the result that coherent objects tend to be attended as a whole.

Mack *et al.* (1992) contested this view and argued that there is absolutely no grouping prior to attention. This argument was based on performance with groups of displays like those used in the Gestalt studies but in which subjects also had to discriminate an additional central character. Subjects were then asked the surprise question of how the background elements were grouped in the preceding display. Their performance was at chance level, indicating that no grouping of these displays had occurred pre-attentively. However, Driver and Tipper (1989) point out that subjects may simply have forgotten the ignored stimulus and that this does not therefore imply that processing may not have occurred at the time. This may be tested if the question is instead made prospective instead of recollective, as in the negative priming studies of Driver (1984). In one experiment designed to test this (Driver and Baylis, 1989) subjects had to judge a central target while ignoring flanking letters. The flankers impaired performance more when they were grouped with the target by various factors, such as good continuation, common colour or common motion, than when they were not so grouped. This indicates that grouping affects the spatial distribution of attention and suggests that it can indeed precede selection.

Driver and Baylis (1989) also found that distant distractors can produce more interference than distractors which lie between the target and those distractors but which are not grouped with them. This finding is problematic for a strict spotlight view, since the spotlight would have to specifically exclude certain areas ('black holes') within the attended region of space. This finding is, however, not always made (Kramer *et al.*, 1991) and appears to depend on stimulus parameters, but has been demonstrated in a number of studies (Driver and McLeod, 1992; McLeod *et al.*, 1991). Driver (1996) concludes that these search results 'show unequivocally that attention can select a spatially dispersed group to the exclusion of a separate but spatially intermingled group'.

2.12 Perception, attention and consciousness

A new look at a new look

Greenwald (1992) claims that 'unconscious cognition is now solidly established in empirical research, but it appears to be intellectually much simpler than the sophisticated agency portrayed in psychoanalytic theory'. This telling remark reveals the lengthy history of the issue of unconscious processes which can in large measure be traced back to Freud and the psychoanalytic school of psychology, for whom unconscious psychic forces were the main determining influences on thought and behaviour. Bruner and Postman (1947) introduced an empirical approach to the role of unconscious processes in cognition, a development which was termed the 'New Look' at unconscious mechanisms. A number of further 'New Looks' have been taken at the issue of unconscious cognitive processing, known as New Look 2 (Erdelyi, 1974, Dixon and Henley, 1980), and New Look 3 (Greenwald, 1992, Loftus and Klinger, 1992). In these studies unconscious cognition has been demonstrated using experimental paradigms such as subliminal perception, in which behaviour or physiological responses are shown to be influenced by stimuli which fall below the subject's threshold of awareness. This is achieved by presenting stimuli of very low intensity or very short duration, or at frequencies beyond the range of conscious perception, by visual or auditory masking, or by the use of unattended channels as in dichotic listening. The sorts of behavioural or physiological reactions that have been elicited in response to subliminal stimuli have included GSRs, invoked EEG potentials, verbal behaviour and conscious perception of above-threshold stimuli, all of which have been shown to be influenced by subliminal stimuli.

Automaticity is another example of non-conscious processing. When a task becomes automated, that is, when it makes minimal demands on attention as when driving a car under routine conditions, highly practised procedural (or implicit) knowledge is employed with conscious control available as a back-up strategy under difficult conditions. How then does the operator know when such conditions pertain? In order to switch from automatic to conscious control the subject must be monitoring the environment unconsciously. This consideration harks back to the cocktail party scenario (p. 45) in which background conversations are unconsciously monitored for mention of a salient word such as one's own name.

Dixon (1981) argues that subliminal perception implies that the processes responsible for conscious perceptual experience are not the same as those which mediate the transmission of information through the brain from receptors to effectors, since the former also require a coincident excitation from the ascending reticular activating system of the brain (which controls the brain's level of arousal or alertness) in order to produce that awareness.

Subliminal stimuli may be subjected to extensive preconscious processing involving long-term memory and emotional responses (Dixon, 1990). This is particularly evident in the phenomenon of perceptual defence, in which the perception of disturbing or embarrassing material is selectively inhibited. Groeger (1988) has effectively dismissed the possibility that subliminal perception may be based on the conscious perception of fragments of the stimulus, since greater semantic influences were found following a subliminal stimulus than were found following a supraliminal one.

A further technique that has been used for the study of subliminal effects is priming. This refers to the effect of prior exposure to a priming stimulus on the recognition of a subsequent stimulus. A considerable literature exists on the 'costs' and 'benefits' of priming on subsequent performance in terms of impairments or facilitation of that performance. Cheesman and Merikle (1986) have demonstrated that priming effects may occur even if the primes are presented too briefly for conscious identification. This technique has been used on brain-damaged patients who may be primed by stimuli that they fail to identify explicitly. Neuro-psychological syndromes such as blindsight (see Chapter 3) may also involve the processing of stimuli of which subjects are not consciously aware.

Marcel (1983) conducted some studies using visual masking that in many ways are among the most convincing as well as the most controversial examples of semantic-level processing in the absence of conscious awareness. He adapted an associative priming paradigm first used by Meyer and Schvaneveldt (1971). Subjects were presented with a masked prime and the time taken to make a lexical decision (such as word/non-word) was measured. Under normal conditions, a prime such as 'bread' facilitates the lexical judgement of a related word such as 'butter' but not of unrelated words such as 'nurse'. Marcel applied masking such that the priming word could not be detected on more than 60 per cent of trials. However, when the primes were masked by a pattern mask, there was clear evidence of priming. This did not occur with a random noise mask, consistent with the suggestion that priming may operate via two different mechanisms of interruption and interference (Turvey, 1973). Marcel proposed that the pattern mask did not prevent automatic, unconscious access to stored semantic knowledge but that it did disrupt perceptual integration and hence entry to consciousness. Similar suggestions are made by Allport (1977) and Coltheart (1980a).

Greenwald (1992) distinguishes two senses of the term 'unconscious'. Firstly, material is unconscious if it falls outside of the 'spotlight' of attention. Secondly, the term 'unconscious' may be used to imply failure to access or report material via introspection. According to Greenwald, the two senses of unconscious cognition are explicable within a network representation. In the first sense of conscious attention, consciousness is defined as corresponding to network operation that boosts activation to high levels in subnetworks. Secondly, in the sense of intro-spection, Greenwald argues that by virtue of having verbal outputs which are connected to 'hidden units' the network can report on, or 'introspect' on its own internal network status. These outputs provide the capacity for introspection but provide no assurance that the reports which result are valid.

The connectionist approach overcomes the basic paradoxes of serial-stage accounts. These include, for example, the seemingly paradoxical operation of a late stage in processing (semantic analysis) when an earlier stage (feature analysis) is not complete. In contrast, by permitting semantic and feature analysis to occur in parallel rather than in series, the network paradigm can account non-paradoxically for semantic analysis without the need for absence–presence discrimination of the unattended object.

Greenwald (1992) argues that unconscious cognition has been demonstrated to have achieved nothing more cognitively sophisticated than the analysis of partial meaning of single words. Although unconscious perceptual processing is clearly possible, the extent of its sophistication appears to be considerably less than psychoanalytic theory gave it credit for.

Summary

- The visual system is specialised for the parallel analysis of multiple attributes ('features') of stimuli including colour, motion, orientation, form and spatial frequency.
- The visual system has two distinct pathways concerned with the processing of 'what' and 'where' aspects of stimuli called the ventral and dorsal routes.
- The visual system employs grouping procedures, extracts depth cues from the environment, and applies operations such as constancy scaling in order to construct a representation of the objects in the world.
- Marr's theory is perhaps the best worked out model of how this representation is constructed.
- Visual illusions may be based on misapplications of knowledge, or of mechanisms (such as constancy scaling) employed by the visual system. They may also derive from physiological fatigue or be the result of poor stimulus quality.
- Object recognition may be achieved by matching the output of feature analysis with stored representations of objects,
- Attention helps guide processing to important objects.
- The role of attention in perception may be to 'glue' features together in a coherent form or to appropriately direct perception–behaviour linkages.
- Attention may be directed to spatial locations, as in the spotlight model, but convincing evidence also exists for the direction of attention to objects.
- Awareness of an object may not be a necessary condition for the activation of semantic-level representations of that object.

Further reading

Gazzaniga, M.S. Ivry, R.B. and Mangun, G.R. (1998). *Cognitive Neuroscience: The Biology of the Mind*. New York: Norton. This book covers the neuroscience of perception and attention in considerably more detail.

Gordon, I.E. (1997). *Theories of Visual Perception* (2nd edn). Chichester: Wiley. There are many textbooks on perception but this is a particularly good one.

Styles, E.A. (1997). *The Psychology of Attention*. Hove: Psychology Press. In contrast, there is a distinct lack of introductory textbooks devoted to attention. This is probably the best.

Chapter 3

Disorders of perception and attention

3.1 Introduction

In Chapter 2 we considered some of the processes involved in perception and attention, and learned a little about how we construct an internal representation of the world around us. Given the complexity of these processes, it is not surprising to learn that brain damage can disrupt perception and attention. However, what is surprising is the range and nature of the deficits that can be observed. By systematically studying these deficits, we are able to learn much about the processes that must be occurring in the intact brain. The emphasis in this chapter is to study the pattern of disorders, and relatively little attempt has been made to locate functions within the brain. I have taken the view that we are interested in *how* we perceive not *where* we perceive.

In structuring this account the approach adopted has been to study increasingly specific disorders. We will start by considering rather general disorders which prevent conscious perception or distort attention. We will then consider disorders which affect the ability to recognise objects and finally discuss disorders which appear to affect the ability to recognise one particular category of object or the ability to encode one particular type of information.

3.2 Blindsight

As we saw in Chapter 2, the striate cortex is central to visual perception. Damage to the left striate cortex will result in blindness in the right visual field of both eyes and damage to the right striate cortex will result in blindness in the left visual field of both eyes. These areas of blindness are called **scotoma**. In order to imagine the effect of such damage, look straight ahead, close your left eye and cover the left half of your right eye. The very restricted visual field you now experience is similar to that which you would experience following damage to your right striate cortex. To see anything to your left side you will need to turn your head (the patient would be able to move his or her eyes).

Now imagine that you were asked to point to a flash of light that had occurred somewhere to your 'blind' left side. If persuaded to take part in this puzzling experiment, you would expect to perform at chance levels, sometimes guessing the correct location but more often being wrong. Poppel *et al.* (1973) studied a group of ex-servicemen who suffered visual field deficits as a result of gunshot wounds to the striate cortex, and asked his participants to make just such judgements. Lights were flashed in the defective area of the visual field of each participant. Because the servicemen could not see the flashes, the light was paired with the sound of a buzzer, and on hearing the buzzer the servicemen were asked to move their eyes in the direction of the light source. The servicemen found this a difficult task, but to their surprise all were able to direct their gaze towards the light which they could not see.

In the following year, Weiskrantz *et al.* (1974) described a patient, DB, who seemed to demonstrate the same remarkable ability. DB was blind in his lower left visual field following surgery to remove part of his right striate cortex to relieve very severe migraine headaches. What was remarkable about DB was the extent to which he could report details of objects appearing in the blind areas of his visual field despite no conscious experience of seeing them. Weiskrantz coined the term 'blindsight' to describe this phenomenon.

In a series of experiments over many years (see Weiskrantz, 1986) Weiskrantz and his colleagues were able to systematically investigate the perceptual abilities preserved in the 'blind' areas of DB's visual field. DB was able to detect the presence of an object, and indicate its location in space by pointing. He could discriminate between moving and stationary objects, and between horizontal and vertical lines, and he could distinguish the letter 'X' from the letter 'O'. However, he was unable to distinguish between 'X' and a triangle, suggesting that the ability to distinguish between X and O was dependent on some low-level characteristic of these stimuli rather than any residual ability to discriminate form. DB's inability to discriminate form is further demonstrated by his failure to distinguish between rectangles of various sizes or between straight and curved-sided triangles.

Blindsight – a sceptical perspective

Some scientists have questioned the existence of blindsight, arguing that there are several possible explanations for blindsight which need to be considered carefully. This limited ability to respond to an object presented in the 'blind' areas of the visual field could either result from the action of the normal, undamaged areas of the visual system or indicate that some sight is preserved in the 'blind' area of the visual field.

Campion *et al.* (1983) favoured the first of these alternatives, suggesting that blindsight was achieved by the subject responding to 'stray light' which was reflected from the object on to the functioning areas of the visual field (remember that patients such as DB are only partially blind, and can see normally in large areas of their visual field). Campion *et al.* described one patient who reported that he was using such a strategy to distinguish between vertical and horizontal bars presented to the blind areas of his visual field. This patient claimed that he could see a faint glow in the preserved areas of his visual field and used this cue to undertake the task. Campion *et al.* also convincingly demonstrated that such a strategy could lead to the accurate detection of the location of a light in a 'blind' area of the visual field of normal subjects whose vision had been masked. Like blindsight patients, these volunteers were able to accurately point to the location of lights that occurred within the masked areas of their vision. These individuals could not have been responding directly to the objects they pointed to and must therefore have been reacting to some perceptual artefact, such as 'stray light' falling into their unmasked visual field. However, it is difficult to see how this stray light could explain DB's ability to distinguish letters such as 'X' and 'O' or two different spatial frequency gratings (two different patterns of black and white stripes which have the same average brightness). In addition, DB could locate objects even against a bright background, whereas Campion *et al.*'s normal subjects could only locate a light source against a low level of background illumination.

Paradoxically, the best evidence against the stray light explanation came from DB's *inability* to respond accurately to objects whose image fell on to his

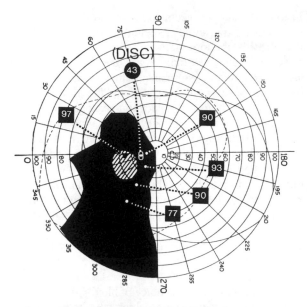

Figure 3.1 Weiskrantz's investigation of DB's blindsight

Note: The dark area indicates the 'blind' area of DB's visual field. The hashed area indicates that region in which DB had some partial awareness of the presence of the light. When the light occurred at his blindspot (marked DISC) DB performed at chance level, correctly reporting the presence of the light on less than 50 per cent of occasions. However, performance at all other locations was well above chance. The stray light hypothesis would predict that performance at the blindspot should be well above chance.

Source: Weiskrantz (1986), reproduced by permission of Oxford University Press

blindspot. The blindspot is the place where the optic nerve passes through the retina. As there are no receptor cells at this location, we are totally blind to images falling on this part of the retina. If DB's blindsight was explained by stray light, then we would expect him to perform equally well whether the image of the object fell on the blindspot or in the scotoma. In fact, DB showed no evidence of being able to detect the presence of objects or lights presented at his blindspot, yet could accurately detect objects or events occurring within the scotoma immediately adjacent to the blindspot (see Figure 3.1).

The sensation of blindsight

It is very difficult to imagine what a patient such as DB experiences when a stimulus is presented within the 'blind' regions of his visual field. It is clear that the experience is very different from that of normal vision; for example, Weiskrantz records DB as saying that he 'felt' movement rather than saw it. As far as we can tell, blindsight patients are learning to respond to very subtle experiences which have little in common with the normal perceptual experience. Indeed, it has been suggested that one reason why reports of blindsight are so rare (most patients with damage to the striate cortex do not report blindsight – a point emphasised by Gazzaniga, 1994) is that patients have to learn to associate these subtle experiences with events in the visual world (Weiskrantz, 1980).

So how can we imagine the experience of blindsight? Suppose you are sitting reading this book when suddenly, in your peripheral vision ('out of the corner of your eye'), a spider scuttles across the floor. Before you are conscious of the motion, you move your head and eyes towards the spider. You did not 'see' the spider but your visual system was able to guide you towards it. Perhaps this is a reasonable analogy to the experience of blindsight. Patients such as DB do not have any conscious experience of perception, yet at some level below that accessible to introspection, the visual system does have access to information about the outside world.

The implications of blindsight: one visual system or two?

The fact that an individual can respond to the visual characteristics of an object without being conscious of seeing it is remarkable. However, more importantly, blindsight provides us with some clues about the workings of the perceptual processes that occur in the intact brain, and about the relationship between perception and conscious experience.

One possible explanation for blindsight is that we have two separate visual systems, one primitive non-striate system and a more advanced striate system. The primitive non-striate system might be sensitive to movement, speed, direction and other potentially important characteristics of a stimulus without giving rise to conscious perception. A frog can catch a fly because it can locate its position in space very accurately, but we do not imagine that the frog consciously perceives the fly. Perhaps blindsight represents the working of this primitive visual system whose functioning is normally masked by the conscious perception which results from the action of the striate visual system.

A slightly different explanation would be to see the striate and non-striate systems as having evolved to fulfil different roles, and this explanation has the advantage that it does not require us to accept that evolutionary process has preserved a now redundant system. But what might the function of the non-striate, blindsight system be? One possibility would be that the striate system has evolved to allow the identification of an object whereas the non-striate system has evolved to allow the localisation of that object in space. There is some evidence from non-human animal studies to support this view. Based on a series of lesion studies in hamsters, Schneider (1969) suggested that there were two separate visual pathways, one responsible for the identification of objects, the other for the location of objects in space.

As we shall see later in this chapter, Goodale and Milner (1992) have also suggested that there are two different visual pathways in the human. However, they believe the distinction is between a system which is responsible for the recognition of objects and one which is responsible for the control of actions such as picking up an object. Intriguingly, Goodale and Milner suggested that object recognition and the control of action might be mediated by different and mutually incompatible types of representation. In this case, they reasoned, it might be *necessary* to separate these two pathways and only allow one of them to have access to consciousness.

3.3 Unilateral spatial neglect

As we saw in the previous section, patients with blindsight are able to respond to a stimulus they cannot see. In unilateral spatial neglect the opposite seems to be true – patients fail to respond to stimuli which they can see. The patient with unilateral neglect has normal visual acuity, but fails to observe objects or events to one side of the body. Neglect occurs following damage to the contralateral hemisphere; most commonly damage to the right hemisphere results in left spatial neglect. A typical patient with left neglect will simply fail to notice objects to the left side of space, for example, only eating the food on the right-hand side of the plate or only drawing the right-hand side of an object.

A classic demonstration of spatial neglect is to ask a patient to draw a clock face. Neglect patients will tend to either omit the numbers between 7 and 11, or if they notice their error, will try to squeeze these numbers on to the right side of the clock (see Figure 3.2).

A disorder of attention?

At first sight unilateral spatial neglect seems to be a failure of attention. The patient is failing to attend to any object which appears in the left half of the visual field. However, there are several reasons to reject this description of the problem. Firstly, there is the phenomenon of extinction where patients are able to respond to a

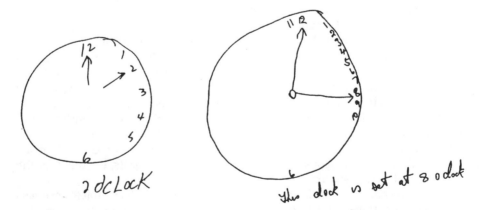

Figure 3.2 Examples of drawings of clock faces produced by patients with unilateral visual neglect
Source: Halligan and Marshall (1993), by permission of Psychology Press Limited, Hove, UK

stimulus in their neglected field when presented on its own, but fail to respond to a stimulus in the neglected field when it is paired with an identical stimulus occurring in the preserved field. Baylis *et al.* (1993) demonstrated that an object would be recognised in the left visual field if it was paired with a different object appearing in the right visual field. However, if the objects in the left and right visual fields were identical, the patient would only report the existence of the object in the right visual field.

Secondly, it is clear that some patients with left spatial neglect are not simply failing to report objects to the left of fixation, but rather are failing to report the left side of an object, regardless of where this falls. For example, Marshall and Halligan (1993) asked patients with left neglect to copy pictures of plants. They found that patients would fail to draw stems or leaves on the left-hand side of the plant, but would also fail to draw the petals on the left-hand side of a flower even if that flower was on the right-hand side of the plant. Thus, the neglect seems to be at the level of the object or part of the object (flower) rather than simply in terms of space relative to the patient.

Thirdly, recent studies have observed a dissociation between peri-personal space (areas of space within reach of the patient) and extra-personal space (space which is beyond reach). Halligan and Marshall (1991) demonstrated that their patient showed left unilateral neglect for peri-personal but not extra-personal space. Cowey *et al.* (1994) demonstrated the reverse pattern, showing that in some patients left neglect was worse in extra-personal than peri-personal space.

In addition, spatial neglect has been shown to occur for stimuli that are imagined rather than observed. Bisiach and Luzzatti (1978) asked neglect patients to describe a piazza in Milan from memory. The patients were asked to describe the piazza from two different perspectives. Buildings which were neglected from one perspective were described from the other perspective as the patients only described buildings which would appear to their right.

Finally, there is some evidence that patients show insight to aspects of a neglected stimulus. Marshall and Halligan (1988) showed a patient pairs of drawings of a house. The patient failed to notice when the house on the left was on fire, but when asked which house they would prefer to live in indicated the non-burning house.

Explaining spatial neglect

It is becoming clear that unilateral spatial neglect may be a group of deficits rather than a single unitary disorder. Halligan and Marshall (1994) reviewed some of the many explanations which have been offered, but it seems unlikely that any one of these theories is ever going to explain all of the deficits reported to date. When studied systematically patients seem to demonstrate a range of different deficits, and it may be that in the future it will be possible to classify these deficits in some systematic manner which will aid our understanding of attention and perception. In the following section we will consider a disorder for which attempts to classify the deficits observed have been rather more successful, leading to a better under-standing of the processes involved in normal perception.

3.4 Visual agnosia

A patient suffering from visual agnosia is unable to recognise everyday objects despite having apparently normal visual acuity, memory, language function and intelligence. An agnosic patient can move around without bumping into things, and can reach for and pick up objects which they are unable to recognise. Farah (1990) defined the condition as 'an impairment in the higher visual processes necessary for object recognition, with relative preservation of elementary visual functions'. Farah's use of the word 'relative' is important. As we shall see, the question of whether it is possible to observe a 'pure' agnosia in which there is no degradation of basic perpetual function is unresolved.

At first sight, this inability to recognise an object might appear to be a failure of language or of memory (see chapters 9 and 5 respectively). However, visual agnosia differs from these memory or language disorders in that agnosic patients retain their knowledge about objects, and so can, for example, name an object when allowed to touch it, or describe an object when told its name.

For the cognitive neuropsychologist, visual agnosia is an important condition because it provides an insight into the inner workings of the perceptual system in the intact brain. As we shall see, the fact that brain damage can result in an inability to recognise particular types of object or to recognise objects from a particular angle while preserving other perceptual abilities provides a powerful demonstration of the modular nature of perception.

Visual agnosia is in fact only one of a set of conditions. The word 'agnosia' roughly translates as 'not knowing', so visual agnosia is 'not knowing by vision'. In tactile agnosia a patient cannot recognise objects by touch, and in auditory agnosia a patient is unable to recognise an object by its sound (such as a bell ringing). Some patients show symptoms in more than one modality (for example, not being able to recognise an object by either sight or touch). However, in this chapter we shall exclusively consider visual agnosia in an attempt to understand better the nature of visual perception in the normal brain.

Apperceptive and associative agnosia

Lissauer (1890) was the first person to study this condition systematically. He adopted the term 'mindblindness' which was originally coined by Munk (1881) to describe a similar condition produced by the removal of the occipital lobes of a dog. In an early attempt to classify the variety of visual agnosias that he observed, Lissauer distinguished two patterns of deficit: **apperceptive agnosia** and **associative agnosia**.

In apperceptive agnosia it is thought that the failure to recognise an object is due to an inability to perceive the form. Patients suffering from this condition cannot draw an object (see Figure 3.3), match similar objects, or even describe the component parts of the object despite normal visual acuity. The patient can form an image of the object but not build a representation based on that image.

Associative agnosia is thought to result from a failure at a later stage in the object recognition process. A patient suffering from associative agnosia is able to

Figure 3.3 The attempts of a patient with apperceptive agnosia to copy six simple figures
Source: Farah (1990), reproduced by permission of MIT Press

draw an object, match similar objects and describe the component parts of an object, yet is unable to recognise the object. In associative agnosia, the perceptual process results in a stable representation, but the patient then fails to associate this representation with the stored knowledge about the object. Teuber (1968) described this condition as 'a precept stripped of its meaning'.

Although first proposed over a hundred years ago, Lissauer's distinction between individuals who cannot form a stable representation of an object, and individuals who can achieve a stable representation but cannot then link this representation to their semantic knowledge about the object, is still regarded as a useful one. The distinction relates well to David Marr's (1982) description of visual perception described in Chapter 2. Adopting Marr's terminology, apperceptive agnosia would result from an inability to form a stable 3-D representation of the object. This failure to achieve a 3-D representation could be either due to a failure to achieve an adequate viewer-centred 2.5-D sketch or because of an inability to progress from the 2.5-D sketch to a full 3-D sketch. By contrast, the associative agnosic would be seen as having achieved a stable 3-D representation but would then be unable to link this representation to stored knowledge about the object – the very last stage of the perceptual process.

In practical terms, the decision to categorise patients as apperceptive or associative is often based on their ability to copy a drawing. Apperceptive patients cannot copy a drawing due to their inability to perceive a picture accurately. Associative patients, on the other hand, can accurately copy a drawing despite being unable to recognise either the object or their drawing of it.

The localisation of lesions in patients with apperceptive agnosia

Jankowiak and Albert (1994) examined the reports published by nine authors describing a total of twelve patients who had been classified as suffering from apperceptive visual agnosia and who had been scanned (using either MRI or CAT scans) to determine the location of the lesion. They concluded that: 'Lesion Localisation in apperceptive visual agnosia tends to be posterior in the cerebral hemispheres, involving occipital, parietal, or posterior temporal regions bilaterally. Small focal or unilateral lesions rarely, if ever, produce this syndrome' (p. 436).

It is interesting to note that carbon monoxide poisoning seems to be a particularly common cause of apperceptive agnosia (for example, Adler, 1950; Benson and Greenberg, 1969; Campion and Latto, 1985; Mendez, 1988; Sparr *et al.* 1991). Carbon monoxide poisoning can result in a large number of widely spread small lesions, sometimes called 'salt and pepper' lesions. Campion and Latto (1985) suggested that these lesions might result in tiny scotomas scattered across the entire visual field which would make it difficult for the patient to discern the contours of an object. Possibly because it results from bilateral lesions, apperceptive agnosia is much rarer than associative agnosia. Jankowiak and Albert (1994) note that because of the lack of autopsy or (more accurate) PET scan data, any conclusion concerning the exact location of lesions responsible for apperceptive agnosia must be tentative at this stage.

The localisation of lesions in patients with associative agnosia

Associative agnosia is more frequently diagnosed than apperceptive agnosia, and the lesions responsible for this condition seem to be less varied or widespread. Jankowiak and Albert (1994) suggested that associative agnosia normally results from bilateral posterior lesions in the areas of the posterior cerebral artery which supplies blood to the visual cortex and temporal lobe, and that lesion size might be critical, with large lesions in this area resulting in general perceptual deficits rather than a 'pure' agnosia. They further suggested that lesions in this region might damage the pathways which connect visual information with stored visual memories in either the left or the right posterior hemisphere,

Concerns over the validity of visual agnosia

Visual agnosia has not always been recognised as a 'real' condition. The diagnosis of agnosia came under particularly strong attack from Bay (1953), who argued that patients who were thought to be suffering from visual agnosia had not been adequately screened for deficits of visual acuity. Bay was also worried by the inconsistent behaviour exhibited by agnosic patients who recognised some objects but not others and failed to recognise an object on one occasion yet correctly identified it on another. He considered this to be evidence that agnosia was actually a mild form of dementia. Although some patients with dementia can show symptoms which are similar to those of agnosia (Mendez *et al.*, 1990), many agnosic patients are highly intelligent and motivated and show no evidence of intellectual impairment (e.g. patient HJA described by Humphreys and Riddoch (1987) – see case study below). Bender and Feldman (1972) shared Bay's doubts and argued that all the cases they had encountered showed evidence of visual field deficits, problems with fixation, dementia or a lack of attention.

Bay's concern that many visual agnosics had unrecognised sensory deficits which could account for their problems has remained topical. Warrington (1982, 1985) has been particularly careful to rule out the possibility that patients may be suffering from sensory deficits which could account for their difficulties in object recognition. Warrington has argued that an inability to discriminate colour, shape or orientation suggests a sensory deficit which may be sufficient to explain the apparent agnosia, and patients showing one or more of these deficits are classified as pseudo-agnosic. However, this very clear distinction between sensory and perceptual disorders is not widely supported. For example, patient HJA described by Humphreys and Riddoch became completely colour-blind following his stroke. This is a very common condition in patients with object recognition difficulties, but Humphreys and Riddoch would not describe their patient as suffering from pseudo-agnosia. Although there is little doubt that the inability to perceive colour did on occasions hamper HJA's attempts to name objects, this deficit cannot fully account for his problems, and most colour-blind people show no evidence of visual agnosia. Warrington's insistence that a deficit in shape discrimination must result in the classification of pseudo-agnosia is particularly controversial, but is supported by the work of Efron (1968) who described a patient, Mr S, who showed symptoms that might have indicated apperceptive agnosia. However, Efron considered that Mr S's inability to distinguish between two shapes when matched for brightness indicated a sensory deficit in shape discrimination. As we shall see later, Humphreys and Riddoch (1987) proposed a new classification of visual agnosia that included 'shape agnosia'. It is clear from Humphreys and Riddoch's description that they would classify Mr S as suffering from shape agnosia. Thus, the very symptom that would result in Warrington describing a patient as pseudo-agnosic is the defining symptom of Humphreys and Riddoch's classification of shape agnosia.

HJA – a case history in visual agnosia

Humphreys and Ridoch's research on visual agnosia has been greatly influenced by their work with one famous (among neuropsychologists at least) patient, HJA. In a fascinating account of their work wih HJA, Humphreys and Riddoch (1987) provide a vaulable insight into the life of an individual with visual agnosia.

HJA suffered damage to both occipital lobes following a post-operative stroke which affected his posterior cerebral artery. On waking up in hospital HJA was faced with a confusing and unfamiliar world. HJA described how he felt that his inability to recognise his surroundings must be due to some 'hangover' or 'bang on the head'. Despite some improvement over the next few weeks, HJA remained unable to recognise many familiar objects. When formally assessed, it was found that he was blind in the top half of both visual fields, but this alone could not account for his problems in recognising objects, as simple movements of his eyes or head would have been sufficient to reveal those aspects of his environment previously hidden by this visual field deficit. HJA could move around without bumping into objects and could reach out and pick things up, but he had considerable difficulty in naming objects on the basis of their appearance alone. Although he could recognise some objects many were a mystery to him, and he had particular difficulty in differentiating between members of a class of object with common characteristics (such as animals or plants). This problem is illustrated by the fact that HJA was capable of successfully trimming the garden hedge with shears, but would fail to notice the difference between the hedge and the roses, which he would decapitate.

It is clear that HJA's difficulty in naming objects was not due to a memory deficit as he was able to give detailed definitions of named objects, demonstrating that his memory for both the function and the appearance of objects was intact. However, when shown these very same objects HJA failed to recognise them (see Figure 3.4).

HJA offered the following definition of a carrot:

'A carrot is a root vegetable cultivated and eaten as human consumption world wide. Grown from seed as an annual crop, the carrot produces long thin leaves growing from a root head; this is deep growing and large in comparison with the leaf growth, some times gaining a length of 12 inches under a leaf top of similar height when grown in good soil. Carrots may be eaten raw or cooked and can be harvested during any size or state of growth. The general shape of a carrot root is an elongated cone and its colour ranges between red and yellow.' (p. 64)

However, HJA was unable to identify a line drawing of a carrot, saying:

'I have not even the glimmerings of an idea. The bottom point seems solid, and the other bits are feathery. It does not seem to be logical unless it is some sort of a brush.' (p. 59)

Figure 3.4 HJA's definition of the word 'carrot' and his attempt to recognise a line drawing of a carrot (as recorded by Humphreys and Riddoch, 1987)

It is clear that HJA could form a stable representation of the major components of the image and could deduce form and texture from a simple line drawing. However, he appeared to be unable to integrate these parts into a single representation which he could relate to his memory of common objects. Critically, when blindfolded and asked to identify objects by touch he was able to name many objects which he could not identify by sight alone, demonstrating that his problem was not some form of anomia (loss of memory for the names of objects).

HJA was able to describe a favourite etching of London which had hung on his living room wall for many years, and was still able to pick out some characteristic aspects of objects in the picture (such as the dome of St Paul's Cathedral), but he commented poignantly:

> But now it does not 'fit' my memory of the picture nor of the reality. Knowing that I should be able to identify the general design of the dome-headed, high circular central tower covering a particularly cruciform building, I can point out the expected detail but cannot recognise the whole structure. On the other hand I am sure I could draw a reasonable copy of the picture.
>
> (Humphreys and Riddoch, 1987, p. 33)

HJA also described a visit to an aircraft museum. During the war he had served in the RAF and at the museum he was able to describe the shape of his bomber to his friends, and was able to recount various stories and describe technical aspects of the aircraft. It is clear that he had a detailed memory for the aircraft and its appearance; however, HJA stated that 'in all honesty, I did not recognise the "whole"'.

When asked to copy a picture, such as the etching of London described above, HJA could produce a reasonable likeness (see Figure 3.5), but this image took six hours to complete by a laborious process of line-by-line reproduction which did not seem to be guided by any knowledge of the form of the object. It was as if he was being set the task of copying a complex pattern of random lines. However, when drawing from memory rather than attempting to copy, HJA produced very recognisable and detailed drawings (see Figure 3.6), indicating that he retained a good visual memory for the objects which he could no longer recognise. He stated:

> I don't find [drawing from memory] too difficult, bearing in mind that I never had much drawing ability. . . . My mind knows very clearly what I should like to draw and I can comprehend enough of my own handiwork to know if it is a reasonable representation of what I had in mind.

Humphreys and Riddoch's classification of agnosia

In some ways, HJA is not a typical agnosic patient, and Humphreys and Riddoch were concerned that his symptoms did not fit the classic description of either apperceptive or associative agnosia. Because HJA could copy a drawing, he would normally be classified as suffering from an associative agnosia. However, the fact that HJA might take many hours to copy a drawing in a slavish way suggests fundamental perceptual problems which he is seeking to overcome using a

Figure 3.5 HJA's copy of his favourite etching showing St Paul's Cathedral, London which took six hours to complete by a laborious process of line-by-line reproduction
Source: Humphreys and Riddoch (1987), reproduced by permission of Psychology Press Limited, Hove, UK

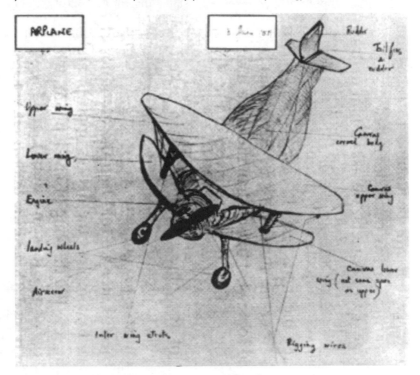

Figure 3.6 An example of one of HJA's drawings from memory
Source: Humphreys and Riddoch (1987), reproduced by permission of Psychology Press Limited, Hove, UK

non-standard strategy. It is clear that HJA can perceive the fine details of the drawing he is copying, but he seems unable to relate these local details to the whole shape of the object.

Humphreys and Riddoch suggested that there are two discrete steps in normal perception. In the first of these the global form of an object is encoded, while in the second the spatially distributed local features are 'bound' together into a more detailed representation. It is in this 'feature binding' that HJA's deficit was thought to lie.

This description of HJA's deficit was supported by other experiments. In one study, Humphreys and Riddoch asked HJA to indicate whether a drawing or a silhouette was of a real or made-up object which combined components of two real objects (see Figure 3.7). Control subjects find this object decision task very easy and perform slightly faster with drawings than with silhouettes. HJA showed the opposite pattern, being quicker and more accurate with the silhouettes than with the line drawings. When presented with a silhouette HJA was able to recognise the global shape without being confused by local detail, but when local detail was present in the drawings it seemed to distract him from the global shape of the object.

Thus it seems that Lissauer's distinction between apperceptive and associative agnosia is inadequate in HJA's case. Humphreys and Riddoch went on to propose a different and more detailed account of visual object agnosia. They proposed that five different types of agnosia could be identified: shape agnosia, integrative agnosia, transformational agnosia, semantic agnosia and semantic access agnosia. The first of these new categories, shape agnosia, covers patients who are unable to copy drawings, and so would previously have been described as having an apperceptive agnosia (or, as we saw earlier would be classified as pseudo-agnosics by Warrington). The second new category, integrative agnosia, covers

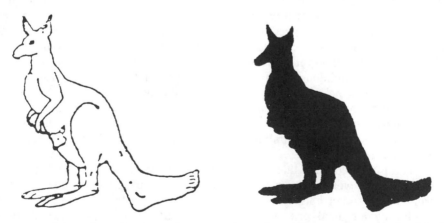

Figure 3.7 Items from the object decision task employed by Humphreys and Riddoch (1987). Patients are required to decide whether either drawings (left) or silhouettes (right) are of real or made-up objects.
Source: Humphreys and Riddoch (1987), reproduced by permission of Psychology Press Limited, Hove, UK

patients like HJA, whose problem seems to lie in an inability to combine information from the local and global scales. Although able to copy pictures, these patients will be abnormally slow in their drawing.

The third new category, transformational agnosia, was offered to describe cases where patients were unable to recognise unusual views of an object. In this case it is assumed that the perceptual processes are intact and the problem lies with the matching of the unusual view to the more normal representation of the object. The fourth category, semantic agnosia, is used to describe patients whose only problem seems to be an inability to access stored knowledge about the objects they perceive. Such patients would be able to copy a drawing and match two different views of an object they were unable to name. Finally, Humphreys and Riddoch suggest that in semantic access agnosia we see patients with intact perceptual processing and intact semantic knowledge about objects, but with an inability to match the perceptual representation to the semantic representation. Such a patient will be able to report that an object is familiar, and will perform well when asked to distinguish between real and made-up objects. They will be able to identify objects by touch, describe the function of a named object and demonstrate an intact semantic representation and an unimpaired perceptual process. However, they will not be able to name objects because they cannot progress from their perceptual representation to their stored knowledge.

Farah's classification of agnosia

Farah (1990, 1991) offered a different account of agnosia in which no attempt was made to distinguish between apperceptive and associative agnosia. Farah considered the frequency with which patients showed symptoms of visual object agnosia, prosopagnosia (an inability to recognise faces – see below) and alexia (the inability to recognise written words). If these three conditions are independent of each other, we should expect to see patients demonstrating all possible combinations of these deficits. Farah observed that, while certain combinations were common, others had never been reliably reported. Of the seven possible combinations of these conditions, five are frequently reported. However, Farah identified only one case in which object agnosia was claimed to occur without prosopagnosia or alexia, and only one reported case of a patient suffering from prosopagnosia and alexia but not agnosia. Furthermore, in both of these cases Farah was able to show inconsistencies in the authors' accounts of their patient's abilities, suggesting unreliable reporting.

Farah argued that this pattern of co-occurrence suggested that these three conditions were not independent of each other, but rather resulted from the disruption of two separate processes. Faces are thought to be recognised using **holistic** or **configural processes** (see Bruce and Humphreys, 1994) whereas the recognition of words is dependent on the recognition of the individual features (letters). Thus we can think of objects as arranged along a continuum, with words which are (almost) entirely recognised on the basis of part-based processing at one end and faces, which are recognised on the basis of whole-based processing at the other end (see Figure 3.8). Farah suggested that object recognition is mediated by two separate processes, one holistic and one feature based. Thus, damage to either system can result in visual object agnosia, which will be seen in combination with either prosopagnosia or alexia depending on whether the holistic- or feature-based system is damaged. Widespread brain injury might damage both systems, leading to all three conditions being observed in the same patient. However, according to this account it should not be possible to observe object agnosia without either alexia or prosopagnosia, as object agnosia would result from damage to either the holistic or part-based process which would also cause problems in either face or word recognition. Thus the observed pattern of occurrence of these three conditions supports Farah's view that two separate processes underlie object recognition.

This account has several merits, but is not widely supported. Rumiati *et al.* (1994) described a patient, Mr W, who was unable to recognise either pictures or real objects, but showed no evidence of prosopagnosia or alexia. This is an important observation because, according to Farah, this should be an 'impossible' combination as agnosia must arise as the result of damage to either the holistic- or the feature-based system – and any such damage would result in either alexia or prosopagnosia. In addition, HJA was profoundly prosopagnosic, but could read short words. This would suggest that his problems were the result of damage to his holistic system. However, the evidence we considered earlier concerning HJA's ability to discriminate real from made-up objects when presented as either line drawings or silhouettes provides evidence that he is able to perceive the more holistic structure of an object. Indeed, HJA's problem seemed to result from his inability to relate the global and local details, rather than an inability to perceive the global form *per se*.

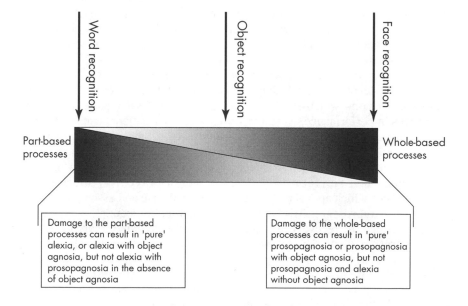

Figure 3.8 A diagrammatic representation of Farah's (1991) explanation of the pattern of co-occurrence of alexia, object agnosia and prosopagnosia

The experience of visual agnosia

It is very difficult to guess just what it is like to suffer from visual agnosia. Indeed, the experience must vary greatly with the type of agnosia. Apperceptive agnosics clearly experience a very confused and distorted visual world in which almost nothing seems familiar and even basic forms are indistinguishable from each other. However, it is rather more difficult to imagine what the perceptual experience of a patient such as HJA must be. Perhaps the best analogy would be to imagine looking at the world through a very powerful microscope. To look at an object you would have to scan the microscope around, trying to remember what each view of the object has revealed. To form a representation of the object in order to allow recognition you would have to assemble a mental picture of the overall structure of the object by piecing together the independent microscopic views. In this way, despite being able to see accurately the component details of the object, you would find it very difficult to recognise the whole, and the more complex the local detail the harder the recognition task would become.

The specificity of perceptual deficits in visual agnosia

So far we have discussed visual agnosias as if all visual agnosics were unable to recognise any objects. In fact, the picture is rather more complicated. As Bay (1953) noted, patients can be very variable in their performance. There are differences in performance between patients, and within single patients there can be variations in performance over time and between different types of object. Of these three sources of variation, the latter, differences in performance with different types of objects, will be discussed at some length in the following sections. However, it is interesting to consider what the study of individual differences in performance and changes in performance over time can tell us about agnosia.

Individual differences in performance are normally attributed to differences in the size and location of the lesion and the study of these differences can help us localise the lesions which can be responsible for different patterns of deficit. Differences in performance over time within particular patients can be difficult to explain, and it was this inconsistent behaviour that led Bay to doubt the existence of visual agnosia. It is quite normal for patients to show quite marked recovery in the first few months after their brain injury, and the pattern of recovery of function can be interesting. Several patients show a pattern of recovery which suggests that the deficits which are seen as signifying apperceptive and associative agnosias might actually represent the two ends of a continuum. For example, Larrabee *et al.* (1985) described the recovery of a patient who, a few days after infarction (damage resulting from a disruption to the blood supply), was showing clear signs of apperceptive agnosia, being unable to name, draw or match objects. However, by forty-eight days' post-infarction she was able to match pictures (and would thus be described as having an associative agnosia) and two years later was even able to name real objects (but not drawings: see also Kertesz, 1979)

Recognising living and non-living objects

The suggestion that some patients may be able to recognise some categories of object better than others is of particular interest. Prosopagnosia, the inability to recognise faces, is one possible example of a category-specific disorder which will be discussed in detail below. However, it has also been suggested that some patients have difficulty in recognising particular categories of non-face objects. Warrington and Shallice (1984) caused considerable interest when they reported that the ability of one of their patients, JBR, to name drawings varied depending upon the category of object that the drawing depicted. In particular, Warrington and Shallice had noticed that although JBR could name drawings of many non-living objects (such as a spade or hairbrush), he couldn't name drawings of living things (such as a dog or fly), or musical instruments (such as a trumpet). Several other authors have since reported that their patients have particular difficulty in naming living things (e.g. Farah *et al.* (1989) reporting the case of LH; Farah *et al.* (1991) reporting the case of MB; Stewart *et al.* (1992) reporting the case of HO). This is an intriguing result which suggests that different processes and/or different parts of the brain are involved in the recognition of living and non-living objects. There is some evidence from studies involving PET scans of the brains of normal subjects to support this notion. Martin *et al.* (1996) showed that the areas of the brain involved in the recognition of tools seemed to differ from those involved in the recognition of animals. However, caution should be exercised here. The evidence suggests a *dissociation* between the ability to name living and non-living things. To date there is no evidence of a *double dissociation*. That is, there are no reported cases of patients who can recognise living but not non-living objects. This suggests the possibility of some other explanation. In particular, the fact that JBR also had difficulty naming musical instruments (as did HO) suggests this is not a living/non-living category distinction.

More recent research has suggested that this apparent category-specific effect may actually be an artefact of the materials used to demonstrate it. Stewart *et al.* (1992) pointed out that although the living and non-living categories of pictures used to demonstrate this effect were matched for the familiarity of the object names, they were not matched for the familiarity of the pictures themselves. Some items, and perhaps especially living things, might be more familiar as words than as images. To take an extreme example, although you will probably be fairly familiar with the name 'Duckbilled Platypus', how often have you seen a picture of this animal? (which, coincidentally, looks rather like a test item from Humphreys and Riddoch's object decision task!) In addition, Stewart *et al.* pointed out that there is a tendency for line drawings of living things to be more complex than drawings of non-living things. When Stewart *et al.* re-tested their patient HO with a new set of materials which were matched for familiarity of both name and picture as well as image complexity, they found that he no longer demonstrated a category-specific agnosia. Funell and Sheridan (1992) re-tested Warrington and Shallice's patient JBR, and found that by using materials which controlled for item familiarity there was no evidence of the category-specific naming deficit that Warrington and Shallice had originally observed.

In a particularly clever test of the possibility that category-specific agnosias might be explained by systematic differences in the pictures used, Gaffan and Heywood (1993) trained monkeys to respond to pictures of living and non-living things. They found it easier to train the monkeys to respond to non-living than living things, indicating that the monkeys could more easily discriminate between members of the non-living than the living category. This strongly suggests that the difference in the living and non-living categories lay in the characteristics of the images rather the semantic associations made to those images. Thus the difference might not be between living and non-living things (a semantic categorisation), but between images which are more or less complex and difficult to individuate.

Farah *et al.* (1989) were also concerned that differences in the complexity of the stimuli making up the living and non-living categories might be contributing to the category-specific deficit apparent in LH's performance. They tackled this problem by asking LH questions about living and non-living objects. They found that LH performed normally except where questions concerned living things *and* the answer required access to visual information (for example, 'Are the hind legs of a kangaroo larger than the front legs?'). A further problem was identified by Farah *et al.* (1991). Farah observed that while a rather general category name was often regarded as a correct response for non-living things (for example, the response 'hat' to a picture of a deerstalker), living things tended to require rather more specific responses (for example, 'lion' rather than 'cat', 'mammal' or 'animal'). They concluded that category-specific performance might be attributable to the level of perceptual and semantic analysis required to identify a living compared to a non-living thing rather than 'differences in aliveness *per se*'.

Thus, the evidence seems to suggest that the category-specific deficits demonstrated by some visual agnosic patients are not a reflection of the organisation of semantic information in the brain, but rather reflect differences in the nature of the encoding required to represent living and non-living things. This is a distinction we shall return to when discussing prosopagnosia.

Recognising typical and unusual views of objects

In a rather different type of deficit specificity, Warrington and Taylor (1973, 1978) demonstrated that some patients who were able to recognise objects when photographed from typical or canonical views (for example, part (a) of Figure 3.9) were not able to recognise these same objects viewed from an unusual angle (part (b) of Figure 3.9). It is important to note that the views were unusual but not completely novel – we have all seen a teacup from above and would have no difficulty recognising it from such a view. The fact that these patients can recognise the canonical view of the object demonstrates that they have no sensory deficits and suggests that they are able to achieve a stable representation of the object.

Warrington and Taylor believed that the unusual views were difficult to recognise because they tended to obscure characteristic features of the object (such as the handle of the cup). They suggested that object recognition was achieved through the process of matching these characteristic features of the object to representations stored in memory. However, this view was not shared by

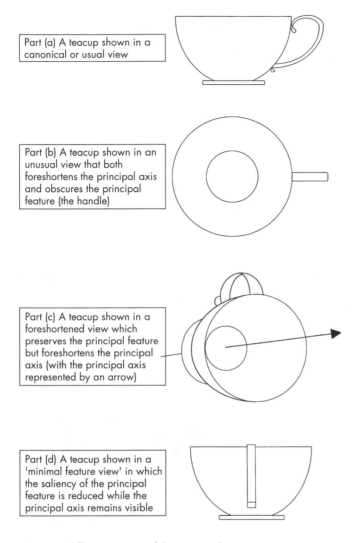

Part (a) A teacup shown in a canonical or usual view

Part (b) A teacup shown in an unusual view that both foreshortens the principal axis and obscures the principal feature (the handle)

Part (c) A teacup shown in a foreshortened view which preserves the principal feature but foreshortens the principal axis (with the principal axis represented by an arrow)

Part (d) A teacup shown in a 'minimal feature view' in which the saliency of the principal feature is reduced while the principal axis remains visible

Figure 3.9 Four different views of the same object

Note: It is possible to draw an object so as to independently manipulate the saliency of the principal axis and the principal feature. Part (a) shows both clearly. Part (b) shows neither clearly. Part (c) shows the principal feature but reduces the saliency of the principal axis, and part (d) shows the principal axis but reduces the saliency of the principal feature. To aid clarity the principal axis has been represented by an arrow in part (c).

Marr, who was influenced by this work when developing his theory of perception (see Marr, 1982). As we saw in Chapter 2, Marr believed that we store a single object-centred representation (the three-dimensional sketch) which allows recognition of an object from any angle of view. He argued that when progressing from the two-and-a-half-dimensional sketch (viewer-centred representation) to the final three-dimensional representation, it was particularly important to identify the principal axis of the object. The unusual views photographed by Warrington tended to obscure or foreshorten the principal axis of the object (which, in the case of a cup, would run vertically through the centre of the base – see Figure 3.9 part (c)). Marr (1984, p. 328) believed that unusual views were more difficult to recognise because they 'corresponded to views in which an important natural axis of the shape is foreshortened in the image, making it difficult for the patient to discover or derive a description in the shape's canonical coordinate system' (and hence to derive a three-dimensional representation). It was this fact, Marr argued, and not the obscuring of the distinctive features that made the unusual views more difficult to recognise.

Thus, the observation that some patients could not recognise unusual views of objects was seen as providing a test of two alternative views of perception. Humphreys and Riddoch (1984[1]) attempted to test these two alternative explanations by producing a set of images consisting of three views of each object. The first, the **canonical view**, clearly showed the object's most distinctive characteristic as well as its principal axis. The second view showed the principal axis clearly, but obscured the object's most distinctive feature (the minimal feature view). The third view showed the distinctive feature while foreshortening the principal axis (the foreshortened view). Examples of these three views are illustrated in Figure 3.9, parts (a), (c) and (d) respectively, and Figure 3.10 illustrates two trials of the type used by Humphreys and Riddoch. Subjects were required to decide if either a foreshortened or a minimal feature view was of the same object shown in canonical view. Five patients were tested. Four of the patients had clear problems in matching the foreshortened stimuli but performed well with the minimal feature match stimuli. The fifth patient (our old friend HJA) was more accurate overall with only slightly more errors in the minimal feature view than the foreshortened view. These results suggest that, for the majority of the subjects, problems in recognising unusual views can be attributed to an inability to identify the principal axis, and this in turn offers some support for Marr's suggestion that object recognition is dependent on a single object-centred representation rather than the identification of characteristic features. However, Humphreys and Riddoch believed that HJA's performance demonstrated that object recognition could also be achieved by the identification of characteristic features.

Mental imagery, perception and visual agnosia

When we recall a mental image from memory, we have the strong impression that we are 'seeing again' – the subjective impression is of looking at an internal screen on which our memories are being projected. However, when we are 'inspecting' a mental image are we really using the same processes that are involved in

---

1 See also Humphreys and Riddoch (1985) which corrects several statistical errors in the original paper.

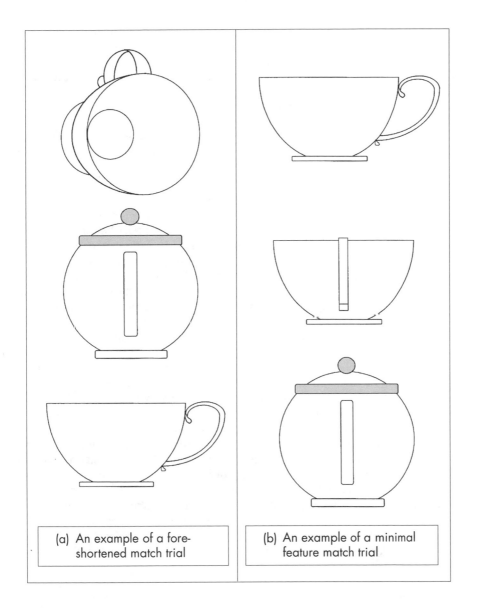

(a) An example of a fore-
shortened match trial

(b) An example of a minimal
feature match trial

Figure 3.10 An illustration of the two types of trials used by Humphreys and Riddoch (1984)

Source: After Humphreys and Riddoch (1984)

Note: Patients were required to determine which two of a set of three photographs were of the same object. One picture showed an object from the canonical view and a second picture showed the same object from either the foreshortened or minimal feature view. The third picture was of a differ-ent object. If obscuring the principal axis makes an object difficult to identify, we would expect patients to find trials such as that shown in part (a) to be more difficult than trials which involved matching principal features such as that shown in part (b).

perception? Evidence from both experimental studies of normal subjects and neuropsychological investigations of brain-injured patients suggests that the answer to this question may be yes.

Levine (1978) suggested that visualisation might use some of the same pathways as direct perception, citing the case of a patient with a variety of deficits including prosopagnosia and visual object agnosia. This patient showed a hierarchy of difficulties in recognising objects, with faces being the most difficult to recognise, followed by animals, then simple objects, and finally letters and colours which she was able to recognise with almost complete accuracy. The patient showed the same pattern of difficulties when asked to describe objects from memory (using her mental imagery). She found it very difficult to describe faces, was able to provide reasonable descriptions and drawings of objects and was able to name accurately the colour of objects from memory. In contrast, other patients seem to show quite different patterns of deficit when perceiving and when imagining an object. For example, Jankowiak *et al.* (1992) described a patient who, though able to visualise and describe objects normally, was unable to recognise them and, as we saw earlier, Humphreys and Riddoch's patient HJA also showed this preserved mental imagery despite profound agnosia. The converse pattern of an inability to form a mental image despite relatively normal perceptual abilities is inherently more difficult to demonstrate, but Hanley *et al.* (1991) described a woman who had a marked inability to learn new visual material. Hanley *et al.* attributed this difficulty to an impairment to the visuo-spatial component of working memory (Baddeley, 1986), that component of memory which allows us to form a mental image on which we can perform mental operations (see Chapter 4). In addition, Farah *et al.* (1988) described a patient who was unable to use mental imagery to decide which of two unseen objects was the larger but was able to recognise these same objects.

This putative evidence for a double dissociation between the ability to form a mental image of an object and the ability to recognise an object undermines any simple notion that mental imagery utilises the same mechanisms that are involved in perception. However, given the evidence of functional equivalence in individuals who have not suffered brain injury, it seems likely that there is some overlap between these systems when working normally. An understanding of the nature of this relationship between mental imagery and perception is probably fundamental to our understanding of both memory and perception; however, for the moment we can only speculate that there is probably some degree of common function.

Perception and action

As noted earlier, even severely agnosic patients frequently retain the ability to interact with objects they are unable to recognise. Most agnosic patients are perfectly capable of navigating themselves around their immediate environment without bumping into things. Goodale and Milner (1992) suggested that the visual recognition of an object and the control of actions directed towards an object might be mediated by quite separate areas of the brain. When we move to pick up an object we direct our actions towards the appropriate position in space and adjust our grip ready to grasp that object. We are unaware of these actions which normally are not under conscious control. Goodale *et al.* (1991) describe a patient, DF, who, following carbon monoxide poisoning, was left with severe visual object agnosia. DF was unable to recognise an object, or to describe its size, shape or orientation. She was unable to distinguish between wooden blocks of different sizes, and could not indicate the width of a block using her index finger and thumb (a task that control subjects could perform accurately and reliably). However, by attaching small infrared light sources to the tips of DF's index finger and thumb, Goodale and colleagues were able to monitor the shape of her grasp as she reached forward to pick up the blocks. This analysis of DF's movements revealed that, like control subjects, she adjusted the shape of her grasp to suit the size of the block she was reaching for. In a second study DF was shown to be unable to indicate the orientation of a large slot by rotating either her hand or a card so that they would fit into the slot. However, when asked to reach out and place her hand or the card in the slot, she was as accurate as the control subjects and analysis of her movements showed that as soon as she initiated the movement she began to orient her hand to match the slot. Thus, although unable to describe the size or orientation of an object, DL was able to use this information to control her movements.

Goodale and Milner (1992) concluded that, while areas of the parietal cortex provide information about the structure and orientation of objects required to control action, the temporal lobe provides the visual information, which mediates conscious perceptual experience. They suggested that these separate channels of information might be giving rise to different types of representation – they noted that the information required to control actions is likely to be viewer-centred, whereas, as we saw in Chapter 2, object recognition requires an object-centred representation. Goodale and Milner suggest that the separation of these two channels might even be necessary to prevent the viewer-centred description used to drive action from interfering with the object-centred description which results in conscious perceptual experience. Finally, they reasoned that if these two systems are separate, it should be possible to observe normal subjects adjusting their motor behaviour to accommodate changes to an object's location or shape which they have not consciously perceived. Goodale *et al.* (1986) demonstrated that normal subjects could adjust their manual aiming to accommodate small movements of a target which had occurred during **saccadic eye movements** (the small automatic movements of the eyes) and which they were quite unable to report.

Goodale *et al.* (1994) found that DL's ability to rotate an object to fit into a slot was limited to perceptually simple objects. DL was unable to manipulate a 'T'-shaped object so that it would fit into a slot. Thus, their hypothesis about separate channels of information mediating action and perception might be limited to very simple perceptual situations with more complex situations requiring higher order object-centred descriptions to be made available in order to control action.

3.5 Disorders of face processing – prosopagnosia and related conditions

Our need to recognise faces probably represents one of the most demanding tasks we set our visual systems. Each of us can recognise thousands of different faces, a remarkable feat when we consider how similar all human faces are. The face is a thin layer of tissue stretched over the skull, and the structure of the skull is very tightly constrained by the position of the eyes, nose and mouth and mechanical considerations such as the requirement to maintain clear air passages. As if to make face identification even harder, we also use our faces for other tasks. We signal our internal state through facial expressions that distort the face and we speak through our mouths, stretching and changing the shape of our face. Given that face perception is such a demanding perceptual task, it is not surprising that brain damage can result in deficits in face processing. However, the pattern and nature of these deficits tell us a great deal about both face processing and perception in general.

Bruce and Young (1986) incorporated the knowledge gained from studying individuals with a variety of face processing deficits with information gleaned from

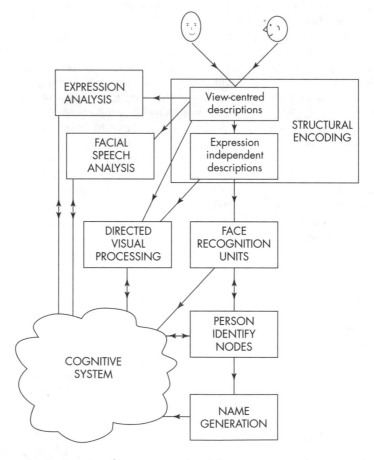

Figure 3.11 Bruce and Young's model of face processing showing independent pathways for face recognition, expression analysis and speech analysis
Source: Bruce and Young (1986), reproduced by permission of the British Psychological Society

experimental studies of normal individuals into a successful model of normal face processing (see Figure 3.11). This model suggests that the recognition of identity, expression and lip-reading (facial speech analysis) are independent processes, and as we shall see below the evidence from brain-damaged patients largely supports this view. However, the model is neutral on the question of whether face processing is dependent on 'special' perceptual processes that are qualitatively different from those involved in the recognition of other non-face objects. This has become a central issue in the field of face processing research, with evidence from experimental studies of normal subjects, developmental studies of neonates and neuropsychological studies of brain-injured patients all being considered. Laboratory studies of face processing have focused on the extent to which image manipulations such as inversion and negation (presenting an image as a photographic negative) affect face recognition. All objects are more difficult to recognise when upside-down or negated, but Yin (1969) demonstrated that face recognition is especially affected by inversion (see Valentine (1988) for a review of this literature). More recently, Kemp *et al.* (1990, 1996) have shown that inversion and negation also affect the ability to make simple perceptual judgements (comparing the location of the eyes) about an unfamiliar face even when the participants are not required to remember the face. However, it is neuropsychological studies of patients suffering from conditions such as prosopagnosia which are seen as providing the most direct test of this question.

Prosopagnosia

Prosopagnosia is an inability to recognise faces that cannot be explained by sensory impairment. Severely prosopagnosic individuals are often unable to recognise members of their immediate family (husbands/wives, children, etc.) and sometimes do not recognise their own reflection. It is not that they have forgotten who these people are; once they hear the voice of a friend or relative they can recognise them and interact normally. A prosopagnosic patient knows that a face is a face, but not whose face, and as we shall see, many can identify facial expressions (such as anger). However, these individuals are unable to link the perceptual representation of the face with their stored knowledge about this individual.

The term 'prosopagnosia' was first used by Bodamer (1947). Bodamer reported three patients who he believed showed a face-specific deficit, apparently being able to recognise non-face objects normally. However, in recent years this claim that prosopagnosia can be observed in a 'pure' form and is face-specific has come under close examination (see Bruce and Humphreys, 1994).

Prosopagnosia – a face-specific disorder?

Face recognition places unusual demands upon the visual system. We have to be able to recognise a chair as a chair, but do not normally need to recognise a particular chair amongst other chairs; that is, we do not need to **individuate** chairs. Face recognition is all about individuation – the task is to identify one specific instance of the class of objects known as faces. Thus, if we are going to conclude that prosopagnosia is face-specific, we need to establish that prosopagnosic patients retain the ability to distinguish between members of a perceptually similar class of objects. If prosopagnosic patients cannot individuate non-face objects then we cannot conclude that theirs is a face-specific disorder.

One prosopagnosic patient who shows some evidence of being able to recognise specific instances of non-face objects is VA reported by DeRenzi *et al.* (1991). VA was able to identify his own possessions from 'line-ups' of similar items (for example, picking out his shaving brush from a line of similar shaving brushes), was able to identify his own handwriting from that of others, was able to identify different cars, and was able to distinguish between coins from different countries despite being profoundly prosopagnosic. Sergent and Signoret (1992) report the case of prosopagnosic patient RM who had a large collection of model cars which he was able to identify more accurately than control subjects (who were interested in cars).

It could be argued that the ability to distinguish between cars or shaving brushes differs from face recognition in that faces are biological rather than manufactured objects. Several cases have been reported where prosopagnosic patients retain the ability to individuate non-human animals. Bruyer *et al.* (1983) reported that Mr W, a prosopagnosic farmer, was still able to recognise his cows. This is in contrast to the report by Bornstein *et al.* (1969) of the case of a prosopagnosic farmer who could not recognise his cows. Assal *et al.* (1984) reported the case of MX, another unfortunate farmer, who initially lost the ability to recognise either humans or his cows; however, six months later he recovered the ability to recognise human faces but remained unable to recognise his cows. Thus, almost unbelievably, we appear to have evidence of a double dissociation between the ability to recognise human and animal faces following brain injury. McNeil and Warrington (1993) described the case of WJ, who took up farming *after* becoming prosopagnosic. The case of WJ, described in detail below, is important because it demonstrates that it is possible to *learn* to distinguish between very similar biological forms (sheep) despite being prosopagnosic and unable to identify even highly familiar human faces.

It is still not clear what conclusions should be drawn concerning the degree of face-specificity in prosopagnosia. The difficulty is in identifying a suitable non-face control stimuli which can be individuated as well as faces by normal subjects. Tests of the ability to individuate non-human animals are interesting but it might be unwise to place too much emphasis on results from a few people who have either preserved or lost the very rare ability to name large numbers of similar farm animals.

Hay and Young (1982) pointed out that the question of whether face recognition is a special process can be subdivided. Firstly, we can ask, does face recognition rely on special processes not involved in the recognition of other objects? A second and separate question is, are there specific areas of the brain devoted to face recognition? Our ability to answer either of these questions will be dependent on our ability to combine evidence from neuropsychological studies of brain-injured patients and laboratory studies of 'normal' subjects.

Covert recognition in prosopagnosia

Some, but not all prosopagnosic patients have been found to show some covert recognition of faces. These individuals report that they are totally unable to recognise faces, and their very poor performance in normal tests of recognition suggests this is the case. However, when tested more carefully it is possible to demonstrate that, at some level below that of conscious awareness, recognition is occurring. For example, Bruyer *et al.* (1983) tried to teach their patient, Mr W, to associate names with faces. If, as Mr W reported, he was totally unable to recognise the faces used in the test, then it should not have mattered which names were paired with which faces. However, Mr W found it much easier to learn to associate a face with its real name than with some other name, thereby demonstrating some unconscious recognition. De Haan *et al.* (1987) showed the same effect with their patient PH, even when tested with the faces of people he had met only after he had become prosopagnosic and had thus never recognised consciously. This suggests that PH is continuing to store the names and faces of people he meets, but that he is unaware of this information to which he has no conscious access.

Bauer (1984) measured the skin conductance of a prosopagnosic patient while he looked at photographs of famous faces and listened to names being read out. Despite being unable to put names to the famous faces the patient showed a greater change in skin conductance when the correct name–face pairing was presented than when false pairings were presented. De Haan *et al.* (1987) used a behavioural rather than physiological measure of the effect of correct and incorrect pairings of faces and names. They presented their patient with pictures of famous faces which included speech bubbles containing a name. PH was asked to classify the name as that of either a politician or an actor. This task does not require face recognition, but, like control subjects, PH found the task more difficult when the face shown was of someone from a different occupational category than when the face and name were of people from the same category (for example, it would take longer to say that the name 'Tom Cruise' was that of an actor when it was presented alongside a picture of Tony Blair than if it was presented next to a picture of Sean Connery). This suggests that, even when the task does not require face recognition this is occurring at some level.

The case of the unknown sheep: a case study in prosopagnosia

McNeil and Warrington (1993) described the case of WJ, a 51-year-old man who suffered a series of strokes which resulted in lesions to the left occipital, left frontal and left temporal lobes causing profound prosopagnosia. When shown a set of three photographs of one famous and two unfamiliar faces, WJ was not able to pick out the famous face. However, when this task was modified by giving WJ the name of the famous person in the trial (asking 'which one is ....?') performance improved significantly, indicating some covert recognition of these famous faces. Following the onset of his prosopagnosia, WJ acquired a flock of sheep which he photographed for McNeil and Warrington. WJ knew his sheep by number, and McNeil and Warrington were able to determine that he could recognise at least eight out of sixteen of the pictures of these 'known sheep' (this is probably an underestimate – McNeil and Warrington report that on several trials WJ could recognise the sheep but not remember its number, making comments such as 'This sheep had three lambs this year.'). This is remarkable evidence of an ability to learn to recognise individual sheep while still being profoundly prosopagnosic for human faces. In order to ensure that this ability was not attributable to some characteristic specific to WJ's own sheep, McNeil and Warrington obtained photographs of 'unknown sheep' and managed to recruit two control subjects who had also acquired flocks of sheep after retiring, together with a number of age and profession matched non-sheep owning subjects. These subjects were all shown photos of eight of the sheep and then shown these eight randomly mixed with eight 'distractor' sheep. The subjects were required to say whether each picture was of one of the original eight or was a distractor sheep. Understandably, the control subjects, both sheep-owning and 'normal', found this a difficult task and their performance was poor compared to that with human faces. WJ showed the opposite pattern of results, performing rather well on the sheep task (correctly recognising 81 per cent of unknown and 87 per cent of the known sheep – better than any other subject), and performed very badly with human faces.

This remarkable case, and McNeil and Warrington's ingenious investigations of it, thus provide clear evidence that WJ was able to recognise individual sheep on the basis of their photographs, despite being profoundly prosopagnosic for human faces. McNeil and Warrington conclude that WJ provides 'further evidence that prosopagnosia can occur as a face-specific deficit' (p. 445).

Facial expression, lip-reading and face recognition

Bruce and Young's model proposes that expression analysis occurs in parallel to, but independently of face recognition. There is evidence from a number of clinical cases to support this view, with some prosopagnosic patients being able to identify the expressions posed by faces they couldn't recognise (e.g. Bruyer *et al.*, 1983) while other patients have shown the reverse pattern, being unable to identify the expression on a face they could recognise (e.g. Kurucz *et al.*, 1979)

There is also evidence of a double dissociation between facial speech analysis, or lip-reading, and face recognition. Although not normally aware of it, we all tend to lip-read when attending to a speaker. The extent of our reliance on lip-reading was elegantly demonstrated by McGurk and MacDonald (1976), who showed that if we hear one phoneme, such as 'ba', while watching the speaker make the mouth movements normally associated with the production of a different sound, such as 'ga', then we tend to perceive a sound which is a combination of the phoneme heard and that predicted by the mouth movements, in this case 'da'. This effect is known as the McGurk illusion, and is of interest to us because some prosopagnosics have been shown to be susceptible to the illusion (and hence can be assumed to be lip-reading normally), while other patients have been identified who are apparently immune to the McGurk illusion (and hence are not lip-reading) yet can recognise faces normally (Campbell *et al.*, 1986).

The dissociation between expression analysis and person identification makes good sense. We need to be able to recognise a face regardless of which expression it is displaying – it would be no good if we could only recognise a friend if they posed a particular facial expression (although I am reminded of a particularly miserable student whom I failed to recognise on the day of her graduation – the only time I had seen her smile!). Rather more surprising is the evidence of a similar dissociation between expression analysis and lip-reading. An accurate assessment of the shape of the mouth is critical to both these tasks, yet it appears that particular lesions can affect the ability to perform one of these tasks and not the other. For example, Campbell *et al.* (1986) described two female patients identified as D and T. Patient D could neither recognise familiar faces, identify facial expressions nor identify the sex of individuals from their facial appearance. However, despite these profound deficits D could read and speak normally and, critically for our discussion here, she could identify the phoneme being mouthed by a speaker and was susceptible to the McGurk illusion. Patient T showed a very different pattern of abilities, being immune to the McGurk illusion and unable to lip-read, but having a preserved ability to identify facial expression.

Young *et al.* (1993) were concerned that our understanding of the processes underlying face processing was dependent on comparisons of individual case histories, often described by different authors and assessed using a variety of different tests. Young *et al.* decided that what was required was a more consistent approach in which a standardised set of assessments was administered to each of a group of patients. Furthermore, Young *et al.* decided to deploy two separate assessment tests of familiar face recognition, two tests of face matching and two tests of expression processing to ensure that an apparent deficit was not due to problems associated with a particular test. Young *et al.* only classified participants as having a deficit if they performed significantly worse than normal control participants on *both* tests of the ability, and only accepted that the deficit was selective if performance on *all* the other tests was the same as that of the normal control participants. Using this very stringent test of impairment, Young *et al.* tested a group of thirty-four ex-servicemen who had sustained brain injuries during the Second World War. Of these subjects they were able to identify one individual who was impaired only in his ability to recognise famous faces, one with a selective impairment for matching unfamiliar faces, and five with a selective impairment in expression analysis. This is very compelling evidence for the independence of these three functions, but Young *et al.* were concerned that a subject might be able to achieve normal levels of performance in a task by adopting a non-standard strategy, such as laboriously checking each part of the image. The fact that a participant is having to fall back on such a strategy suggests that they are suffering from some impairment, but this impairment might not show up in the performance data. For patients to be recognised as having a selective impairment they had to demonstrate not only normal levels of performance on the unaffected tests, but also to complete these tasks as quickly as normal participants. Using this even stricter criterion there was still evidence of the dissociation between the ability to identify facial expression and to recognise identity. However, there was no longer any evidence of a dissociation in the recognition of famous faces and the matching of unfamiliar faces.

Thus, we can be confident that the ability to recognise an individual is independent of the ability to recognise facial expressions. The form of the visual deficit demonstrated by some patients is therefore specific to a particular task based on a particular object. This is remarkable, but could it be that some patients might show an even finer level of specificity, being able to recognise some facial expressions but not others?

Deficits in the perception of specific facial expressions

Ekman and colleagues identified a set of universal facial expressions (happiness, surprise, fear, sadness, disgust and anger) which they argued were recognised in all cultures (Ekman, 1982). Ekman believed that the identification of a facial expression is a categorical process, with any expression always being recognised as one of these six. This gives rise to the possibility that a deficit in expression analysis might be specific to one particular expression.

Calder *et al.* (1996) investigated this possibility. They produced a series of images based on Ekman and Friesen's (1976) original photographs. These photographs were computer-manipulated to produce a sequence which included **interpolated** images bridging the gap between one image and another. For example, a sequence could be produced which started with the standard fear response and over a number of images changed into the standard sadness image. These images are reproduced in Figure 3.12. Normal observers are very consistent in their judgements concerning these interpolated images, categorising them as one expression rather than seeing the image as a mixture of two expressions (which it is). You might like to check this finding yourself. Most people report that the first three images in the top row all show happiness with the fourth and fifth images 'switching' over to show surprise. In reality this sequence of five images progresses smoothly from happiness to surprise – the apparent discontinuity between images 3 and 4 is illusory.

Calder *et al.* (1996) presented these images to two individuals with amygdala damage. These two patients show a deficit in the recognition of expressions of

---

Figure 3.12 *(opposite)* The computer-manipulated images used by Calder *et al.* (1996)

Source: Reproduced by permission of Psychology Press Limited, Hove, UK

Note: These images were produced by manipulating the original images that Ekman and Friesen (1976) produced to illustrate prototypical facial expressions. In this sequence each image is a mixture of two of different prototypical expressions. As we move from left to right across the images in the top row, we progress from happiness to surprise. The leftmost image is made up of 90 per cent of the happiness image and 10 per cent of the surprise image. The next image is 70 per cent happiness and 30 per cent surprise, and the middle image in the row is made up of equal proportions of happiness and surprise. The fourth image shows 30 per cent surprise and 70 per cent happiness and the final

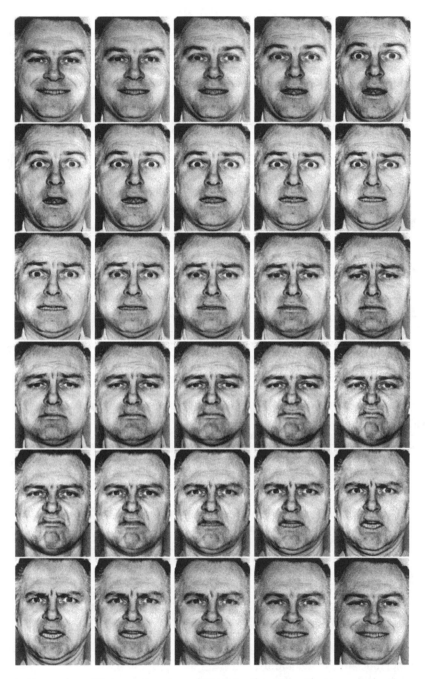

image in this row shows 10 per cent surprise and 90 per cent happiness. The images in the other rows show the same proportions of surprise-fear (second row), fear-sadness (third row), sadness-disgust (fourth row), disgust-anger (fifth row) and anger-happiness (sixth row). Most people see these images as illustrating one expression or another rather than a mixture of two expressions.

fear or anger, tending to identify the images from these parts of the sequence as showing some other expression. This is in line with several other findings which have suggested that the amygdala might be particularly involved in the recognition of fear and anger.

Adolphs *et al.* (1995) described one individual who, following bilateral damage to the amygdala, had particular difficulty in recognising or drawing a face showing fear, and Morris *et al.* (1996) have shown that the pattern of blood flow in amygdala is related to the degree to which a facial stimulus shows a fearful expression. In addition, Sprengelmeyer *et al.* (1996) have demonstrated an apparent deficit in the ability to recognise expressions of disgust in a group of people with Huntington's disease, a degenerative neurological disorder.

Thus, we have some early evidence that neurological disorders can result in a loss of sensitivity to one particular facial expression while preserving the ability to recognise other expressions.

Summary

The disorders we have considered in this chapter are debilitating and distressing conditions which severely disable the individuals who suffer them. However, for cognitive neuropsychologists these individuals afford an invaluable opportunity to glimpse the inner workings of the processes of perception and attention. Although there is disagreement about the nature of some deficits, a clear picture is beginning to emerge.

- There is an increasing degree of convergence between the models proposed by cognitive psychologists to account for the behaviour of their normal subjects and those proposed by neuropsychologists to account for their patients' disabilities.
- A striking example of such convergence is provided by the account of object recognition offered by Marr and that of object agnosia offered by Humphreys and Riddoch.
- The experimental cognitive and neuropsychological evidence both seem to describe a **modular system** in which a series of independent processes each contribute towards the goal of perception.
- This point is best illustrated in the case of face perception, where the recognition of expression is quite separate from that of identity.
- The distinction made by Marr between viewer-centred and object-centred representations has proved to be particularly useful and has assisted attempts to characterise and classify the disorders we have observed.
- The study of disorders of perception and attention has also provided evidence of a dissociation between conscious experience and the ability to respond appropriately to a stimulus.
- This dissociation which characterises the condition of blindsight was also seen in prosopagnosia, where it is called covert recognition, and in unilateral neglect, where some patients show evidence of partial insight into the nature of neglected objects.

- Finally, there is some evidence that the nature of the representation formed might be dependent on the task to be performed, and in particular there may be an important distinction between the perceptual processes that mediate action and those which result in recognition.

Further reading

Weiskrantz, L (1986). *Blindsight: A Case Study and Implications*. Oxford: Oxford University Press. This book gives a detailed consideration of blindsight.

Farah, M.J. (1990). *Visual Agnosia: Disorders of Object Recognition and What they tell us About Normal Vision*. Cambridge, MA.: MIT Press. Research into the various forms of visual agnosia, including prosopagnosia, is described in further detail in this book.

Young, A.W. (ed.) (1998). *Face and Mind*. Oxford: Oxford University Press. This gives a fuller description of Prosopagnosia, and related conditions including some not covered in this chapter.

Robertson, I.H. and Marshall, J.C. (eds) (1993). *Unilateral Neglect: Clinical and Experimental Studies*. Hove: LEA. Includes a very detailed description of unilateral neglect.

Memory

4.1 The nature and function of memory

Memory and its importance in everyday life

Memory is the process of storing information and experiences for possible retrieval at some point in the future. This ability to create and retrieve memories is fundamental to all aspects of cognition, and in a broader sense it is essential to our ability to function properly as human beings. Our memories allow us to store information about the world so that we can understand and deal with future situations on the basis of past experience. The process of thinking and problem-solving relies heavily on the use of previous experience, and memory also makes it possible for us to acquire language and to communicate with others. Memory also plays a very basic part in the process of perception, since we can only make sense of our perceptual input by referring to our store of previous experiences. Even our social interactions with others are dependent upon what we remember. In a sense it can be said that our very identity relies on an intact memory, and the ability to remember who we are and the things that we have done. Almost everything we do depends on our ability to remember the past.

Encoding, storage and retrieval of memory

The memory process can be divided into three main stages (see Figure 4.1). First of all there is the *input* stage, where newly perceived information is being learned or encoded. Next comes the *storage* stage, where the information is simply held in preparation for some future occasion. Finally there is the *output* stage, where the information is retrieved from storage.

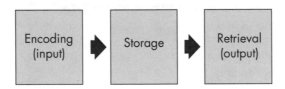

Figure 4.1 The encoding, storage and retrieval stages of memory

Those who have had any experience of using a computer will probably be able to see clear parallels between these three stages of human memory and the input/storage/output processes involved in storing a computer file on disk. Perhaps the most important reason for distinguishing between these three stages is that each stage will need to be successfully completed before we can retrieve a memory. This means that when we find we are unable to recall some item, the cause could be either a failure at the input stage (i.e. faulty learning), a failure at the output stage (i.e. faulty retrieval), or even a failure of the storage mechanism.

Methods of testing memory

There are three main ways of testing memory performance, and the type of test chosen has a strong influence over the retrieval scores obtained. The three methods are:

1 *Free recall* In free recall (also called spontaneous recall) you are required to generate the test items from your own memory without any outside help.

2 *Cued recall* Cued recall also requires you to generate test items from your own memory, but with the aid of reminders or 'retrieval cues' which may help to jog your memory.

3 *Recognition* In a recognition test the original test items are re-presented at the retrieval stage, and you are merely required to indicate whether or not you recognise them.

It is generally found that people can recognise far more items than they can recall, with cued recall scores tending to fall somewhere in between recognition and free recall scores (Tulving, 1976). These findings, and the possible reasons for them, will be examined in more detail in Section 4.7.

How many types of memory store are there?

Some psychologists have suggested that there are several different types of memory store, each with its own function and with its own distinct characteristics. Others maintain that there is only one memory store, which must adapt itself to all possible applications. The debate between the 'multistore' and 'single store' theorists has been going on since the earliest days of memory research, and it is one of the most fundamental questions that we can ask about memory. These theories, and the evidence for them, will therefore be considered in detail in Section 4.2.

4.2 Multistore models and working memory

Multistore models of memory

William James was one of the first psychologists to put forward theories about the structure of human memory. More than a century ago he suggested (James, 1890) that a distinction should be made between two types of memory store, which he called 'primary memory' and 'secondary memory'. These terms have more recently been replaced by the terms 'short-term memory' and 'long-term memory', defined roughly as follows:

Short-term memory (STM) refers to the memories which we are holding in conscious awareness, and which are currently receiving our attention.

Long-term memory (LTM) refers to the memories which we are not presently holding in conscious awareness, but which are held in storage ready to be recalled.

James made this distinction essentially on the basis of subjective experience, and it was left to later psychologists to provide scientific evidence for it. However, James was a psychologist of great intuitive genius, and like many of his theories the distinction between primary and secondary memory remains plausible to this day.

The distinction between STM and LTM is sometimes referred to as a 'dual-store' theory, because it proposes two distinct forms of memory storage. It therefore constitutes one of the first 'multistore' theories of memory, describing memory as a number of related structures rather than as a single entity. Over the years evidence has gradually accumulated in support of the dual-store theory, the most convincing evidence coming from the study of amnesic patients. Those suffering from organic amnesia (a memory impairment caused by physical damage to the brain), are characterised by their inability to form any new long-term memories. In contrast, their immediate short-term memory is usually unimpaired (Scoville and Milner, 1957; Baddeley and Warrington, 1970). Such patients are able to remember what has been said to them during the previous few seconds, but not much else. The finding that STM can remain intact despite severe impairment of LTM suggests that they are separate and independent memory stores. This view receives further support from the finding that some patients show the reverse of this dissociation, with an intact LTM but a severely impaired STM (Warrington and Shallice, 1969). Taking the two types of evidence together, it is apparent that either the STM or the LTM can be separately impaired whilst the other store remains intact. A 'double dissociation' of this kind is regarded as being far more convincing than evidence of a single dissociation (Warrington, 1979), and it is the main reason why most cognitive psychologists accept that STM and LTM are largely independent memory stores.

Evidence for the existence of two separate memory stores led memory theorists to propose various hypothetical models of memory structure. One popular model was that of Atkinson and Shiffrin (1968), and a simplified version of their model is shown in Figure 4.2. Their model incorporates STM and LTM stores, and also includes a preliminary store of sensory information held in unprocessed form. There is some evidence for such a sensory store (Sperling, 1960).

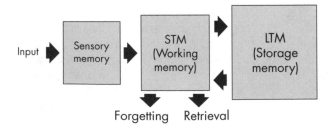

Figure 4.2 The multistore model of memory
Source: Adapted from Atkinson and Shiffrin (1968).

Earlier models of memory storage had seen the STM as little more than a 'port of entry' into the LTM, but in this model the STM store is also used for retrieval of memories from storage. This notion of STM as a focus of both input and output of memories is of central importance to more recent multistore models, which have developed the concept of the STM as a conscious working memory (Baddeley and Hitch, 1974).

Measuring STM performance

Most traditional tests of memory, such as the recall of wordlists or stories, provide what is predominantly a measure of LTM. Tests of STM are harder to devise, but one of the most popular is the testing of immediate memory span. The subject is simply read a series of items (such as digits) and is then required to repeat them immediately, in the correct order. Since there is no time delay, immediate memory span is thought to depend mainly on STM, and has become widely accepted as an approximate measure of STM performance. However, it is probably not a pure measure of STM, since there is evidence that LTM may make some contribution to span performance (Hulme *et al.*, 1991).

You may wish to test your own digit span as a demonstration of the procedure. Read the five digits in the top row of the list below, then cover up the list and try to write them down. If you get them all right, try moving on to the next row, in which the number of digits is increased to six. Keep on going until you start getting some of the digits wrong. Your digit span is the largest number of digits you can get right in one trial.

Digit span test

71504
284936
8351609
25736184
940627135

Experiments have shown that the average normal person has a maximum digit span of about seven digits (and in fact their maximum span for letters or words tends to be fairly similar), though there is some variation in the general population, with scores varying typically from five to about nine items (Miller 1956).

Another measure of STM performance is the recency effect in free recall. When subjects are presented with a list of items which exceeds memory span, they are bound to forget some items when tested straight afterwards. However, it has been established that they are more likely to remember items from the end of the list than from the middle, a phenomenon known as the recency effect and first demonstrated by Ebbinghaus (1885). A likely explanation for the recency effect is that items at the end of the list are still being held in the STM, whereas items presented earlier in the list will have been lost unless the subject has managed to put them into LTM storage. This theory received convincing support from the

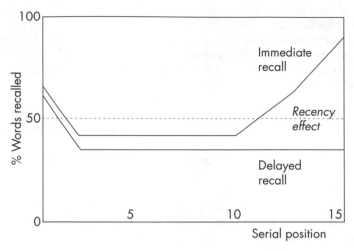

Figure 4.3 Serial position curves for immediate and delayed recall
Source: Adapted from Glanzer and Cunitz (1966)

finding that the recency effect tended to disappear when a delay was introduced between learning a wordlist and recalling it (Glanzer and Cunitz, 1966). A delay of thirty seconds, which was filled with a simple task (counting backwards) to prevent subjects from rehearsing the wordlist, was found to be sufficient to entirely eliminate the recency effect. The results of this experiment are summarised in Figure 4.3.

Another method of measuring STM performance is the Brown–Peterson task (Brown, 1958; Peterson and Peterson, 1959). This is a technique for measuring the duration of STM rather than its capacity, and more specifically its duration in the absence of rehearsal. The subject is presented with a test item which is well below maximum span (such as three letters), and is then immediately required to perform a distraction task (such as counting backwards in threes) which prevents rehearsal of the test item. After a short retention period a signal is given to the subject to repeat back the three letters. The results obtained by Brown and the Petersons showed that in the absence of rehearsal forgetting took place surprisingly quickly, in fact within a few seconds. After a retention interval of eighteen seconds, fewer than 10 per cent of the test items were recalled. Two main conclusions can be drawn from these results. In the first place, STM storage apparently requires rehearsal of some kind in order to keep the item in conscious attention. Secondly, when rehearsal is prevented items are lost from the STM very rapidly. In fact Muter (1980, 1995) has shown that most items are forgotten within three or four seconds if the subject is not expecting to be tested. Muter claims that this is probably a more accurate estimation of STM duration since the use of an unexpected test may help to eliminate the contribution of LTM. Multistore theories of memory were popular for many years (for a review of multistore models see Healy and McNamara, 1996), but in recent years they have given way to the 'working memory' model.

The working memory model

Early versions of the dual-store model tended to regard STM and LTM as two stores differing mainly in their duration. However, Baddeley and Hitch (1974) emphasised the different functions of these stores. They saw the STM as an active 'working memory', a kind of mental workspace in which a variety of processing operations were carried out on both new and old memories. In contrast, the LTM was seen as a 'storage memory', maintaining information in a fairly passive state for possible future retrieval. A useful analogy is to think of the working memory as resembling the screen of a computer, a space in which various operations are performed on current data, whilst the storage memory serves a similar purpose to the computer's memory disks, holding large amounts of information in long-term storage.

Baddeley and Hitch (1974) regarded the working memory as a workspace where analysis and processing of information would take place. As might be expected, they found that its processing capacity had a finite limit. Performance on a task involving the working memory was found to be severely disrupted by performing a second similar task at the same time, because the two tasks were in competition for limited processing capacity. However, there was found to be very little interference between two tasks which involved different sensory inputs. Baddeley and Hitch concluded that the working memory must have separate stores for different sensory modalities. They proposed a model of working memory (see Figure 4.4) comprising a central executive served by two short-term stores, the 'phonological loop', which holds auditory and speech-based information, and the 'visuo-spatial sketchpad', which holds visual images.

The existence of the phonological loop is suggested by the finding that the immediate recall of a list of spoken words is severely disrupted by the simultaneous performance of a second verbal task, for example, an articulatory suppression task such as repeating 'the, the, the' over and over again (Baddeley and Lewis, 1981). It is assumed that the second task disrupts the first because they are both competing for the same phonological loop.

The phonological loop is seen as being the mechanism underlying tasks such as digit span or word span, which was previously believed to have a limit of about

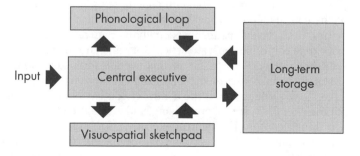

Figure 4.4 The working memory model
Source: Adapted from Baddeley (1986)

seven items (Miller, 1956). However, Baddeley *et al.* (1975) found that the word span limit is greater for short words than for long words (a phenomenon known as the 'word length effect'), which led them to suggest that the phonological loop was limited not by the number of items it could hold but by the length of time taken to recite them. In fact, the word span was found to be limited to the number of words that could be spoken in about two seconds. The phonological loop thus seems to work in a rather similar way to a short loop of recording tape, which explains how it got its name.

Baddeley and Lewis (1981) found that articulatory suppression interfered with a subject's ability to detect errors of logic or word order in a sentence. This suggests that the function of the phonological loop may be to hold on to a sentence for long enough to analyse it for logic, word order and overall meaning. This view is supported by clinical studies. Vallar and Baddeley (1984) investigated a subject, 'PV', who appeared to have a severely impaired phonological loop, as demonstrated by a very small memory span. PV was found to have great difficulty in under- standing long and complex sentences, but had no trouble with short and simple sentences. It seems therefore that the problem was not one of basic compre- hension, but an inability to retain and examine a long sentence. Other studies have found evidence of reduced phonological memory performance in children with language problems (Raine *et al.* 1992), and in normal children with poor linguistic ability (Gathercole and Baddeley, 1990; Adams and Gathercole, 1996). Patients suffering from a deficient phonological span have also shown impaired arithmetical ability in some cases (McCarthy and Warrington, 1987), though not all patients show this impairment (Butterworth *et al.*, 1996).

Investigation of the visuo-spatial sketchpad has shown that short-term visual recall is severely disrupted by performing a second visual task at the same time, but is not greatly disrupted by a non-visual task. For example, Logie (1986) found that the ability to learn words by using imagery was greatly disrupted by a second visual task but not by a speech task, and Robins *et al.* (1996) found that the ability to recall positions on a chessboard was disrupted by a secondary spatial task (manipulation of a keypad) but not by a task involving the repetition of words.

Recently Logie (1995) has argued that the working memory stores contain distinct active and passive components. For example, there is evidence suggest- ing that the visuo-spatial working memory contains separate visual and spatial components, with the more active spatial component being involved in movement perception and the control of physical actions whilst the more passive visual compo- nent is concerned with visual pattern recognition. Similarly the phonological working memory may comprise separate articulatory and auditory components.

The experiments described so far in this section give some indication of the sorts of tasks that make use of the phonological loop and the visuo-spatial sketchpad. Rather less is known about the central executive, but it is thought to be concerned with the overall control of processing, and is assumed to be in control of the two memory loop systems. The central executive is thought to be involved in many of the higher mental abilities, such as decision-making, problem-solving and making plans. Baddeley (1996) suggests that more specific cognitive functions of the central executive may include coordinating performance on two separate tasks, attending selectively to one input and inhibiting others, switching retrieval strategies, and manipulating and holding information in long-term memory. Most of these functions are thought to involve the frontal lobes (Shallice, 1988; Baddeley, 1996), since they tend to be impaired in patients with frontal lobe damage, who have difficulty in producing controlled and flexible responses and instead rely extensively on automatic processing. The role of the frontal lobes in executive functions will be considered in more detail in Chapter 7.

4.3 Ebbinghaus and the first long-term memory experiments

The work of Ebbinghaus

The scientific study of memory began with the work of Hermann Ebbinghaus (1885), whose methods were to have a huge influence on memory research for many years. Using himself as the experimental subject, Ebbinghaus carried out a number of classic experiments in which he attempted to measure memory performance in a scientific and quantified manner. He also made an attempt to control all unwanted variables out of his experimental design. Ebbinghaus realised that the use of verbal items in a memory test would add an uncontrolled variable to the design, since the words used would all be of different meaning and would therefore differ in their memorability. He decided to eliminate this variable by using nonsense material instead of meaningful words in his experiments. Ebbinghaus devised lists of test items known as 'nonsense syllables', so-called because they are pronounceable syllables but have no meaning, such as VOP or TUV. Ebbinghaus considered that all nonsense syllables were of similar memorability, since they were meaningless. Having devised a suitable form of test item,

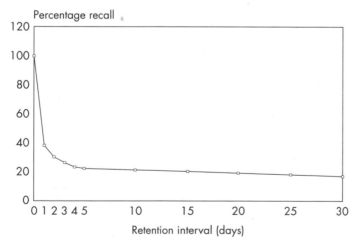

Figure 4.5 The forgetting curve
Source: Ebbinghaus (1885)

Ebbinghaus used it to investigate the way that forgetting took place with the passage of time. A list of syllables would be learned and then retested after a certain retention interval, and scores were plotted as a 'forgetting curve', as shown in Figure 4.5.

As the graph shows, forgetting was extremely rapid at first, but as the retention interval increased the rate of forgetting gradually levelled off. This same basic forgetting curve has been confirmed in many subsequent experimental studies (Slamecka and McElree, 1983), and it is now generally accepted that newly learned material is initially forgotten at a very rapid rate, but that forgetting becomes far more gradual at longer retention intervals.

Interference and decay

The forgetting curve demonstrates that memories tend to dissipate over a period of time, and Ebbinghaus suggested two main theories to explain why this might occur, which can be summed up as follows:

Spontaneous decay – memories deteriorate with the passage of time, regardless of other input.

Interference – memories are actively disrupted by the influence of some other input.

Ebbinghaus was able to demonstrate experimentally that interference did indeed have a significant effect on memory. He showed that memory scores for the learning of one list were considerably reduced by the subsequent learning of a second list, a phenomenon known as retro-active interference. Another experiment showed that the memory for a list was also subject to interference from a previously learned list, a phenomenon known as pro-active interference. In summary, the interference effect could be caused by any additional input occurring either before or after the target list. The design used in these interference experiments is summarised below. The inclusion of a control condition in both experiments is quite crucial, because without it we would not know whether forgetting in the experimental condition was caused by learning the second list or by the passage of time. In both experiments Ebbinghaus found that memory scores in the experimental condition were lower than those in the control condition.

Experiment 1 (Retroactive interference)

EXPERIMENTAL	Learn list A	–	Learn list B	–	Test A
CONTROL	Learn list A	–	Distractor task	–	Test A

Experiment 2 (Proactive interference)

EXPERIMENTAL	Learn list A	–	Learn list B	–	Test B
CONTROL	Distractor task	–	Learn list B	–	Test B

Although Ebbinghaus was able to obtain evidence for the occurrence of inter-ference, producing evidence for the occurrence of spontaneous decay has proved to be rather more difficult because of the difficulty of separating its effects from those of other forms of forgetting which also inevitably take place over time. However, the interference and decay theories both remain plausible.

Many subsequent studies have confirmed the effects of interference, which has been shown to depend on the degree of similarity between the target item and the items interfering with it (McGeoch, 1932; Underwood and Postman, 1960). A simpler way of describing this phenomenon is that similar items just get muddled up with one another. More recent versions of the interference theory suggest that interference does not actually affect the memory trace as such, but merely makes it harder to retrieve. One such theory is that of Anderson *et al.* (1994), who propose that the retrieval route which would have been used for the target item is blocked by the retrieval of a similar item. This may explain why we often find we are unable to recall a name once we have recalled a similar but incorrect one. For example, a person attempting to recall the name of the basketball player Michael Jordan might initially come up with the similar name of singer Michael Jackson. Having once blocked their retrieval route in this way the real name cannot be brought to mind. Evidence that the retrieval of one trace can interfere with the retrieval of a rival trace has been reported by Chandler and Gargano (1998), who suggest as a possible explanation that the interfering item may interact with the retrieval cue, altering it in some way so that it becomes less effective in cueing other traces.

A revised version of the decay theory was put forward by Thorndyke (1914), based on the idea that memory traces decay if they are not used. A new version of this 'decay with disuse' theory has recently been proposed by Bjork and Bjork (1992), who suggest that it is not the memory trace itself which deteriorates with disuse but our access to it. Frequent retrieval of a memory trace is assumed to strengthen the retrieval routes leading to it. Memories which we have retrieved frequently in the past thus remain accessible, but access to unretrieved memories becomes more and more difficult as time passes. This version of decay theory obviously ties in closely with the interference theory of Anderson *et al.* (1994) mentioned above, since both depend on retrieval route accessibility.

The experiments and theories proposed by Ebbinghaus over a century ago had a tremendous influence on subsequent memory research. However, psychologists eventually came to question one very central feature of his research method, namely his use of nonsense items as test material. By controlling out the effects of meaning and knowledge, Ebbinghaus had eliminated what was possibly the most important single feature of memory function.

4.4 The role of knowledge, meaning and schemas in memory

Meaning and mnemonics

It has been known for many years that people are very bad at learning things which they find meaningless. The human brain does not appear to be well suited to rote-learning, or 'parrot learning' as it is sometimes called. For example, if you read the number 1984747365 just once, there is very little chance that you will still remember it in ten minutes' time. In fact you have probably forgotten it already. However, try looking at the number again and this time try to imagine George Orwell (1984) sitting on a jumbo jet (747) for one year (365). By adding these associations to the numbers they become more meaningful and thus more memorable. Consequently you are not only likely to remember these numbers in ten minutes' time, but it is entirely possible that you will still remember them in ten years' time (I offer my apologies if this turns out to be the case). Essentially what we have done here is to make use of knowledge that is (probably) already in your LTM store, to add meaning to a list of otherwise meaningless digits. Many techniques and tricks have been devised over the years to enable us to add some meaning to an otherwise meaningless list of numbers or words. These techniques are known as **mnemonics**, and you probably already know and use several. One good example is the use of mnemonics to assist with the recall of the sequential order of the colours of the spectrum, by turning it into a sentence such as 'Richard Of York Gave Battle In Vain'. The first letters of these seven words may help the retrieval of the colours of the spectrum in their correct order (red, orange, yellow, green, blue, indigo and violet). It will be noticed that in this case the colours themselves are not devoid of meaning but their sequential order is. There are other popular mnemonics for remembering the notes on the musical scale, the number of days in each calendar month, the twelve cranial nerves, and many other items which are either meaningless or else occur in a meaningless sequence. A number of books have been written which offer mnemonic systems to enhance memory performance (e.g. Lorayne and Lucas, 1974; Gruneberg, 1992). These mnemonic techniques almost invariably involve some method of adding meaning to items which otherwise contain very little meaning, and their effectiveness provides evidence for the view that people are much better at memorising information which has meaning, and to which they can apply their previous knowledge.

Bartlett's story recall experiments and the schema theory

The first clear experimental demonstration of the importance of meaning and knowledge on memory was provided by Bartlett (1932) in a now famous study which is regarded by many as the first step towards the modern cognitive approach to memory. Bartlett investigated the way that his subjects remembered a short story, using a very simple design in which each subject would hear the story read out to them and after a short interval would be required to write down all they could remember from it. Bartlett also used a method known as serial reproduction, in which the first subject to hear the story would then pass on their version of it to a second subject, and then on through several more subjects until a point was reached where hardly any of the original story was left. In order to make the experiment more interesting Bartlett used slightly unusual stories such as the one below, which is a Red Indian folk tale called 'The war of the ghosts'. If you wish to try the experiment on yourself you should read through the story once, then cover it over and write down as much of it as you can remember.

The war of the ghosts

One night two young men from Egulac went down to the river to hunt seals, and while they were there it became foggy and calm. Then they heard war-cries, and they thought, 'Maybe this is a war party.' They escaped to the shore, and hid behind a log. Now canoes came up, and they heard the noise of paddles, and saw one canoe coming up to them. There were five men in the canoe, and they said, 'What do you think? We are going up the river to make war on the people.' One of the young men said, 'I have no arrows.' 'Arrows are in the canoe,' they said. 'I will not go along. I might be killed. My relatives do not know where I have gone. But you,' he said, turning to the other, 'may go with them.' So one of the young men went, but the other returned home. And the warriors went up the river to a town on the other side of Kalama. The people came down to the river, and they began to fight, and many were killed. But presently the young man heard one of the warriors say: 'Quick, let us go home: that Indian has been hit.' Now he thought: 'Oh, they are ghosts.' He did not feel sick, but they said he had been shot. So the canoes went back to Egulac and the young man went ashore to his house, and made a fire. And he told everybody and said: 'Behold I accompanied the ghosts, and we went to fight. Many of our fellows were killed, and many of those who attacked us were killed. They said I was hit, and I did not feel sick.' He told it all, and then he became quiet. When the sun rose he fell down. Something black came out of his mouth. His face became contorted. The people jumped up and cried. He was dead.

This story is rather strange to the average person from a Western cultural background (i.e. someone who is not a Red Indian), as it contains references to various supernatural entities such as ghosts, magic and states of invulnerability, all concepts which are rather unfamiliar to most of us. Bartlett's most important finding was that his subjects tended to recall a changed and distorted version of the story. However, the changes noted by Bartlett were not random, but were systematically directed towards the creation of a more rational and sensible story. Bartlett concluded that subjects tended to rationalise the story to make it fit in with their expectations, based on their own past experience and understanding of the world. Typically the story which emerged from a subject of Western cultural background would be a far more straightforward account of an expedition which was relatively free from ghostly or magical interventions. Some of the more unfamiliar parts of the story tended to be left out altogether. Bartlett explained these findings in terms of his schema theory (see Chapter 1), which proposes that we perceive and encode information into our memories in terms of our past experience. Schemas are the mental representations that we have built up from all that we have experienced in the past, and according to Bartlett we compare our new perceptual input with these schemas in an effort to find something there which is meaningful and familiar. Thus any input which does not fit the existing schemas will either have to be distorted until it does fit, or else it will not be retained at all.

These findings have quite important implications for a variety of real-life situations, as they raise questions about whether we can rely on eyewitness testimony. We should expect, for example, that witnesses presenting evidence in a court of law will be likely to produce a distorted and rationalised version of events they have witnessed. We should also question the accuracy of any eyewitness account such as news reports, and accounts of historical events. Indeed we should even question the accuracy of our own memories of the past, since there is every likelihood that much of what we think has happened in our lives has in fact been subject to distortion and rationalisation of which we are unaware. On those rare occasions where we do actually get a chance to check the accuracy of our memories, as, for example, when chatting with a friend about some shared experience from the past, we often discover quite major discrepancies between two people's accounts of the same event. Bartlett's experiments showed that we should never expect memory to be entirely accurate, since it will tend to reflect our own efforts to make sense of its content. Bartlett also gave us an insight into the way memory actually works. He showed us that memory appears to be stored in terms of its meaningful content, and thus depends on the extent to which the subject's knowledge can be used to make sense of the incoming information.

The effect of meaning and knowledge on memory

Bartlett's theories were not widely accepted at first, partly because they concerned inner mental processes (such as schemas) which were unacceptable to the behaviourists who dominated mainstream psychology at that time. Moreover, Bartlett's experiments were rather poorly designed. For example, the main variable in his story recall experiments was the meaningfulness of the story content, but as this was determined purely on the basis of subjective opinion, it is perhaps not surprising that it met with some criticism.

In recent years there have been a number of studies which offer a more scientific basis for Bartlett's theories, by providing an objective means of varying the meaningfulness of the narrative. Bransford and Johnson (1972) tested their subjects' ability to recall a short passage, which made relatively little sense unless the subject was provided with some kind of explanatory context, in this case a picture (see Figure 4.6). Two groups of subjects were used in this experiment. One group was shown the helpful picture, but the other group was not. The group which had seen the picture was subsequently able to recall far more of the passage than the other group, probably because the picture helped to make sense of the passage. The passage is reproduced below, and you may wish to try out the experiment on yourself.

The balloons passage

If the balloons popped the sound wouldn't be able to carry since then everything would be too far away from the correct floor. A closed window would also prevent the sound from carrying, since most buildings tend to be well insulated. Since the whole operation depends on the steady flow of electricity, a break in the middle of the wire would also cause problems. Of course, the fellow could shout, but the human voice is not loud enough to carry that far. An additional problem is that the string could break on the instrument. Then there would be no accompaniment to the message. It is clear that the best situation would involve less distance. Then there would be fewer potential problems. With face to face contact, the least number of things could go wrong.

In this experiment the subject's ability to find meaning in the passage was scientifically controlled by giving helpful information to one group but not to the other. This method of controlling the variable of meaningfulness was thus quite objective and did not rely at all on the subjective opinion of the experimenter as was the case in Bartlett's story recall experiments. Since the two groups of subjects were read exactly the same passage in exactly the same conditions, the only major

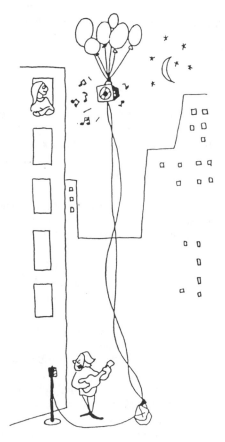

Figure 4.6 The picture used to make the balloons passage meaningful
Source: Bransford and Johnson (1972)

variable was the degree of meaningfulness, which was systematically controlled by the experimenter.

These experiments on story recall suggest that a passage is more memorable if we can make use of our knowledge and experience to increase its meaningfulness. Other studies have shown that subjects who possess a great deal of expert knowledge about a subject are particularly good at remembering material which relates to their field of expertise. Chase and Simon (1973) compared expert chess players with chess novices for their ability to recall the positions of chess pieces, after being shown an uncompleted game of chess. Their results showed that chess experts were able to remember the positions of the pieces with great accuracy, whereas chess novices produced far less accurate recall. However, the chess experts only achieved superior recall when the test material consisted of real or plausible chess games, but not when the chess pieces were placed in random positions. This suggests that the real games were probably more memorable to the chess experts because they held more meaning and significance for the expert player, full of implications for the subsequent development of the game. Similar benefits of expert knowledge have been reported for the memories of experts on football (Morris *et al.*, 1981) and experts on television soap operas (Reeve and Aggleton, 1998).

Schemas and scripts

Schank and Abelson (1977) proposed a form of schema called a script, which combines a sequence of events which might normally be expected in a particular situation. Scripts can therefore guide our behaviour by enabling us to anticipate what will happen next. For example, a visit to a restaurant typically involves the following sequence of events and actions:

> Enter restaurant / Find table / Choose seat / Sit down /
> Receive menu / Choose food / Order from waiter / Wait for food /
> Food arrives / Eat food / Waiter brings bill / Pay Bill / Leave restaurant.

This sequence provides us with a general idea of what to expect when we go to a restaurant. It will therefore come as no great surprise when a bill is presented after the meal (though the size of the bill may well be a surprise). Scripts may help us to organise our plans and our actions, by providing us with a general framework with which to organise them. They also help us to understand events and the behaviour of others.

Of course, events in real life do not always follow a script in a precise and invariant manner, so it is better to think of scripts as a set of 'default' options, which may be liable to alteration or even substitution. Schank (1982) recognised this point by suggesting that scripts contain various sub-components which are to some extent interchangeable. This version of script theory makes allowances for the variable nature of real-life experience and allows script theory to explain how people manage to deal with unusual or even quite novel situations.

Although schema and script theories remain popular as general theoretical principles, a major criticism is that they do not make very specific and testable predictions, because we cannot possibly know all of the schemas that are held by any one person.

4.5 Input processing and encoding

Levels of processing theory

Craik and Lockhart (1972) proposed a theory to explain the role of knowledge and meaning in memory, which in some ways borrows from schema theory in that it stresses the importance of extracting meaning from the perceptual input. Their 'levels of processing' theory suggests that the processing of new perceptual input involves the extraction of information at a series of levels of increasing depth of analysis, with more information being extracted at each new level (see Figure 4.7). Thus initial processing will be shallow, extracting only the more superficial features of the input such as the shape of an object (structural processing) or the sound of a word (acoustic processing). However, the input may subsequently be processed at a deeper level where more complex features are analysed, such as the meaningful content of a word (semantic processing).

The main prediction of the levels of processing theory is that the retention of a memory trace will depend on the depth to which it has been processed during the encoding stage. It is therefore a theory that emphasises the importance of input processing, and in fact Craik and Lockhart suggest that the memory trace is essentially a by-product of perceptual processing. Like schema theory, the levels of processing theory is able to explain the well-established finding that meaningful material is more memorable than non-meaningful material, by postulating that meaningful material can be more deeply processed. However, unlike schema theory, the levels of processing theory specifies a number of distinct stages in the processing sequence, and then makes a firm prediction that memory performance will depend on the level to which processing has progressed.

The levels of processing theory has been criticised for its inadequate definition of the dimension of processing depth, and the consequent lack of any objective means of quantifying it (Baddeley, 1978; Eysenck, 1978). One approach which goes some way towards answering this criticism is the use of orienting tasks, which provides the main supporting evidence for the levels of processing theory.

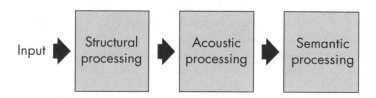

Figure 4.7 The levels of processing model
Source: Adapted from Craik and Lockhart (1972)

Orienting tasks

An **orienting task** is essentially a set of instructions which is intended to direct the subject towards a certain type of processing. For example, Craik and Tulving (1975) presented the same list of sixty words to three different groups of subjects, but gave each group a different orienting task to carry out. The orienting tasks were as follows:

1   *Structural orienting task* (e.g. is word in block capitals?)
2   *Acoustic orienting task* (e.g. does word rhyme with 'bat'?)
3   *Semantic orienting task* (e.g. does word fit the sentence 'The cat sat on the. . . .'?)

The results are shown in Figure 4.8.

These results showed that tasks which require deep processing tend to produce better retrieval than do tasks which involve shallower processing, and this general finding has been confirmed by other orienting task studies (e.g. Hyde and Jenkins, 1973; Craik, 1977; Parkin, 1983).

The design used by Craik and Tulving for their orienting task experiment required the subjects to read through the wordlist without realising that their memory of it would later be tested. In other words it was a test of incidental learning rather than intentional learning. This technique was used in order to prevent subjects from deliberately trying to learn the wordlist, since subjects motivated to learn the words might tend to disregard the instructions to carry out a particular orienting task. It is interesting to note that when Craik (1977) instructed a group of subjects to try to learn the list deliberately, their recall scores were no better than those of the group performing a semantic orienting task.

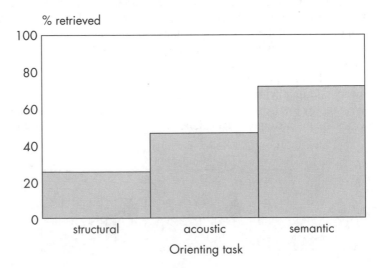

Figure 4.8 The effect of orienting tasks on retrieval
Source: Craik and Tulving (1975)

The effect of processing depth is not limited to verbal test items. For example, Winograd (1976) showed that face recognition scores were higher for subjects rating the pleasantness of each face than for subjects who were required to report on a more superficial structural feature of each face, such as whether or not it had curly hair.

Orienting tasks continue to be widely used as a means of inducing semantic or non-semantic processing, and many different kinds of encoding task have been employed for this purpose. These can be divided into two main types of task (Hunt and McDaniel, 1993). Firstly, there are 'item-specific' tasks which involve processing the target item in isolation, such as rating its pleasantness or forming a picture image of the item alone. Secondly there are 'relational' tasks which involve relating the target item to other items, such as category sorting or the use of imagery for the item in a context. Whilst both types of processing have been found to assist subsequent retrieval, there is evidence that item-specific processing assists the discrimination of the item from others during retrieval, whilst relational processing helps to create a retrieval route to the item by connecting it with others (Hodge and Otani, 1996).

Elaborative encoding

In its original form the levels of processing theory proposed a strict sequential order of processing, beginning with structural processing and then proceeding to acoustic and finally semantic processing. However, this processing sequence is not entirely plausible, since the three types of processing are qualitatively different and thus discontinuous with one another. The suggestion that structural, acoustic and semantic processing somehow blend into one another does not seem convincing. Furthermore there is some evidence (e.g. the Stroop effect – see Chapter 1) that semantic processing can sometimes take place before the 'shallower' stages are complete. It was partly in answer to these criticisms that the original sequential model of processing depth was replaced by a parallel model, known as the **elaborative encoding** theory (Craik and Tulving, 1975), in which elaboration of the trace is assumed to take place simultaneously in the structural, acoustic and semantic domains, rather than in sequence (see Figure 4.9).

This theory assumes that any new input will be subjected to several different types of processing at the same time, and that depth of processing depends on the

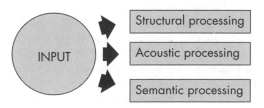

Figure 4.9 The elaborative encoding theory
Source: Adapted from Craik and Tulving (1975)

amount of elaboration within each processing domain. This view is supported by the finding (Craik and Tulving, 1975) that complex semantic orienting tasks produce better retrieval than simple semantic orienting tasks.

Although this parallel model abandons the concept of a sequence of processing mechanisms, it can still explain the general superiority of semantic processing, since there is obviously far more scope for extensive semantic elaboration than there is for structural or acoustic elaboration.

This revised version of the theory overcame some of the criticisms made of levels theory, but it did so at the expense of becoming even more vague in its predictions. Processing depth was now even harder to specify or measure, since it was no longer possible to use different processing domains as a simple criterion of depth.

Elaborative encoding theories of memory propose that extensive processing leads to a more elaborated memory trace, due to the formation of a large number of associative links with other items in the memory. Since each of these associative links can serve as a potential retrieval route, the trace will be more easily retrieved because there are so many possible pathways back to it. Recent versions of the theory have therefore tended to place emphasis on the strengthening of inter-item associations and the consequent creation of additional retrieval routes which are brought about by elaborative processing (Lockhart and Craik, 1990; Hodge and Otani, 1996).

An alternative view was proposed by Eysenck (1979), who provided evidence that in some cases the value of extensive input processing was that it produced a more distinctive and unique memory trace, which could be more easily retrieved because it stood out clearly from other items in storage. At the present time both the 'elaboration' and 'distinctiveness' accounts of processing depth remain plausible, and it is possible that both mechanisms may operate together. However, both models emphasise the view that deep processing is effective because it creates a trace which can be more easily retrieved.

Elaborative and maintenance rehearsal

Rehearsal is commonly employed as a method of retaining a piece of information, as, for example, repeating a telephone number over and over to yourself until you have the chance to write it down. Craik and Lockhart (1972) made a clear distinction between 'maintenance rehearsal' of this kind, in which the input is merely repeated without further processing, and 'elaborative rehearsal', in which elaborative processing is carried out on the input. They argued that only elaborative rehearsal would lead to long-term retention of the information, and that maintenance rehearsal served only to hold it temporarily in conscious awareness and did not help to strengthen the trace. There is some evidence that the mere repetition of an item without active processing does not leave a lasting trace (Craik and Watkins, 1973), though some studies have failed to confirm this finding (Greene, 1987).

One example of the importance of elaborative processing is the common finding that people are surprisingly poor at describing or recognising common objects, such as the coins in their own pockets. Although we see the more common coins on a regular basis, most people are unable to remember any details about their appearance, such as the position of the writing and whether the face on the coin is looking right or left (Nickerson and Adams, 1979). This shows that mere repetition without elaborative encoding is not enough to ensure retrieval.

Several studies have shown that recall scores are particularly high for test items which the subjects have used in reference to themselves (Rogers *et al.*, 1977; Klein *et al.*, 1989; Kahan and Johnson, 1992), as, for example, when an orienting task requires subjects to decide whether adjectives can be used to describe them personally. This is known as the self-reference effect. It has also been found that subjects are more likely to remember items which they have generated themselves in a word association test, a phenomenon known as the generation effect (Slamecka and Graf, 1978; Smith and Healy, 1998).

Transfer-appropriate processing

The levels of processing theory, at least in its original form, proposes that semantic orienting tasks should provide better retrieval under all circumstances than will acoustic orienting tasks. However, a number of studies (e.g. Fisher and Craik, 1977; Morris *et al.*, 1977) have shown that this prediction only holds true when the retrieval test also involves the use of semantic cues, where the subject is required to recall the items by making reference to their meaning. When the retrieval cues are acoustic in nature, as, for example, when the subject is asked to recall a word similar in sound to a cue word, then acoustic orienting tasks are found to produce superior retrieval (see Figure 4.10). The most effective type of input processing is found to be that which best matches up with the processing at the retrieval stage, a phenomenon referred to as transfer-appropriate processing.

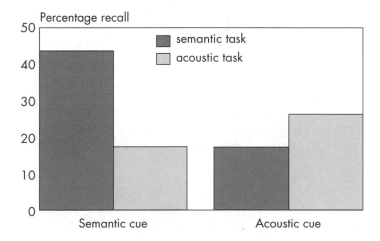

Figure 4.10 Recall as a function of input task and retrieval cue
Source: Fisher and Craik (1977)

This finding cannot be adequately explained by the levels of processing theory, but it is entirely consistent with another theory known as the encoding specificity principle, which will be examined in Section 4.6.

4.6 Retrieval cues and feature overlap

The encoding specificity principle

Tulving (1972) proposed that the retrieval of an item from memory depended on the availability of retrieval cues which matched up with some aspects of the stored memory trace. Tulving called this the **encoding specificity principle** (often abbreviated to 'ESP'), since it proposes that retrieval cues will only be successful if they contain some of the same specific items of information which were encoded with the original input. Of course it is not necessary for *all* the stored features of the item to be available in the retrieval cues too, but some of them must be if retrieval is to be successful. Tulving suggested that the chance of retrieving a memory trace depends on the amount of **feature overlap** between input and retrieval information, which is the extent to which features of the trace stored at input match those available at retrieval.

There are a number of analogies which can help us to visualise the concept of encoding specificity. For example, the need for input and output information to match up can be seen in a more concrete form when we are searching for a particular book in a library (Broadbent, 1966). In order to find the book, we need to have some information about it. We may know the name of the author and possibly the title, and this retrieval information should enable us to find the book, so long as the librarian has stored and catalogued the books in terms of their authors and titles. However, if we know only the colour and size of the book, we are unlikely to find it since our retrieval information will not match up with the information used to store the book (unless of course we are dealing with a rather strange library in which the books are shelved according to their colour and size, but in real life this is not how libraries operate). The vital factor in determining our success in retrieving a memory (or for that matter a book) is the degree of feature overlap between the retrieval and storage information. There must be a match between input and output features if we are to retrieve a memory, in much the same way as there must be a match between a lock and a key if we are to succeed in unlocking a door. Figure 4.11 illustrates the principle of encoding specificity in diagrammatic form. It shows how each of the features encoded with the original memory trace can serve as a potential retrieval route, providing that a matching retrieval cue is available.

You may find it helpful to consider Figure 4.11 in terms of your own efforts to recall items from the past. For example, try to recall the names of as many British prime ministers as you can. Your memory trace for a very well-known prime minister such as Winston Churchill will be easy to recall, because the trace will have been extensively elaborated with a large number of associations, any of which can provide a potential connection with your memory trace for Churchill. Thus any mention of the war, spitfires, cigars, bowler hats or vee-for-victory signs might be

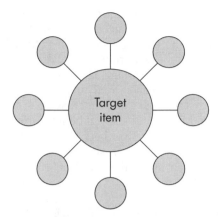

Figure 4.11 Diagram to illustrate the relationship between a target item and its associations

expected to provide direct access to the 'Churchill' memory trace. However, a less well-known prime minister such as Stanley Baldwin would be far harder to recall, since there are probably very few things that you associate with him and thus very few potential retrieval routes.

The ESP theory can thus provide a satisfactory explanation of the effects of processing depth on retrieval (see Section 4.5), by assuming that elaborative processing creates a rich network of associations, each one increasing the like-lihood of subsequently matching up with a retrieval cue. The ESP theory can also provide a convincing explanation for many of the other observed phenomena of memory function. For example, it can explain the well-established finding that recognition is usually superior to recall (see Section 4.7), since a recognition test provides far more retrieval cues and thus an increased chance of feature overlap between input and output information.

Another finding which can be readily explained by ESP theory is the phenomenon of transfer-appropriate processing (see Section 4.5), since feature overlap will obviously be maximised if the encoding task and retrieval cue are both of the same type (i.e. the acoustic/acoustic and semantic/semantic conditions), but will be minimised when input and output processing are different in nature (i.e. the acoustic/semantic and semantic/acoustic conditions).

The ESP theory receives much support from its considerable explanatory power. Possibly the most convincing evidence for ESP theory however is the phenomenon of context-dependent memory.

Context-dependent memory

It is a common observation in everyday life that returning to some earlier contextual setting can serve as a powerful cue for the retrieval of memories. You may have noticed that when you revisit some place where you spent part of your earlier life, old memories from that period tend to come flooding back, cued by the sight of a street or a building that you have not seen for many years. Sometimes a particular piece of music may bring back old memories, or even a smell or a taste which you have not experienced since childhood. These are all examples of contextual cueing, and they rely on revisiting or reinstating an earlier context.

In one of the first experimental studies of the effect of context on retrieval, Greenspoon and Ranyard (1957) tested the recall of two groups of children who had both learned the same test material in the same room. However, for the retrieval test one group returned to the room where it had carried out the learning, whereas the other group was tested in a different room. It was found that the group whose learning and retrieval took place in the same room showed better retrieval than the group tested in a different room. This finding has been confirmed by subsequent studies (e.g. Smith *et al.*, 1978), and it has been shown that merely imagining the original room and its contents can assist the recall of what was learned in that room (Jerabek and Standing, 1992).

One experiment which demonstrated the phenomenon of context-dependent memory in a particularly clear manner was that of Godden and Baddeley (1975), who carried out their research on divers. The divers were required to learn a list of forty words, either in a 'wet' context (i.e. under the sea) or in a 'dry' context (i.e. on the seashore). Similarly, recall of the list of words could be tested in either the 'wet' or 'dry' settings. The recall scores are shown in Figure 4.12. It is clear from these findings that divers who learned the wordlist underwater recalled it best when they were also tested underwater, and those who learned on dry land also produced the best recall when they were tested on dry land. The main conclusion of this experiment was that recall of the wordlist was maximised when the context of learning (i.e. wet or dry) was reinstated for the recall test. However, a subsequent experiment suggested that context reinstatement tended to assist recall but not recognition (Godden and Baddeley, 1980), possibly because contextual features act as retrieval cues, which are particularly scarce in a recall test.

The phenomenon of context-dependent learning has now been convincingly demonstrated by a large number of studies. Davies and Thomson (1988) reviewed

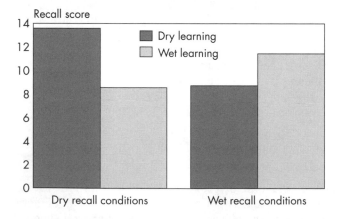

Figure 4.12 The recall of words by divers under 'wet' and 'dry' conditions during learning and retrieval
Source: Godden and Baddeley (1975)

twenty-nine context reinstatement studies, and they reported that twenty-seven of them had confirmed the occurrence of improved recall with context reinstatement, and only two studies failed to find such an improvement. Eich (1985) suggested that such negative findings might reflect a failure of the test item to become strongly connected to its learning context. Eich showed that the effect of context reinstatement was increased when subjects were instructed to form images of the test items in their context rather than alone. The degree of contrast between two contexts might also help to determine the size of any context effect. For example, moving from one room to another may not have much effect on retrieval if the two rooms are fairly similar. On the other hand, there are very obvious differences between sitting on the sea bed in full diving equipment and sitting on the seashore without it.

The occurrence of context-dependent memory clearly fits in very well with ESP theory, which predicts that retrieval depends on the amount of feature overlap, including that for contextual information.

State-dependent and mood-dependent memory

A phenomenon related to context-dependent learning is the finding that retrieval can be assisted by the reinstatement of a particular mental state at retrieval which was also present at the learning stage. For example, several studies have shown that subjects who were in a state of alcoholic intoxication at the learning stage of the experiment would recall the test items more readily if they were again intoxicated during the recall test (e.g. Goodwin *et al.*, 1969; Lowe, 1981). Apparently the experience of being drunk constitutes a form of inner context which can help to cue memories. This phenomenon is known as 'state-dependent memory', and it has also been reported with other variations in mental state, such as depression. Bower *et al.* (1978) found that retrieval of a wordlist was slightly better if the subjects were in the same depressed mood at retrieval as they had been in at the learning stage. In this experiment depressed mood states were induced by the use of hypnosis. Another study (Bower, 1981) showed that when asked to recall events from earlier in their lives, subjects in a depressed mood tended to recall a disproportionate number of sad and depressing events, whereas non-depressed subjects tended to recall rather more of their happier experiences. This phenomenon is more accurately referred to as mood-congruent memory rather than mood-dependent memory, since the subject retrieves words which are congruent with their present depressed mood but which are not actually known to have been present during a previous depressed phase.

The finding that memory can be mood-dependent has significance not only for theories of memory and retrieval but also for theories of depression. It has been suggested that some people are prone to depression because they have a cognitive bias to perceive the more depressing aspects of their experience and not to notice the more positive aspects (Sacco and Beck, 1985). Mood-dependent retrieval might perpetuate this selective cognition, by making a depressed person more likely to recall experiences from previous periods of depression, thus trapping them in a cycle of selective cognition leading to further depression. The phenomenon of mood-dependent retrieval is not a particularly strong or reliable effect (Bower and Mayer, 1989), but it has important implications.

Crime reconstructions and cognitive interviews

The principle of context-dependent memory has recently been put to practical use in the field of crime detection. In an attempt to jog the memories of possible witnesses, crime reconstructions are often organised in which every effort is made to replicate the original events and context of the crime as exactly as possible. Actors play out the roles of the participants, usually in the setting where the actual crime took place. Such reconstructions are often shown on television in the hope that witnesses may be reminded of some relevant piece of information by the strong contextual cues.

Similar principles are used in a technique known as the **cognitive interview** (Geiselman *et al.*, 1985; Fisher and Geiselman, 1992). Unlike the traditional police interview in which the witness is simply questioned about the actual crime, the witness undergoing a cognitive interview is also encouraged to recall various aspects of the context of the crime, and is wherever possible cued with contextual information. The witness may be reminded of various details of the crime setting, what the weather was like on the day in question, and even the newspaper headlines on that day. They may be shown photographs of the crime scene, or they may actually be taken back to it. There may also be an attempt to replicate their mental state during the crime, by asking them to try to remember how they felt at the time. An additional advantage of cognitive interviews is that they not only increase the amount of context reinstatement but also the variety of different retrieval cues, which may help to activate alternative retrieval routes.

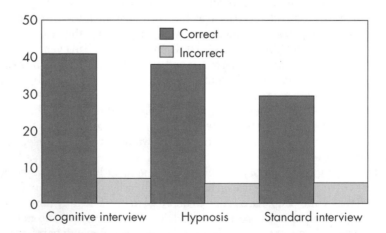

Figure 4.13 The number of correct and incorrect statements made by witnesses under three different interview conditions
Source: Geiselman *et al.* (1985)

Geiselman *et al.* (1985) have shown that the cognitive interview does in fact succeed in coaxing more information from the witness than does the traditional police interview (see Figure 4.13).

As these results indicate, a possible drawback of the cognitive interview is that whilst it usually generates a larger number of correct responses it also tends to produce more incorrect responses. This is a problem which clearly requires some caution when cognitive interviews are used in real-life police investigations, especially when the witnesses are young children (Memon *et al.*, 1997). However, the technique of cognitive interviewing has none the less proved to be of value and is being used increasingly by police forces (Roy, 1991).

Episodic and semantic memory

It may seem rather surprising that contextual cues, often of a very peripheral nature, can have a strong influence on retrieval. However, in many recall situations the context is actually the main thing that we are required to remember. Tulving (1972) pointed out that memory retrieval in everyday life frequently involves the retrieval of context, and this is equally true of most laboratory experiments on memory. For example, in a typical experiment on the retrieval of a list of words, you might be asked if the word 'dog' was on the list. Despite what you might think, you are not being asked to recall any information about dogs, or even what the word 'dog' means. You are being asked whether the word 'dog' was on that particular wordlist, presented in a particular place and time. In other words, you are being asked to recall the *context* in which you heard the word 'dog'. Tulving (1972) called this type of memory **episodic memory**, because it refers to a specific episode or event in our lives associated with a specific context. In contrast, there are occasions where we are required to retrieve general knowledge about some item without reference to any specific context or event, as, for example, if you were asked to explain what a 'dog' is, or whether it has four legs and a tail. This type of retrieval is essentially context free, and Tulving has given it the name **semantic memory**. Other psychologists have come up with their own terms for episodic and semantic memory, notably Warrington (1986), who refers to 'memory for events' and 'memory for facts'. With the benefit of hindsight the distinction between episodic and semantic memory seems perfectly obvious, but it still appears to have been largely disregarded by cognitive psychologists until quite recently.

The distinction between semantic and episodic memory received some initial support from reports that patients suffering from organic amnesia appeared to be selectively impaired in their ability to recall specific episodes and events, whilst showing little impairment in their ability to recall semantic knowledge (Warrington, 1986). However, these findings have been questioned in recent years (see Chapter 5). Rather more convincing evidence for a dissociation between episodic and semantic memories has come from brain scan studies, which have shown that episodic and semantic recall tasks produce activation in quite different areas of the brain. It has been found that the recall of semantic knowledge produces activation primarily in the left temporal lobe, whereas the recall of contextual episodes causes activation of the right pre-frontal area (Shallice *et al.*, 1994).

The exact relationship between semantic and episodic memory remains uncertain. Tulving originally regarded them as two quite separate memory stores, but more recently (Tulving, 1987) he has come to accept that semantic and episodic memories probably represent different processes within essentially the same memory storage system, with each semantic memory being derived from the occurrence of a series of memories for related episodic events.

4.7 Retrieval mechanisms in recall and recognition

Recall and recognition performance

The distinction between recall and recognition was briefly discussed in Section 4.1. Recall and recognition are two different forms of retrieval, which are commonly employed not only in experiments but in everyday life. The main difference between them is that in recognition the test material is reinstated at the retrieval stage and subjects must decide whether or not it is familiar from the test session, whereas in a spontaneous recall test subjects are required to generate test items purely from their own memory. Between these two extremes lies cued recall, where the subject is given cues (i.e. reminders) of the target items but not the actual items themselves.

It is usually found that recognition is much easier than recall, and yields higher retrieval scores. For example, Mandler *et al.* (1969) presented their subjects with a list of a hundred words, which were repeated five times. The average recall score obtained was only 38 per cent, whereas the average recognition score was 96 per cent. It is worth noting that cued recall performance usually tends to fall somewhere in between recall and recognition performance, though the actual score will depend largely on the quality of the retrieval cues (Tulving, 1976).

ESP and GR theories of retrieval

The apparent superiority of recognition performance over recall performance is so striking that clearly any theory of retrieval must provide an explanation for it. The encoding specificity principle (ESP) model of memory assumes that recognition is superior to recall because it offers more feature overlap between input and output, since a recognition test provides more retrieval cues (Tulving, 1976). This model therefore explains the difference between retrieval scores for free recall, cued recall and recognition by proposing different amounts of feature overlap, as shown in Figure 4.14.

An alternative approach is the 'generate and recognise' (GR) theory (Kintsch, 1968; Anderson and Bower, 1972), which proposes that in recall the subjects must first generate possible target items spontaneously, following which the items generated are subjected to a recognition task in order to discriminate between correct and incorrect items. In a recognition test, however, there is no need for subjects to generate possible test items since the items are already in front of them. Thus recall is seen as having two stages (i.e. generate and recognise), whilst

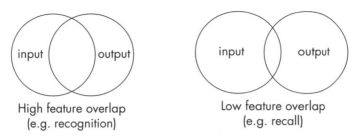

High feature overlap
(e.g. recognition)

Low feature overlap
(e.g. recall)

Figure 4.14 The overlap between features of the stimulus encoded at input and the features available in the retrieval cue at output

recognition has only one (i.e. recognise). This could explain why recall is more difficult than recognition.

An important feature of the GR theory is that it makes the assumption that recognition is actually one of the sub-processes of recall. This means that in theory any item that can be recalled should also be recognisable. However, it has been shown that in certain situations subjects are unable to recognise items which they can recall (Tulving and Thomson, 1973). This phenomenon is known as 'recognition failure' (short for 'recognition failure of recallable items'), and it provides strong evidence against the GR theory. Recognition failure is most easily demonstrated with a design in which strong retrieval cues are provided for recall but not for recognition. Subjects are typically required to learn weakly associated word pairs, essentially consisting of a cue word followed by a target word (e.g. black–engine). They are later required to recognise the target word of each pair (e.g. engine) from a checklist, but without the benefit of the cue word being presented. However, in a subsequent recall test the cue word is presented, which is often sufficient to induce recall of the target word despite the inability to recognise it. Recognition failure has now been demonstrated with a number of different experimental designs (for a review see Nilsson and Gardiner, 1993), and it is one of the main reasons why GR theory is no longer widely accepted. Although not entirely discredited, GR theory cannot rival the explanatory power of ESP theory.

4.8 Automatic and controlled memory processes

Familiarity and recollection as retrieval processes

Both the GR and ESP theories of retrieval assume that recognition is essentially a single process, but Mandler (1980) suggests that recognition may involve two alternative retrieval routes. The first is a **familiarity** rating, which simply involves making a judgement as to whether or not an item has been encountered before. The second is the **recollection** of actual occasions when the item was encountered. The distinction between these two processes is well illustrated by a phenomenon that all of us have probably experienced at some time, which is the inability to identify a familiar person seen outside of their normal context. For example, if you happen to meet your local greengrocer on the bus, you may find, at least for a moment, that although his face is very familiar you cannot remember who he is. At this stage the person's familiarity has been established but the setting from which he is familiar cannot be recollected. This may come to you later with a bit of effort, but it requires the recollection of actual occasions when you have previously met the person. The fact that familiarity can occur without recollection demonstrates that these are two separate retrieval processes. Familiarity and recollection might therefore operate as two independent retrieval routes, which may be used either separately or in combination.

Mandler (1980) pointed out that a familiarity judgement seems to be an automatic process, something which occurs without any conscious effort or volition (see Chapter 1 for the differences between automatic and controlled processes). When you recognise someone's face in a crowd, their familiarity seems to jump out at you automatically. No effort is required, and you cannot prevent yourself from making this familiarity judgement. Recollection, on the other hand, seems to be a controlled process, and one which requires some degree of volition, conscious attention, and effort. The main differences between the familiarity and recollection processes can thus be summarised as follows :

| *Familiarity*: | Automatic | Effortless | Involuntary | Unconscious |
| *Recollection*: | Controlled | Effortful | Voluntary | Conscious |

It could also be argued that familiarity ratings are essentially context free, whereas recollection normally involves retrieval of the context in which the item was encountered. There is thus some overlap here with the episodic/semantic distinction discussed in Section 4.6.

The familiarity/recollection theory of recognition gains some support from the fact that it provides a plausible explanation for real-life phenomena such as the inability to identify a familiar face. There are also experimental studies which lend further support, notably those employing the 'remember and know' (R & K) procedure (Tulving, 1985), in which subjects are in effect asked to indicate whether their responses are based on recollection or on familiarity. The R & K procedure (also known as the 'Recognition and conscious awareness' test) normally consists of a recognition test in which subjects must decide whether they consciously 'remember' (i.e. recollect) an item being presented, or whether they merely 'know' the item (i.e. from its feeling of familiarity). Using this procedure, Gardiner and Parkin (1990) found that 'remember' (R) scores for verbal items were significantly reduced when the subject was distracted by a second task during the learning of the list, but divided attention had no discernible effect on the 'know' (K) scores. Similar results were obtained by Parkin *et al.* (1995) using face recognition rather than verbal items. These findings suggest that recollection requires full and un-divided conscious attention at the learning stage, whereas familiarity judgements do not.

A number of other dissociations have been found between these two forms of retrieval. For example, semantic and non-semantic orienting tasks produce similar 'K' scores, whereas 'R' scores benefit greatly from semantic processing (Gardiner and Java, 1993; Gardiner *et al.*, 1994).

The distinction between the familiarity and recollection components of recognition receive further support from reports that amnesic patients appear to have relatively unimpaired familiarity judgements but severely impaired context recollection (Huppert and Piercy, 1976; Parkin *et al.*, 1990a). These findings will be discussed in Chapter 5.

These experiments all demonstrate 'dissociations' between familiarity and recollection, supporting the view that they involve distinct processes.

Implicit and explicit memory

Most tests of memory involve the direct testing of what the subject is able to consciously remember and report, which is known as **explicit memory**. Tests of recall and recognition are both examples of explicit memory, and for many years this was the only type of memory to be studied. However, recently there has been an increasing interest in the use of indirect memory tests which can provide evidence of memories that the subject is unaware of having. This is known as **implicit memory**.

Tulving *et al.* (1982) provided evidence for the existence of implicit memory by testing the effect of repetition priming on the completion of fragmented words. After being presented or 'primed' with a list of words (e.g. 'telephone'), the subject would later be required to complete a series of fragmented words, half of which had been on the priming list (e.g. '-el-p-o-e'). Subjects were able to complete far more of the fragmented words which had been previously primed, even for words which they were unable to identify in a recognition test. Indeed, subjects were found to be equally likely to complete a fragmented word with the previously primed target word, regardless of whether or not that word could be recognised. Thus a primed word that could not be recognised explicitly could still apparently influence performance on a test of implicit memory.

Parkin *et al.* (1990b) investigated the effect of divided attention on implicit and explicit memory, by priming subjects with a list of target words whilst distracting them with a second task involving the detection of changes in pitch of an audible tone. They found that divided attention during priming caused a marked deterioration in the subsequent recognition of target words, but had no effect on the number of target words produced in a fragment completion task. These findings suggest that implicit memory does not require conscious attention.

Graf *et al.* (1984) have produced evidence that implicit and explicit memories differ in their optimal level of input processing. Their subjects were primed with target words, and presented with either a semantic or a non-semantic orienting task. They were then given a form of word fragment completion test, in which subjects were cued with a wordstem (i.e. the first few letters of the target word) which could serve as either a word completion cue or a simple retrieval cue. When subjects were instructed to deliberately try to recall target items in response to the cues (i.e. an explicit memory test), the semantic orienting task produced better recall than the non-semantic task, as would be expected. However, when subjects were simply asked to respond with any word that seemed to fit the wordstem (i.e. an implicit memory task) the number of target words produced was not affected by the nature of the orienting task. Similar results have been obtained in an experiment using memory for non-verbal items (e.g. sounds such as a clock ticking) with the semantic task again assisting explicit memory but not implicit memory (Chiu and Schacter, 1995). These studies suggest that explicit memory may require deeper processing than does implicit memory, and supports the suggestion that implicit memory draws mainly on data-driven processing (such as the identification of perceptual features of the target item), whilst explicit memory may depend more on schema-driven processing (Hayman and Tulving, 1989; Schacter *et al.*, 1990).

Further evidence for the distinction between implicit and explicit memory arises from the finding that they differ in their sensitivity to retention interval. Tulving *et al.* (1982) showed that implicit memory tends to be far more durable over a long period than does explicit memory, often continuing to influence responses long after the subject has lost any ability to retrieve the target items explicitly. Their results are shown in Figure 4.15. The differential effect of retention interval on implicit and explicit memory has been confirmed by other studies (Tulving *et al.*, 1991; Deschepper and Treisman, 1996). It seems that memories can remain in store at an unconscious level for very long periods, but that people may gradually lose the ability to access them consciously.

The distinction between implicit and explicit memory has received further support from reports that organic amnesic patients show impaired explicit memory but relatively intact implicit memory (Graf *et al.*, 1984; Schacter, 1987; Vaidya *et al.*, 1995). These findings will be examined in Chapter 5.

It is interesting to note that the dissociations found between implicit and explicit memory closely resemble those found between familiarity and recollection (see Section 4.7). In both cases there are differential effects of divided attention, processing depth and (possibly) amnesic impairment. It might therefore be speculated that these two dimensions overlap. Certainly it seems likely

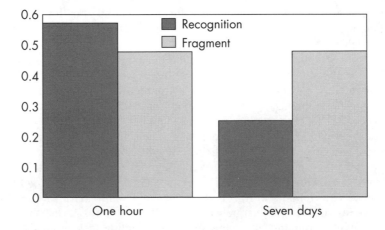

Figure 4.15 Scores for recognition and fragment completion after retention intervals of one hour and seven days
Source: Tulving *et al.* (1982)

that implicit memory and familiarity ratings share a dependence on automatic processes, responding to the general level of activation of a memory trace and its basic perceptual features. In contrast, explicit memory and recollection seem to share a dependence on controlled effortful processes, and make use of associative or contextual inter-item connections. However, whilst an overlap between these two dimensions seems highly plausible, their exact relationship still awaits clarification.

The process dissociation procedure

Jacoby (1991) pointed out that the procedures which have been used to distinguish between automatic and controlled memory processes do not in fact measure those underlying processes in a pure and uncontaminated form. Jacoby argues that the comparison of measures such as R & K scores and explicit/implicit memory are *task* distinctions rather than *process* distinctions, and the tasks employed may not directly correspond with underlying cognitive processes. For example, scores obtained on an explicit recognition task are likely to reflect a mixture of conscious and unconscious retrieval.

Jacoby *et al.* (1993) devised a method known as 'process dissociation procedure' (PDP), which is intended to distinguish between pure retrieval processes rather than merely between tasks. A wordlist is presented which is later subjected to two different types of retrieval test, known as the 'inclusion' and 'exclusion' tasks, as follows:

Inclusion task: subjects are instructed to respond to cues by making deliberate use of the previously primed words where possible.

Exclusion task: subjects are instructed to respond to the cues, deliberately *avoiding* the use of the previously primed words where possible.

It is argued that the 'inclusion' condition measures the combined efforts of conscious and unconscious retrieval, both working in the same direction (i.e. both helping to add words to the retrieval score). However, in the 'exclusion' condition conscious and unconscious memory are working in opposite directions (i.e. the subject is consciously excluding primed words but is unconsciously including them). Thus, any of the primed words which do appear in the word completions of the exclusion task will be words that were not consciously recalled. This rather complex manipulation is intended to allow the contributions of conscious and unconscious retrieval to be calculated in a reasonably pure form.

Jacoby *et al.* (1993) made use of the process dissociation procedure to confirm that divided attention during priming has different effects on the conscious and unconscious components of retrieval. Their results are shown in Figure 4.16. Under full attention learning conditions the inclusion task produced far higher scores than did the exclusion task, presumably because conscious recollection helps the former but hinders the latter. However, with divided attention the influence of conscious recollection is reduced, so inclusion scores and exclusion

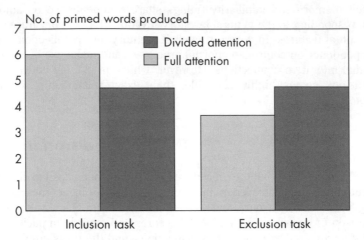

Figure 4.16 Scores obtained on inclusion and exclusion tasks following encoding under conditions of full or divided attention
Source: Jacoby *et al.* (1993)

scores are virtually the same now that both are reduced to a largely unconscious response.

The process dissociation procedure (PDP) has been widely used in the last few years, but some of its basic assumptions have been questioned. For example, Graf and Komatsu (1994) have cast doubt on the claim that PDP can isolate pure measures of the conscious and unconscious components of memory. Richardson-Klavehn and Gardiner (1995) have also found evidence for an involuntary effect of conscious memory in a process dissociation task, thus disputing the previous assumption that conscious memory was always voluntary and that unconscious memory was always involuntary. The original authors however maintain that process dissociation procedure still provides the best available means of separating conscious and unconscious memory processes (Toth *et al.*, 1995). It remains to be seen whether the process dissociation procedure will stand the test of time or whether it will turn out to be a blind alley.

4.9 Memory in real life

Ecological validity

One major criticism which can be directed at the majority of memory research is that it tends to involve rather artificial situations which are unlikely to occur outside a laboratory. You might like to consider when was the last time you were asked during your normal day-to-day life to retain three letters in your memory whilst counting backwards (Peterson and Peterson, 1959), or how often you have been asked to complete wordstems whilst deliberately trying to exclude previously primed words (Jacoby *et al.*, 1993). Unless your life is very different from mine,

I suspect that these will not have been common events; they are tasks that simply do not occur in everyday life. Of course, laboratory experiments do have an important function, as they enable us to study processes like implicit memory which are not otherwise seen in a pure form. Such processes probably do play a major part in everyday memory but usually in combination with other processes, hence the need for artificial experiments to isolate them. However, whilst accepting the value of laboratory experiments, Neisser (1976) has argued that memory should also be investigated in real-life settings where the conditions are completely natural. He describes this approach as having **ecological validity**. In recent years there has been an increasing amount of work on memory in real-life settings, including studies of autobiographical memory, flashbulb memory and eyewitness testimony.

Autobiographical memory

How much can you remember about the events in your life up to now? How well can you remember your school days? How many of your teachers and schoolmates can you name? You might like to spend a few moments testing yourself on these questions, and you will probably be surprised how much you can retrieve from the distant past, often about people and events you had not thought about for many years.

Autobiographical memory is concerned with our memory for events from our own lives. The methods used to investigate this very personal kind of memory usually involve asking subjects to freely recall events from the past, or alternatively to recall events in response to some sort of retrieval cue, which gives more control over the type of items to be retrieved. Using such methods, it has been found (Rubin, *et al.*, 1986; Conway, 1990) that subjects tend to recall more information from recent years than from the distant past, and in fact there seems to be a direct relationship between the amount of information recalled from a given year and its recency. These findings are consistent with decay and interference theory (See section 4.3), both of which predict that older memories will become less accessible. One exception to these general findings is that older subjects tend to recall relatively few recent events but an increased amount from their early adult years (Rubin *et al.*, 1998). A possible explanation for this effect is that their earlier years may have been more memorable because they were more eventful or pleasant. Another interesting finding is that most people can remember virtually nothing of the first few years of their lives, a phenomenon known as 'childhood amnesia'.

One problem with the study of autobiographical memory is that it is often difficult to check its accuracy. You may be quite sure that you remember the events of your sixteenth birthday clearly and accurately, but this does not mean that your memories are correct. A number of investigators, notably Linton (1975) and Wagenaar (1986), deliberately kept very detailed diaries of their own daily experiences over a period of many years, which could later be used to check the accuracy of their retrieval. Wagenaar (1986) also took the trouble to record retrieval cues for later use, and was able to establish that the likelihood of retrieval depended on the number of retrieval cues available. With suitable cues Wagenaar recalled about half of the events recorded over the previous six years. Linton (1975) found that items which had been tested previously were far more likely to be retrieved later on, presumably because retrieval provided reactivation of the item and kept retrieval routes open. Both Linton and Wagenaar noted that their recall of past events showed a strong bias towards the recall of pleasant events rather than unpleasant ones. There are several possible explanations for this retrieval bias. Psychoanalytic theory suggests that we tend to repress our more unpleasant memories as a means of self-protection (Freud, 1938). Another theory is that unpleasant memories have often been acquired in stressful situations, which may have inhibited memory input (Williams *et al.*, 1988; Hertel, 1992). A third possibility is that pleasant memories are more frequently retrieved and rehearsed than unpleasant ones because people prefer to think about pleasant events when reminiscing about the past (Searleman and Herrmann, 1994).

Clearly memory for past events is likely to be affected by the emotional significance of those events to the subject. The most extreme cases of emotionally significant events are not only memorable themselves, but may leave a lasting memory of trivial aspects of the context which happened to coincide with them. These are known as **flashbulb memories**.

Flashbulb memories

It is something of a cliché that all Americans are said to remember what they were doing when they heard the news of President Kennedy's assassination. Brown and Kulik (1977) decided to test this out, and they found that all but one of the eighty subjects they tested were indeed able to report some details of the circumstances and surroundings in which they heard the news of Kennedy's death. Similar findings have been reported for a range of other major news events, including the explosion of the space shuttle *Challenger* (McCloskey *et al.*, 1988; Neisser and Harsch, 1992), the resignation of Mrs Thatcher (Conway *et al.*, 1994), and the Hillsborough football disaster (Wright *et al.*, 1998). This apparent capacity of a major news event to illuminate trivial aspects of the subject's environmental context is known as 'flashbulb memory'. The significance of flashbulb memory is not that the major news event itself was well remembered (which it fairly obviously would be), but that subjects were able to remember trivial details of their own lives at the time of the event, such as where they were and what they were doing.

In an effort to explain the occurrence of flashbulb memory, Brown and Kulik (1977) suggested that a special memory mechanism was involved, which could create a memory trace that was unusually accurate and immune to the normal processes of forgetting. This special mechanism was assumed to be brought into action only by events which were very emotionally shocking and which held great personal significance for the subject. It was argued that such a memory mechanism might have evolved because it would convey a survival advantage, by enabling individuals to remember vivid details of past catastrophes which would help them to avoid similar dangers in the future. However, the notion of flashbulb memory as a special process has been challenged by studies showing that flashbulb memories seem to be no more accurate than any other type of memory. For example, Neisser and Harsch (1992) used a questionnaire to test the ability of American subjects to recall details of the circumstances in which they first heard news of the *Challenger* disaster. They tested their subjects on the day after the disaster and then tested them again about three years later. The results showed that recall in the long-term follow-up test was by no means immune to forgetting, since roughly half of the details remembered disagreed with the information recalled the day after the crash.

Whilst the special mechanism theory still has supporters (Conway *et al.*, 1994), others feel that the phenomenon can be adequately accounted for by the mechanisms underlying normal memory. Neisser (1982), for example, proposes that the memory of a very significant event would be likely to benefit from frequent recall and retelling of the memory. Another possible explanation for flashbulb memory is that the occurrence of a very dramatic event could serve as an exceptionally powerful contextual cue for otherwise trivial events. Although our surroundings and activities may not be very memorable in themselves, they could be made far more retrievable by their association with highly memorable contextual cues.

Eyewitness testimony

A courtroom is one place where memory can be of crucial importance. The testimony given by an eyewitness frequently provides the decisive evidence which determines whether or not the defendant is convicted. But there is a great deal of evidence to suggest that eyewitness testimony is fairly unreliable and does not justify the faith placed in it by the courts. The pioneering work of Bartlett (1932) demonstrated that story recall was extremely inaccurate (see Section 4.4), and particularly prone to distortion by the subject's prior knowledge and expectations. Eyewitness testimony is also prone to contamination from information acquired after the event. For example, Loftus and Palmer (1974) showed subjects a film of a car accident, and later asked them questions about it. Their answers were found to be quite strongly influenced by the wording of the questions. For example, subjects were asked to estimate how fast the cars had been travelling, but the question was worded differently for different subject groups. Subjects who were asked how fast the cars were travelling when they 'smashed into one another' on average gave a higher estimate of speed than did subjects who were asked how fast the cars were travelling when they 'hit one another'. Furthermore, they were far more likely to report having seen broken glass (although in fact none was shown) when tested a week later. In a similar experiment, Loftus and Zanni (1975) found that subjects were far more likely to report seeing a broken headlight if they were asked if they saw '*the* broken headlight' rather than '*a* broken headlight' (in fact there was no broken headlight in the film). Merely changing a single word was sufficient to influence subjects, essentially by making an implicit suggestion to them about what they should have seen.

Distortion tends to be even more marked when the events witnessed involve violence (Loftus and Burns, 1982), since witnesses are likely to be less perceptive when in a frightened or emotional state. Furthermore, like other forms of memory, eyewitness testimony becomes increasingly unreliable with the passage of time.

Flin *et al.* (1992) found that eyewitness reports became less accurate after a five-month delay, and although this applied to all age groups tested, small children were found to be particularly susceptible. Some studies have suggested that child witnesses may be generally more prone to suggestion and memory distortion (Loftus *et al.*, 1992). Children have also been found to be more likely to make a positive identification of the wrong person in an identity parade, though interestingly they are also more likely to make correct identifications (Dekle *et al.*, 1996), suggesting that children have a general tendency to make positive identifications more readily than do adults. Despite these limitations, Davies (1994) concludes that children can provide valuable testimony provided that care is taken in questioning them.

From a consideration of these findings it is easy to see how easily a witness in a court case might be influenced by police questioning, or by information from other sources such as newspapers, lawyers or other witnesses. In fact there are many examples on record of this sort of distortion occurring in actual court cases, and Fruzzetti *et al.* (1992) estimate that thousands of innocent people are probably convicted every year on the basis of mistaken identity.

There are obviously important lessons to be learned from these studies. In the first place, judges and juries should realise that witnesses cannot be expected to have infallible memories, and they should not place too much reliance on the evidence of eyewitness testimony alone. Statements should be taken from witnesses as soon as possible after the incident in question, and witnesses should be allowed to use notes when giving their evidence in court at a later date. Finally, police interviewers should be particularly careful about their methods of questioning, and should avoid the use of leading questions or suggestions which might implant misleading information in the heads of the witnesses.

Memory, real life and amnesia

In recent years there has been an increasing trend towards the study of memory in naturalistic settings, though these studies may in turn suggest scientific experiments to isolate certain key variables in controlled conditions. In some cases there has been a genuine interaction between laboratory studies and real-life applications, an interaction which can be of benefit to both approaches. One example is the interaction between experimental studies of context reinstatement and their application in police reconstructions and cognitive interviews (described in Section 4.6).

Perhaps the most valuable source of knowledge about memory function has been the study of individuals who suffer from a memory disorder, which can tell us a great deal about the working of normal memory. This will be the subject of Chapter 5.

Summary

- There is evidence for the existence of two different types of memory store, comprising a short-term working memory and a long-term storage memory.
- Processing an input to a deep level, making use of schemas from past experience to analyse its meaningful content, will increase the likelihood of retrieving that input in the future.
- Feature overlap between retrieval cues and information stored with the memory trace will determine whether or not the trace can be retrieved.
- The reinstatement of the context in which a memory trace was acquired will be of great assistance in retrieving the trace.
- Retrieval involves both automatic processes (such as familiarity judgements) and controlled processes (such as context recollection).
- Studies of memory phenomena in real-life settings, such as eyewitness testimony and autobiographical memory, provide an important complementary approach to laboratory studies because of their greater ecological validity.

Further reading

Parkin, A.J. (1997). *Memory and Amnesia*. Oxford: Blackwell. A thorough account of recent research into both normal and abnormal memory. A rather theoretical approach, but clearly written and quite suitable for students at undergraduate level.

Searleman, A. and Herrman, D. (1994). *Memory from a Broader Perspective*. New York: McGraw-Hill. As the title suggests, this book includes a number of topics which are not fully dealt with in most other texts, especially aspects of everyday memory such as childhood memory, mnemonics, and the effects of stress on memory. A very readable book, at times actually amusing.

Baddeley, A.D. (1997). *Human memory: theory and practice*. Hove: Erlbaum. A thorough account of recent work on memory, and a particularly good source of research on working memory.

DISORDERS

Disorders of memory

5.1 Amnesia

The tragic effects of amnesia

'**Amnesia**' is the name given to disorders of memory. Amnesia normally involves severe forgetfulness which goes beyond the everyday forgetting observed in normal people, to the extent that it may interfere with the activities of normal life. We are all prone to moments of forgetfulness, but most people with intact cognitive functioning can remember quite a lot about the events in their lives, especially their most recent experiences and events which are important to them. However, a person suffering from amnesia may be quite unable to remember any recent events in their lives, even the most important ones. You can probably recall quite easily where you were five minutes ago, or the person you just chatted with, or even what you did yesterday evening. Many amnesics would be unable to remember these simple things, and may have no idea of what they have done with their day so far. In severe cases they may be quite unable to commit any new experiences to memory, and this can be very disruptive to their lives. Without an intact memory it can become impossible to keep a job, to keep up relationships with family and friends, or even to look after oneself and maintain an independent existence. In fact it is clear from the study of severely amnesic patients that memory is quite crucial to our ability to function properly as human beings. Amnesia is a very disruptive and distressing condition. However, it is also a disorder from which a great deal can be learned about the nature of memory function.

Case study: Ronald Reagan

Ronald Reagan was probably one of the most successful and powerful people of all time. He first became famous as a film actor, appearing in many popular films. After retiring from the acting profession, Reagan began a new career in politics, and he was elected President of the United States in 1980. He remained in office until 1988, and during this eight-year period he was arguably the most powerful man in the world.

As president of the United States Ronald Reagan came to be regarded as an outstanding communicator, the skills from his acting days clearly standing him in good stead in his new career as a politician. But in 1994, a few years after he had left office, he was told that he had the early signs of Alzheimer's disease, a progressive dementia which first destroys the memory and then all other cognitive abilities.

Ronald Reagan announced the news in a brief handwritten letter to the American public. He wrote: 'I have recently been told that I am one of millions of Americans who will be afflicted with Alzheimer's disease. I now begin the journey that will lead me into the sunset of my life.' Within three years Ronald Reagan's memory had deteriorated so badly that he no longer remembered that he had once been the President of the United States. He was unable to understand why people waved at him in the street, and why strangers seemed to know him and wished to shake his hand. He was also no longer able to recognise friends or former aides. In 1997 he was visited by George Schultz, his former Secretary of State, but Mr Reagan did not seem to recognise his visitor, despite their many years of working closely together. However, it is possible that some glimmer of recognition remained, perhaps a slight feeling of familiarity somewhere below the level of conscious recollection. At one point during the visit the former president had returned to the room where his wife Nancy was chatting with Mr Schultz. Mr Reagan turned to his nurse and said, 'Who is that man sitting with Nancy on the couch? I know him. He is a very famous man.'

Organic and psychogenic amnesias

Organic amnesia is caused by physical damage inflicted on the brain. This may arise from a variety of different causes, including brain infections, accidental injuries, and degenerative disorders such as Alzheimer's disease (see Section 5.2 for a more detailed list). Organic amnesias tend to be severe and disabling, and they are also irreversible in the majority of cases because the brain lesion does not heal. **Psychogenic amnesias** are quite different in their origin, as the causes are psychological and tend to involve the repression of disturbing memories which are unacceptable to the patient at some deep subconscious level. Psychogenic amnesias can be disorientating and disruptive to the patient, but they are rarely completely disabling, and as there is no actual brain damage they are reversible and in most cases will eventually disappear. The organic amnesias are far more serious, and since they are also particularly instructive in helping us to understand the nature of memory function they will provide the main substance of this chapter.

5.2 The causes of organic amnesia

The aetiology of amnesia

The term 'aetiology' refers to the origins and causative factors of a disorder. The main aetiologies of organic amnesia are summarised below.

- *Alzheimer's disease (AD)* is the most common cause of amnesia. It is a degenerative brain disorder which first appears as an impairment of memory, but later develops into a more general dementia, affecting all aspects of cognition. AD occurs mostly in the elderly, and in fact it is the main cause of senile dementia, eventually affecting as many as 20 per cent of elderly people. Although seen mainly in people who are at least 60 or 70 years old, in rare cases AD may affect younger people, when it is referred to as pre-senile dementia. It was first identified by Alois Alzheimer (1907), though the cases he described in fact concerned the pre-senile form. It was only later realised that the same basic degenerative disorder, with its characteristic pattern of tangled neural fibres, was also responsible for most senile dementias. Since the amnesic symptoms of AD patients are usually complicated by additional symptoms of general dementia, they do not present a particularly pure form of amnesia and for this reason they are not the most widely researched amnesic group.
- *Korsakoff's syndrome* is a brain disease which usually results from chronic alcoholism, and it is mainly characterised by a memory impairment. It was first fully described by Korsakoff (1887), and it has become one of the most frequently studied amnesic conditions, mainly because it presents as a relatively pure form of amnesia without the complication of extensive dementia. However, recent studies have suggested that other cognitive functions besides memory may be impaired, though not usually to the extent seen in Alzheimer's cases.
- *Herpes Simplex Encephalitis (HSE)* is a virus infection of the brain, which can leave the patient severely amnesic. One important characteristic of HSE amnesia is its relatively sudden onset, which means that in many cases the date of onset of amnesic symptoms is known fairly precisely, in contrast to the very gradual onset of degenerative disorders such as Korsakoff and Alzheimer cases.
- *Temporal lobe surgery.* A very small number of patients have become amnesic as a result of brain lesions caused by deliberate surgical procedures, usually

involving the temporal lobes. Such cases are fortunately very rare, but they have been extensively studied because they provide a particularly valuable source of knowledge about memory. This is because the precise moment of onset of their amnesia is known, and furthermore the location and extent of their lesions is also known fairly accurately. One individual suffering from such temporal lobe amnesia, HM, has probably been more extensively investigated than any other amnesic patient (Scoville and Milner, 1957; Milner, 1966).

- *Post-ECT amnesia*. ECT (Electroconvulsive therapy) is a treatment used to alleviate depression, usually in patients who have failed to respond to any alternative form of therapy. ECT involves the administering of an electric shock across the front of the patient's head, and it has been found that a period of amnesia may follow the administering of the shock. Although it is possible that post-ECT amnesias are different in nature to the true organic amnesias, they have been widely investigated because they represent a serious side-effect of a deliberately administered treatment. It is therefore important for ethical reasons to establish the severity and duration of post-ECT amnesia as part of the evaluation of the treatment.

- *Other causes of organic amnesia*. Since any condition which damages the appropriate areas of the brain can cause amnesia, there are many other possible causes, though none of them have been as widely studied as those listed above. For example, strokes and tumours can occasionally lead to amnesia, as can head injuries, brain damage caused by cardiac arrest, HIV infection, and degenerative conditions such as Huntington's Chorea and Parkinson's disease.

Brain lesions associated with amnesia

The brains of amnesic patients have been extensively studied in an effort to identify the main sites where **lesions** (i.e. injuries) have occurred. The traditional method of doing this was by post-mortem examination, but in recent years a variety of brain imaging techniques have been developed which have made it possible to examine the brains of living patients. Brain scans of this kind have been able to detect a number of lesion sites which had not previously been identified by post-mortem studies. Such localisation techniques have identified two main areas in the brain where lesions tend to be found in cases of organic amnesia. These are the temporal lobes and the diencephalon, and their position is illustrated in Figure 5.1.

The temporal lobes contain the **hippocampus**, and this structure is of particular importance to the creation of new memories. Surgical removal of the hippocampus and parts of the medial temporal lobes of the patient HM was found to have a devastating effect on his memory, especially his ability to acquire and store new memories (Scoville and Milner, 1957). Since HM's lesions were deliberately inflicted (though of course without the realisation that their effect would be so devastating) their location is well known, and it can therefore be concluded that damage restricted to the medial temporal and hippocampal zone is sufficient to cause such severe amnesia without any other lesion being present. In patients with

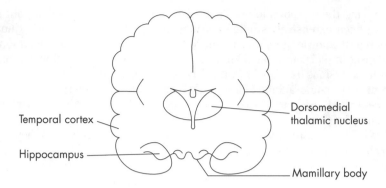

Figure 5.1 A cross-section through the human brain showing areas most often damaged in organic amnesics

amnesia caused by HSE (Herpes Simplex Encephalitis) it has been found that the medial temporal region also tends to be the main site of lesions (Damasio *et al.*, 1985), though the lesions are usually more extensive and involve most of the temporal cortex. Similar lesions are found in the early stages of Alzheimer's disease (West *et al.*, 1994), though in the later stages of this progressive condition there are more extensive lesions, extending into the forebrain at first and later affecting many areas of the brain.

The other main area of the brain where lesions tend to produce amnesia is the **diencephalon**, a region which includes the thalamus and mamillary bodies. These are the areas which are damaged in most Korsakoff patients, though their lesions may be quite diffuse and frequently also include lesions of the frontal cortex (Victor *et al.*, 1989).

In fact the lesions found in two cases of the same amnesic aetiology are by no means always identical. For example, some Korsakoff patients have frontal lesions whilst others do not. However, most amnesics are found to have lesions in either the temporal lobes or the diencephalon, and the characteristics and symptoms of their amnesia will be determined by the location of their lesions rather than by their actual cause. It is therefore quite possible for two Korsakoff patients to have quite different amnesic symptoms, and it is equally possible for two amnesic patients to have similar amnesic symptoms despite having different aetiologies.

It may seem rather surprising that there are two different areas of the brain (i.e. temporal lobes and diencephalon) where lesions can produce severe amnesia, and that damage to either one of these areas alone can cause amnesia without damage to the other. It seems highly unlikely that these two brain areas both have the same function, and a more likely explanation is that they probably work together in some way so that both areas are vital to intact memory function. One hypothesis based on known connections and lesion outcomes is that the hippocampus is probably responsible for creating new memories for storage elsewhere in the temporal lobes. Parts of the diencephalon may be important in processing and retrieving memories from these storage sites, which could explain why both hippocampal and diencephalic lesions are capable of causing amnesia.

The main symptoms of amnesia

Although there are many different causes of organic amnesia, there are some general symptoms which seem to be common to most cases, regardless of their aetiology. This suggests the possibility that there may be a general pattern of memory impairment which is common to all organic amnesics, and this is referred to as the 'organic amnesic syndrome'.

The main characteristic of the organic amnesic syndrome is known as **anterograde amnesia**, which means an inability to remember events occurring since the onset of the disorder. There may also be **retrograde amnesia**, which is an inability to remember events from the period before the onset of amnesia. However, any retrograde amnesia is usually less severe than the anterograde amnesia, and in fact its severity varies considerably from patient to patient. A third characteristic of the amnesic syndrome is that sufferers usually retain an intact short-term memory, despite the severe impairment of long-term memory. More recently it has been discovered that certain other memory functions may remain relatively unimpaired in organic amnesia, notably procedural memory and implicit memory.

Recent studies have revealed that there is actually considerable variation between amnesic patients. Although most organic amnesics suffer from the symptoms listed above, the relative severity of each of the symptoms can vary dramatically from one patient to another, so it may be more accurate to regard the main symptoms of amnesia as separate and independent types of impairment.

Perhaps the most interesting feature of organic amnesia is that it does not involve a universal impairment of memory function. There are many aspects of memory which seem to remain largely unimpaired in a typical case of organic amnesia, and these islands of intact functioning are of great interest because they not only tell us a great deal about the nature of the underlying memory dysfunction, they also shed light on the mechanisms underlying normal memory function.

Case study: Temporal lobe surgery (HM)

On 23 August 1953 a 27-year-old man, referred to in the literature by his initials 'HM', underwent a surgical operation to remove both of the medial temporal lobes of his brain in an effort to alleviate his severe epilepsy. Although the surgeon did not realise it at the time, this operation was to have a devastating effect on HM's memory. Since that fateful day he has been unable to learn anything new. Consequently he has no intact memories for any of the events of his life since 1953, indicating a profound anterograde amnesia. HM is virtually untestable on most measures of LTM, and it was reported that he 'forgets the events of his daily life as fast as they occur' (Scoville and Milner 1957). Because of this HM will watch the same television programme several times without recognising it, and he frequently does the same crossword puzzle many times without realising he has done it before. Even after several years of regular visits from clinicians such as Brenda Milner, he is still unable to recognise them.

In contrast to this very severe anterograde amnesia, HM only has a fairly limited retrograde amnesia. Although he remembers nothing that has happened to him since 1953, his memory is reasonably good for events preceding that date, especially for his childhood. In fact HM's recall of the first sixteen years of his life appears to be quite normal, and his retrograde impairment seems to be restricted to the eleven years preceding the date of his surgery (Ogden and Corkin, 1991). HM is a particularly interesting case for the comparison of anterograde and retrograde amnesia, since the date of onset of his amnesia is known precisely. We can therefore be confident about these estimates of the extent of his anterograde and retrograde impairments.

Despite his inability to register any new memories in his long-term memory, HM seems to have an intact short-term memory and his STM span is completely normal (Wickelgren, 1968). However, this only allows him to hold on to his experiences for a few seconds. HM is able to carry on a fairly normal conversation, but he can only remember the last sentence or so, which obviously limits his conversational range. He also has a tendency to repeat something he has just said a few moments earlier.

Because of his severe amnesia HM is unable to live a normal life, and he requires continual care. However, he does retain some memory capabilities. Apart from his intact STM and childhood memories mentioned above, he also retains the ability to learn new motor skills such as mirror drawing, though he has no recollection of actually learning them. He also shows some learning in tests of implicit memory, such as completing the stems of previously primed words. In addition, HM shows some vague familiarity with a few major news events from the period since 1953, such as the assassination of President Kennedy (Ogden and Corkin, 1991). These studies indicate that HM's amnesia is actually quite selective, an observation which has important implications for our understanding of the modular nature of memory processes.

5.3 Short-term and long-term memory impairments

Intact STM in organic amnesia

One of the most striking features of typical organic amnesics is that they are usually able to carry on a fairly normal conversation, despite having virtually no recollection of any recent events. The ability to keep up a conversation demonstrates that patients are able to remember what has been said in the last few seconds, although they may be unable to recall anything that took place any earlier than that. Such observations can be explained by the fact that organic amnesics usually retain an intact short-term working memory.

Early observations of the preservation of STM (short-term memory) were largely anecdotal, but more recently they have been supplemented by objective measurements of STM function, such as digit span. Talland (1965) carried out a study involving no less than twenty-nine Korsakoff patients, all of whom proved to be significantly impaired in a whole battery of long-term memory tests such as story recall, wordlist recall and picture recognition. However, their digit span scores were similar to those of normal subjects, averaging about seven items. Baddeley and Warrington (1970) again reported apparently normal STM span in Korsakoff patients, and in addition they found a normal recency effect in a test of free recall. As explained in Chapter 4, the recency effect is thought to reflect the STM component of free recall, so this provided further confirmation of the apparent preservation of STM.

HM, the patient whose amnesia was brought about inadvertently by temporal lobe surgery, has been found to retain a normal digit span despite his extremely dense anterograde amnesia (Wickelgren, 1968). On the other hand, when presented with a list of digits which was just one item larger than his span, HM was unable to learn this list even after twenty-five repetitions (Drachman and Arbit, 1966). This task is known as the 'extended digit span', and most normal subjects have no difficulty in learning such a list within a few trials, and can even learn lists of fifteen or twenty digits if given a few repetitions of the list.

Patients suffering from HSE (Herpes Simplex Encephalitis) amnesia have also been found to have a normal STM in the face of a severe LTM impairment (Starr and Phillips, 1970; Wilson and Wearing, 1995). Similar findings of preserved STM span have been obtained with patients in the early stages of Alzheimer's disease (Miller, 1977), though in the later stages Alzheimer patients do show a deterioration of STM performance (Corkin, 1982), reflecting the general dementia which eventually pervades all aspects of their cognitive functioning.

From a consideration of all these studies it would appear that in virtually every type of organic amnesia there is severe LTM impairment but a relatively unimpaired STM or working memory.

Short-term memory impairment

The above findings suggest a dissociation between STM and LTM, since STM can remain intact despite severe LTM impairment. However, there are a few cases on record which exhibit the reverse of this dissociation. As mentioned in Chapter 4, the patient KF suffers an impaired STM but an apparently normal LTM (Warrington and Shallice, 1969). Following damage to the left parietal region of the brain caused by a motorcycle accident, KF was found to have a digit span of only one or two digits, despite having an apparently unimpaired LTM. Several other patients have been studied who show a similar pattern of impaired STM in contrast to an apparently intact LTM (Basso *et al.*, 1982; Vallar and Baddeley, 1982). These patients represent a reversal of the more usual pattern of impaired LTM with intact STM as seen in typical cases of organic amnesia, indicating a 'double dissociation' between STM and LTM (as mentioned in Chapter 4) which provides strong confirmation of the independence of these two stores.

However, such conclusions should be treated with caution, since the methods used to measure STM and LTM have serious limitations. Measurements of STM performance are particularly suspect, since tests like digit span are probably not pure measures of STM and may include an LTM component. Furthermore, the STM is no longer regarded as a simple unitary store but as a complex 'working memory' with several sub-systems (see Chapter 4). Tests such as digit span probably measure the capacity of the phonological loop, which is only one of the sub-systems of working memory. Since there are no satisfactory methods of measuring STM in a pure and complete form, conclusions drawn from these measurements must remain tentative.

Patients with STM deficit have usually been found to be capable of functioning fairly well in normal life, because there are few everyday tasks which make major demands on STM and (as explained previously) these individuals tend to retain normal LTM function. However, some recent studies have shown that individuals with STM deficit may have difficulty in fully understanding long sentences (Vallar and Baddeley, 1982), and in very severe cases may have difficulty in learning new vocabulary or a new foreign language (Baddeley *et al.*, 1988). These findings may possibly provide a clue as to the function of the STM 'working memory', since it is apparently necessary to be able to hold new input briefly in the STM in order to process the information it contains and to transfer it to the LTM 'storage memory'.

5.4 Anterograde and retrograde amnesia

Distinguishing anterograde from retrograde amnesia

There are two main types of amnesic memory loss, namely anterograde and retrograde amnesia (see Figure 5.2).

Anterograde amnesia (AA) refers to the impairment of memory for events and experiences which have occurred *since* the onset of an amnesic illness.

Retrograde amnesia (RA) is an impaired ability to remember events and experiences which occurred *before* the onset of the amnesic illness.

The distinction between AA and RA is most important, because it offers a possible means of distinguishing between learning disorders and retrieval disorders. Patients suffering from a disorder of learning would be expected to have AA but not RA, since they should have no difficulty in retrieving memories from the period

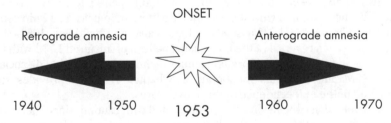

ONSET

Retrograde amnesia   Anterograde amnesia

1940   1950   1953   1960   1970

Figure 5.2 Anterograde and retrograde amnesia shown in relation to the moment of onset

Note: In this example the subject is HM, who became amnesic in 1953.

before onset when their learning ability was unimpaired. On the other hand, patients suffering from a disorder of retrieval would have difficulty in retrieving memories from any period in the past, and would thus be expected to have both AA and RA. It is possible that learning and retrieval disorders could occur together in the same patient, in which case both AA and RA would be expected but with the AA component probably being more severe.

Testing for AA is fairly easy and straightforward. The patient is simply required to learn some form of test material (e.g. words, stories, pictures, etc.) and is then tested for their retrieval performance at some later time. However, tests of RA are more problematic, since the test material must have been learned by the patient prior to the onset of amnesia. The presentation of test material is therefore usually beyond the control of the tester, who must try to find some information that the patient is likely to have encountered in the distant past. In practice this normally involves testing the patient's memory for events which happened many years before the test session, a procedure referred to as a test of 'remote memory', as opposed to the testing of 'recent memory' in more typical AA test procedures.

Tests of remote memory

Remote memory tests can either involve the testing of past *personal* events, which tend to be unique to each individual, or past *public* events, which are likely to have been familiar to most people.

Tests of past personal events focus on autobiographical memory, for example, asking a patient about events from their school-days. Because of the unique and personal nature of these items, the scores of amnesics and those of normal subjects are not directly comparable, since they will be recalling different events. Another problem is that it is often difficult to check the accuracy of the responses given. Some refinement of this approach has been achieved by using a standard questionnaire to sample specific events in a typical person's life (Kopelman *et al.*, 1990), which are confirmed where possible by interviewing relatives.

Tests of past *public* events, such as major news events from the past, allow the same test items to be given to many different people. By choosing test material which virtually everybody is likely to have been exposed to at some earlier time, it is possible to devise a standardised test with known performance norms, so that amnesic and control subjects can be compared using exactly the same test. Various different test materials have been used for this purpose, including news events from the past (Sanders and Warrington, 1971; Squire and Slater, 1975), famous faces from the past (Sanders and Warrington, 1971; Albert *et al.*, 1979) and television shows which were shown only once (Cohen and Squire, 1981). These tests sample different time periods from the past by selecting items which were widely publicised at a particular period, but which have received no subsequent publicity. The Boston Remote Memory Test (Albert *et al.*, 1979) is a widely used test battery which includes tests of famous faces from the past as well as information about people and events from earlier times.

It is important to bear in mind that tests of past personal memory tend to involve specific events from an individual's autobiographical memory, which consist mainly of episodic memories. Past public memories on the other hand may sometimes involve semantic memory, in which items of general knowledge are retrieved without any specific episodic context (see Chapter 4 for the distinction between episodic and semantic memory). This distinction has not always been recognised in the past, and some earlier investigators made the mistake of comparing episodic measures of anterograde amnesia (e.g. 'Where did you go yesterday morning?') with semantic measures of retrograde amnesia (e.g. 'What was the name of your primary school?') without realising that they were not comparing like with like. However, tests of personal and public events have both proved to be valuable measures of retrograde amnesia, offering the added possibility of assessing the relative impairment of episodic and semantic memory.

Retrograde impairment in organic amnesics

Ribot (1882) observed that patients with senile dementia often had clear memories of childhood and early adulthood but were unable to remember more recent periods in their lives. Ribot concluded that these patients suffered RA with a 'temporal gradient', since the degree of impairment increased with the recency of the event. This observation has become known as 'Ribot's law', though it is perhaps more a guiding principle than a law since it does not apply to all amnesic patients.

Korsakoff patients have usually been found to exhibit a fairly severe RA, and this finding has been confirmed by studies using a variety of different test materials (Albert *et al.*, 1979; Cohen and Squire, 1981). Moreover, items from the more distant past were usually better remembered, indicating a temporal gradient in accordance with Ribot's law. Some typical results are presented in Figure 5.3, which shows the performance of Korsakoffs and normal control subjects on the Boston Famous Faces Test (Albert *et al.*, 1979).

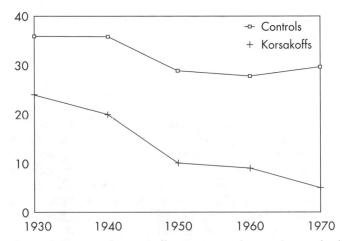

Figure 5.3 The performance of Korsakoff amnesics and normal control subjects on a test of the identification of famous faces from the past
Source: Albert *et al.* (1979)

Severe RA has also been found in studies of HSE (Herpes Simplex Encephalitis) patients (Cermak and O'Connor, 1983; Wilson and Wearing, 1995) and also in Alzheimer patients (Wilson *et al.*, 1981; Hodges *et al.* 1993), though in the latter case the temporal gradient is less marked. However, this pattern of severe retrograde amnesia is not found universally. For example, the temporal lobe surgery patient HM has been found to have very severe AA but a rather more limited RA (Milner *et al.*, 1968, Ogden and Corkin, 1991).

Learning-deficit theories of amnesia

As explained in the case study above, HM appears to suffer a profound AA but with a relatively mild RA. On the basis of this observation, Milner (1966) argued that HM's impairment was essentially an inability to learn and store new information. More specifically, Milner hypothesised that HM's amnesia reflected a failure to consolidate memories from a temporary STM trace into a permanent LTM trace, bearing in mind his intact STM.

This hypothesis raised the interesting possibility that other amnesias (such as Korsakoff's disease) might be explained by the same underlying consolidation problem. It was argued that the apparent occurrence of RA in Korsakoff patients might actually be an anterograde (learning) impairment which had not been detected in earlier years (Piercy, 1977). Since the onset of Korsakoff's disease is slow and insidious, AA could well go undetected for many years and thus later be mistaken for retrograde amnesia. This would also provide an explanation for the temporal gradient of RA, since the increasing impairment would reflect the gradual onset of the condition.

However, the consolidation-deficit theory lacks credibility as a general theory of amnesia. One problem for the theory is the finding that even HM does definitely have some retrograde amnesia (Ogden and Corkin, 1991), and so do HSE patients (Wilson and Wearing, 1995). Since the date of onset of amnesia is known with considerable accuracy in these cases, it has been possible to establish that there is a genuine retrograde amnesia for events preceding that date. There is also evidence that the RA reported in Korsakoff patients is genuine, although the date of onset is not normally known with any accuracy. Butters and Cermak (1986) were able to test a Korsakoff patient, PZ, whose memory prior to the onset of amnesia had been objectively recorded. PZ had been an eminent scientist and author before becoming amnesic, and he had written his autobiography shortly before the onset of his disorder. Proof therefore existed that he had been able to remember many events and names of colleagues prior to onset which he could no longer recall after onset, proving that in his case there was evidence of a genuine RA.

Retrieval-deficit theories of amnesia

In contrast to Milner's consolidation-deficit theory, Warrington and Weiskrantz (1970) proposed a retrieval deficit as the basis of organic amnesia. An impairment of retrieval could in theory explain both the anterograde and the retrograde components of amnesia, since a failure of the retrieval mechanism would be expected to affect all previous memories regardless of when they were acquired. However, a retrieval-deficit theory would predict equally severe AA and RA, which is not borne out by the many studies which indicate that AA tends to be far more severe than RA for most organic amnesics (e.g. Marslen-Wilson and Teuber, 1975; Ogden and Corkin, 1991). This could possibly be explained by the fact that earlier memories are for some reason more durable, perhaps because they have been heavily overlearned by years of retrieval and rehearsal, so that they can even survive in the face of a retrieval impairment. This hypothesis also offers a possible explanation for the occurrence of a temporal gradient in RA. Developing this idea, Squire *et al.* (1984) suggest that older memories will probably have been retrieved from time to time over the years, with each act of retrieval creating more copies of the memory and more retrieval routes by which it may be accessed. Whilst this remains a satisfactory explanation for the occurrence of temporal gradients, the retrieval-deficit theory does not seem to provide an adequate general explanation for all organic amnesias. It cannot readily explain the dramatic variations in the relative severity of AA and RA between different patients, which suggests that AA and RA may be fairly independent of one another. Nor can it explain how anterograde and retrograde impairments can sometimes occur in isolation.

Isolated retrograde and anterograde amnesia

In fact there is some evidence that either RA or AA can occur in isolation. Examples of isolated RA without AA are extremely rare, but a few such cases have been reported in patients who have suffered head injuries (Goldberg *et al.*, 1981; Kapur *et al.*, 1992; Papagno, 1998), and in one case following HSE infection (O'Connor *et al.*, 1992).

In contrast, Mair *et al.* (1979) studied two rather unusual Korsakoff patients with severe AA but no RA. Cohen and Squire (1981) also reported similar findings with their patient NA, an ex-law student, who has severe AA but no extensive RA, as evidenced by the fact that he still retained a good knowledge of the law. In fact NA was injured in a freak accident by a friend who accidentally stabbed him with a fencing foil, which he thrust at NA as a joke, intending to stop short. Unfortunately the foil entered NA's nostril and penetrated his brain, with devastating effects.

From these admittedly somewhat unusual cases it would appear that deficits of learning and retrieval are separate and fairly independent disorders, since either type of disorder can occur in isolation. If this is the case, it is possible that the majority of organic amnesics may actually suffer from a mixture of encoding and retrieval deficits, though there may be considerable variation in the relative severity of these two components.

Brain lesions and impaired learning and retrieval

It is now clear that all organic amnesics are not alike, since they vary considerably in the relative severity of AA and RA which they exhibit. The obvious conclusion to be drawn from these observations is that disorders of learning and retrieval are separate, and may have different underlying causes. Indeed there is some evidence that these two types of amnesia may be associated with lesions in different regions of the brain.

Patients whose lesions are restricted to the hippocampal area are usually found to suffer severe AA but very little RA, as in the case of the temporal lobe surgery patient HM (Scoville and Milner, 1957) and the patient RB, whose hippocampus was damaged by a stroke (Zola-Morgan *et al.*, 1986). In contrast, HSE patients whose lesions extend beyond the hippocampus to include large areas of the temporal cortex are usually found to exhibit severe RA in addition to their dense AA (Cermak and O'Connor, 1983; Wilson and Wearing, 1995). Based on such findings Parkin (1996) suggests that the hippocampus is primarily concerned with the consolidation of new memories, whereas the temporal cortex which surrounds it may be the main site of storage of these memories. Damage to the hippocampus would thus be expected to impair the acquisition of new memories, whereas extensive damage to the temporal cortex would disrupt the storage and retrieval of past memories. This theory is consistent with the occasional occurrence of cases of isolated retrograde amnesia (i.e. severe RA with hardly any AA) in patients with lesions in the temporal cortex but not in the hippocampus (Kapur *et al.* 1992, Hokkanen *et al.*, 1995).

Korsakoff patients typically have lesions in the diencephalon rather than the temporal lobes or hippocampus, yet they still tend to exhibit both AA and RA. This would seem to suggest that the diencephalon also plays a part in memory retrieval and possibly storage too, though its contribution may not be identical to that of the temporal lobe structures. Indeed, there is some evidence that the diencephalon may be particularly concerned with the retrieval of context (Parkin *et al.*, 1990a), a theory which will be explored in more detail in Section 5.5.

Case study: Severe amnesia following Herpes Simplex Encephalitis infection (Clive W)

The case of Clive W is extremely well known, as he has been the subject of two television documentaries. Before his illness Clive was a professional musician, and his energy and brilliance had made him extremely successful. He was chorus master to the London Sinfonietta, and he worked as a music producer for the BBC. But in March 1985 Clive developed a flu-like illness, complaining of a severe headache and fever. The illness was eventually identified as Herpes Simplex Encephalitis (HSE), a rare viral infection of the brain. Unfortunately, by the time a diagnosis had been made Clive's brain had already sustained terrible damage, and he would never be able to return to his previous life again.

Brain scans have subsequently revealed that Clive's left temporal lobe has been completely destroyed, together with some damage to his right temporal lobe and parts of his frontal lobes. These lesions have robbed Clive of his memory, in fact making him one of the most severely amnesic patients ever recorded.

As with most organic amnesics, Clive suffers a severe anterograde impairment, though rather unusually the impairment is total, and he is completely unable to acquire new memories. In the words of his wife, 'Clive's world now consists of just a moment. He sees what is right in front of him, but as soon as that information hits the brain it fades. Nothing registers.' This makes life incredibly confusing for Clive. Any conversation he has with another person is immediately forgotten, as though it had never taken place. A visitor who leaves the room for a few minutes will be greeted afresh by Clive on re-entering the room, as if he or she were a new visitor. If Clive is allowed to go out into the street alone, he rapidly becomes lost. This is a risky situation for him, since he cannot find his way back and he cannot ask for assistance as he does not remember where he lives.

Unlike many amnesics Clive also suffers from a very severe retrograde amnesia. He cannot remember any specific episodes from his life prior to the onset of his amnesia, and he no longer recognises most of his former friends. This retrograde impairment even extends to famous public figures. Clive says that he has never heard of John F. Kennedy or John Lennon. He was also unable to recognise a photograph of the Queen and Prince Philip, though when pressed he suggested that they might have been singers. However, Clive's retrograde amnesia is not total. He does remember a few facts about his childhood (such as the fact that he grew up in Birmingham), though he cannot remember any specific events. In contrast to these limited recollections, Clive still clearly recognises his wife and he treats her with the same familiarity and affection as in earlier times.

In addition to his episodic memory impairments Clive also shows clear evidence of a semantic memory disorder. He is unable to provide definitions of a number of common words such as 'tree' and 'eyelid'. He also has difficulty in recognising some common objects, for example, jam and honey which he cannot distinguish from one another.

One aspect of Clive's memory which does seem to have remained surprisingly intact is his musical ability. He is still able to play the piano and sight-read music with great skill, despite the fact that he has virtually no memory of his previous career as a musician.

Before he became amnesic, Clive was a person of considerable intelligence, and he remains highly intelligent despite his lost memory. Perhaps this is why he is so acutely aware of the limitations of his present state. Clive does not know what has caused his problems, because when it is explained to him he immediately forgets. However, he is very well aware that there is something wrong with his ability to think, and he has tried hard to find explanations for it. One of his conclusions is that he must have been unconscious until the last few seconds. At every moment of his life he feels as though he has just woken up, and his diary contains repeated entries of the same observation:'I am now fully awake for the first time.' For most of us it is difficult to imagine what it must be like to experience such a state of mind, trapped in a few seconds of existence.

For a more detailed account of Clive's memory disorder see Wilson and Wearing (1995).

5.5 Memory functions preserved in amnesia

Motor skills

They say you never forget how to ride a bicycle. Certainly motor skills tend to be very durable in normal people, but there is considerable evidence that learned skills are also preserved in organic amnesics. Not only do amnesics tend to retain their old skills from before onset, they also retain the ability to learn new skills and procedures, even in patients who find most other forms of learning impossible.

Corkin (1968) reported that HM was able to learn a number of new motor skills such as mirror drawing. Mirror drawing involves drawing a shape on a piece of paper viewed through a mirror, which is a very difficult skill to learn since all the normal visual feedback is reversed. HM succeeded in learning this new skill to a reasonable level of competence, though significantly he remained unaware that he had learned it, and he did not recognise the apparatus when it was shown to him on a later occasion. This ability to learn skills and procedures without being aware of having learned them seems to be a common finding in studies of amnesics. For example, Starr and Phillips (1970) described a patient known as PQ, who had been a concert pianist before becoming amnesic as a result of an HSE infection. PQ not only retained his ability to play the piano, but proved to be quite capable of learning to play new pieces of music, though he remained quite unaware that he was able to play them.

Glisky *et al.* (1986) reported that amnesics had been successfully trained to carry out simple computer tasks, though the training had required a great deal of time and patience. It was also noted that although these patients had been able to learn the meanings of several computer commands, this learning was only demonstrated while operating the computer and showed no generalisation to other contexts. This suggests that skill learning in amnesics is highly inflexible, possibly because it does not take place at a conscious level. In view of the many studies showing intact skill learning in amnesics, Cohen and Squire (1980) have suggested a distinction between **procedural memory**, which can be demonstrated by performing some skilled procedure, and **declarative memory**, which can actually be stated in a deliberate and conscious way. Cohen and Squire suggest that amnesics have an intact procedural memory, but an impaired declarative memory. This would explain the fact that they can learn new skills and procedures but reveal no conscious awareness of it.

The preservation of procedural memory in amnesics represents an example of learning which remains intact at an unconscious level, and in this respect it resembles implicit memory.

Implicit and explicit memory

There are a number of other types of behaviour which amnesics seem to be able to learn in addition to motor skills, though again without any conscious memory of the learning event. Such learning can sometimes be demonstrated by tests of implicit memory (see Chapter 4), in which patients' behaviour is shown to have been influenced by some previous experience despite their inability to consciously recall it. An early demonstration of this phenomenon was reported by Claparede (1911), who carried out a rather bizarre experiment in which he greeted an amnesic patient with a handshake, made rather painful for the patient by the presence of a pin concealed in Claparede's hand. Claparede noted that the patient who had fallen foul of this trick refused to shake hands with him the following day, but could not explain the reason for this unwillingness. The cautious behaviour of the patient thus revealed evidence of learning without any conscious awareness of the learning episode.

Similar effects were later demonstrated by Warrington and Weiskrantz (1968) using the technique of repetition priming. They showed Korsakoff patients a series of degraded pictures of common objects or words (see Figure 5.4 for an example), starting with the most incomplete version and then showing increasingly complete versions until the word or object was correctly identified.

Figure 5.4 An example of an incomplete or fragmented word stimulus
Source: Warrington and Weiskrantz (1968). Reproduced by permission of Macmillan.

When the same procedure was repeated at a later time, the Korsakoff patients showed a marked reduction in the number of trials required to identify the object, thus providing clear evidence of learning. A similar study was carried out on the patient HM, who also showed an improvement in the identification of degraded pictures following repetition priming (Milner et al., 1968).

Graf *et al.* (1984) used the priming of verbal material to demonstrate intact implicit memory in Korsakoff patients. Following a priming task, subjects were presented with word fragments and asked to complete them with the first word that came into their heads. In most cases the Korsakoff patients were found to respond with previously primed words, even though they revealed no memory of those words in a test of explicit recall or recognition (see Figure 5.5). In fact the Korsakoff patients achieved similar wordstem completion scores to the control subjects. Graf *et al.* concluded that implicit memory was unimpaired in Korsakoff patients, whereas explicit memory was severely impaired. Several other studies have confirmed that implicit memory, but not explicit memory, appears to be preserved in amnesics (Graf and Schacter, 1985; Cermak *et al.*, 1985).

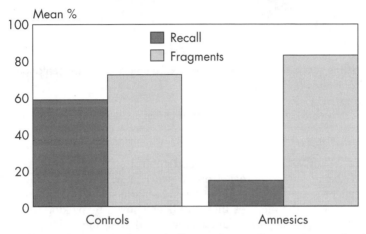

Figure 5.5 The performance of Korsakoff amnesics and normal control subjects on tests of explicit memory and implicit memory (word fragment completion)
Source: Graf *et al.* (1984)

Familiarity and context recollection

As explained in Chapter 4, Mandler (1980) suggested that familiarity and recollection represent two alternative routes to recognition. An item may be judged familiar when we feel that we have seen it before, without necessarily remembering where or when. Recollection involves remembering the actual occasion in which the item was encountered. Recollection therefore involves the retrieval of context, whereas a familiarity judgement does not. Mandler argued that a familiarity judgement was an automatic process, which occurred without conscious effort or volition. Recollection on the other hand was considered to be a controlled process, which requires conscious effort and is carried out deliberately.

A number of studies have suggested that organic amnesic patients retain the ability to detect the familiarity of a previously encountered item but have particular difficulty recollecting the context from which it is familiar. Huppert and Piercy (1976) performed a classic experiment demonstrating the poor context retrieval

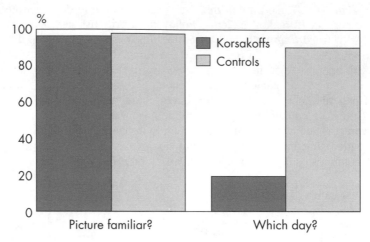

Figure 5.6 The recognition of pictures and discrimination of presentation context in Korsakoff amnesics and normal controls
Source: Huppert and Piercy (1976)
Note: Scores shown are number of correct responses minus number of incorrect responses.

of amnesics. They showed Korsakoff and control subjects two sets of pictures, the first set being shown on day 1 of the experiment and the second set on day 2. Shortly after the presentation of the second set, the subjects were tested for their ability to recognise the pictures they had been shown, by picking them out from a mixture of previously presented pictures and new ones that had not been previously presented. As Figure 5.6 shows, both the amnesics and the normal control subjects proved to be very good at identifying the pictures they had seen before. However, when asked to discriminate the pictures shown on day 2 from those shown on day 1, the performance of the amnesics fell to little more than chance level, whilst the control subjects still achieved a high level of accuracy. Most of us would have little difficulty in distinguishing between something we saw yesterday and something we saw today, but contextual judgements of this type seem to be particularly difficult for amnesics.

Huppert and Piercy (1978) carried out a follow-up experiment which showed that the recognition performance of the Korsakoff patients was mainly based on a judgement of the general familiarity of the pictures. The experiment was basically similar to their previous one, except that this time some of the pictures presented on day 1 were presented three times, in order to increase the strength of their familiarity. When requested on day 2 to pick out the recently presented (day 2) pictures, the amnesic subjects often chose pictures which had been presented three times on day 1, and in fact were just as likely to pick them as they were to pick out pictures presented once only on day 2. These results suggest that Korsakoff patients respond to a recognition test by making a judgement of the general familiarity of a test item, without knowing whether that familiarity arose from frequent presentation or from recent presentation.

One method of distinguishing familiarity-based responses from context recollection is the process dissociation procedure (Jacoby *et al.*, 1993), which was described in Chapter 4. This procedure makes use of inclusion and exclusion tests, the former reflecting a conscious recollection of context and the latter an automatic familiarity judgement. Using this procedure, Verfaellie and Treadwell (1993) confirmed the earlier findings that amnesics were largely restricted to familiarity-based recognition responses and were unable to recollect context.

Parkin *et al.* (1990a) devised a test of recency judgement in which subjects were shown four pictures which they had to pick out from an array of sixteen pictures presented one minute later. However, in subsequent trials the pictures which had originally been presented as distractors were now used as targets, whilst target items now became distractors. All the pictures thus became familiar to the subjects, so that in subsequent trials the subjects were only able to identify the target items by recalling the recency of their presentation. The procedure therefore tested the judgement of temporal context. Parkin *et al.* administered this test to both Korsakoff and HSE patients, and they found a severe impairment of recency judgements in the Korsakoff patients but relatively little impairment in the HSE patients. On the basis of these findings, Parkin *et al.* concluded that context retrieval seemed to be particularly difficult for Korsakoff patients (who have diencephalic lesions), but not for HSE patients (who have temporal lesions). Further support for this view came from a study by Hunkin *et al.* (1994), using the list discrimination procedure, in which subjects are presented with two lists of sentences separated by a filled three-minute interval. Whilst Korsakoff and HSE amnesics obtained similar scores for correctly recognising target sentences, the Korsakoff group were far worse than the HSE group at discriminating between list 1 and list 2 sentences. In view of these findings, Parkin (1996) drew the tentative conclusion that the impairment of context retrieval may be specifically associated with diencephalic lesions, noting that most previous reports of impaired context retrieval had in fact involved Korsakoff subjects.

Semantic and episodic memory

The distinction between semantic and episodic memory (Tulving, 1972) was explained in Chapter 4. Episodic memory refers to memory for specific events in our lives, and it therefore involves the retrieval of context (i.e. where and when the event took place). Semantic memory refers to the store of knowledge we possess (such as the meaning of a word), and requires no contextual retrieval.

It has been suggested (Tulving, 1989) that amnesics exhibit a selective impairment of episodic memory, whilst their semantic memory remains intact. This theory is consistent with the general observation that amnesics usually retain a normal vocabulary despite their inability to remember specific events from their lives. However, although a person's vocabulary is certainly part of his or her semantic memory, it is mostly acquired in early childhood. Since memories of any type which date back to early childhood are usually found to be preserved in amnesic patients (see Section 5.4), an intact vocabulary does not in itself provide proof of a generally intact semantic memory. It is more likely that an intact vocabulary in amnesics merely reflects the well-established preservation of early learning, and possibly also the fact that language is practised and overlearned throughout life.

In fact there is evidence that amnesics do reveal an impairment of semantic memory when tests focus on more recently acquired vocabulary. Gabrielli *et al.* (1988) reported that the temporal lobe patient HM was unable to learn new words, and he was usually unable to define words and phrases which had been introduced since the onset of his amnesia in 1953 (e.g. 'jacuzzi'). Similar impairments of semantic memory have been reported in Korsakoffs (Verfaellie and Roth, 1995), and in HSE amnesics (Wilson *et al.*, 1995).

Studies of retrograde amnesia (Kopelman, 1989) have also revealed impairment of semantic memory (e.g. identifying famous people) as well as episodic memory (e.g. retrieval of personal autobiographical events). In view of these findings, it would appear that both semantic and episodic memory are impaired in organic amnesics, so there is no clear support for the hypothesis that amnesia involves a selective impairment of episodic memory.

Explaining preserved memory function in amnesia

The findings reported so far in this section suggest that amnesia is not usually an all-pervasive impairment, but tends to impair certain specific memory functions whilst leaving others intact (see Figure 5.7). Each of the dichotomies shown in Figure 5.7 represents a contrasting pair of functions, of which one is impaired and the other intact in most amnesic patients. One exception to this distinction is the episodic/semantic dichotomy, since (as explained above) both episodic and semantic memory seem to be impaired in amnesics.

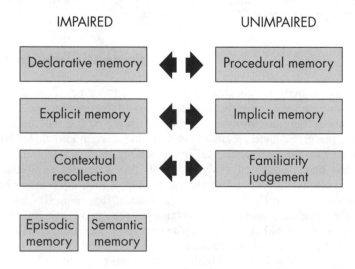

Figure 5.7 Dissociations between impaired and unimpaired memory functions in amnesia

These findings have provided the basis for several different theories of amnesia which are summarised below:

1   *Declarative memory* is impaired in amnesics but *procedural memory* remains intact (Cohen and Squire, 1980).
2   *Explicit memory* is impaired in amnesics but *implicit memory* remains intact (Graf *et al.*, 1984).
3   *Context recollection* is impaired in amnesics but *familiarity judgements* are unimpaired (Huppert and Piercy, 1976; Mandler, 1989).

All three of these theories are supported by extensive research evidence, which was summarised earlier in this section. However, it is clear that there is substantial overlap between these theoretical approaches, and efforts have therefore been made to find a common underlying factor which might make it possible to combine them into a single general theory. One such approach (Cohen and Squire, 1980) argues that the impaired functions (i.e. declarative memory, explicit memory and context recollection) all require the conscious retrieval of memory, which can therefore be classified as 'declarative' in the broadest sense. In contrast, the preserved functions (i.e. procedural memory, implicit memory and familiarity judgements) all involve memories which can be demonstrated without conscious awareness, and which can therefore be generally described as 'non-declarative'. Cohen (1997) therefore argues that the declarative/non-declarative distinction can provide the basis of a general theory of organic amnesia which to a large extent subsumes other related theories. (NB: It should be noted that Cohen has adopted a slight change in terminology for this more broadly based theory, preferring to use the terms 'declarative'/'non-declarative' memory in order to allow for the inclusion of concepts such as implicit memory which cannot easily be categorised as 'procedural' in nature.)

Mandler (1989) has emphasised the role played in these memory functions by 'automatic' and 'controlled' processes (see Section 4.6). He suggests that the memory functions which are impaired all require the use of consciously controlled processes, whereas the preserved functions can all apparently operate at an automatic level. Mandler therefore concludes that organic amnesia is essentially 'a disease of consciousness'. In his view amnesics have lost the ability to carry out consciously controlled retrieval and are thus forced to rely mainly upon unconscious automatic processes.

It has also been argued (Cohen and Eichenbaum, 1993; Cohen, 1997) that declarative memory involves the learning of associative connections and relationships between memories (such as linking two memories together, or linking an item with its context). In contrast, non-declarative memory seems to be restricted to the strengthening of a single response mechanism (such as a motor skill or the level of activation and familiarity of a word). An important consequence of this distinction is that declarative memory can be applied in a flexible way to fit novel situations, whereas non-declarative responses tend to occur in an inflexible manner as a reaction to one particular stimulus situation.

Cohen (1997) suggests that the hippocampus performs the associative binding function of declarative memory, whereas non-declarative memory involves the cortex and cerebellum. This view has received some support from MRI brain imaging studies (Cohen *et al.*, 1994; Kim *et al.*, 1994).

Until recently the episodic/semantic distinction provided the basis of a widely accepted theory of amnesia, which proposed that *episodic memory* was impaired in amnesics whilst *semantic memory* remained intact (Warrington, 1979; Tulving, 1989). However, this theory has lost much of its credibility because (as explained in Section 5.4) it has now been established that both episodic and semantic memories are usually impaired in amnesics. This finding lends weight to the view (Cohen, 1984) that episodic and semantic memory are both forms of declarative memory, as indicated in Figure (5.7).

5.6 Other types of amnesia

Frontal lobe lesions

Most of the effects of organic amnesia described so far have been the result of lesions in either the temporal lobes or the diencephalon, which are known to be the main areas of the brain concerned with memory. However, it has also been found that patients with frontal lobe lesions often show some impairment of memory, though these tend to be rather different in nature to those associated with the classic amnesic syndrome.

One characteristic of patients with frontal lobe lesions is a tendency to **confabulation** (Moscovitch, 1989), which is the reporting of memories that are incorrect and apparently invented. For example, an elderly patient who is asked whether he has any grandchildren may reply that he has, although this is actually untrue. To the observer it may appear as if the patient is making up these false memories, but they are actually the result of a retrieval fault rather than any intention to deceive. If patients have difficulty in recalling the information requested, they may attempt to fill the gap in their memory with the most likely possibility. Thus an elderly person who is unable to recall whether he has grandchildren may reply that they he has because this would seem likely for a person of his age. Confabulation could thus be seen as a tendency to use general knowledge from the semantic memory to fill in the gaps which have appeared in the episodic or autobiographical memory. This is a mechanism which probably occurs to some extent even in perfectly normal people, but crucially they are usually able to distinguish between genuine events from their lives and their general knowledge of what is likely. Frontal lobe patients appear to have difficulty in making this distinction.

Another characteristic of frontal lobe patients may help to explain their tendency to confabulation, and this is their inability to recall the source of the information they recall. Impaired source memory in frontal lobe patients has been demonstrated by a number of studies in which subjects were provided with a list of facts with which they were not previously familiar. When tested a few days later, frontal lobe patients showed no impairment in their recall of the facts but, unlike normal subjects, they could not remember where or when they had learned them (Schacter *et al.*, 1984; Janowsky *et al.*, 1989). In some cases frontal patients would claim to have known the facts for many years, or to have learned them on some other occasion. This inability to distinguish one source of learning from another may help to explain confabulation, where there is apparently a similar inability to distinguish between autobiographical episodes and general knowledge.

Another finding which appears to fit in with this general inability of frontal patients to discriminate the source of a memory is their inability to remember temporal order. When presented with a series of test items, frontal lobe patients are usually able to recognise the items a short time later, but are unable to recall the order in which they were presented (Shimamura *et al.*, 1990; Swain *et al.*, 1998).

Overall, it would seem that frontal lobe patients have a general inability to discriminate between the sources and origins of the memories they retrieve. They are usually able to retrieve memories in an adequate fashion, but they lack the normal ability to monitor and verify the source of their retrieved memories. One possible explanation (Shallice, 1988) for this defect of discrimination is that frontal lobe patients have an impairment in the central executive of their working memory. The central executive (which was discussed in Chapter 4) is assumed to be responsible for conscious decision-making processes. This might possibly include decisions about the source or accuracy of a retrieved memory. The central executive is also thought to control the conscious override of automatic processes, and this is also an ability which is thought to be impaired in frontal lobe patients. However, these impairments tend to have their main effect on thinking and problem-solving, so they will be taken up again in Chapter 6.

The impairments which have been described in this section are those which are associated with frontal lobe lesions, and the studies presented have all focused on patients with damaged frontal lobes. However, it is important to bear in mind that frontal lobe lesions can frequently coexist with other types of lesion. For example, it has been found that some Korsakoff patients have frontal lobe lesions in addition to their diencephalic lesions (Shimamura *et al.*, 1988), and these particular individuals often exhibit a marked tendency to confabulation and other frontal symptoms coexisting with the more usual characteristics of Korsakoff's syndrome.

An impairment in frontal lobe functioning is also thought to occur in many otherwise normal elderly people, and this will be considered below.

Memory loss in the normal elderly

It is widely accepted that memory tends to decline in older people, and there is some evidence for such an age-related decline. However, deterioration of memory is not readily detectable until the age of about 65 or 70, and the degree of impairment is not usually very great, at least not among the normal elderly. The popular view of old age leading to dementia is certainly not supported, and it is important to recognise the clear distinction between the dementing elderly (such as those with Alzheimer's disease) who suffer a very severe memory impairment, and the normal elderly who show only a relatively small impairment. Studies have indicated that the normal elderly tend to have particular difficulty with retrieval, and tend to show a decline in recall ability though not in recognition (White and Cunningham, 1982).

It has also been reported that the normal elderly tend to have difficulty in remembering the temporal order of events (Naveh-Benjamin, 1990), and also tend to have an impaired source memory (McIntyre and Craik, 1987).

These findings are similar to those observed in frontal lobe patients (see above), which is consistent with the finding that neuron loss in the elderly tends to be more extensive in the frontal lobes. Another study which produced evidence for the theory that the elderly tend to suffer frontal lobe deterioration was that of Parkin and Walter (1992), who used the 'Remember and Know' procedure. As explained in Chapter 4, a 'remember' response indicates recollection of context, whereas a 'know' response merely indicates a feeling of familiarity. Parkin and Walter found that elderly subjects (mean age 81) produced far fewer 'remember' responses than did their young subjects, but gave a similar number of 'know' responses. These results suggested that the elderly subjects rely on familiarity rather than recollection when attempting to recognise something. An interesting feature of these results was that the amount of decline in recollection was found to be related to measures of frontal lobe impairment, such as the Wisconsin card-sorting test. One possible explanation of age-related memory decline consistent with the above findings is that the elderly lose some of their capacity for consciously controlled processing and attention (Hartley, 1993). However, an alternative view is that the main cause of cognitive decline in the elderly is a reduction in their processing speed (Salthouse, 1994). Either of these views would be consistent with the general finding that the elderly are more reliant upon automatic processes as a consequence of declining processing ability.

Concussion amnesia

Concussion is one of the most common causes of amnesia, though fortunately the memory disturbance tends to be temporary. A person who is knocked unconscious by a blow on the head will typically suffer from both anterograde and retrograde amnesia, which may be extensive at first but which then usually shrinks to leave only a very limited period of time from which memory is never recovered. For example, a footballer who is concussed by a collision with another player will probably be unable to remember the events immediately following the collision (e.g. being taken off the pitch and driven to hospital) and more interestingly he will probably be unable to remember the events which preceded it (such as the actual tackle which caused the collision). Typically, retrograde amnesia might extend backwards in time about a minute or two before the accident, and this brief gap in the player's memory would almost certainly be permanent.

Amnesias of this kind are known as concussion amnesias, and they fall within a broader category known as post-traumatic amnesias (PTA), which include any type of closed-head injury. Russell (1971) surveyed a large number of PTA victims and found that in most cases retrograde amnesia extended only a minute or two before the accident, though in a few cases it extended back over a period of days or even weeks. In all probability these cases of very extensive retrograde amnesia reflect some other form of memory disturbance in addition to the temporary effects of concussion, and either involve an organic brain lesion or alternatively a psychogenic amnesia.

In many respects the characteristics of concussion amnesia resemble a temporary version of the organic amnesic syndrome. For example, during the period immediately following the concussive accident, the patient is likely to show an impairment in LTM tasks such as learning wordlists (Gasquoine, 1991), but will perform normally on tests of STM such as digit span (Regard and Landis, 1984). However, the very limited extent of retrograde amnesia suggests that there is no lasting impairment to the patient's retrieval. The most probable explanation of the pattern of amnesia associated with concussion is that the patient is temporarily unable to consolidate memories from the STM working memory into the LTM store. This would explain why events following the concussive injury are not stored, but it also explains why events held in STM immediately before the injury are also lost. In all probability the contents of the STM working memory at the time of the accident are lost because they have not yet been transferred to the LTM, and the STM working memory (which depends on conscious awareness) is put out of action during the period of unconsciousness.

ECT and memory loss

ECT (electroconvulsive therapy) involves the passing of an electric current through the brain in an effort to alleviate depression. This treatment has been in fairly widespread use for over forty years, and its value in the treatment of depression is well established despite the lack of any clear explanation of how it actually works. However, there has long been concern about the possible side-effects of ECT, and in particular the possibility that it might cause brain damage. The main evidence for such damage is the observation that ECT can apparently cause memory impairment. In the period immediately following the administration of an ECT shock, the patient typically shows a temporary amnesia rather similar to that seen following concussion. There is usually both anterograde and retrograde amnesia (Squire and Chace, 1975; Squire *et al.*, 1981), which may be extensive at first but which then shrinks to leave only a fairly limited amnesia for the treatment period itself and for the few days preceding it. It therefore appears that for most patients there is only a temporary impairment of memory. Follow-up tests of memory performance a few weeks after the completion of ECT treatment have usually failed to detect any lasting anterograde impairment (Squire and Chace, 1975; Weeks *et al.*, 1980; Warren and Groome, 1984). Indeed there is usually a clear improvement in memory scores compared with pre-ECT levels, because memory performance improves with the alleviation of depression.

For example, Warren and Groome (1984) found that patients showed a steady improvement in their memory scores over the period of their ECT treatment, which was probably a consequence of the alleviation of their depression over this period (see Figure 5.8). There is a slight dip in performance in some tests following the administering of ECT, but this effect is subsequently counteracted by a general improvement in memory as depression lifts. Unfortunately it is very difficult to separate the effects of ECT and depression on memory, and this has been a serious problem for such studies. For example, the control subjects used in ECT studies tend to differ from the experimental group not only in their freedom from ECT but also in their level of depression.

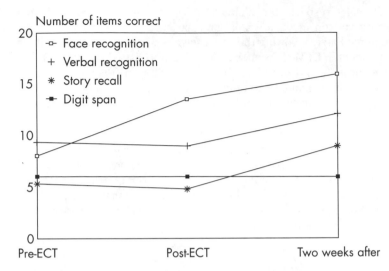

Figure 5.8 Performance on a battery of memory tests before ECT, shortly after ECT, and two weeks after the completion of a course of ECT treatment
Source: Warren and Groome (1984)

Despite the fact that objective tests of memory usually fail to detect any lasting memory impairment following ECT treatment, patients often report that they still feel subjectively that their memories have been damaged (Freeman *et al.*, 1980). One possible explanation for this discrepancy (Squire *et al.*, 1979) is that patients who have gone through a period of temporary amnesia during ECT treatment may become more sensitive to the normal imperfections of memory which afflict everyone, and they may wrongly attribute such memory failures in everyday life to their ECT treatment. Whilst this may certainly be a factor, there is also a possibility that ECT does, at least in some patients, leave a lasting memory impairment which is not detected by the available memory tests.

Summary

- Organic amnesia is caused by brain damage of some sort, usually affecting the temporal lobes, hippocampus and diencephalon. Such brain lesions may arise from a variety of different causes, such as Alzheimer's disease, Korsakoff's syndrome, Herpes Simplex Encephalitis, strokes and tumours.
- Organic amnesia is characterised by an impairment of long-term memory, but the short-term working memory usually remains intact.
- Most amnesics suffer from an anterograde impairment, so that they have difficulty in learning new information from the time period subsequent to onset.
- In many cases there is also retrograde amnesia, so that memories are also lost from the period preceding onset. However, the retrograde impairment is

often relatively mild, and memories of earlier time periods such as childhood frequently remain intact.

- The anterograde and retrograde components of amnesia appear to be fairly independent of one another, so that their relative severity can vary considerably from patient to patient. In rare cases either retrograde or anterograde amnesia may occur in isolation.

- Although most amnesics suffer a severe impairment of conscious 'declarative' memory processes such as recall or context recollection, there is usually no impairment of unconscious 'non-declarative' processes such as motor skill learning, implicit memory and familiarity judgements.

- In addition to the amnesias which are characteristic of the organic amnesic syndrome, memory impairment may also be caused by other factors, such as ageing, frontal lobe lesions, concussion and ECT. However, these impairments tend to have their own distinct characteristics, and differ somewhat from the pattern of symptoms seen in the classic amnesic syndrome.

Further reading

Campbell, R. and Conway, M.A. (1995). *Broken Memories*. Blackwell. A book of individual case studies. Each chapter contains a detailed study of a single patient with some kind of memory disorder, including a detailed account of the HSE patient Clive W (written by Barbara Wilson and Deborah Wearing).

Baddeley, A.D. Wilson, B.A. and Watts, F.N. (1996). *Handbook of Memory Disorders*. Chichester: Wiley. A large handbook, providing comprehensive cover of all aspects of amnesia for the specialist. Aimed primarily at clinicians and researchers, but useful for undergraduate students as a reference book.

Gazzaniga, M.S. (1998). *Cognitive Neuroscience: The Biology of the Mind*. New York: Norton. This text focuses on the biological bases of cognition. A useful source for students who wish to find out more about brain structure and function. Very well illustrated, with plenty of detailed drawings, photographs and scans of the brain structures which underlie cognitive processes.

Martin, G.N. (1998). *Human Neuropsychology*. New York: Prentice Hall. Another neuropsychology book which includes a lot of detail about brain anatomy and function in addition to the disorders relating to brain damage.

Chapter 6

Thinking

Problem-solving and reasoning

6.1 Introduction

Most of us would suggest that 'thinking' covers a range of different mental activities, such as reflecting on ideas, having new ideas, theorizing, arguing, making decisions and working out problems. An important feature common to all of these is that they are under our own control and we can run through actions symbolically rather than in actuality. Some of our thinking is directed towards specific goals, for example, solving crossword problems or composing the answers to questions. However, much of our thinking is comprised of imaging, wishing and daydreaming, and here there is often a feeling of an uncontrolled drifting of our thoughts.

This chapter will confine itself to providing an overview of the key findings of research into problem-solving and reasoning. Creativity and imagery, which are also aspects of our thinking and constitute alternative research areas, are not considered here. It should be noted that whilst many have used problem-solving as an operational definition of thinking, such a narrow definition does restrict discussion to findings of research on goal-directed thought processes. However, constructing a theory of problem-solving alone is comparable with trying to provide a theory of art broad enough to cover everything from ceramics to opera (Cohen, 1983).

6.2 Early research on problem-solving

Thought processes have been studied from many different theoretical points of view. Oswald Kulpe was one of the first to examine thought processes, such as the making of judgements, using specially trained adult human subjects and the classical introspective report as his research methodology. Here, subjects were asked to focus on the component sensations and this tended to lead to conflicting reports. Gilhooly (1996) comments that, in particular, the issue of thinking without images led to considerable controversy, with some introspectionists reporting imageless thought and others claiming that thought was always accompanied by imagery, albeit very faint images.

Frequently, we are conscious of the products of thinking rather than the processes themselves, and the behaviourists offered a completely different approach, which of course focused on observable behaviour and 'learning' rather than 'thought'. Thorndike (1898) argued that the process of problem solution occurred through trial and error; in other words responses to the problem are simply random responses until one of them proves successful. A cat placed in a box with a trapdoor was not observed to show behaviour approximating thinking, but instead performed all kinds of behaviours until the appropriate response was made accidentally, the trapdoor would then open and food was available as a reward. With practice, the cat would escape quite quickly by reproducing those learned responses. Whilst some problem-solving may indeed occur through trial and error, alternative means of arriving at problem solution were investigated by the Gestalt psychologists who conducted a number of well-known and widely cited experiments in this field of research. Their research revealed some of the reasons why people can have difficulty in finding the correct solution to a problem.

The Gestalt approach to problem-solving

Research conducted by Wolfgang Köhler, one of the three founder members of the Gestalt school, took place on the island of Tenerife. He was trapped there during the First World War and became the director of an animal research station. He founded a colony of chimpanzees and studied their problem-solving behaviour. For example, one chimp named Sultan was able to use a stick to obtain some bananas that were placed on the outside of his cage. When provided with two poles, neither of which was long enough to reach the bananas, the ape first 'sulked', then eventually put one pole inside the other to create a longer pole. Köhler (1925) used the term **insight** to refer to the ape's discovery. Other apes were observed when provided with bananas hanging from the ceiling out of their reach. Again, intense thinking typically preceded a flash of insight (the 'aha') and the apes would stack crates on top of each other to provide a staircase to the bananas. According to the Gestaltists, the process of some problem-solving requires the reorganising or restructuring of the elements of the problem situation in such a way as to provide a solution. This is known as productive thinking or insight. Reproductive thinking, on the other hand, relies on the rote application of past solutions to a problem.

The Gestalt ideas inspired the work of Maier, Duncker and Luchins. Maier (1930, 1931) investigated the 'two-string' problem. This involved human subjects who were introduced to a room that had two strings hanging from the ceiling. Other objects in the room included pliers and poles. The subjects were told to tie the two strings together, which was not easy as it was not possible to reach one string whilst holding the end of the other string. One solution is to attach the pliers to the end of one string so that it can swing like a pendulum. Maier waited until subjects were obviously stuck and then brushed against the string to make it swing. Although not necessarily noticing his action, many went on to arrive at the pendulum solution, and Maier claimed that his subtle hint resulted in a reorganisation or restructuring of the problem.

Functional fixedness

Some subjects were unable to solve Maier's problem, even if he handed them the pair of pliers and explicitly told them that by using the pliers and no other object they could solve the problem. This was because they were unable to shift from seeing pliers as a tool for gripping things to seeing it as a weighty object. Duncker (1945) termed this **functional fixedness** and defined it as the inability to use an object appropriately in a given situation because of prior experience of using the object in a different way. Functional fixedness is a good example of stereotypical thinking and is a 'block' to problem solution.

A well-known study conducted by Duncker (1945) concerns a problem where subjects are handed a candle, a box of nails and other objects. The task is to fix the candle to a wall by a table but so that it does not drip on the table. His observations revealed that few thought of using the box which contained the nails as a candle holder. Subjects were therefore considered to be 'fixated' on the usual function of the box, namely to hold the nails.

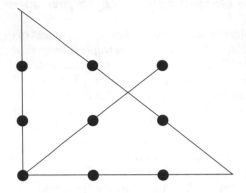

Figure 6.1 A solution to the nine-dot problem. Subjects find it hard to connect the dots with lines that go beyond the matrix.
Source: Adapted from Scheerer (1963)

The nine-dot problem is another famous Gestalt problem. Scheerer (1963) presented subjects with nine dots arranged in a 3×3 matrix. The task is to join all the dots in four straight lines without lifting the pencil from the paper. Most subjects could not do this, as they attempted to keep their lines within the matrix or square created by the dots; the solution to the problem required that they drew lines beyond the matrix (see Figure 6.1).

Problem-solving set

Another potential 'block' to problem-solving is referred to as 'set' which is the rote application of learned rules. Luchins (1942) asked subjects to imagine that they had an unlimited supply of water and three jugs with which to measure out a certain quantity of water (see Figure 6.2). The volumes of the three jugs are specified for each separate problem. Subjects were trained on a series of problems which either

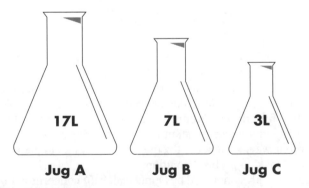

Figure 6.2 An example of the water jug problem
Source: Adapted from Luchins (1942)
Note: The problem requires a quantity of water to be measured out. For example, to measure out 4 litres of water you can either fill B and then pour 3 litres into C or follow a more complicated method due to set which is to fill A, pour 7 litres of water into B and then two lots of 3 litres into C.

had the same complex solution method (the set condition) or on a series of problems that were solved using different methods (the control condition). Subjects were then presented with critical problems, which could be solved either with the complex solution method or with a shorter, simpler method. To solve the critical problems, those in the control condition chose the simpler method. In contrast, those in the set condition used the complex method, providing evidence of reproductive thinking, which in this case hindered problem solution.

The research inspired by the Gestalt ideas demonstrates that some problems cannot be solved through reproductive thinking and that our past experience can hinder problem solution. However, this early research did not provide us with an explicit account of the processes underlying productive thinking, insight; such attempts arose later with research conducted within the information processing framework.

6.3 Problem-space theory of problem-solving

In the 1960s, Newell and Simon initiated research that resulted in the information processing view of problem-solving. Their work involved creating a computer program called the General Problem Solver (GPS). They demonstrated that most simple problems consisted of a number of possible solutions and each of these solutions could be broken down into a series of discrete steps or stages.

The stages they identified included:

1   Representing the problem – a **problem space** is constructed which includes both the initial state and the goal state, the instructions and the constraints on the problem and all relevant information retrieved from long-term memory. To assist such representation, symbols, lists, matrices, tree diagrams, graphs and visual imagery can all be used.
2   Selection of operators – operators are actions that will achieve a goal, and are used for transforming the initial state.
3   Implementation of the selected operators – this results in a new current state within the problem space.
4   Evaluation of the current state – if it corresponds to the goal, a solution is reached.

Newell and Simon claimed that the key features of GPS were also characteristics of human problem-solving. They asked human subjects to solve the problems whilst thinking out loud and, when comparing the verbal protocols with the way the GPS solved these same problems, they found remarkable similarities.

Problem-solving strategies

According to Newell and Simon (1972), most problems are solved by the use of a small number of general purpose **heuristics**, which are basically 'rules of thumb'. Heuristics are methods or strategies which often lead to problem solution but are not guaranteed to succeed. They can be distinguished from algorithms, which are methods or procedures that will always produce a solution sooner or later. Our knowledge of the rules of arithmetic provides us with algorithms to solve problems such as 998 multiplied by 21. However, in certain situations we might estimate the solution to be in the region of 20,000. There are many situations in real life where we use heuristics as either our memory constraints or other processing limitations do not allow us to use algorithms, or simply because there are no algorithms available.

Well-defined problems, where the initial state, the available operators and the goal state are clearly specified, could be solved by deciding which moves are possible, starting from that initial state, and thinking through the consequences of each of these moves. A diagram showing all the possible sequences of actions and intermediate states can be constructed. This is called a **state–action tree**. Such a tree will allow one to find a sequence of actions that leads from the initial state to the goal state. Applying such a 'check-every-state' algorithm would be very time-consuming and impossible for complex problem-solving activities such as playing chess. Instead, many problems can be solved through **problem reduction**, a sort of 'divide-and-conquer' approach. The problem is converted into a number of sub-problems and each of these are further subdivided unless they can be solved by the available operators.

Means–end analysis is one method or heuristic for developing sub-problem structures. First, the difference between the current state and the goal state is noted, a sub-goal is then identified that will reduce this difference and a mental operator is selected to achieve the sub-goal. Choosing appropriate sub-goals to achieve the main goal is important to successful problem-solving. Gilhooly (1996) suggests that making travel plans constitutes a real-life example of means–end analysis. The desire to travel from London to New York will require one to note the large distance between the two and to select air travel as the operator to reduce the difference. The sub-goal of 'ticket purchase' is then constructed which in turn leads to the sub-goal 'choose travel agent'. Clearly, a number of subsidiary problems have to be resolved in order to arrive at the desired destination.

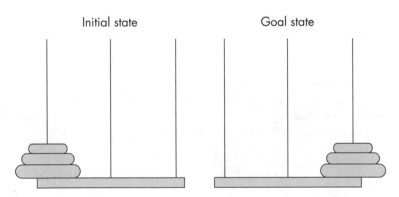

Figure 6.3 The Tower of Hanoi problem
Note: Only one disc can be removed at a time and a larger disc cannot be placed on top of a smaller disc.

Several well-defined problems that have been researched include the Tower of Hanoi and the Missionaries and Cannibals; both are 'move' problems (problems of transformation). The GPS program, which incorporated means–end analysis, was able to solve these problems. The Tower of Hanoi problem consists of three discs placed in order of size on the first of three pegs (see Figure 6.3). The goal state is for these three discs to be placed in the same order on the last peg. Only one disc may be moved at a time and a larger disc cannot be placed on top of a smaller disc. These two rules restrict which mental operator can be selected so that, for example, there are only two possible first moves: to place the smallest disc on the middle or on the last peg. According to means–end analysis, a reasonable sub-goal is to place the largest disc on the last peg.

The difficulty that we humans face is being flexible in our choice of strategies and in being prepared to depart from strategies that entail moving towards closer approximations of the goal. This was demonstrated in the Missionaries and Cannibals problem, where three missionaries and three cannibals need to be transported across a river in a boat. The constraints are that the boat can only hold two people and the number of cannibals on either bank of the river must never exceed the number of missionaries. At one point, the problem-solver has to transfer one cannibal and one missionary back to the starting point (see Figure 6.4), and this move increases the difference between the current state and the goal state. Thomas (1974) found that subjects experienced difficulty in making this move when they were presented with a variant of the problem involving hobbits and orcs (the orcs wanted to eat the hobbits). However, subjects also took longer and made more mistakes when there were a number of possible alternative moves. They were also observed to perform a sequence of moves quite rapidly, then pause for a while and then perform another sequence of moves, suggesting that to solve the problem several major planning decisions were required.

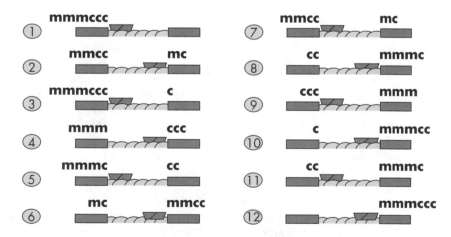

Figure 6.4 The Missionaries (m) and Cannibals (c) problem

Note: Moving from step 6 to step 7 often causes difficulty for problem-solvers as this involves transferring one cannibal and one missionary back to the starting point, hence moving away rather than towards the goal.

Simon and Reed (1976) asked their subjects to solve an extended version of the problem involving five missionaries and five cannibals, a more complex version than that studied by Thomas, and they did not observe extensive forward planning. Subjects were observed to make 'local' move-by-move decisions and to shift strategy. They found that initially subjects employed a balancing strategy, ensuring that there were equal numbers of missionaries and cannibals on each side of the river. Since this strategy could not result in successful problem solution, they then switched to a means–end strategy to move as many as possible to the goal side of the river. Finally, subjects switched to an anti-looping heuristic, which involved avoiding any moves that reversed the immediately preceding move. Subjects could not solve this complex version of the problem successfully unless they were flexible and prepared to shift from one strategy to a different strategy.

The problem reduction approach and the various heuristics are useful means of problem solution given the limitations of our working memory. Efficient solution may depend on our willingness to shift strategy. However, flexibility is not the only constraint. We are influenced by the language used to describe the problem, as there is evidence suggesting that subjects construct a representation of a problem that is very similar to the wording of the problem instructions (Hayes and Simon, 1974). In real life, however, expertise and experience will also affect both problem representation and problem solution. This is because the sorts of problems we actually encounter require considerable amounts of knowledge or require us to go and find the relevant information.

6.4 Problem-solving and knowledge

Expertise

The discussion of problem-solving has so far focused on well-defined problems, where the problems are well specified and, like puzzles, the knowledge required to find the solution is present in the instructions given. The heuristics used to solve them have been termed *general-purpose* or *domain-independent*, in that they can be applied to a wide range of situations or domains and do not involve specific knowledge of the domain. There are other kinds of problems that require expertise, such as chess, and here people will acquire and use *domain-specific rules* when becoming experts. These sorts of problems will be solved differently by experts and novices (and GPS).

Research that studies expertise is a move towards studying everyday, ecologically valid problems. Many studies have looked at chess and examined why grandmasters play chess better than others. DeGroot (1965) collected protocols from some of the best chess players and examined their memories for chess positions. DeGroot found that rather than spend time considering and discarding alternative moves, the grandmasters usually select the best move within the first five seconds of looking at the board, and then spend fifteen minutes checking the correctness of the move. Their prior knowledge allows them to avoid considering irrelevant moves. This contrasts with weaker players who select their best move after much thought, a move which is not as good as that of the grandmaster. It would appear that the two groups of players differ in the way they pe. chess positions, as grandmasters were found to accurately reconstruct position from memory after only five seconds of study. When doing s. repositioned the pieces in small groups, placing four or five pieces on the b. then pausing and then positioning another four or five pieces. In other words grandmasters seemed to remember the chessboard in chunks. Other research ha. shown that the grandmasters do not simply have better memories. If the pieces were arranged in a random way, in non-legal configurations of chess pieces, then the performance of the grandmasters and weaker players was comparable (Chase and Simon, 1973a).

Studies of novices and experts solving physics problems have also demonstrated the importance of specific knowledge structures or schematic knowledge. Chi *et al*. (1981) gave expert physicists and novices the task of categorising problems in mechanics. They found that novices tended to group problems together that shared the same key words or objects, for example, pulleys, springs, friction or ramps. Experts, on the other hand, classified problems according to the principles involved, for example, the conservation of energy principle or Newton's force laws. The experts would solve the problems four times faster than novices despite the fact that they would spend more time analysing and understanding the problems by drawing on their available knowledge. Larkin *et al*. (1980) found that experts used a different strategy to solve a problem and would work forwards to a solution, unlike novices who tended to work backwards.

Problems that require expertise are thus solved differently by experts and novices; experts have available relevant schematic knowledge and domain-specific rules which assist in the representation and solution of problems.

Problem-solving by analogy

Research on expertise has shown that knowledge structures based on past experiences can determine how we approach and solve problems. Frequently, in everyday life, the problems we face are not well defined and we will draw on existing knowledge in our attempts to solve them. However, we do not always have knowledge that is directly relevant to the problem. Often, though, a problem will resemble in some way a problem that we have previously encountered, and drawing on that by analogy may help us. The use of analogy in solving problems has been of considerable interest since the early 1980s.

Gentner and Gentner (1983) were among the first to consider how analogies might assist the way problems are solved. Subjects learning how electricity flowed through the wires of an electrical circuit were taught either with a water flow analogy or with a moving crowd analogy. They were then presented with battery and resistor problems. In the water flow analogy, subjects were told that the flow of electricity was like water flowing through pipes, with water pressure acting like voltage and flow rate like current. They were able to use this analogy to understand the effects of combining batteries, as separate batteries could be modelled by separate sources of water pressure. In the moving crowd analogy, subjects were told that the flow of electricity was like a crowd of people moving through a passage, and this group subsequently showed a better understanding when presented with resistor problems than with battery problems. They could see a resistor as analogous to a turnstile and the electric current as analogous to the rate of movement of people.

The processes of analogy or analogical mapping can be broken down into four parts (Stevenson, 1993). Firstly, the problem to be solved, the target problem, has to be interpreted and represented and here language comprehension plays a role. Secondly, a possibly useful source analogue has to be selected and retrieved from long-term memory. Thirdly, some similarity between source analogue and target problem has to be noted and the elements of the source analogue mapped on to the target problem. This mapping is most successful when the best set of correspondences is found between source analogue and target problem. Fourthly, the novel information provided by the source allows inferences to be drawn and transferred. It might be the case that the target problem is in an unfamiliar domain, so that the problem-solver will transfer as much as possible. Alternatively, the mapping may involve matching relationships rather than conveying new knowledge. Gick and Holyoak (1983) proposed that when we are provided with two examples of one type of problem, we will extract a schema based on their similarity or dissimilarity; this schema then assists analogical transfer and hence the successful solving of similar problems in the future.

The extent to which successful retrieval and mapping occurs is governed by several constraints. Evidence has highlighted the importance of structural constraints. For example, Gick and Holyoak (1980) used Duncker's (1945) *tumour problem*. To solve the problem, medical knowledge is not useful. The problem concerns a patient who has a malignant tumour that cannot be operated on. The tumour can only be removed by radiation, but radiation destroys healthy tissue at the same rate as diseased tissue. Gick and Holyoak (1980) found that presenting a completely different story, from a completely different domain of knowledge, could facilitate solution by analogy as both stories were structurally similar. In the *General story*, a General is attempting to attack a fortress which is well defended and can only be reached by a number of different roads. Each of these roads is mined and can only be crossed safely by a small group of men. The General splits his force into small groups, which approach simultaneously from different directions to converge at the fortress and win the battle. There was, however, little spontaneous use of the analogy; subjects had to be provided with a cue as to how this different story was relevant. Although the analogy was not spontaneously retrieved, it was successfully mapped on to the target problem because of the structural similarity of the two problems.

In addition to structural constraints, there are also semantic and pragmatic constraints. If an argument in the target problem is a synonym of that in the source analogue then the two are semantically similar. Gentner and Toupin (1986) found that once a child had acted out one simple story about an animal (the source), he or she could act out the same story but with different characters (the target). The experimenters manipulated semantic similarity by altering the similarity of the animals in the various roles. Performance declined as similarity decreased. Keane (1987) found that when presented with a problem about a stomach tumour, subjects were more likely to benefit from a story about destroying a brain tumour than the story about the General. The influence of pragmatic constraints was demonstrated in a study by Keane (1990). Subjects were provided with one of two versions of a story about a fire and then asked to solve Maier's two-string problem. The story describes two ways in which a helicopter was used to save people trapped on the upper floors of a burning skyscraper. Which method failed and which was successful was reversed in the two versions. Subjects typically used the successful method as a source analogue for the string problem, irrespective of its specific content, confirming the importance of pragmatic goals in problem-solving.

In summary, research on problem-solving has revealed that whilst well-defined problems can be solved by using general-purpose, domain-independent heuristics, our expertise and experience will determine the extent to which we can draw on relevant schematic knowledge and domain-specific rules. Our stored knowledge is searched when the problem space is constructed. The importance of knowledge structures for successful problem-solving in real life has come to light with research on the use of analogy.

6.5 Deductive and inductive reasoning

There appear to be three main criteria for deciding that an individual is engaging in problem-solving activities (Anderson, 1980), and a great variety of tasks meet these:

1   The activities must be goal directed, i.e. the individual attempts to attain a particular end state.
2   The attainment of the goal or solution must involve a sequence of mental processes rather than just one.
3   These processes should be discernibly cognitive.

In many reasoning experiments, subjects are asked to solve problems which have a well-defined structure in a system of formal logic. This qualifies as problem-solving, since the behaviour of anyone tackling this task is goal directed and the task solution requires a number of intervening cognitive processes.

Research has considered both **deductive reasoning tasks** and **inductive reasoning tasks**. The distinction between deductive and inductive reasoning is that whereas with deductive reasoning the conclusion is certain, with inductive reasoning the conclusion is highly probable but not necessarily true. Deductive reasoning entails problems for which a normative solution is available, namely that required by the logical systems, and the subjects' responses can be measured as either correct or incorrect against such a criterion. Certain statements or premises are provided and the task is to decide on whether the validity of the conclusion that follows is true. Inductive reasoning entails reaching conclusions which the subject cannot be certain are true, and in this sense the conclusion may be regarded as a hypothesis, the validity of which would have to be tested.

In general, research on inductive reasoning has demonstrated that we are capable of abstracting concepts logically, whilst research on deductive reasoning has found our reasoning to differ from that prescribed by a system of formal logic. However, before examining the errors that have been revealed in this type of thinking, it is worth noting that they should not be considered to reflect unintelligent behaviour. Evans (1989, p. 111) wrote:

> errors of thinking occur because of, rather than in spite of, the nature of our intelligence. In other words, they are an inevitable consequence of the way in which we think and a price to be paid for the extraordinary effectiveness with which we routinely deal with the massive information-processing requirements of everyday life.

Deductive reasoning

Research involving deductive reasoning has examined whether conclusions that are drawn from certain premises are indeed logically valid. The information required to perform these reasoning tasks is provided and there is no need for the subject to draw on any stored information from long-term memory. An inference is made, and this simply entails making explicit something that was initially implicit in the premises. The following is one example of a valid deductive inference:

> Hannah is older than Francesca (premise 1);
>
> Joseph is younger than Francesca (premise 2).
>
> Therefore, Hannah is older than Joseph (conclusion).

This example simply requires us to know that the relation older–younger is *transitive*, which means that objects can be ordered in a single line. (Other transitive relations are smaller–larger, warmer–colder and darker–lighter.)

Another example of a valid deductive inference is:

> The kettle will only work if it is switched on;
>
> The kettle is not switched on.
>
> Therefore, the kettle will not work.

This example simply requires us to understand the connective 'only if'. The actual content is not important; only the form of the argument. We might of course wish to dispute the conclusion of the following example:

> If the cake is made of chocolate then the cake tastes bad;
>
> The cake is made of chocolate.
>
> Therefore, the cake tastes bad.

Although the inference is logically correct, we will find it difficult to ignore the actual content (especially if we like chocolate cake).

With this sort of deductive reasoning, known as propositional logic, there are different rules of inference. The most important is known as *modus ponens*:

> If the bell is ringing, then the dog is barking;
>
> The bell is ringing.
>
> Therefore, the dog is barking.

Given the premise 'If X, then Y', and also given X, one may correctly infer Y.

Another rule of inference is *modus tollens*:

> If the bell is ringing, then the dog is barking;
>
> The dog is not barking.
>
> Therefore, the bell is not ringing.

Given the premise 'If X, then Y', and the premise 'Y is false', the conclusion 'X is false' necessarily follows.

There are two other inferences, the *affirmation of the consequent*:

> If the bell is ringing, then the dog is barking;
>
> The dog is barking.
>
> Therefore, the bell is ringing.

and the *denial of the antecedent*:

> If the bell is ringing, then the dog is barking;
>
> The bell is not ringing.
>
> Therefore, the dog is not barking.

Most would suggest that these two conclusions are indeed valid (Evans, 1989); however, both are invalid. The bell does not have to be ringing for the dog to be barking (a letter might have been delivered). Equally, just because the bell is not ringing does not mean the dog is not barking. Experiments have also demonstrated that most of us do not make errors with *modus ponens* but the error rate can exceed 30 per cent for *modus tollens* (Evans, 1989).

Other research has been conducted using syllogistic reasoning problems and this has also revealed that people often make errors. Subjects are presented with two premises and a conclusion, and these must be in one of four forms: All A are B;

Some A are B; No A are B; Some A are not B. The task is to determine whether the conclusion logically follows. For example:

> All sweets are bad for your teeth.
>
> All mints are sweets.
>
> Therefore, all mints are bad for your teeth.

Although the following is also valid:

> All vegetables are good for you.
>
> All chocolates are vegetables.
>
> Therefore, all chocolates are good for you.

One key finding to emerge is that the content of the syllogism is important. Evans *et al.* (1983) found that beliefs affected reasoning. They found that 71 per cent of subjects accepted invalid arguments when the conclusion was believable. For example:

> No addictive things are inexpensive.
>
> Some cigarettes are inexpensive.
>
> Therefore, some addictive things are not cigarettes.

Arguments with an identical syllogistic form but an unbelievable conclusion were accepted by only 10 per cent. For example:

> No police dogs are vicious.
>
> Some highly trained dogs are vicious.
>
> Therefore, some police dogs are not highly trained.

Although the effect of beliefs was also observed when the conclusions were valid, it was most marked when the given conclusion was invalid, suggesting that subjects are more likely to check the validity of unbelievable conclusions and accept believable conclusions uncritically.

The question that arises is whether we make these errors because we are thinking illogically. Henle (1962) has argued that many of the errors on deductive reasoning tasks occur simply because the reasoning task itself may be mis-understood or misrepresented; after this initial misunderstanding the reasoning itself is logical. There may be 'failure to accept the logical task', so that the focus is on the truth or falsity of the conclusion (as in not accepting that chocolate cake tastes bad). Research has shown that our beliefs, feelings and knowledge affect our ability to deduce correctly, only because they influence the acceptability of certain conclusions.

Braine *et al.* (1984) have suggested that many of these errors occur because of failures of comprehension; we expect to find all the information we need to know. If we are told 'If the bell is ringing, then the dog is barking' then we will assume that it is just a bell ringing that makes the dog bark. Braine *et al.* (1984) showed that if we are provided with an additional premise, we are less likely to consider the following affirmation of the consequent valid:

> If the bell is ringing, then the dog is barking;
>
> If the child is laughing, then the dog is barking;
>
> The dog is barking.
>
> Therefore, the bell is ringing.

These results provided further support for Braine's (1978) view that we use a natural logic; that we have a repertory of abstract rules that we will use unless tutored in standard logic.

Mental models

Rather than argue that our deductive reasoning is logical when we find the correct solution and illogical when we find the wrong one, Johnson-Laird (1983) suggests that we either use the appropriate **mental model** or an inappropriate one. We construct the mental model or representation according to what is described in the premises and this will depend on how these are interpreted. We can use imagery to create this representation. For example, according to the following set of premises:

> The milk is to the right of the margarine.
>
> The yoghurt is to the left of the milk.
>
> The cheese is in front of the milk.
>
> The cream is to the left of the cheese.

We could therefore imagine the food on a shelf in a fridge to be laid out as:

margarine	yoghurt	milk
	cream	cheese

From this mental model we could conclude that the cream is in front of the yoghurt even though this is not explicitly stated in the premises. To test this we would need to search for an alternative model that would also fit these premises; if none is found we can stick with that conclusion. However, a search would yield an alternative model, namely:

yoghurt	margarine	milk
	cream	cheese

We would have to conclude that we are not sure whether the margarine or the yoghurt is behind the cream.

This approach distinguishes between firstly comprehending the premises and secondly reasoning with the models. If we are not trained in logic we will find it difficult to reason with negation. Johnson-Laird *et al.* (1992) found that negation could either affect comprehension or it could affect reasoning. The statement 'it is not the case that there is no cream in the fridge' is difficult to comprehend and takes longer to comprehend than its logical equivalent 'there is cream in the fridge'. However, once the premises have been understood and represented as mental models, reasoning will depend on whether you have searched for all possible models. For example, 'it is not the case that there is cheese or there is yoghurt' only needs one mental model:

no cheese	no yoghurt

However, the statement: 'It is not the case that there is both cheese and yoghurt' actually yields three models:

no cheese	yoghurt

cheese	no yoghurt

no cheese	no yoghurt

So although negation makes comprehension difficult, it is the number of mental models which have to be considered that makes reasoning more difficult. The limits of our working memory restrict the number of models we can construct and hold in our working memory.

In summary, research on deductive reasoning has shown that we do not always reason logically. We often fail to reach the conclusions which formal logic would prescribe and often fail to follow the rules of inference. We make errors, but these errors do not appear to be random and a variety of explanations have been proposed. We might misrepresent the problem, we might be unable to accept the conclusion because of our beliefs or knowledge or we may inadequately understand the meanings of the premises. The extent to which we search among alternative conclusions or create mental models will be subject to working memory limitations.

Inductive reasoning: hypothesis generation and testing

Inductive reasoning has been investigated by looking at the processes of hypothesis generation and hypothesis testing. One area of research relates to concept learning, which here does not entail concept formation (how classes or categories are constructed) but concept attainment or identification, the search for attributes or qualities that are associated with a particular concept. In experiments, several stimuli will be identified as either positive or negative instances of the concept. The subject has to use the accumulating information from the positive and negative instances to decide what the concept is.

Bruner *et al.* (1956) were the first to conduct research on concept learning. They used stimuli consisting of rectangular cards containing various objects and these cards varied on specific dimensions:

- the number of borders around the edges of the cards (1, 2 or 3)
- the number of objects in the middle of the cards (1, 2 or 3)
- the shape of objects (square, circle or cross)
- the colour of objects (red, black or green).

The experimenters also altered the way in which the cards were shown to the subjects. The *selection paradigm* involved showing the subject all the cards and asking the subject to select one at a time to show to the experimenter. The subject would then be told if that card was a positive and negative instance of the concept. This procedure allows one to see the pattern of selections and hear the hypotheses volunteered during the task, from which the problem-solving strategy being used can be inferred.

Bruner *et al.* (1956) noted that subjects used a limited number of strategies. *Conservative focusing* is where subjects focus on the first positive instance and then select another card that differs from it in only one attribute. If the second card is also a positive instance, then the attribute that differentiates the two cards must not be part of the concept. *Focus gambling* is a similar but riskier strategy, where the subjects change two or more of the attributes of the first positive instance when selecting the next card. If the second card is also a positive instance, a lot of information has been gleaned. However, if it is a negative one, subjects cannot infer which of the changed attributes was responsible. *Successive scanning* involves formulating a hypothesis and selecting cards accordingly. This strategy tends to be less efficient as it makes considerable demands on memory and subjects tended to pick cards that verified rather than falsified their hypotheses.

The selection paradigm has not been without criticism. Subjects may be ascribed a certain strategy even though not all of their selections were consistent with that strategy. The procedure itself is also not one encountered in everyday life. Of more relevance is the *reception paradigm*, where the experimenter provides a sequence of positive and negative instances of the concept. Bruner *et al.* (1956)

found that subjects would either use the *wholist* or *partist* strategy. The wholist strategy is where all of the features that are present with the first positive instance are included in the hypothesis that the subjects formulate; this hypothesis is then adapted to exclude any features that are found to be absent in subsequent positive instances. The partist strategy involves taking part of the first positive instance as a hypothesis. If a subsequent card does not comply with the hypothesis, then a new hypothesis is selected on the basis of the features in that and previous cards. The wholist strategy tended to be more effective as a strategy since it makes fewer demands on memory and indeed was seen to be the preferred strategy of many subjects.

The experiments of Bruner *et al.* (1956) demonstrate that we seem to select logical strategies when confronted with an inductive reasoning task. Which strategy is adopted will however depend on a range of factors, including the complexity of the problem and the cognitive skills of the person adopting the strategy. A tendency towards verifying rather than falsifying was observed in how we seek to test the hypotheses we form and other research has provided evidence for this bias.

In a classic study, Wason (1960) informed subjects that the three numbers '2 4 6' conformed to a simple relational rule (three numbers in increasing order of magnitude). Subjects were then asked to generate sets of three numbers and to explain why they had chosen that set of three numbers. The experimenter in turn indicated whether each set conformed to the rule. Subjects were told that when they thought they had discovered the correct rule, they were to reveal it. Wason found that most subjects would generate a hypothesis, and then seek to generate sets of numbers that were consistent with the hypothesis. Only 21 per cent of subjects guessed the rule correctly with their first attempt. Most subjects did not attempt to disconfirm the hypothesis, which is actually the best way of testing its correctness. In a later study, Wason (1968) asked subjects how they would determine whether or not their hypotheses were incorrect and only a quarter gave the correct answer. Wason went on to suggest that this confirmation bias is a very general tendency in human thought, and one possible explanation for why prejudices and false beliefs are maintained. Other research has shown that it is possible to encourage disconfirmation (e.g. Gorman and Gorman, 1984), and it should be noted that in real life, whilst scientists may seek to falsify established theories, they find confirmatory evidence beneficial when developing a new theory (Chalmers, 1982). The confirmation bias will be discussed further in relation to a different task devised by Wason.

The Wason Selection Task: hypothetico-deductive reasoning

Wason (1960) devised a very famous task requiring subjects to test hypotheses via deductive reasoning, known as the four-card selection task (see Figure 6.5). Four cards are shown with R, G, 2 and 7 printed on them. The following rule is given:

If there is an R on one side of the card, then there is a 2 on the other side of the card.

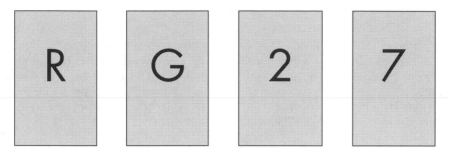

Figure 6.5 The Wason Selection Task
Source: Adapted from Wason (1960)
Note: The rule is: 'If there is an R on one side of the card, then there is a 2 on the other side of the card.' Select only those cards that would need to be turned over in order to decide whether or not the rule is correct.

Subjects are told to select only those cards that would need to be turned over in order to decide whether or not the rule is correct. R (modus ponens) and 7 (modus tollens) is the correct answer – an answer selected by only 5 per cent of university students. The starting point for solving the problem is to test whether any of the cards fail to obey the rule. Most subjects chose R alone, or R and 2. There is however nothing to be gained by turning 2 over (affirmation of the consequent), since the rule does not claim that an R must be on the other side of a 2.

Originally, Wason explained the choice of cards in terms of a confirmation bias: that subjects were trying to confirm rather than disconfirm the rule. However, an alternative explanation emerged later, namely that of a 'matching bias' (Evans and Lynch, 1973). Subjects selected R and 2 because they were biased towards those items mentioned in the rule. Linguistic cues to relevance determine which cards the subjects attend to and hence those they will consider for selection. Support for the explanation was offered by modifying the rule as follows:

> If there is an R on one side of the card, then there is NOT a 2 on the other side of the card.

Most subjects would correctly select R and 2. They also incorrectly selected these cards when the rule was:

> If there is not an R on one side of the card, then there is a 2 on the other side of the card.

The correct response is G and 7.

However, the perceptual matching hypothesis cannot explain why more concrete everyday versions of the rule tend to elicit correct solutions. The ease with which people conform to logical principles when testing a hypothesis depends crucially on the content of the problem. Wason and Shapiro (1971) used cards with 'Manchester', 'Leeds', 'Car' and 'Train' printed on them. The rule was:

Every time I go to Manchester I travel by car.

Sixty-two per cent of subjects stated correctly that the Manchester and Train cards needed to be turned over, against only 12 per cent when a logically equivalent problem was given in an abstract form. One explanation offered is that reasoning is facilitated by the use of concrete and meaningful material. Support for this was provided by Johnson-Laird *et al.* (1972), when subjects were shown envelopes in place of cards, together with the following postal rule:

If the letter is sealed then it has a 5d stamp on it.

(The British postal rule stipulated that unsealed envelopes were allowed to carry a 4d stamp. Subjects were asked to imagine that they were postal workers sorting letters and checking to see if the rule had been violated.) Four envelopes were shown, two of which were front side up, with a 5d or 4d stamp, and two were rear side up showing sealed or unsealed (see Figure 6.6). The task was to choose which envelopes to turn over in order to decide whether the rule was true or false. Of the twenty-four subjects who took part in the experiment, twenty-two correctly selected the one showing a 4d stamp and the sealed envelope, whereas only seven subjects were able to solve the abstract version of the task correctly.

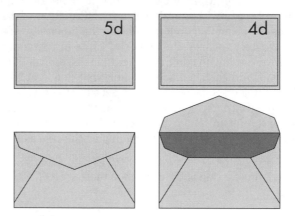

Figure 6.6 The postal version of the selection task. The rule is: 'If the letter is sealed then it has a 5d stamp on it.'
Source: Adapted from Johnson-Laird *et al.* (1971)

An alternative explanation, however, is that reasoning is facilitated when the problem relates directly to the subject's own experience. Griggs and Cox (1982) provided support for this explanation. They failed to replicate the findings of Wason and Shapiro (1971) among a group of American students in Florida, who would not have had any direct experience of Manchester or Leeds. They then introduced the rule:

If a person is drinking beer, then the person must be over 19 years of age.

The four cards were: 'drinking a beer', 'drinking a coke', '16 years of age' and '22 years of age'. The rule introduced corresponded with the Florida law on drinking and 73 per cent of the subjects produced the correct answer against 0 per cent on an abstract version of the problem.

Other research has found that this alternative explanation does not account for all cases where a problem content facilitates reasoning. It is not the case that subjects must have direct experience of the context. Griggs and Cox (1983) used the Sears Problem which entails asking subjects to play the role of a store manager (the store being Sears), who has to check that a certain company rule has been adhered to. The rule is:

> If a purchase exceeds $30, then the receipt must be approved by the departmental manager.

Four receipts are then displayed, two of which are front side up with totals of above and below $30. The other two receipts are front side down, one with and one without the signature of the departmental manager. Even though subjects did not have any direct experience of working as a manager in a department store, about 70 per cent correctly chose the receipt for more than $30 and the one receipt that had not been signed. Therefore, analogous rather than direct experience assisted performance on this task.

Two conclusions can be drawn from research based on the card selection task devised by Wason. Firstly, that the original abstract version was solved with a bias towards thinking about positive evidence to confirm their hypothesis rather than negative evidence to disconfirm their hypothesis. Secondly, introducing a concrete version of the task that has thematic content, and associated prior knowledge, can sometimes produce a more logical performance. Research by Evans (1996) has shown that subjects actually spend little time thinking about the cards they do not select; cards with higher selection frequencies also had longer inspection times, as if subjects were taking the time to rationalise their choice. Therefore, although subjects have selected the correct cards in some experiments using versions of Wason's task and hence showed evidence of logical reasoning, the recent findings of Evans suggests that their performance may not be the result of considering the consequences of alternative selections. Simply judging the correctness of our decisions according to a system of formal logic does not tell us whether the underlying process, our thinking, is logical.

Pragmatic reasoning schemata

Cheng and colleagues (Cheng and Holyoak, 1985; Cheng *et al.*, 1986) have argued that we do develop abstract rules for reasoning from our experiences, but these are not at a logical or syntactic level but at a pragmatic level. People often reason using **pragmatic reasoning schemata** and these are clusters of rules that are highly generalised and abstracted but defined with respect to different types of relationships and goals. For example, in our everyday lives, we are exposed to situations involving permission (we need certain qualifications for certain professions), and these are situations in which some action A may be taken only if some precondition B is satisfied. Cheng *et al.* (1986) explain that if we encounter a problem where the semantic aspects suggest that this is a permission situation then all of the rules about permissions in general can be called on, including 'If action A is to be taken, then precondition B must be satisfied', 'Action A is to be taken only if precondition B is satisfied', 'If precondition B is not satisfied, then action A must not be taken', and so on. We are also exposed to situations involving obligation (if our child is ill for a while, we must inform the school they attend), and from these we note that the occurrence of some condition A incurs the necessity of taking some action B. Cheng *et al.* (1986) point out that rules about obligations are not quite the same but similar to rules about permissions. The rule 'If condition A occurs, then obligation B arises' implies 'If obligation B does not arise, then condition A must not have occurred', but not 'Condition A occurs only if obligation B arises'.

The rules of some of the pragmatic reasoning schemata will lead to the same solution as do the rules of standard logic. Therefore, we will appear to provide responses that would be classified as logical. However, the underlying process has not entailed the application of logical rules and errors will arise when the rules of the schemata differ from those that follow from standard logic. Of relevance here is that the 'abstract permission rule' will allow us to solve Wason's selection task, but this rule needs to be invoked by the rules stated in the task, and this is unlikely to occur with the standard abstract version of the task. Instead, we can solve versions of the task even if we do not have the direct experience of the rules, as long as the rules can be rationalised as giving permission.

6.6 Statistical reasoning

A further area of research which has shown how 'error-prone' our thinking can be has concerned our ability to judge probabilities. Here, the mathematical theory of probability has been used as the yardstick against which to measure our performance. A probability is a number in the range of 0 to 1, and the probabilities of all the possible events in a given situation should add up to make 1. Thus, the probability of tossing a coin and it coming down heads is one-half, the probability of throwing a die and it coming up 3 is one-sixth and the probability of it coming up either 3 or 4 is one-third. The mathematical theory can provide us with equations for calculating the probability of two independent events both happening and the probability of one event happening given that another has happened (conditional probability). The widely cited work of Kahneman and Tversky has revealed that rather than basing our judgements on probability theory, we use heuristics when asked to assess probabilities. As observed previously, whilst heuristics are short-cut rules of thumb, their use can lead to systematic errors and biases.

One important rule of thumb is the **availability heuristic**, whereby judgements are made on the basis of how available relevant examples are in our memory store, in other words the ease with which we can think of instances. Tversky and Kahneman (1973) asked subjects whether the letters K, L, N, R and V occur more often in the first or the third position in English words. The common response was that each appears more often in the first position than the third, even though the reverse is the correct response, probably because it is easier to think of words starting with a certain letter. When asked to listen to a list of thirty-nine names (either nineteen famous women and twenty fairly well-known men or nineteen famous men and twenty fairly well-known women), Kahneman and Tversky (1973) found that subjects judged incorrectly that there were more of the 'famous' individuals than of the 'fairly well-known' individuals. The better known names were more easily recalled. This heuristic is likely to make us overestimate the frequency of highly publicised events that are in fact comparatively rare, such as winning the lottery or dying in an air crash.

Other research has shown that we may make decisions between alternative possibilities on the basis of which appears more representative, regardless of other information; representative or typical instances of a category are judged to be more probable than unrepresentative ones. This **representativeness heuristic** can explain the *gambler's fallacy*, that after a run of losses there will be a good chance of a win. Similarly, when shown the following two sequences of coin tosses:

(1) *HTHTTH*   (2) *TTTTTT*

and asked which is more likely if the coin is fair, then the first sequence is usually picked. Although both are equally probable, the sample more representative of a larger run of coin tosses is preferred; namely the first sequence with equal numbers of 'heads' and 'tails'. Generally, we fail to acknowledge the random fluctuations observable in small samples.

Kahneman and Tversky (1972) presented the following problem:

> A certain town is served by two hospitals. In the larger hospital about forty-five babies are born each day and in the smaller hospital about fifteen babies are born each day. As you know, about 50 per cent of all babies are boys. However, the exact percentage varies from day to day. Sometimes it may be higher than 50 per cent, sometimes lower. For a period of one year, each hospital recorded the days on which more than 60 per cent of the babies born were boys. Which hospital do you think recorded more such days?

Most subjects judged the number of days to be roughly equal in the two hospitals. They expected the samples in both hospitals to reflect the proportions seen in the general population of births. The correct answer is the smaller hospital, because its fifteen babies constitute the smaller sample and hence has a greater chance of not being representative of the population; the proportion of male babies will be more variable.

This heuristic means that we make judgements on the basis of the extent to which the salient features of a person or object are representative of the features thought to be characteristic of some category. Kahneman and Tversky (1973) provided subjects with brief descriptions of five people and told them that these descriptions had been chosen at random from a total of a hundred descriptions. Half of the subjects were told that this total consisted of descriptions of seventy engineers and thirty lawyers, whereas the others were told the opposite, that the descriptions were of seventy lawyers and thirty engineers – this is referred to as *base-rate* information or the *prior odds*. The subjects' task was to decide the probability that the person written about in each description was an engineer or a lawyer. Some of the descriptions were similar to the stereotype we have of an engineer and dissimilar to that of a lawyer. In response to such a description, subjects in both conditions would decide that there was approximately a .9 probability that the person was an engineer. The base-rate information about the sample composition was ignored – since Jack resembles an engineer he is probably an engineer. This is known as the **base rate fallacy**.

Alternatively, if they were provided with an uninformative description which did not correspond to the stereotype of either an engineer or a lawyer, then one might predict that subjects would provide a response based on the base-rate information. However, results showed that subjects would typically rate the chance of Dick being an engineer or lawyer as equally likely, at .5 probability. However, if subjects were asked to estimate the probability that an individual chosen at random was an engineer, and were provided with no information about the person, then they would estimate correctly either .7 or .3 probability depending on the base-rate data that had been given. This suggests that unless prior odds are the only relevant information, the representativeness heuristic guides our probability judgement.

Tversky and Kahneman (1980) found further evidence to support this conclusion. They told their subjects that there were two taxi companies in a town; these were the Blue Cab Company and the Green Cab Company. An accident involving a taxi occurred, and the subjects' task was to judge the likelihood that the taxi had been blue. Some subjects were told that the town had an equal number of blue and green taxis but that 85 per cent of the taxi-related accidents involved green taxis. They were told of eye-witness evidence, namely that a witness said that a blue taxi was involved but that there was a 20 per cent chance that this witness was mistaken. These subjects would use the prior odds, the base-rate information, to arrive at an estimate which was close to the correct figure. Other subjects were told that 85 per cent of the town's taxis were blue and the remaining 15 per cent were green and they relied mainly on the eye-witness evidence, ignoring the base-rate information they had been provided with. Such results suggest that people may be more inclined to take account of base-rate information when it seems to be causally relevant.

Garnham and Oakhill (1994) point out that more serious errors of judgement can be explained in terms of the representativeness heuristic, as illustrated by the following problem (Tversky and Kahneman, 1982):

> Linda is 31 years old, single, outspoken, and very bright. She majored in philosophy. As a student, she was deeply concerned with issues of discrimination and social justice, and also participated in anti-nuclear demonstrations. Which of the following statements about Linda is more probable: (1) She is a bank teller. (2) She is a bank teller who is active in the feminist movement.

Although the first statement is more probable (it is reasonable to assume that there are some bank tellers who are not active in the feminist movement), many have been found to prefer the second statement. This is known as the **conjunction fallacy**, the failure to acknowledge that everything that is both A and B must also be A.

It would appear that when presented with statistics, we frequently respond in a biased way and use heuristics to arrive at answers. We do not seem to possess the appropriate algorithms, as prescribed by probability theory, to solve the problems correctly. It should be noted that there is some evidence that we are less likely to make errors when the statistics are presented as frequency rather than probability information (see Gigerenzer and Hoffrage, 1995). We are more likely to deal with frequencies than probabilities in everyday situations.

6.7 Everyday reasoning

In our daily lives, we are required to draw conclusions or inferences and to make decisions. Research on formal, well-defined reasoning problems has shown, as outlined above, that we make errors. The question then arises as to whether we perform as poorly with everyday real-world problems. Wagenaar (1994) reported on how the probability of guilt is determined in criminal courts and concluded that different heuristics are applied, with the availability heuristic being used most frequently. The confirmation bias is also apparent in that there is a preference for verification of guilt rather than falsification; for example, the positive identification in a line-up by a few witnesses is likely to be believed even though the suspect was not recognised by a large majority of other witnesses. Hill and Williamson (1998) reported on the decisions that players make when taking part in the National Lottery. They demonstrated that many of the heuristics and biases noted above are apparent in the Lottery number selections. For example, the tendency to choose numbers which have been least drawn can be explained in terms of the gamblers' fallacy, whereas the tendency to choose numbers that appear 'random' rather than adjacent numbers can be explained in terms of the representativeness heuristic.

Research that has considered our ability to develop convincing arguments about everyday issues has also revealed many errors. Perkins *et al.* (1991) presented an overview of studies that asked subjects questions of general social and political significance (for example, would providing more money for state schools significantly improve the quality of teaching and learning?). Consistently, subjects were found to perform poorly, with many providing only one-sided arguments or worse still, biased arguments. Furthermore, education, maturation and life experience did not seem to improve the quality of the reasoning. Kuhn (1991) provided support for such findings when examining the effect of expertise on everyday reasoning skill. Subjects were asked questions such as 'what causes unemployment?' Few presented alternative accounts or counter-arguments demonstrating a 'my-side' bias, 'my-side' arguments being those that support our initial judgements. Kuhn also selected subjects who would be regarded as experts on the problems posed. However, again results showed that detailed knowledge of a topic is not necessarily linked to an improvement in their thinking.

It would appear that our decision-making and our reasoning about general issues is error-prone and incomplete; instances of confirmation bias and belief bias are also evident. There are similarities between formal and everyday reasoning, and the theory of mental models does provide us with a framework with which to examine both. There are of course differences. Firstly, everyday reasoning requires us to generate premises, evaluate the premises we generate and take on board our existing emotions and beliefs attached to these premises or to the conclusions we reach. Secondly, in contrast to formal reasoning, we can revise or supplement the premises as we gain more information. Thirdly, whereas formal reasoning problems permit only one single conclusion, with everyday reasoning counter-arguments can be developed.

Oaksford (1997) proposes that we make errors on reasoning problems in the laboratory because we are applying our normal non-logical yet rational strategies to these unfamiliar logical problems. The strategies we employ in everyday reasoning might not conform to standard logic or probability theory, but this does not mean that our reasoning is not rational. Of relevance here is Simon's (1957) notion of 'bounded' rationality: that we would be rational but within the limits in our ability to process information. Evans and Over (1996) have offered several ways of conceiving of rationality. They distinguish between two kinds of rationality: a personal rationality (rationality$_1$), when we are successful in achieving our goals and an impersonal rationality (rationality$_2$), when we reason according to normative theory (formal logic or probability theory). They argue that whilst we have a considerable amount of the former, we have only a restricted capacity for the latter.

Summary

- The study of problem-solving has shown that we use a limited number of strategies and heuristics to solve a range of problems and these allow us to work within the limitations of our memory system.
- Successful problem-solving requires us to be willing to switch strategies and to avoid functional fixedness and set.
- The use of strategies and heuristics is also evident in how we solve reasoning tasks, but as with problem-solving, these can lead to error and bias.
- The theory of mental models provides us with a framework for understanding the processes underlying both formal and everyday reasoning.
- It is important to acknowledge that in our daily lives the problems we attempt to solve do have a content and a context.
- Our existing knowledge may allow us to solve new problems through analogy. The extent to which we can do this is restricted by structural, semantic and pragmatic constraints.
- Domain-specific rules such as pragmatic reasoning schemata may emerge with experience and explain why the content and the context of the problem is important.
- Our thinking should not only be assessed according to formal logic or probability theory.

Further reading

Garnham, A. and Oakhill, J. (1994). *Thinking and Reasoning*. Oxford: Blackwell. This book provides a fuller account of the issues and research identified here.

Gilhooly, K.J. (1996). *Thinking: directed, undirected and creative* (3rd edn). London: Academic Press. This book provides more detail on the research described here, as well as chapters on creativity and daydreaming not covered here.

Evans, J. St. B.T. and Over, D.E. (1996). *Rationality and Reasoning*. Hove: Psychology Press. This book provides an overview of the research relevant to its title, and a full account of their view of rationality.

Stevenson, R. (1993). *Language, Thought and Representation*. Chichester: John Wiley. This book provides a broader overview of thinking and its links to language and representation.

Chapter 7

Disorders of thinking

Executive function and the frontal lobes

7.1 Introduction

Earlier chapters have looked at deficits of specific cognitive processes such as language, perception and memory. Thinking can involve all of these cognitive processes, although this depends on its definition. As noted in Chapter 6, thinking is seen as comprising a great range of cognitive activities, only some of which are goal directed such as problem-solving and reasoning. It is not surprising then that there is no single deficit of thinking equivalent to aphasia, agnosia or amnesia. Increasingly, however, reference is made to 'executive' deficits and to the 'executive' function of the frontal lobes. This chapter will consider the important contribution of the frontal lobes to the organisation of cognitive skills in everyday problem-solving. A major section will outline research looking at the effects of frontal lobe damage, showing that such patients display impairments in tests involving attention, abstract and conceptual thinking, cognitive estimation and strategy formation. Section 7.2 will therefore focus on the frontal lobes and consider early clinical and experimental work with reference to the notion of a **frontal lobe syndrome**.

7.2 The frontal lobes

Anatomy and physiology

The frontal lobes constitute approximately one-third of the mass of each cerebral hemisphere, encompassing all tissue anterior to the central sulcus. It is not surprising, therefore, that patients with damage to the frontal lobes area show a great diversity of impairments that may affect motor, emotional, social or cognitive processes. The lobes comprise a variety of areas which are functionally and anatomically distinct (see Figure 7.1) and which can be grouped into three broad categories (Kolb and Whishaw, 1996). The first category is the motor cortex, which was classified by Brodmann as area 4. The second category is the premotor cortex (area 6 and some of area 8), and in humans the lateral premotor area includes Broca's area (area 44). The motor and premotor areas play an important role in the control of limb, hand, foot and digit movements as well as influencing the control of face and eye movements.

The third category is the prefrontal cortex, which in primates can be subdivided into the dorsolateral prefrontal cortex (areas 9, 46); the ventral (or inferior) prefrontal cortex (areas 11, 12, 13, 14); and the medial frontal cortex (areas 25, 32). Studies conducted in the early decades of the twentieth century revealed rich and complex afferent and efferent connections to a variety of other areas of the brain. The prefrontal cortex receives afferent pathways from the auditory, visual, gustatory, olfactory and somatosensory areas. There are connections to and from many subcortical areas including the limbic system (which plays an important role in arousal, motivation and affect), the caudate nucleus (the part of the basal ganglia involved in the integration, programming, inception and termination of motor activity) and the amygdala (which is implicated in the control of fear, rage and aggression).

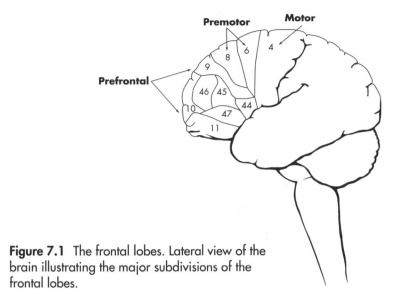

Figure 7.1 The frontal lobes. Lateral view of the brain illustrating the major subdivisions of the frontal lobes.

Is there a 'frontal lobe syndrome'?

Many of the changes in behaviour thought to be characteristic of frontal lobe damage are actually related to lesions in the prefrontal cortex. Sometimes these changes are labelled the **frontal lobe syndrome**, but such a term is rather misleading as there is great variation in the functional results of frontal lobe damage. This variation is hardly surprising given the size and complexity of the prefrontal cortex, and was apparent in studies conducted in the nineteenth and early twentieth centuries. Some of these will be described below.

Early clinical work revealed wide-ranging changes in personality. Some found a pattern of aggression, bad temper and viciousness whereas others described a lack of concern and inappropriate cheerfulness. The most famous case concerning frontal lobe damage is that of Phineas Gage, described by Harlow (1848, 1868). Prior to his injury, Phineas Gage was a conscientious and industrious railroad engineer, whose responsibilities included placing and detonating explosives. A fuse and a tamping iron, an iron bar 3.5 feet long and 13.5 pounds in weight were used to set off the explosive. Accidentally, Gage placed the tamping iron on the explosive, prematurely detonating the explosive, and the result was that the tamping iron penetrated his skull. It entered through the side of his face, passed through the left frontal lobe and exited from the right frontal bone (see Figure 7.2 and Macmillan, 1986). Gage survived and the injury did not appear to have any major long-term effects, with the exception of a change in his personality. Following the accident he was no longer reliable or considerate and showed poor judgement and poor social skills. Harlow (1868) suggested that these changes in behaviour were a result of the frontal lobe's responsibility for planning and the maintenance of socially acceptable behaviour.

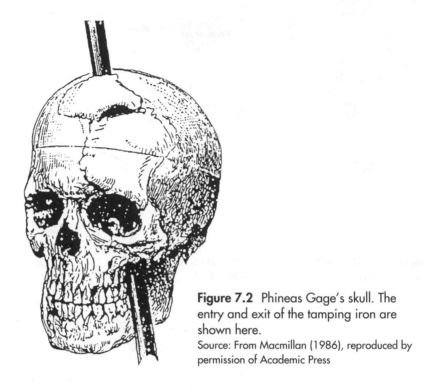

Figure 7.2 Phineas Gage's skull. The entry and exit of the tamping iron are shown here.
Source: From Macmillan (1986), reproduced by permission of Academic Press

A change in personality was noted by Welt (1888) when reporting the case of a 37-year-old man, presumed drunk, who had fallen from a fourth-storey window. He suffered a severe penetrating frontal fracture. Five days after sustaining this injury he showed a change in personality. He went from being an honest, hard-working and cheerful man to being aggressive, malicious and prone to making bad jokes (the term 'Witzelsucht' was used to describe this addiction to joking). He teased other patients and played mean tricks on the hospital staff. After about a month of such objectionable behaviour he reverted to his old self, only to die some months later from an infection.

In contrast, Jastrowitz (1888) reported a form of dementia in patients with tumours of the frontal lobe, which was characterised by an oddly cheerful agitation. He used the term 'moria' (meaning stupidity) to describe this behaviour. Others, including Zacher (1901) and Campbell (1909), emphasised the lack of concern and apathy shown by their patients. Brickner (1936) described a patient, whose pre-frontal region was almost completely excised in an operation. The fundamental disability that emerged appeared to be a problem with synthesising essentially intact cognitive processes. Ackerly (1937) found no decline in 'general intelligence' in a 37-year-old woman, whose entire right prefrontal region had been amputated and left prefrontal region damaged. She also continued to be the same sociable, likeable and kind-hearted person; instead the key change in her behaviour was that once she had started a task she had to complete it, reflecting an abnormal 'lack of distractibility'.

Early experimental work by physiologists on animals led to a variety of conclusions. Goltz (1892) experimented with dogs and, together with his assistant Loeb (1902), concluded that the prefrontal region did not contain the neural mechanisms underlying intelligence or personality traits. Ferrier (1876) found ablations of the prefrontal region in monkeys to result in changes that were difficult to describe precisely. Despite appearing normal, they seemed more apathetic and less attentive and intelligent. Bianchi (1922) conducted experimental studies on monkeys and dogs across three decades. He found unilateral prefrontal ablations to be without effect and, whilst bilateral ablations did not result in any sensory or motor defects, they did result in marked changes in character. The animals became less affectionate and sociable and more fearful and agitated; furthermore, they tended to perform repetitive, aimless movements rather that purposeful actions. Bianchi suggested that these changes were linked to the disintegration of the total personality rather than to a loss of 'general intelligence' or of a specific ability.

With the rise of animal psychology, many other studies examining the effects of experimentally produced prefrontal lesions were conducted during the first half of the twentieth century. These confirmed that unilateral ablation had no significant effect. Bilateral lesions were found to impair animals on tasks where they were required to keep in mind an environmental event for a short period of time. Jacobsen *et al.* (1935) found in one female chimpanzee a change in personality and behaviour as a result of a bilateral prefrontal ablation. Behaviour suggestive of Witzelsucht was observed alongside a change in her affective reactions. Like Bianchi, Jacobsen *et al.* found that prefrontally injured monkeys and dogs did show changes in personality, alongside certain cognitive deficits that were detectable but not easy to describe. Previously, the chimpanzee had become upset to the point of having temper tantrums when she made mistakes on complex tasks. After the bilateral lobectomy, she no longer showed such behaviour when making mistakes.

Both early clinical and experimental studies revealed a range of different behavioural deficits, pertaining to both cognitive processing and personality; however, no single pattern of deficits emerged that would justify the use of the term 'frontal lobe syndrome'. Benton (1991) noted that the term 'was adopted to refer to this aggregation of deficits, perhaps as much as a convenient label as from any conviction that it represented a true syndrome, i.e., a conjunction of inherently related symptoms' (p. 26). Since this early work, advances have been made in understanding the functions of the frontal lobes. There is evidence to suggest that this area is responsible for the highest forms of human thought, for the 'executive' or 'supervisory' functions of cognition. Recently, it has been suggested that Spearman's 'g', the concept of 'general intelligence', when measured by tests of 'fluid intelligence', is largely a reflection of these particular functions of the frontal lobe (Duncan *et al.*, 1996).

More recent clinical work highlights not just the change in personality, but rather that decision-making appears to be affected, despite the fact that there is no indication of any significant impairment in any specific cognitive skill. Eslinger and Damasio (1985) described the case of an accountant who underwent an operation to remove part of his frontal lobes. Afterwards, he was very poor at organising his life, even though he performed extremely well on a wide range of neuropsychological tests and achieved an IQ of over 130. He was unable to hold down a job, went bankrupt and was twice divorced. He was frequently unable to make decisions over relatively simple matters such as which restaurants to dine in or what clothes to wear.

Schindler *et al.* (1995) reported two cases that also demonstrate this effect of frontal lobe damage. Both patients showed a change in personality and, despite having intact language, memory and perceptual skills, each showed impaired decisional capacity. Both patients were able to describe their medical problems and their need for treatment, and both felt they could provide adequate self-care. Neither patient wanted to give up their familiar surroundings and change their way of living. However, on several occasions one patient had been found in her house lying on the floor with inadequate heating and rubbish filling some of the rooms. The other patient had failed to prepare meals for herself, despite the fact that her son ensured that food was available in her apartment. The patients appeared to be competent, demonstrating verbal fluency and intact memory, but in reality were unable to care for themselves.

Section 7.3 will review empirical findings concerning deficits in problem-solving and reasoning. Research has shown that patients with frontal lobe lesions can be impaired in a range of attention, concept attainment and strategy formation tasks, although there is no single test that will be failed by all frontal patients. It is also worth bearing in mind that although impairments on these tasks can be attributed to dysfunction of the frontal lobes, there are many different kinds of damage as the frontal lobes are large structures. Therefore, frontal patients are heterogeneous in terms of both the site of damage and their behavioural symptoms. Before moving on to the next section, I give below the case histories of three such patients.

The case histories of AP, DN and FS

In a paper by Shallice and Burgess (1991a), three patients with traumatic injuries to the prefrontal structures are described. All three found the organisation and planning of everyday life activities problematic and their specific difficulties are described here.

AP was 23 years of age when he was involved in road traffic accident. A CT scan revealed considerable bifrontal damage. He was unable to return to his job and a year later he attended a hospital as a day patient for rehabilitation. Although he was well motivated and keen, he was unable to complete the simplest of activities as he was unable to maintain his concentration on the task at hand. For example, instead of returning to the therapy room after fetching coffee, he was found on the local golf course. Shopping was impossible because he was unable to buy more than one item before returning to his car. Three months later he was transferred to a different rehabilitation clinic as an inpatient, where he remained for a year. Although there was some improvement in his ability to organise daily activities, he went home to live with his parents. He later reported in a clinical interview that he is unable to keep his room tidy, to file his magazines or to carry out shopping, cleaning and laundry duties. He is not able to plan ahead for his social life or to provide any example of organising something in advance.

DN was 26 years of age when he was involved in a road traffic accident. Six months after sustaining his injuries, he found that he was unable to continue with his previous employment. Despite some success at studying and obtaining a teacher's certificate, he spent five years doing a variety of jobs and being dismissed from most of them. A CT scan performed twenty-two years later, when he was 48, revealed considerable damage to the right frontal lobe and some to the left frontal lobe. It emerged in a clinical interview that he is untidy, and shaves, washes his hair and changes his clothes only when told to do so by his wife, bathing only if going out somewhere special. Domestic chores are rarely undertaken spontaneously and if his wife goes out he will usually leave the food preparation to his 10-year-old son. When asked to do something by his wife, she has to give specific instructions and even then he might only complete some aspects of the task. The organisation of their social life is left to his wife. He is rarely successful at buying items needed, despite his wife preparing a shopping list, and she reports that he is occasionally irresponsible with money.

FS sustained injuries in two separate incidents. She suffered a skull fracture when thrown from a horse in her twenties and then at the age of 53 she was knocked off her bicycle by a car, hitting her head on the road. A CT scan was conducted two years later and revealed a large lesion to the left frontal lobe and some atrophy to the left temporal lobe. It was revealed that she has kept the same job for the previous twenty-five years and lives by herself in a single room. In a clinical interview she reported that she is very untidy, that she shops every day to buy just a few things and never goes to the supermarket. She seldom goes out in the evenings and almost never travels away from her home town. She generally does not undertake inessential or novel activities and in the interview reported no plans for the following weekend. She could not recall an incident where someone relied on her to do something, and reported leaving the organising of any joint activity to others.

We will return to these three cases later in the chapter, when examining their performances on the specific neuropsychological tasks devised by Shallice and Burgess.

7.3 Problem-solving and reasoning deficits

Impairments in attention

Successful problem-solving and reasoning require both goal-directed thinking and an ability to correctly direct and sustain attention. The ability of brain-damaged patients to monitor what is happening in the environment, and their ability to sustain their concentration and not be distracted, has been examined using a variety of tests. Characteristically, patients with lesions to the frontal lobes have shown evidence of impaired performance.

Salmaso and Denes (1982) asked subjects to perform a vigilance task, namely to detect a target stimulus which was interspersed infrequently among repeated presentations of other stimuli (a signal detection task). The stimuli were either pairs of sloping lines or pairs of letters, and were presented only briefly. Subjects were required to respond on those occasional trials when the pairs of lines or letters were different. Some of the patients with bilateral frontal lobe damage could not reliably detect the targets. This suggests that their ability to sustain their attention was adversely affected.

An impairment in concentration in a simple counting task was observed in patients with right frontal lobe damage (Wilkins *et al.*, 1987). In particular, subjects had difficulty in counting either auditory clicks or tactile pulse stimuli when they were presented at a rate of one per second. The involvement of the right frontal lobe in sustaining attention has also been reported in a more recent study. Rueckert and Grafman (1996) gave patients with left and right frontal lobe lesions three sustained attention tasks. The first was a simple reaction time task requiring subjects to respond when they saw an 'X'. The second was a continuous performance test asking subjects to respond to an 'X' but not to any other letter. The third required subjects to respond to a specified target when reading a story. For all three tests, patients with right frontal lobe lesions missed more targets and showed longer RTs compared with matched control subjects. Furthermore, their performance in the continuous performance test worsened with time.

The reduction in the ability of patients with frontal lobe damage to sustain their attention is complemented by evidence of their distractibility. During testing, their attention frequently wanders and they will often report irrelevant things. In addition, frontal patients have been observed to grasp or use objects placed near them (Lhermitte, 1983), providing evidence that the patient's habitual responses are being triggered even in situations where they are not required. This is termed 'utilisation behaviour' and has been observed even when the patient has been instructed to do something else, such as complete a psychometric test. One such patient, LE, was described by Shallice *et al.* (1989). LE was observed to pick up and deal out a pack of cards appropriately for the number of people present in the room. The pack of cards present in the clinical interview acted as an environmental trigger.

An inability to suppress the most salient response was observed when frontal patients were administered the Stroop colour word test. If shown the word 'red' written in 'blue', we usually have no trouble in saying what the word is, but find naming the colour of the ink more problematic because we need to suppress our habitual reading response (see Chapters 1 and 2 for further information). Patients with left frontal lesions have been found to perform very poorly on the Stroop test (Perret, 1974). The involvement of the frontal structures in this task has been confirmed in an experiment using normal volunteers; activation of anterior right hemisphere and medial frontal structures was observed using positron emission tomography (Bench *et al.*, 1993).

Perret (1974) found that those patients who performed poorly on the Stroop test also failed to perform well on a verbal fluency test (to search for words beginning with a certain initial letter). He suggested that this could be because the verbal fluency test makes similar cognitive processing demands, namely to suppress the habitual response of searching for words according to their meaning. Burgess and Shallice (1996a) considered this issue further, using a task which allowed them to examine both verbal inhibitory as well as verbal initiation abilities. They presented subjects with sentences in which the last word was missing (the Hayling test). The missing word is strongly cued by the rest of the sentence; for example, the word 'stamp' is cued by 'He mailed the letter without a . . . '. For the first half of these sentences, subjects were asked to provide the word which they thought could fit at the end of the sentence (response initiation condition). For the second half they were asked to provide a word which made no sense at all in the context of the sentence (response suppression or inhibition condition). In comparison to patients with posterior lesions, patients with frontal lobe lesions took longer to complete the sentences in the response *initiation* condition. They also performed worse in the response *inhibition* condition, providing significantly more straightforward completions of the sentence. Even when the answers were not completions, the words they selected were more likely to be semantically related to the sentence. The inability to suppress a current response provides a possible explanation of frontal lobe patients' failure on other tasks, for example the Wisconsin Card Sorting Test described below.

Impairments in abstract and conceptual thinking

Successful problem-solving and reasoning requires us to go beyond the information provided and to engage in abstract thinking. One commonly used method of assessing abstraction involves classification or sorting tasks. Such tasks require participants to abstract the concept or rule used for sorting. These are similar to the inductive reasoning tasks described in Chapter 6. The ability of frontal patients to formulate and test hypotheses as to what the correct rule may be is usually impaired. An early study by Halstead (1940) asked patients with bilateral frontal lesions to perform a fairly simple sorting task, namely to sort the items that were similar amongst sixty-two miscellaneous objects into separate groups. Some patients did not include all the items in their groupings, and the groupings themselves were not meaningful; there was no apparent coherent organising principle.

Other sorting tasks use an array of tokens which vary in dimensions such as shape and colour. In a study by Cicerone *et al.* (1983) patients with bilateral frontal lobe lesions were shown stimuli that varied on four dimensions, namely size, colour, form and position. The task was to abstract the critical dimension. On each trial, patients were shown four pairs of stimuli and asked to choose one according to what they thought the critical dimension might be (see Figure 7.3). On specified trials they were told if their choice was right or wrong, and negative feedback would require them to switch to a different hypothesis and to select a different dimension. Results showed that patients with tumours of the frontal lobe were impaired on this task compared to subjects with posterior tumours. Those with frontal lobe lesions used fewer hypotheses and frequently failed to shift from an irrelevant hypothesis, even when told their choice was incorrect. They continued to select the stimulus using the same dimension on subsequent trials despite negative feedback, as if they were failing to attend to all of the relevant dimensions.

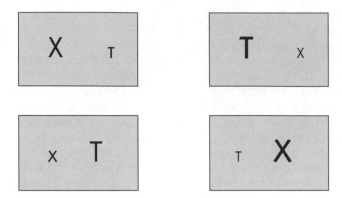

Figure 7.3 Card sorting task
Source: Adapted from Cicerone *et al.* (1983)
Note: The task is to abstract a single critical dimension from stimuli varying on four dimensions: size, colour, form and position.

Failure to make effective use of feedback was also noted in earlier research using the Wisconsin Card Sorting Test, where patients are presented with four cards which can vary along three dimensions, namely number, colour and shape (see Figure 7.4). The number of items on the card range from 1–4, the shape of the items is either a circle, triangle, cross or star and the colour of the items is either red, green, yellow or blue. The task is to sort a stack of cards into four piles, with one pile below each card on the table.

As with the previous test, the subject has to hypothesise the rule, for example, sort according to colour, and the experimenter provides feedback as to whether each card is being placed correctly in one of the four piles. After a specific number of cards have been correctly placed (for example, ten consecutive correct responses), the experimenter changes the rule without warning. Neurologically intact individuals quickly detect such rule changes and switch to a new hypothesis accordingly. Patients with frontal lobe damage have been found to continue with their original rule despite the negative feedback they were receiving (Milner,

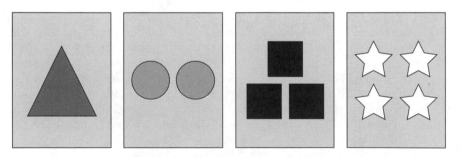

Figure 7.4 Wisconsin Card Sorting Test
Note: The cards vary along three dimensions – number, colour and shape, and the task is to sort a stack of cards according to a rule.

1964). They may continue to sort according to their first hypothesis for as many as a hundred cards, showing an inability to shift response strategy (known as **perseveration**) and a lack of flexibility in their behaviour.

Perseverative responses were also observed in a recent study by Miller and Tippett (1996), when employing the Matchstick Test of Cognitive Flexibility. This test is a visual problem-solving task and therefore very different from the sorting tasks described above. It requires the subject to show different ways of removing sticks from a two-dimensional geometric figure so that a particular shape emerges (see Figure 7.5). Their results showed that patients with damage to the right frontal lobe were impaired in their ability to shift strategy. Those with left frontal lobe damage displayed no significant difficulty. These results are consistent with earlier research that has found the right frontal lobe to be more important than the left when the tasks entail minimal verbal requirements.

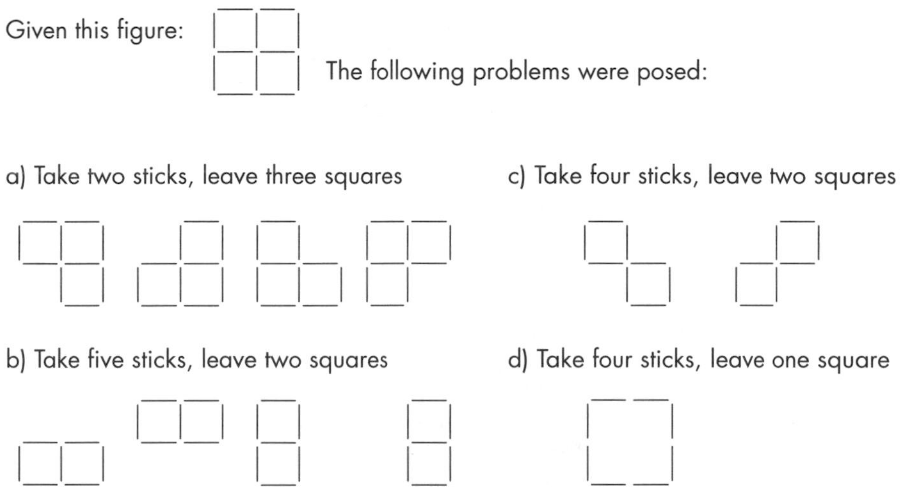

Figure 7.5 Matchstick Test of Cognitive Flexibility
Source: Adapted from Miller and Tippett (1996)
Note: The four problems associated with one of the geometric designs used in the Matchstick Test of Cognitive Flexibility are shown.

Other research has attempted to identify the extent to which the perseveration observed in concept formation tasks is a result of not attending to the feedback provided. Findings have revealed that when a modified version of the Wisconsin Card Sorting Test is used, so that patients are warned and explicitly told of a change in the rule (Nelson, 1976), or are told explicitly which dimension to use to sort the cards (Delis *et al.*, 1992), a significant number of frontal patients still continued to show perseveration. Although patients are able to abstract a rule or formulate an hypothesis when presented with the Wisconsin Card Sorting Test, they do not use the feedback they are given to modulate their behaviour and shift to a different rule. Indeed the results of Delis *et al.* suggest that patients are impaired both in their ability to use the feedback provided and in their ability to shift to a different rule.

Delis *et al.* used a new sorting task requiring participants in one condition to sort 6 cards spontaneously and to report the rule they employed; in a second condition to report the rules for correct sorts performed by the examiner and in a third condition to sort the cards according to abstract cues or explicit information provided by the examiner. Their results revealed no single deficit, such as perseveration, could account for their findings. The authors conclude that although impaired abstract thinking was not the primary deficit, it is one of several 'higher level' functions that collectively disrupt the problem-solving ability of frontal patients.

Matters are complicated further by the findings of Owen *et al.* (1991). They found that frontal patients were not impaired if the shift involved the same dimension. This is termed an intra-dimensional shift and occurs when a participant is required to transfer a rule involving a stimulus dimension such as colour or shape to a novel set of examplars of that same stimulus dimension. Patients were however impaired when they were required to shift response set to an alternative, previously irrelevant dimension. This is termed an extra-dimensional shift and is a core component of the Wisconsin Card Sorting Test. The authors wrote that 'The behaviour of the frontal lobe group . . . was observed to be characterized by a total disregard for the correct, previously irrelevant dimension' (p. 1003). Barceló *et al.* (1997) suggested that frontal lobe patients may be impaired mostly in making extradimensional shifts because of their inability to suppress previous incorrect responses; thus the poor performance of frontal patients on the Wisconsin Card Sorting Test may be linked to problems in inhibitory control. Helmstaedter *et al.* (1996) found impaired response inhibition (known as **disinhibition**) to be one characteristic of patients with frontal lobe epilepsy that differentiated them from patients with temporal lobe epilepsy.

Finally, using a different rule-detection task, Burgess and Shallice (1996b) failed to find significant differences in the incidence of perseverative responses when comparing patients with different cerebral lesions. They designed the Brixton Spatial Anticipation Test which, unlike the Wisconsin Card Sorting Test, allows the amount of guessing to be estimated. Patients were presented with a booklet containing fifty-six pages, with each page showing a 2×5 array of circles numbered 1 to 10 (see Figure 7.6). Pages differed in terms of which circle was filled. The task was to predict which circle would be filled on the next page. The rule would apply to a certain number of pages, and this number would vary in an unsystematic way from 3 to 8. Therefore changes in the rule could not be anticipated. The errors made by participants were scored either as perseverations, or as applications of other incorrect rules, or as bizarre responses and guesses. Patients with anterior lesions made more errors overall, with a significantly higher absolute number and proportion of the third type of errors. In addition, having detected a correct rule, they were more likely to abandon it. However, their performance did not demonstrate a greater tendency to perseverate.

Although the Brixton Spatial Anticipation Test resembles the Wisconsin Card Sorting Test in that the subject has to learn arbitrary rules which change, there are important differences. Relevant rules can be abstracted from the perceptual display in the sorting task, for instance, to sort by colour or by shape; this is not the case in the Spatial Anticipation Test. One possible explanation for their results, one of the three offered by Burgess and Shallice, is that the creation of an appropriate rule

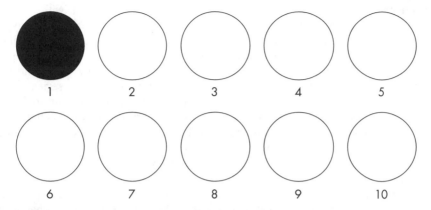

Figure 7.6 Brixton Spatial Anticipation Test
Source: Adapted from Burgess and Shallice (1996)
Note: Each page of the test shows a 2 × 5 array of circles. The task is to predict which circle will be filled on the next page.

is a more abstract process in the Brixton test. Alternatively, one of their other suggestions is consistent with findings from studies involving cognitive estimation described below, namely that anterior patients are more willing to think of bizarre hypotheses which they do not disconfirm.

Impairments in cognitive estimation

A different kind of reasoning is employed in tasks involving cognitive estimates, where deductions or inferences about the world are drawn from known information. Shallice and Evans (1978) asked questions such as 'What is the largest object normally found in a house?', 'How fast do racehorses gallop?', 'What is the height of the Post Office Tower?' and 'What is the length of the average woman's spine?' – in other words questions that cannot be answered directly from information stored in memory. Instead, a realistic estimate can be inferred from other knowledge. For example, a reasonable answer to the last question can be arrived at by first using knowledge about the average height of a woman, then realising that the spine runs about one-third to half the length of the body, allowing one to judge the answer to be somewhere between 22 to 33 inches. Shallice and Evans found that patients with frontal lesions would perform worse than those with posterior lesions, sometimes providing absurd or outrageous values, for example, that the spine is about '5 feet long' and that the largest object in the house is 'a ceramic toilet seat'. Shallice and Evans suggested that poor performance was a result of poor strategy formation – although the questions could be answered by drawing upon general knowledge, no immediate obvious strategy was available.

Poor cognitive estimation has also been observed in a task involving the price of goods. Smith and Milner (1984) showed individuals with frontal lobe damage miniature replicas of real-life products, such as a sewing machine and a car. Results showed that patients with right frontal lobectomies responded with bizarre estimates of price on about 25 per cent of trials. Again, poor performance is hypothesised to result from poor strategy formation. In a later study, Smith and Milner (1988) asked patients to estimate the frequency of an event or item. A series of nonsense items was shown and some of the items appeared only once, whereas others appeared three, five, seven or nine times non-consecutively. A series of test items followed and for each test item the patient had to state whether or not it was included in the initial sequence and furthermore, if this response was positive, they were asked to estimate how often it had been shown. Whilst patients with lesions in both left and right frontal lobes were able to accurately remember the presence or absence of the test item in the initial sequence, they had difficulty estimating its frequency of occurrence.

Thus, although these patients showed a normal ability to recognise an abstract design, they could not estimate accurately how many times they had seen that particular design. Closer inspection of the results reveals that their estimates were not significantly different at lower frequency levels; differences only emerged when the design had been shown at least seven times. Smith and Milner suggest that the patients' performance may reflect a difficulty in cognitive estimation. Alternatively, frontal patients may find it difficult to carry out an orderly search for the representations of the designs in memory or in remembering information with a temporal component. Other research outlined in the next section does, however, support the notion that it is poor strategy formation that results in poor performance in cognitive estimation tasks.

Impaired strategy formation

Other tests have been developed to investigate how well frontal patients can formulate a strategy to obtain a goal, and performance in such tests is a good indication of how well the individual can produce a plan of action, which can involve sub-goals, suited to the particular task presented. Shallice (1982) devised the Tower of London task (a task related to the Tower of Hanoi problem described in Chapter 6). The problem involves an apparatus with three beads and three pegs of varying heights so that each peg can hold one, two or all three beads. The task requires one to move the three beads which are placed on one part of the apparatus to a different position (for example, see Figure 7.7). These beads can only be moved one at a time and can only be moved to a different peg. The difficulty of the task is graded according to the number of moves necessary to achieve the solution. Frontal patients, specifically those with left frontal damage, were found to be both inefficient and ineffective at performing this task. In particular, they engaged in moves that only directly led towards their goal.

Owen *et al.* (1990) used a computerised version of this task and found no differences between left and right frontal lobe patients. However, whereas normal subjects and both groups of frontal patients spent the same amount of time planning their first move, the frontal patients spent considerably longer planning subsequent moves. Not only were they observed to have significantly longer thinking times overall, they needed more moves to solve the problem.

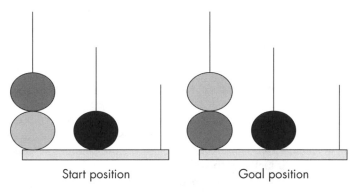

Start position   Goal position

Figure 7.7 An example of a problem from the Tower of London task
Source: Adapted from Shallice (1982)

Morris *et al.* (1993) provided corroborative evidence of the involvement of the frontal regions in the Tower of London task by measuring regional blood flow in neurologically intact individuals. Subjects performed a computerised touch-screen version of the task that entailed two conditions. In the first they were guided by the computer to solve the problem (a control task that requires no planning activity) whereas in the second they were asked to perform the task without guidance. Morris *et al.* found significantly higher levels of activation, i.e. a greater increase in regional cerebral blood flow, in the left frontal cortex in the second condition, when subjects had to actively plan the moves. Furthermore, a relatively greater increase was shown by those subjects who spent more time planning the solution and also in those who solved the problem in fewer moves.

The evidence presented so far implicates the frontal lobes in 'planning', at least in the case of the Tower of London task. Goel and Grafman (1995) presented twenty patients with lesions in the prefrontal cortex with a computerised five-disc version of the Tower of Hanoi puzzle and found them to be impaired in this task in comparison to normal controls. Their individual moves to solve the problems were analysed and both patients and controls were found to use the same strategy. However, the patients' poor performance could be attributed to a failure to spot and/or resolve the counterintuitive backward move. To achieve the goal, a move has to be made that takes you away from the goal and the conflict between the sub-goal and goal has to be acknowledged. This counterintuitive backward move was discussed in Chapter 6 in relation to the Missionaries and Cannibals problem; many of us experience difficulty in implementing this move as it contravenes our favourite heuristic: to reduce the difference between the current state and the goal state. Goel and Grafman point out that the patients' response to satisfy the goal rather than a conflicting sub-goal is consistent with explanations of impaired performance on other tasks, namely that frontal patients have a particular problem with suppressing their current, salient or habitual response. They also stress that the Tower of Hanoi problem does not test planning ability in the sense of constructing and evaluating a particular plan, because unless the counterintuitive backward move is spotted the problem cannot be solved. Below is outlined research that does consider planning ability in relation to real life problems and, in line with the case studies described earlier, supports the notion that planning ability is impaired as a result of frontal lobe damage.

Deficits in everyday higher order planning

Shallice and Burgess (1991a) have developed other tests to explore higher order planning deficits, and these mimic everyday problem-solving. The Six Element Test is undertaken in a standard hospital office. It requires the patient to complete three different but not difficult tasks, each with two components, within a specified time period, namely fifteen minutes. The tasks are: dictating a route into a recorder; carrying out arithmetic problems and writing down the names of approximately a hundred pictures of objects. One key aspect of the instructions given to subjects is that all the tasks should be completed and that the important thing is to do a little of each of the components of each of the tasks.

The Multiple Errands Test requires the patient to carry out certain tasks in situations where minor unforeseen events can arise. The patient is given a card with eight tasks written on it and then sent to a shopping precinct to carry out these tasks. There are six simple requests (for example, buy a lettuce), the seventh tasks requires the patient to be somewhere in fifteen minutes and the eighth task requires the recording of four pieces of information during the errands (for example, the price of a pound of tomatoes or the rate of exchange of the French franc yesterday). Patients are instructed to spend as little money as possible (within reason) and to take as little time as possible (without rushing excessively). They are told to only enter a shop when wanting to buy something, and to tell the experimenter when they leave the shop what they have bought. They are informed that they cannot use anything not bought in the street, other than a watch, to help them. Finally, they are told that they can do the tasks in any order.

These tests were used in a study of three frontal head injury patients (AP, DN and FS) described earlier (see p. 198). All three had WAIS IQs of between 120 and 130, and in thirteen tests considered to be sensitive to frontal lobe damage for instance in the Wisconsin Card Sorting, Stroop and Cognitive Estimation tests, the performance of two of the patients (AP and DN) fell within the normal range. The performance of the third patient (FS) was impaired in four of these tests. In daily life, the three patients planned few activities and showed little spontaneous organisation; two had lost their jobs because of gross oversights. When asked to complete the Six Element Test, all three patients performed at below the normal range; not only were their scores quantitatively lower, their performance was qualitatively different when compared to that of control subjects. AP started by making notes for four minutes, which were then never used. DN spent ten minutes on one task and did not even attempt a second very similar task. FS tackled only three of the six sub-tasks.

The three patients performed equally poorly on the Multiple Errands Test. They made more than three times as many inefficient actions and broke three times as many rules in comparison to normal controls. Again, their behaviour was qualitatively different. Two of the patients experienced difficulties with shopkeepers. AP asked for the previous day's newspaper and on obtaining it angered the shopkeeper by leaving the shop without paying for it, breaking the rule that only bought items can be used. DN asked a shop assistant to give him a birthday card free, breaking the buying rule and resulting in a heated argument. FS broke the rule that no shop should be entered other than to buy something because the shop, a chemist, did not stock the soap she especially liked. She would not buy other cheap soap even though this would have been adequate for the task.

Shallice and Burgess proposed that these patients were able to generate intentions but not to reactivate these intentions later on, when these were not directly signalled or primed by the stimulus situation. The patients lost the facility to activate or trigger markers. Normally, when intentions are created or rules are temporarily created, markers are activated which are then triggered if a relevant situation occurs. This triggering will interrupt ongoing behaviour to ensure that the intention or rule is realised. They explain that 'a marker is basically a message that some future behaviour or event should not be treated as routine and instead, some particular aspect of the situation should be viewed as especially relevant for action' (p. 737). The patients performed poorly on the Six Elements and Multiple Errands Tests, not because of motivational or retrospective memory impairments, but because of processes that bridge these; processes which assist the realisation of goals and intentions.

These findings shed light on why patients with frontal lobe damage can perform well in many laboratory tests that supposedly tap frontal lobe function and yet fail in everyday activities. Duncan *et al.* (1996, p.296) wrote:

> In the laboratory it is often the rule to give strong verbal prompts to task requirements, to repeat these until performance is correct, to gather data over a long series of stereotyped trials, and to have only a modest set of concurrent task requirements. In all these respects, the activities of daily life may often be different: there are no explicit verbal prompts, no stereotyped repetition of closely similar 'trials,' and sometimes multiple, concurrent concerns.

7.4 The executive functions of the frontal lobes

Many of our everyday tasks involve the implementation and monitoring of habitual well-established routines, such as making coffee and cleaning the bath, and these routines are considered to be established in memory and to require little of our attention. Many other tasks, including problem-solving activities such as finding out why the kettle will not work, involve a series of operations such as searching, matching, deciding, evaluating and transforming. Established cognitive skills may have to be reorganised to allow novel patterns of behaviour to be implemented. Exactly how such mental processes are controlled is still open to debate, but several have hypothesised an 'executive mechanism', including Baddeley (1986) when proposing the central executive in his model of working memory.

The term 'executive' function has been used to refer to a range of related abilities, including our ability to plan and regulate goal-directed behaviour, to sustain attention, to remain objective and to use information flexibly, so that we can conceive of alternatives and make choices. Furthermore, the term has proved to be of particular use to neuropsychologists as a means of referring to the constellation of deficits observed in patients with frontal lobe damage. Baddeley (1986) uses the term the **dysexecutive syndrome**. The deficits being referred to here are those outlined in Section 7.3: impaired concentration, impaired concept formation, disinhibition, inflexibility, perseveration, impaired cognitive estimation and impaired strategy formation. Luria (1966) suggested that it was the responsibility of the frontal lobes to programme and regulate behaviour. Baddeley (1986) saw the frontal lobes as having a coordinating, monitoring and organising role in working memory. Stuss and Benson (1987) proposed that such a frontal executive system includes component processes that influence two basic functional systems: drive and sequencing. The most developed notion of an executive is described below.

Supervisory attentional system

Norman and Shallice (1986) adopted an information processing approach to explain these deficits of executive function. Complex but well-established patterns of behaviour are controlled by hierarchically organised schemas or memory representations. High level schemas can call up subordinate programmes or sub-routines, so, for example, 'making dinner' will have component schemas containing at the lowest level instructions on how to use the oven and at higher levels how to make a cheesecake. Fundamental to their approach is the distinction between habitual and novel action routines. They suggested that each of these are selected and integrated in different ways.

Norman and Shallice suggested that we frequently function on autopilot, selecting and integrating cognitive or behavioural skills on the basis of established schemas. Environmental cues trigger certain responses which in turn trigger specific schemas; for instance, a kettle may trigger your 'make a cup of tea' schema. Once triggered, a schema competes for dominance and control of action by inhibiting other schemas which might conflict with it. When there is a clash between two routine activities, an operation they call **contention scheduling** prevents two competing activated schemas from being selected through lateral inhibition. However, it is not always desirable to select schemas on the basis of the strength of their initial activation. Norman and Shallice argued that coping with novelty involves the selection of schemas that are modulated by the operation of a **super-visory attentional system** (similar to Baddeley's concept of a central executive). This system can heighten a schema's level of activation, allowing it to be in a better position to compete with other schemas for dominance and thus increasing its probability of being selected in contention scheduling (see Figure 7.8).

Norman and Shallice indicated five types of situations that would involve the operation of this system:

1   Situations that involve planning or decision-making (e.g. Tower of London task).
2   Situations that involve error correction or trouble-shooting (e.g. Wisconsin Card Sorting Test).

3   Situations that require less well-learned responses or require the involvement of a new pattern of actions (e.g. tasks involving cognitive estimates).
4   Situations that are considered to be dangerous or technically difficult.
5   Situations that require us not to suppress a strong habitual response or to resist temptation (e.g. Stroop Test).

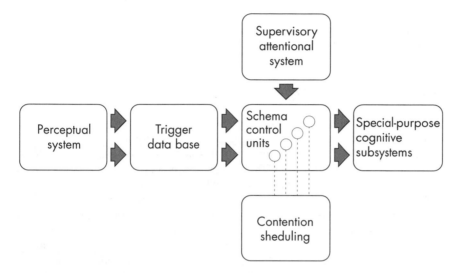

Figure 7.8 A diagram of the Norman and Shallice Model
Source: Adapted from Shallice (1982)

Their approach assumes that we might operate in one mode where potentially demanding but routine action or thought processes are selected by well-learned triggering procedures. When these routine operations will not allow us to achieve our goal then some form of explicit modulation or novel activity must take place, involving higher level processes – the supervisory system. The notion that our cognitive processes might operate on different levels or modes (routine versus non-routine processing) is also contained in artificial intelligence models of problem-solving, e.g. SOAR (Laird *et al.*, 1987). Their use of the concept of 'schemas' is also apparent in other explanations of cognitive behaviour (see Chapter 4).

Shallice (1988) explains how this approach can account for impairments of problem-solving. Lesions to the frontal lobes impair the functioning of the supervisory system so that contention scheduling operates unmodulated. The deficits in sustained attention and distractibility, described above, arise because unless strong trigger-schema contingencies are present, the patient is unable to inhibit irrelevant input. Observations of utilization behaviour, the tendency to pick up and use objects in close proximity, are consistent with this. Perseveration will be observed when the situation triggers a well-learned set of responses. One schema would gain abnormal levels of dominance over others and it would be difficult to switch to a different set of responses. Perseveration has been observed in the performance of frontal patients on the Wisconsin Card Sorting Test. Tasks or situations that require a 'novel' response, for example, those involving cognitive estimates, will be problematic as there is no routine procedure that allows the patient to produce an appropriate response.

Shallice and Burgess (1991b) suggested that the supervisory system should not be considered to act as a single resource. To explain the effects of damage on task performance, the supervisory processes can be subdivided into different classes. This fractionation of the supervisory processes allows this approach to account for dissociations of deficits in problem-solving, and explain why a patient may be impaired on a scheduling test such as the Multiple Errands Test and not on other more standard tests of frontal lobe functioning.

An alternative explanation

Others have proposed accounts of frontal lobe dysfunction that do not specify a damaged central executive mechanism. Goldman-Rakic (1987) conducted extensive research with non-human primates and proposed that the dorsolateral prefrontal cortex is crucial for the working memory, called 'representational memory' in this paper. This framework has been extended by Kimberg and Farah (1993) to account for the range of human cognitive impairments following frontal lobe damage. They proposed that the strength of associations among working memory representations are weakened, specifically those representations of goals, environmental stimuli and stored declarative knowledge. The representations themselves are unaffected; what is deficient are the associations among these different working memory representations. Kimberg and Farah went on to simulate the weakening of working memory associations using a computer model. They selected four tasks that frontal patients failed, and found that their 'damaged' model also failed all four tasks in the same ways as frontal-damaged patients.

Whether or not an explanation of frontal lobe dysfunction specifies a damaged central executive, the challenge faced by theorists is to account for dissociations between the different tasks. Rueckert and Grafman (1996) failed to find significant correlations between any of the three measures of sustained attention and performance on the Tower of Hanoi or the WCST. The authors suggest that the regions of the frontal lobe subserving sustained attention may not be the same regions involved in the problem-solving tasks. In the Burgess and Shallice (1996a) study which employed the Hayling Sentence Completion Test, analysis revealed extremely low correlations between the patients' performance in the response initiation and response inhibition conditions. Such results suggest that initiation and inhibition may be impaired singly and that the two processes are separable. Finally, Burgess and Shallice (1994) reported low correlations between patients' performance on the Hayling Test and the Brixton Spatial Anticipation Test and concluded that the two tests are either tapping differing executive processes or dedicated supervisory resources. They point out, firstly, that we still need to understand the individual processes that are tapped by these executive tasks. Secondly, that we need to find associations between tasks sensitive to frontal lobe function with differing incidental demands. They suggest that finding associations rather than demonstrating dissociations may aid our understanding of frontal lobe function in the future.

Summary

- Frontal lobe damage can affect performance on a wide range of tasks, including many that are considered to be problem-solving or reasoning tasks.
- What appears to be affected does not involve any of the individual cognitive components themselves, giving rise to the notion that the frontal cortex acts as a central executive.
- Norman and Shallice have provided a theory of frontal lobe function that specifies damage to the central executive of working memory.
- Research in this area is problematic, however, partly because problem-solving and reasoning processes can only be investigated using complex tasks which make demands on a variety of cognitive skills.
- Recent findings suggest that the use of laboratory tests may not be tapping those problem-solving and reasoning activities that frontal patients find difficult to perform in everyday life.

Further reading

Kolb, B. and Wishaw, I.Q. (1996). *Fundamentals of Human Neuropsychology* (4th edn). New York: W.H. Freeman. This book will provide information on the physiology, ontogeny and neurochemistry of the brain.

Levin, H.S. Eisenberg, H.M. and Benton, A.L. (eds) (1991). *Frontal Lobe Function and Dysfunction*. Oxford: Oxford University Press. This book includes chapters from key researchers in the area.

Norman, D.A. and Shallice, T. (1986). Attention to action: willed and automatic control of behaviour. In R.J. Davidson, G.E. Schwartz and D.E. Shapiro (eds) *Consciousness and Self-regulation* (Vol. 4). New York: Plenum Press. This chapter provides a full description of an information processing account of executive function.

Language

8.1 Introduction

For the cognitive psychologist, perhaps the most remarkable and intriguing of human abilities is our capacity to use language. Why should this be so? After all, activities involving language are commonplace in our everyday lives. We talk to our families, listen to the news, read the newspaper, chat on the phone, all without conscious effort or obvious premeditation. These activities, however, rely on an ability which, on reflection, is exceptionally clever and impressive. In the words of Steven Pinker (1994), 'Simply by making noises with our mouths, we can reliably cause precise new combinations of ideas to arise in each other's minds' (p. 15). So, by varying those sounds, each of us can tell someone the plot of a film seen last night, ask what they had for breakfast or tell them to 'go and take a running jump'. In the same way each of us can follow that film plot, provide information about what our breakfast consisted of or react to the injunction to take a running jump (without, it should be noted, taking its words literally).

What cognitive processes are involved in such an ability? Language undoubtedly has interconnections with other cognitive capacities discussed elsewhere in this book. For example, in listening to talk and in reading text, working memory processes may be involved in holding the input long enough for it to be analysed and understood (Gathercole and Baddeley, 1993). Information gained through language becomes part of our long-term memory system and helps us make sense of future messages. Thinking and reasoning processes are also closely intertwined with language.

However, many cognitive scientists hold that language processing cannot be understood simply in terms of aspects of memory, reasoning and other cognitive processes that help us make sense of the world. They argue that language must rely on a relatively autonomous set of abilities, each having its own knowledge base and the whole affair functioning, to a large extent, independently of other cognitive processes (Fodor, 1983; Chomsky, 1986).

This chapter will consider the nature of language as a system and review research which has looked at how language is understood, how it is produced, and how it functions in interactional contexts such as conversations. Much of the evidence concerning the language system has come from the study of how language can break down in people who have language disorders resulting from brain injury. Evidence from disorders of language will be reviewed in Chapter 9.

8.2 The language system

Psychologists' main concern is in working out what processes are involved, on the one hand, in understanding speech and in reading and, on the other hand, in producing language when we talk or write. 'The goal is to discover how speakers turn ideas into words and how listeners turn words into ideas' (Clark and Clark, 1977, p. 10). In understanding language (or language comprehension), we can think of the process as beginning with hearing sounds, attaching meaning to the sounds in the form of words, combining the words into a sentence and working out what thought or intention the speaker was trying to convey. In communicating our own thoughts through language (language production), we start with a proposition (a thought), translate this thought into a sentence and produce the speech sounds that express that sentence. A number of levels seem to be involved: speech sounds, words and sentences at the very least.

The discipline of linguistics has provided further insight into the levels of language and the systematic and rule-governed way in which each operates. These levels consist of the sounds of speech (known in linguistics as **phonetics**), the sound system of any particular language (**phonology**), word formation (**morphology**), the combination of words into phrases and sentences (**syntax**), the meanings of words, phrases and sentences (**semantics**), and activities using language which extend beyond individual sentences, such as stories, speeches, newspaper articles and conversations (**discourse**). A diagram showing the different levels is shown in Figure 8.1.

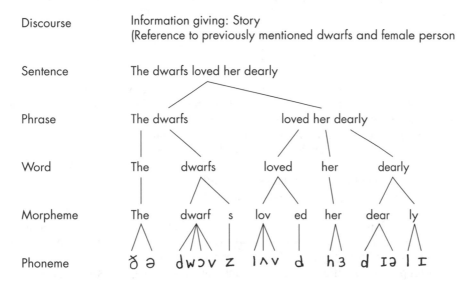

Figure 8.1 Levels of linguistic structure
Source: After Gleitman (1995)

Speech sounds

When we speak we use the lips, tongue, mouth and vocal cords to fashion a column of air from the lungs in such a way as to produce a variety of physical sounds. The field of phonetics investigates this process of the articulation of speech and the physical characteristics of speech as sound waves. Not all of the differences between speech sounds are perceived as making a difference to meaning within a language. For example, the sound of the first letter in 'pin' and the second letter in 'spin' actually differ from one another in that there is a small puff of air (called aspiration) that accompanies the *p* in 'pin' but not in 'spin'. However, in the English language, this is not a distinction that is critical to a difference in meaning. In contrast, the difference between *p* and *b*, actually a difference in voicing, does affect meaning so that we know that 'pin' is not the same word as 'bin'. In English the /p/ and /b/ sounds are two **phonemes**, whereas the two variants of /p/ are not. Every language, then, has a different set of phonemes (English has forty), and learning to pronounce and discriminate them is one of the challenges we face when we try to learn a foreign language.

Phonemes combine to form words. Each language has its own rules about which phonemes can follow others and, although we conform to these rules every time we talk, most of us would have difficulty explaining the rules to someone else. Like many aspects of language they rely on tacit, rather than explicit, knowledge. So, for example, we know implicitly that in English the sound /p/ cannot be followed by the sound /b/ at the beginning of a word and so we would be unlikely to choose a word like 'PBLITZ' if we had to create a brand name for a new product. We make a different sound to form the plural 'cats' (the phoneme /s/) from that for 'dogs' (the phoneme /z/), since /s/ cannot follow 'g' at the end of a word.

Word level

At the level of words, language makes contact with items in the non-linguistic world. Words, sometimes known as **lexical items**, designate things and people, abstract concepts, actions, events and properties of objects.

In addition to analysing words into their component speech sounds, we can also consider units of meaning within words. Take the following sets of words:

Speak, speaks, speaker, speaking, spoke
Ease, easy, easily, easier, easiest, unease

The need to have meaningful units of language that are larger than the phoneme but smaller than the word becomes apparent. The word 'speaks' can be divided into the component 'speak', which it shares with 'speaking' and 'speaker', and the component '-s', the third-person singular ending. Linguists call these units **morphemes**, the smallest linguistic units that carry meaning. Many morphemes, known as free morphemes, can be used on their own as words, for example, 'speak', 'ease', 'cat', 'book'. Others, like '-s', '-ing', '-est' and 'un-' cannot occur on their own and are known as bound morphemes. Bound morphemes can occur at the beginning of a word (**prefixes**) or at the end (**suffixes**) where they are also known as **inflectional endings**.

There is a particular set of free morphemes which cannot have bound morphemes attached to them and which are mostly short common words which function mainly to indicate sentence structure. These include determiners ('the', 'a', 'an'), prepositions ('in', 'by', 'to'), conjunctions ('and', 'but', 'because') and relative pronouns ('who', 'which'). Psychologists have termed these **grammatical function words** (or just 'function words') and contrast them with **content words** which are the words conveying the main semantic content of the message. Content words can be regarded as open-class items since new ones, such as 'eco-warrior', are always being added, whereas function words belong to a relatively fixed, closed class of about 360 items. Whilst the distinction between function and content words is not a strictly linguistic one, psychologists have been interested in whether there may be differences in the way these two sets of words are processed.

A native speaker of a language has a knowledge of words, a vocabulary, which, in terms of words that are recognised, may extend to several hundred thousand items. When a word, say, 'dinosaur', has been learned, the person will have knowledge of how the word is pronounced, how it can function in a sentence (for example, as a noun) and its meaning. This knowledge appears very like the information that would appear in a dictionary entry for 'dinosaur' and this has led to the mental store of words being referred to as a **mental lexicon** in which each word has a lexical entry. The way words are organised in such a mental lexicon and how they are accessed when needed has been a major topic in the psychology of language.

Sentence level

Words are not uttered one at a time but are combined together in phrases and sentences, allowing us flexibility in expressing our thoughts, not having to learn a new word for each thought. Sentences express propositions that convey aspects of events in the world. They may convey to the listener 'who? did what? and to whom?' These basic components of the meaning of a sentence (or thematic roles) are conveyed through syntax. Take the sentence:

(1)   The journalist vexed the drunken politician.

Linguistic intuition tells us that this sentence follows grammatical rules of the English language, whereas the following does not:

(2)   Vexed the drunken the journalist politician.

In (1) we know from the word order that 'the journalist' is the person doing the vexing (the subject of the verb) and 'the drunken politician' the person being vexed (the object). Syntax includes rules for combining words in certain orders and for adding appropriate inflectional endings such as the 'ed' ending on 'vex'. The nature of the linguistic rules which can best characterise the syntactic structures of a language such as English is the focus of much of the endeavours of academic linguists. Psychologists' interest is in the processes by which the brain can crack this complex system of rules efficiently and at great speed.

The level of discourse

We do not speak in individual sentences as isolated units. One sentence links with the last and together they build up a connected discourse. Nor do we talk in monologues. Language is a social activity that allows us to interact and share our thoughts with other people. We relate to other people by linking what we say with what they have just said. Through this process we participate in conversation. To be able to converse effectively with other people we need to know more than just the sounds, words and sentence structures of a language. We have to make subtle adjustments to what we say and make complex inferences about what other speakers are getting at for conversation to proceed smoothly. Cognitive psychologists are becoming aware of the sophisticated cognitive processing involved in such a system.

8.3 Psychology and linguistics

The psychological study of language is often known as **psycholinguistics**. As this name implies, psycholinguistics sprang from an attempt at an integration of the fields of psychology and linguistics, though their differing intellectual traditions have made the relationship between the two a somewhat uneasy one.

The person most responsible for providing insight into the intricacy of language as a system is Noam Chomsky, the linguist who revolutionised the study of language and who has been making major theoretical contributions to linguistics over the last forty years (Chomsky, 1957, 1965, 1981, 1986). Although Chomsky's thinking has evolved over the years and aspects of his linguistic theories have changed considerably, certain aspects of his theoretical position have been maintained. A crucial insight was that people routinely produce and understand utterances that are completely new to them, ones they have never said before or had said to them. This creativity that characterises language must imply that language users have a set of rules which allow them to tackle any sentence that comes along. It is this set of rules, known as the **grammar**, that linguists like Chomsky set out to discover. This set of rules will be powerful enough to create (or 'generate') grammatical sentences in a particular language and, importantly, not generate ungrammatical sentences.

How do linguists go about establishing the laws or 'rules' of language? One way would be to record people talking as they go about their everyday business, transcribe what they say and then attempt to analyse the transcripts for underlying regularities of some sort. Chomsky argues that such an attempt would come to nothing because people's talk is liable to contain grammatical errors along with all sorts of false starts, self-corrections, hesitations and unfinished sentences. He compares this messy and contaminated language **performance** with the more pure and unadulterated language **competence**, the tacit knowledge people have which underpins their performance. Linguists gain access to language competence by asking speakers to judge whether or not strings of words are grammatical. Often, in actual fact, they themselves make these grammaticality judgements, a source of some criticism from cognitive psychologists who consider themselves to be more methodologically rigorous.

Chomsky pointed out that certain sentences seem intuitively to be related to one another, despite being very different in structure. A set of such sentences would be:

(3)   Chomsky analysed this sentence.
(4)   This sentence was analysed by Chomsky.

(5)   It was Chomsky who analysed this sentence.
(6)   It was this sentence that was analysed by Chomsky.

By contrast, two sentences may be identical in form but seem very different, such as:

(7)   Chomsky is easy to please.
(8)   Chomsky is eager to please.

To capture such relationships, Chomsky (1965) argued that every sentence could be given two grammatical descriptions, one a surface structure and the other a deep or underlying structure. Two sentences could have very different structures at surface level but be the same or very similar at a deep structure level of syntax. Similarly, two sentences could resemble each other in the surface form of words but have quite different descriptions at deep structure level. Chomsky's notion of an underlying level of structure has had a strong influence on psychologists' models of language processing, though in Chomsky's own linguistic theory it has diminished in significance in later versions (1981).

Psychologists have been interested in the grammars developed by linguists because of the possibility that they will help in understanding what goes on in speaking and listening. Chomsky (1968), however, believes that there is no direct relation between the rules of grammar (competence) and the way people proceed to produce and understand speech (performance). He says the relation is only indirect and it is up to psychologists of language to discover what it is.

Early psycholinguistic research tried to incorporate linguistic theoretical constructs directly and to test out whether empirical research could validate their role in psychological processing, what was referred to as their 'psychological reality'. Indeed, certain early work seemed to show some success in demonstrating a link between syntactic complexity and processing difficulty (Mehler, 1963; Miller and McKean, 1964; Savin and Perchonock, 1965) (for a review see Harley, 1995). So, for example, passive voice sentences like

(9)   The policeman was shot by the robber

would take longer to process and be more difficult to recall than active voice sentences such as

(10)   The robber shot the policeman.

However, a classic study by Slobin (1966) demonstrated that the situation was not so straightforward. He presented subjects with sentences which had to be judged true or false with respect to a picture, known as a sentence verification task. For example, he presented a sentence like

(11)   The cat is being chased by the dog

and showed a picture of a dog chasing a cat. He confirmed that more complex sentences such as passive voice sentences took longer to verify than syntactically simpler ones. However, this was only the case for sentences like (11) which are said to be reversible because the subject and object could be reversed and still result in a sensible sentence. Other sentences were non-reversible, like

(12)   The flowers are being watered by the girl.

To reverse subject and object in (12) results in a semantically implausible sentence. Slobin found that the non-reversible sentences could be verified more quickly than reversible ones, suggesting that semantic cues facilitated comprehension. In addition, he found that when the sentences were non-reversible, subjects did not take any longer to judge a passive such as (12) than the equivalent active voice sentence,

(13)   The girl is watering the flowers.

It seems that any extra syntactic difficulty associated with the passive voice over the active does not hold when semantic plausibility can be used to work out who is doing what, to whom.

Slobin's study not only cast doubt on the idea that sentence processing mirrored syntactic complexity, it also raised questions about the way syntactic and semantic information interacted in sentence processing. This point will be discussed further below.

8.4 Recognising spoken and written words

Crucial to understanding what people say to us is the ability to recognise the individual words that make up the message. We can usually do this very efficiently, regardless of whether we are familiar with the speaker and regardless of variations in regional accent. The process is very rapid. In one study subjects identified a target word in a spoken passage and pressed a button to indicate that they had done so, on average 275 milliseconds after the start of the word, even though the average duration of the words in the passage was 370 milliseconds (Marslen-Wilson and Tyler, 1980). Similarly impressive is the ability of the reader to recognise written words at tremendous speed, sometimes as fast as 150 milliseconds per word (Rayner and Pollatsek, 1989) and despite variations in font and styles of handwriting. Cognitive psychologists have been particularly interested in the question of what mental processes make such efficient word recognition possible.

The recognition of written and spoken words will be reviewed alongside one another in this section because there is an overlap in the research and theoretical models that have been developed. However, as will be seen in Chapter 9, there is evidence for separate systems for spoken and written word recognition and it cannot be assumed that conclusions based on lexical access in one domain can necessarily be applied in the other (Connine et al., 1990).

What factors influence the efficiency of word recognition? One clearly established finding is that the time it takes to recognise a word depends on the frequency with which that word is encountered in the language. Frequency can be established by referring to counts that have been undertaken of the frequency of occurrence of each word in a sample of books, magazines and other printed material, amounting to some twenty million words in the case of the Thorndike–Lorge Word Frequency Count (1944) and one million words in the case of the more recent Kucera and Francis listing (1967). Words can be selected for experiments that differ in frequency but do not differ in word length (e.g. 'catch' and 'cache'). In a phoneme monitoring task subjects listen to a spoken passage with instructions to understand the passage and to listen out for a target phoneme such as /t/. In a study by Foss (1969) the target phoneme sometimes followed a high-frequency word and sometimes a low-frequency word. Results showed that on average it took longer to identify the target phoneme after low-frequency words, suggesting an increased processing load for accessing them. Rayner and Duffy (1986) investigated the effect of word frequency on reading. By measuring eye fixations during reading they were able to show that low-frequency words were fixated on average for about 80 milliseconds longer than high-frequency words.

An important issue has been whether word recognition is affected by the context in which the word occurs; that is, is it recognised less quickly and accurately in isolation than when it follows a preceding word or is part of a sentence? Many findings in cognitive psychology support the notion that stimuli are recognised better in context. The issue involves the question of the extent to which the processing of 'bottom-up' information such as the component sounds or letters of words is influenced by 'top-down' information, in this case from semantic, syntactic and pragmatic aspects of what is being said.

One way of investigating the effect of context has been to ask whether the meaning of a preceding word or sentence can affect the recognition of a succeeding word, an effect known as semantic priming. Word reading times have been shown to be influenced by sentence context. Zola (1984) measured eye fixations while subjects read pairs of sentences like (14) and (15):

(14) Movie theatres must have buttered popcorn to serve their patrons.
(15) Movie theatres must have adequate popcorn to serve their patrons.

Subjects fixated longer on the target word 'popcorn' in sentence (15) than in (14), probably because in (15) the word 'buttered' limits the range of possible succeeding nouns to a greater extent than the word 'adequate' does in (14) and thus 'popcorn' can be recognised faster in (14) than in (15).

Many studies of semantic priming have used the lexical decision task where the subject sees strings of letters on a screen (e.g. 'RELIEF' or 'RAFLOT') and has to decide whether or not they form a word. Meyer and Schvaneveldt (1971) presented words in pairs and showed that subjects were faster at making such decisions for each word in the pair when the words were related (e.g. 'cat–dog') than when they were unrelated (e.g. 'cat–pen') and many other studies have supported this finding (for a review see Balota, 1992).

A variant on the lexical decision task uses a cross-modal paradigm where the subject receives input from both auditory and visual modalities. A word or sentence is heard through earphones immediately prior to a target string appearing on a screen for a lexical decision to be made. Swinney (1979) presented context sentences that produced a bias towards one of the meanings of an ambiguous target word. For example, immediately following sentence (16) the subject might see either the word ANT, SPY or SEW.

(16) Because he was afraid of electronic surveillance, the burglar carefully searched the room for bugs.

Swinney found that reaction times were faster for words like SPY, which fit with the context, than for neutral words such as SEW. However, he found that words like ANT, which do not fit with the context sentence but are semantically related to the final word in the sentence, were also faster relative to neutral words. Swinney's finding has been taken to show that both senses of the ambiguous word are activated simultaneously and can lead to semantic priming effects, but that these effects are relatively independent of broader contextual knowledge coming, in this case, from the remainder of the sentence.

Fewer studies have investigated semantic priming in spoken word recognition. Although auditory lexical decision tasks have been used (Blumstein *et al.*, 1982), there are problems with the use of this technique because a non-word, when spoken, can often sound like a variation in the pronunciation of some real word. Liu *et al.* (1997) have proposed the use of a single word-shadowing task to investigate semantic priming in lexical access for spoken words. This task involved subjects listening to word pairs or to sentences and repeating a target word. The target word was signalled by a shift in voice from a male to a female speaker (or vice versa). They found evidence of priming effects, with responses being faster when target words followed related words (e.g. water–DRINK) than unrelated words (e.g. fruit–SILVER) and when target words were more predictable from the sentence context (e.g. 'The gambler had a streak of bad LUCK') than when they were less predictable (e.g. 'The kind old man asked us to RACE').

Explaining lexical access

A central concept in explanations of word recognition has been the notion of the mental lexicon, the body of knowledge we hold about words, including their pronunciation, spelling, meaning and typical syntactic roles. Listeners and readers access the lexicon each time they encounter a word in reading or when listening to someone talking. How do we access the appropriate word so efficiently? Do we search right through the lexicon on each occasion? Do other comprehension processes interact with lexical access or is lexical access independent of them i.e. modular? A number of models of how the lexicon is accessed have been put forward.

There are two main types of model of lexical access: *direct access models* and *serial search models*. Direct access models assume that the lexicon contains a detection device for each lexical item within it. Features of words, such as letters or component sounds, activate detectors for many possible candidate lexical entries simultaneously until one becomes pre-eminent. Serial search models, on the other hand, hold that lexical entries are examined one by one to match to features of the input.

One of the most influential models has been the logogen model of lexical access developed by John Morton (Morton, 1969, 1970, 1979; Morton and Patterson, 1987). This model is a direct access model and is based on the concept of thresholds. In the model, each word in the lexicon is represented as a 'logogen'. A logogen acts as a feature counter and passively accumulates evidence. Evidence can be from sensory sources, so that hearing the phoneme /t/ increases the activation levels of all words containing this sound, including, for example, the word 'cat'. Evidence can also be from contextual sources so that hearing the word 'pet' may increase the activation level of the logogens associated with the names of a range of animals including the one for 'cat'. The logogen builds up evidence until its individual threshold level is reached, when it 'fires' and the word is recognised. Each time a word is encountered, the threshold for that word is temporarily lowered and less sensory information would be needed to recognise it. Word frequency has long-term effects which lower the logogen's resting activation level.

The logogen model can be seen as an important precursor of connectionist models of word recognition. As discussed in Chapter 10, the connectionist model of reading of single words put forward by Seidenberg and McClelland (1989) is a highly interactive model with three levels: the input, hidden and output layers. Each unit in these layers has an activation level and is connected to the units in the next layer by a complex web of weighted connections, which can be either excitatory or inhibitory. By being exposed to word-pronunciation pairs, the model is 'trained' to associate spellings with pronunciations and 'tested' on novel letter strings. Seidenberg and McClelland showed that the model mimicked human performance in a number of ways. For example, written words such as 'gave' whose pronunciation is regular, i.e. it follows the pattern of other words ending in 'ave', such as 'brave', 'save' and 'rave', were pronounced faster than irregular ones such as 'have'. Such models have exciting potential for cognitive psychology but, as pointed out by Forster (1994), showing that a network model can successfully learn a complex task such as reading does not necessarily mean that the model corresponds to the way that humans actually do it.

The cohort model (Marslen-Wilson, 1973, 1975, 1987, 1989) was devised to explain the process of spoken word recognition, in a way that captures the sequential on-line nature of speech recognition. According to this model, once the first two phonemes of a word have been heard, listeners develop a set of likely candidates for the word, known as the 'word initial cohort'. Thus, recognition units for all the words that begin in the same way as that word are activated. As successive phonemes are perceived, recognition units for words that no longer fit decline in activation and are eliminated until the cohort becomes smaller and smaller and finally one word is left, the one whose recognition unit has a much higher activation level than the others, and the target word is identified. Like the logogen model, the cohort model allows direct, parallel access to the lexicon. However, unlike the passive process of accumulation of positive evidence in the logogen model, the cohorts actively seek to eliminate themselves.

Although findings suggest that words are recognised more readily in semantic context, it is also the case that we can recognise words even when they arise in unpredictable contexts, an ability capitalised on by poets whose effects are sometimes gained by introducing elements that have an impact on the reader by virtue of being unexpected. Motivated in part by such considerations, Marslen-Wilson (1987), in a later version of the cohort model, proposed that context does not influence the make-up or size of the cohort; it does not make some words more likely to be activated or exclude others. Semantic priming effects can be explained because context does affect the time it takes to integrate the word being processed with the higher order representation of the meaning of what had previously been said.

The other main type of model of word recognition is the search model. Forster (1976, 1979) proposed an autonomous serial search model. In this model the lexicon is seen as containing a master file of words, rather like the way books are organised in a library. This master file links with a series of access files, in the way a library might have a set of card index files. There are orthographic access files, phonological access files and syntactic-semantic access files. When a word is perceived, a search is carried out through the access files until a match is made and directions given to the master file in the lexicon which holds all the information to do with the word, including its meaning. To make the process more efficient, the access files are organised into separate 'bins' on the basis of the initial sound or letter of a word. Items within each of the 'bins' are then ordered by frequency, so that the more frequent items can be examined first. The model is modular in the sense that the search process is independent of other possible sources of information such as sentence context.

8.5 Production of spoken words

When we talk, we convert thoughts into language. How do we match the elements of thought to the words by which they can be expressed? The elements of thought are usually referred to as 'concepts'. Concepts divide the world into units, some of which may correspond to words. If a speaker wishes to convey the information that, for example, a lorry has crashed into a car, the speaker has to match the elements of the thought with the linguistic units, words in English or whatever language is being used. As well as a semantic match with the underlying concepts, the speaker has to take syntax into account. The word to be selected will have to be of a particular grammatical category, such as a noun, verb or adjective in order to fit into the sentence frame that is being constructed. Choice of word is also influenced by such factors as whether the word has already been mentioned in the discourse, thus allowing a pronoun to stand in for it. Different words may even be selected when addressing different listeners; for example, for children as opposed to adults or for close family as opposed to strangers. Despite the range of factors that have to be taken into account in accessing words, the process is accomplished extremely accurately. Estimates suggest that a typical speaker has a production vocabulary of around 20,000 words, yet error data suggest that the wrong word is chosen only about once per million words.

Lexicalisation is the name given to this process by which the thought that underlies a word is turned into the sound of the word. Lexicalisation is widely thought to be a two-stage process (Levelt, 1989, 1992). In the first stage the concept makes contact with an abstract form which includes the semantic representation of the word and the syntactic information associated with it, but does not include the phonological form of the word. This abstract level of representation is known as the **lemma** and the process of making contact with it is known as lemma selection. The second stage of lexicalisation involves specifying the actual phonological form of the word, known as the **lexeme**, by a process known as lexeme selection.

This two-stage model of lexicalisation can help understand a common experience which psychologists refer to as the **'tip-of-the-tongue state'**. This is the experience of being unable to retrieve a particular word despite strong feelings of knowing it. The tip-of-the-tongue state can be seen as the result of success at the stage of lexicalisation that involves contacting the lemma but failure at the stage of making contact with the lexeme (see Harley, 1995).

Evidence to support the distinction between the two stages of lexicalisation comes from research that has used a priming paradigm. Wheeldon and Monsell (1992) investigated lexical priming in lexicalisation. They found that participants were faster at naming pictures when they had recently produced the name of the picture while reading aloud or giving a definition but not if they had produced a word that sounds the same (a homophone such as 'weight' for 'wait'). Thus the effect came about when the priming was semantically and phonologically generated but not when the priming was solely phonological. Whether or not the two stages are independent of one another or whether they interact has been the subject of some debate. An interactive model based on connectionist principles which proposes that processing during speech planning occurs at several levels at once (Dell, 1986; Dell and O'Seaghdha, 1991) is described in Section 8.6.

8.6 Sentence comprehension

Understanding language involves considerably more than just recognising the words. We have to bring to bear syntactic and semantic knowledge as to what each word means in context and work out how the meanings are combined. When we hear on the news a sequence like:

(17)   In a shooting incident in West Belfast today, a policeman was shot at by a gunman.

we need to be able to use syntactic knowledge to find out who did the shooting, the policeman or the gunman, and which of the two was shot at. Moreover, knowledge of the world may have to be employed too, for example, in making sense of newspaper headlines, such as the following:

NOW WE'VE ALL BEEN SCREWED BY THE CABINET

In grasping what this 1993 headline meant, newspaper readers could bring to bear knowledge that it appeared on the day after an announcement of tax changes and in the wake of a sex scandal involving a government minister. Pragmatic knowledge too would be involved in appreciating that this headline is to be regarded as figurative rather than literal in meaning.

There are many challenges in finding methods to investigate sentence comprehension, since the processes involved occur so rapidly and automatically, often while the sentence is still unfolding.

Just as ambiguous stimuli have been used to help us understand visual perceptual processes (Chapter 2), psycholinguists have made considerable use of sentences whose meaning is ambiguous in order to help gain insight into processes involved in sentence interpretation. A sentence such as 'They are racing cars' has a **structural ambiguity** and in one like 'Jane went up the steps to the bank' there is a **lexical ambiguity** since the noun 'bank' can refer to both a river bank and a financial institution. Ambiguities in language are more numerous than most people realise. Advertisers often make use of ambiguous phrases because they may require some extra processing and engage the curiosity of the reader, alerting attention to the product. Sometimes the ambiguity is inadvertent, as in the following which appeared on a newspaper hoarding:

FORGIVE
ME
QUEEN
BEGS
FERGIE

Now consider the following sentence:

(18)   The horse raced past the barn fell.

If you have the same difficulty as most psychology students who have read this sentence since Bever (1970) first quoted it, you will be stumped by that final word 'fell' until you realise the sentence could be paraphrased as

(19)   The horse that had been raced past the barn fell.

Such sentences are known as **garden path sentences**, for the obvious reason that they lead you astray in your initial syntactic parsing.

It is important to consider whether sentences are processed as they are heard or read, on a word-by-word basis over time, or whether we wait until a whole clause or sentence has been completed before processing takes place all in one go. A 'wait and see' approach might be most appropriate because, although we receive words one at a time, sentences are more than just chains of words. The interpretation of one word may depend on other words at some distance within the sentence, known as 'long distance dependencies'. An example would be the referent of the word 'it' in (20):

(20)   If the point of what I am trying to say is obscure, let me assure you that I am going to clarify *it* in a minute.

However, the 'wait and see' approach would place heavy demands on the working memory system. It seems more likely that we follow an 'immediacy principle', making decisions about how each word functions in the sentence as we go along (Just and Carpenter, 1980, 1992). In sentences like (18) we take the first verb we encounter to be the main verb for that sentence and carry on with this assumption until we subsequently come across the second verb and have to revise our strategy. The surprise we experience at encountering the second verb is some indication in itself of the immediacy principle being followed. The immediacy principle is also supported by studies of the duration of people's eye fixations while they read sentences like (18) and (19) which show that longer is spent fixating on the second verb in sentences like (18) than in sentences like (19) (Just and Carpenter, 1992).

The way each type of knowledge – syntactic, semantic and pragmatic – is used in sentence processing and their roles relative to one another has been the basis for considerable research and debate in the psychology of language. There are two points of view on the way syntactic, semantic and pragmatic information apply in the interpretation of a sentence. One view is that the syntactic analysis of the sentence operates independently of, and is not influenced by, semantic and pragmatic knowledge (Frazier, 1989). Such a view is in line with Chomsky's linguistic theory (1986) which sees syntax as an autonomous module. The other point of view is an interactive one which holds that semantic information can guide syntactic analysis (Taraban and McClelland, 1988; Trueswell *et al.*, 1994).

Syntactic processing

When we hear a sentence we have to work out how the incoming words relate together to form a representation in our minds of the syntactic structure of the sentence, a process known as **parsing**. In conceptualising the mental representation of syntactic structure, many psycholinguists have drawn on linguists' proposals for a set of formal rules for creating sentences out of groups of words, the **phrase structure rules** and, in particular, linguists' way of depicting these rules diagramatically in the form of phrase structure trees (see Figure 8.2 for a phrase structure tree diagram). A phrase structure tree is a useful way of expressing the hierarchical structure of the phrase groupings that make up a sentence. Each point at which the tree branches is known as a 'node' and the more syntactically complex the sentence, the more nodes will be present in the tree diagram.

How might the process of parsing work? Early psycholinguistic research (e.g. Sachs, 1967; Slobin, 1966) had shown that we do not use processes that mirror linguistic rules when interpreting sentences (see Section 8.3). Fodor *et al.* (1974) argued that although linguistic rule systems were not blueprints for psychological processing (i.e. were not 'psychologically real'), the end-product of parsing was a syntactic representation and this representation was the deep structure of the sentence as described by Chomsky (1965). They proposed that to recover the syntactic structure of sentences, rather than following systematic rules, we use a number of heuristic strategies, essentially rules of thumb, which generally allow us to arrive at the appropriate structure but are not foolproof and may sometimes fail and lead us astray.

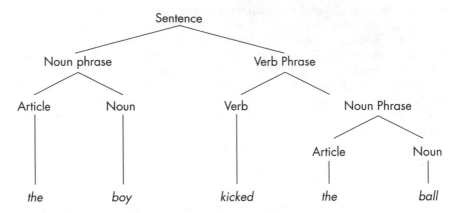

Figure 8.2 A phrase structure tree diagram

One strategy, proposed by Bever (1970), was that, since in English sequences of noun–verb–noun often correspond to active voice sentences, parsing might in the first instance proceed by taking the initial noun in a noun–verb–noun sequence to be the subject (and agent of the action) and the second noun to be the object (and acted-upon element) in the sentence. He argued that young children are sometimes misled by this strategy into misinterpreting passive voice sentences, where the first noun corresponds to the acted upon and not the actor. Kimball (1973) extended the strategy approach and proposed seven principles of parsing. Frazier (1987) argued that our initial attempt to parse a sentence follows the principle: use the simplest, easiest to construct phrase structure tree possible.

Frazier combined a number of the previously proposed strategies for recovering underlying syntax into two basic strategies which people were said to use to keep their initial syntactic parsing as simple as possible. These are the 'late closure strategy' and the 'minimal attachment strategy'. The late closure strategy is stated as: if grammatically permissible, each new incoming term is attached to the clause or phrase currently being processed.

The operation of the late closure strategy can be detected in reading a sentence like (21):

(21) Since Jay always jogs a mile seems like a short distance.

A garden path is created in (21) because the new noun phrase 'a mile' gets attached to the verb phrase 'jogs' and is assumed to be its object, whereas it is, in fact, the subject of the main verb 'seems'. Eye movement studies of people reading sentences like (21) show that after the point of ambiguity people's fixations increase in duration and regressive eye movements show that people backtrack to the area at which ambiguity arises, in this case to 'jogs' (Frazier and Rayner, 1982).

The minimal attachment strategy is stated as: Each new incoming item is added to the phrase structure in a way that requires the minimum of additional nodes. The operation of the minimal attachment strategy is shown in the way a garden path is created in sentence (22):

(22)   The performer sent the flowers was very pleased.

When the word 'sent' is encountered, the reader using the minimal attachment strategy parses it as a verb, attaching a verb phrase to the sentence node in the phrase marker. However, the word 'sent' actually denotes the beginning of a relative clause which involves a more complex parsing with three additional nodes having to be formed. The parsing of sentence (22), therefore, violates the minimal attachment strategy and this is demonstrated in the element of surprise experienced as we read to the end of such a sentence.

Frazier holds the position that syntactic analysis is autonomous and proceeds independently of pragmatic considerations. A study by Rayner *et al.* (1983) compared sentences like (22) with (23):

(23)   The florist sent the flowers was very pleased.

If pragmatic knowledge influences syntactic analysis, then sentences like (23) should be more susceptible to the garden path effect, since florists usually send flowers rather than receive them. In fact, eye movements were very similar for each of the sentences, in terms of the time participants spent inspecting the words 'was very' in each. These findings appear to show that the garden path effect was equally strong in both types of sentence thus supporting the independence of syntactic processing and pragmatic knowledge, rather than an interactive view.

Taraban and McClelland (1988) argue for a parallel, interactive model of parsing and take issue with some of Frazier's conclusions. They cite two sentences used in an experiment by Rayner *et al.* (1983):

(24)   The spy saw the cop with binoculars but the cop didn't see him.
(25)   The spy saw the cop with a revolver but the cop didn't see him.

Rayner *et al.* (1983) had pointed out that in (24) it could be either the spy or the cop who has the binoculars. They had argued that we tend to take it to be the spy who has the binoculars because the phrase structure tree for analysing the sentence according to that reading is simpler than the one for the other reading and thus the minimal attachment strategy leads us to adopt that simpler syntactic analysis. In (25) the minimal attachment strategy would lead to the anomalous interpretation that the spy used a gun to look at a policeman and readers did, indeed, take longer on this sentence and their eye movements showed they backtracked in order to attempt another parsing of the sentence.

Taraban and McClelland (1988) argue that semantic expectations could be responsible for Rayner *et al.*'s finding. The first few words 'The spy saw . . . ' could create the expectation that the sentence may describe what instrument the spy used. They devised pairs of sentences like (26) and (27) and compared performance on them with Rayner *et al.*'s sentences.

(26)   The couple admired the house with a friend but knew that it was overpriced.
(27)   The couple admired the house with a garden but knew that it was overpriced.

In these sentences the semantic expectation set up in the first few words would be that some information about the house would be given and thus (27) would be processed more easily than (26). However, application of the minimal attachment strategy in (27) would lead to semantic expectations being violated and thus (26) might be processed more easily. Taraban and MacClelland found that sentences like (27) were actually read faster than ones like (26), reversing the pattern found by Rayner *et al.* (1983) and supporting the idea that semantic expectations influenced readers' behaviour more than the minimal attachment strategy.

On the basis of these findings, Taraban and MacClelland argue for a parallel interactional model of sentence parsing based on connectionist principles (see Chapter 10). While the evidence suggests that semantic information can guide syntactic analysis, there are still a number of possible ways in which the two types of information might combine in sentence comprehension. It is still argued by Frazier (1990), for example, that syntactic parsing could operate independently to generate a syntactic analysis and then semantic considerations come into play to assess its plausibility and validity.

Why is there such a reliance on ambiguous sentences in research on parsing? Why does psycholinguistic research not draw more on detailed linguistic analyses of our grammatical knowledge? In a review of the area Mitchell (1994) points out that processing takes place so swiftly that our current psycholinguistic techniques are not yet sufficiently subtle to obtain measurable effects with unambiguous structures or to track the subtleties of linguistic accounts.

8.7 Sentence production

Language production differs from the understanding of language in that under-standing begins with a spoken or written message which has to be interpreted to determine the underlying thoughts, whereas when we talk, we start with a thought for which we have to find the appropriate words. It has been relatively difficult to find research strategies for studying this process because its starting point is a thought or idea which cannot be readily detected and observed. The final product, the spoken word, can, however, be observed and one of the most fruitful strategies has been to study speech output for **slips of the tongue**, the errors people make when they talk. Fromkin (1973) said these errors 'provide a window into linguistic processes' (pp. 43–44).

When psycholinguists began to make detailed records of the speech errors made by their friends and acquaintances (Fromkin, 1971; Garrett, 1975) and to make detailed analyses of them, they found that the errors which people make are not just random substitutions, omissions or insertions. In fact slips of the tongue are quite systematic. Figure 8.3 shows some examples of types of slips of the tongue based on errors reported by Fromkin (1973), Garrett (1975), Dell (1986), and Harley (1995).

Slips of the tongue generally involve one word, morpheme or phoneme, being substituted for another word, morpheme or phoneme. Garrett (1975, 1984) studied several thousand such errors and developed a model of speech production based on the most frequent types encountered. Four types which he thought to be particularly important for an understanding of speech production processes were:

- *Word substitutions* such as 'boy' for 'girl' and 'black' for 'white', which only occur with content words and certain prepositions, for example, 'At low speeds it's too light (heavy)'.
- *Word exchanges* such as 'Fancy getting your model renosed' for 'Fancy getting your nose remodelled'. In these errors words from the same categories exchange with one another, for example, nouns with nouns, adjectives with adjectives and verbs with verbs.
- *Sound exchange errors* such as 'shinking ships' for 'sinking ships'. These usually affect adjacent words.
- *Morpheme exchange or 'stranding' errors* such as 'slicely thinned' for 'thinly sliced', 'He is schooling to go' for 'He is going to school' where the 'ing' ending has been stranded in its original position and the verb stem to which it was originally attached ('go' in this example) has been moved elsewhere in the sentence.

Anticipation error:		
take my bike	→	bake my bike
sun is in the sky	→	sky is in the sky
Word exchanges:		
writing a letter to my mother	→	writing a mother to my letter
guess whose name came to mind?	→	guess whose mind came to name?
Perseveration:		
he pulled a tantrum	→	he pulled a pantrum
God rest ye merry gentlemen	→	God rest re merry gentlemen
Word substitutions:		
before the place opens	→	before the place closes
get me a fork	→	get me a spoon
Morpheme exchange:		
I sampled some randomly	→	I randomed some samply
a weekend for maniacs	→	a maniac for weekends

Figure 8.3 Examples of types of slips of the tongue
Source: From Fromkin (1973), Harley (1995), Dell (1986), Garrett (1975)

The production of a sentence according to Garrett's model (Garrett, 1975, 1984) involves a series of levels of processing which operate independently of one another (see Figure 8.4).

The basic ideas the speaker wants to talk about are conceptualised at the 'message level'. At the 'functional level', concepts are matched up with semantic representations of lexical items and with the thematic roles, such as agent or object,

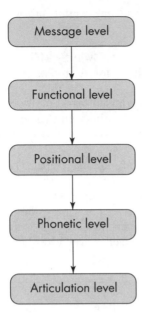

Figure 8.4 Garrett's model of speech production
Source: Adapted from Garrett (1984)

which those lexical items will take. At the 'positional level' information about the phonological form of words and about the syntactic form the sentence will take is specified and lexical items are ordered in terms of particular syntactic structures, such as the active or the passive voice. At the 'phonetic level', the phonological form of the words is specified in greater detail to yield a phonetic level of representation and, finally, at the 'articulation level' commands to the vocal apparatus to speak the sentence are put in place.

Garrett suggested an important difference between the way function words and bound morphemes on the one hand, and content words on the other hand, are introduced into the sentence plan. According to his formulation, at the functional level only semantic representations associated with content words are involved. At the positional level, when the syntactic form of the sentence is selected, it comes with the phonological form of the grammatical function words and bound morphemes already specified and they are already in position. The phonological forms of the content words, however, are not yet specified and in position. The phonological form of each content word has to be specified and inserted into the syntactic form of the sentence within the positional level of sentence generation.

This distinction helps explain some of the types of slips of the tongue that have been documented. Word substitutions, for example, are thought to arise at the functional level, explaining why they occur only with content words and occurring at the stage of lexicalisation when lemmas are being identified (see Section 8.5). Sound exchange errors, according to this model, are thought to arise during the positional level when content words are being inserted into syntactic structures and do not apply to function words because function words are already in position in the syntactic structure when it is specified. Stranding errors also occur while content words are being positioned in the sentence structure. The wrong position may be selected for the content word but the grammatical ending does not move with the remainder of the word. It is 'stranded' because it was already in position when the syntactic form was selected.

Whether planning during speech production proceeds in a serial fashion, along the lines set out by Garrett and in a later model proposed by Levelt (1989; Bock and Levelt, 1994), or whether planning involves interaction between different levels is a matter for debate. Dell (1986) and Dell and O'Seaghdha (1991) propose an interactive model based on connectionist principles by which processing during speech planning occurs at the same time at semantic, syntactic, morphological and phonological levels. This spreading activation model allows feedback from later levels such as phonological levels to earlier levels of planning as is characteristic of a connectionist network (see Chapter 10). When at a certain point in a sentence frame a verb, say, is to be inserted, activation is set up within the lexicon, which takes the form of a connectionist model. When a node within the lexicon becomes activated, activation spreads to all the nodes connected to it. The most highly activated node belonging to the verb category is chosen. Once a word has been selected, its activation reduces to zero for a time, preventing it from being selected repeatedly. Sometimes an incorrect word will have a higher level of activation than the correct one and this would give rise to a speech error such as a word substitution. Categorical rules constrain the types of items that are activated at each level within the model, explaining why errors usually occur within one category with, for example, nouns replacing nouns. Exchange errors can be explained by the idea that once an item has been selected its activation reduces to zero. Thus, because all the elements of the sentence will have become activated during planning, a word (or a phonological element) may be spoken earlier in a sentence than is appropriate. The activation level for that word (or phonological element) will reduce to zero so it is unlikely to be repeated in its intended slot and one of the other words (or phonological elements) which were highly activated takes its place.

Dell (1995) points out that some speech errors, such as 'The competition is a little strougher' appear to reflect both semantic and phonological processes. These 'mixed errors' may be best explained by an interactive model of speech production allowing simultaneous activation of different levels. Such a conclusion, however, is contested by those like Levelt and colleagues (Levelt, 1989; Bock and Levelt, 1994) who hold to a modular, sequential speech production system.

Critical of the heavy reliance on spontaneous error data in studies of speech production, Levelt et al. (1991) reported a study in which people were asked to name pictures as quickly as possible, while also listening to spoken words through earphones and pressing a button as soon as they recognised this word. Some of the words they heard were semantically related to the picture, some were phono-logically related, some were unrelated and some were 'mediated', linked through a semantic and phonological connection. For example, given the picture of a sheep, the word heard was 'goal' which is phonologically related to 'goat' which in turn is semantically related to 'sheep'. Levelt et al. argued that an interactive model of lexicalisation would predict that naming of the sheep picture would be facilitated by the presentation of the mediated stimulus 'goal'. However, such facilitation did not occur. The findings seemed to support a sequential model since semantically related words facilitated naming only when presented after a very short delay (less than 100 milliseconds) and phonologically presented words had an effect only after a longer delay (more than 600 milliseconds). These findings appeared to support the idea of two separate stages, the earlier lemma stage of semantic activation and the later lexeme stage of phonological activation.

8.8 Discourse level

Discourse is the term for a set of sentences related to one another in a meaningful way. In investigating language processing at discourse level, we go beyond the study of word and sentence processing to the level at which speakers and listeners integrate the thoughts and ideas expressed in sentences into topics and follow the flow of ideas from one topic to the next. Topics can be negotiated and developed across speakers, the process normally referred to as 'having a conversation' or 'chatting'.

At discourse level, the processes of sentence comprehension and production which we have been discussing still come into play but the picture becomes more complex. The speaker has to present what he or she has to say in a way that allows the listener to work out the purpose intended. This purpose, known as the communicative intention, may be, for example, to provide information, to request the listener to do something or to request information. There is no one-to-one matching between linguistic structure and communicative intention. For instance, a listener has to infer that an utterance in the form of a question may be intended to convey information, as in 'Would you believe that England have just lost two more wickets?' or to request that an action is carried out, as in 'Can you pass me the newspaper?' or one of a range of other communicative intentions which can be conveyed in the form of a question.

If the intention is to convey information as, for example, for an item in a news bulletin, the propositions expressed must be presented in an organised way, rather than as a random list of statements. The listener has to be able to do the work of understanding each proposition, relating it to the broader topic.

Cues that help us connect ideas from different sentences together are known as **cohesive devices**. Halliday and Hasan (1976) have outlined a range of such devices in English. A commonly used one is that of pronominal reference, where pronouns such as 'she', 'her', 'it', 'their' refer to items mentioned earlier:

(28)   The little girl opened her present. *She* became very excited.

Another cohesive device is that of demonstrative reference where 'the', 'that', 'those' may be used to refer back to something that has gone before, as in (29):

(29)   Once there was a handsome prince. *The* prince was lonely.

Psychologists have made a distinction between given and new information. Given information refers to information the speaker assumes the listener already knows, while new information is information the listener is assumed not to know as yet. Clark and Haviland (1977) suggested a model of sentence integration known as the 'given/new strategy' by which the given and new information in each incoming sentence is identified, an antecedent in memory is found for the given information and the new information is attached to that antecedent. They measured the time taken to read pairs of sentences like (30) and (31):

(30)   We got some beer out of the car.
      The beer was warm.

(31)   We got some picnic supplies out of the car.
      The beer was warm.

The use of 'the' in the second sentence of each pair establishes that 'the beer' is given information. Establishing the antecedent for 'the beer' is more straight-forward in (29) than in (30) because it can be easily matched with the beer mentioned in the first sentence. In pairs like (30), Clark and Haviland suggest that we have to make a 'bridging inference' that, since beer is sometimes included in picnic supplies, 'the beer' referred to must have been part of those picnic supplies. Time taken to read the pairs of sentences was indeed longer for pairs like (31) than for those like (30).

Many other complex inferences are involved when two or more people are conversing. For communication to proceed smoothly, a speaker needs to make relatively accurate inferences about what the other person already knows about the topic and what needs to be explained. The partner in the conversation needs to have a working model in mind of the speaker's line of thought to be able to determine what the speaker 'is getting at' and to work out 'why she is telling me this'. Listeners have to be able to determine when someone is speaking figuratively rather than literally and to work out the figurative or metaphorical meaning (Clark and Lucy, 1975). Complex knowledge of the world may also have to be brought to bear, as in this telling example from Pinker (1994), who asks us to imagine having to program a computer to understand an exchange like the following:

Woman: I'm leaving you.
Man: Who is he?

There is enormous potential for confusion and misunderstandings in conversational exchanges, as another exchange quoted by Pinker (1994) indicates:

First guy: I didn't sleep with my wife before we were married, did you?
Second guy: I don't know. What was her maiden name?

Yet, for the most part, conversations proceed smoothly. In order for this to be the case, people must have some implicit, shared assumptions about the way each will contribute to the joint conversational enterprise. Grice (1975) identified four such shared assumptions which he called 'maxims':

1   *The maxim of quantity*: say as much as is needed to be informative but no more than is needed.
2   *The maxim of quality*: only say what you believe to be true.
3   *The maxim of relation*: make your contribution relevant to what has gone before and the aims of the conversation
4   *The maxim of manner*: be clear, brief and to the point.

Of course, speakers do not always conform to all these maxims but they do provide one way of conceptualising the basic ground rules for being able to participate with others in conversational interaction. It is when conversation becomes awkward that we become aware that some convention has been violated, that someone is being too long-winded, too terse or is frequently straying from the point. The possibilities for characterising difficulties that may arise at the level of discourse for people with brain injury, with dementia, schizophrenia or with autism are beginning to be explored.

Summary

- The use of language provides us with a subtle and sophisticated tool for communicating with other people. The relative independence of cognitive processes involved in language from other aspects of cognition is a matter of debate.
- Language involves a complex system operating at a number of levels from the basic sounds of speech, through word, sentence and discourse levels.
- Linguists focus their study on language competence, the knowledge of the grammar of language that is thought to underlie our ability to use language creatively. Psycholinguists are more interested in studying aspects of language performance, our production of language and the way we understand and remember what is said to us.
- A number of variables have been identified which can affect the speed with which a word is recognised, including frequency and context effects and a number of models of lexical access have been proposed.
- The process of lexicalisation by which the thought underlying a word is turned into the sound of the word appears likely to be a two-stage process of semantic followed by phonological activation.
- The study of sentence comprehension has been heavily based on studies of processing of ambiguous and 'garden path' sentences. There is evidence for an 'immediacy principle' and two major processing strategies have emerged from research: the 'late closure strategy' and the 'minimal attachment' strategy. The extent to which sentence comprehension involves sequential as opposed to interactional processing is still in dispute.
- Much of the research on sentence production has involved studies of spontaneous slips of the tongue and the characteristics of typical slips have led to progress in the development of models of speech production processes.
- Cognitive psychologists are becoming aware of the complex processes

involved in managing the production and comprehension of connected discourse, particularly where interaction between conversational partners is involved.

Further reading

Carroll, D.W. (1994). *Psychology of Language* (2nd edn). Belmont, CA: Brooks/Cole. This is a good introductory textbook covering a wide range of topics in an accessible way.

Clark, H.H. (1994). Discourse in production. In M.A. Gernsbacher (ed.) *Handbook of Psycholinguistics*. London: Academic Press. An authoritative review of the use of language in discourse by the leading researcher in the field.

Harley, T.A. (1995). *The Psychology of Language: From Data to Theory*. Hove: Psychology Press. This is an excellent textbook on the psychology of language, with more advanced coverage than the Carroll or Whitney texts and with its roots in British research and theory.

Mitchell, D.C. (1994). Sentence parsing. In M.A. Gernsbacher (ed.) *Handbook of Psycholinguistics*. London: Academic Press. A very comprehensive review of this aspect of language processing.

Pinker, S. (1994). *The Language Instinct: The New Science of Language and Mind*. Harmondsworth: Penguin. A fascinating and exceptionally well-written exploration of the nature of language and its role in our mental make-up. A really good read.

Whitney, P. (1998). *The Psychology of Language*. Boston, MA: Houghton Mifflin. An excellent introductory text, more recent than the Carroll or Harley texts.

Chapter 9

Disorders of language

9.1 Introduction

In Chapter 8 it was stressed that, though talking and listening to others are natural, effortless activities to most people, analysis from a psychological point of view reveals a complexity and diversity of component processes. These include sound and word identification, production of complex sound patterns, accessing intricate networks of word meanings, comprehension processes and, in addition, personal-social considerations. Language is closely involved in problem-solving and thought as well as in communicating with others.

For some people, neurological disease or traumatic injury to the brain causes this natural, effortless use of language to be disturbed and to become effortful and fraught with difficulties. In this chapter we will consider the ways in which the ability to use language can be impaired, focusing on what can be learned about language processes in the brain by studying the patterns of difficulty demonstrated by people with **aphasia**, impairment of language ability caused by brain injury. Evidence about brain–language relations from neuro-imaging studies using PET and fMRI techniques will also be drawn upon.

Early work on language impairment was largely concerned with neurological issues, identifying which parts of the brain were most involved in language function, and these issues remain an enduring interest. However, much of the recent work on language disorder has been concerned with what such language disturbances can tell us about brain function, about what processes are involved in using language and how these processes interrelate. Again the issue of modularity is central to the debates in this area: is language separate from the central system that performs nonlinguistic cognitive processing and are components of the language processing system modular in the sense that they function separately and can be selectively impaired?

9.2 Historical perspective

Since ancient times it was known that damage to the brain could affect language functioning but a major breakthrough occurred in 1861 when Paul Broca, a surgeon and anthropologist in Paris reported an autopsy he had carried out on the brain of a man who had had severe loss of language for more than twenty years. The man's nickname was 'Tan' because, although he could answer some questions with gestures, all he could say were a few swear-words and the syllable 'tan'. Broca found that an infection had left 'Tan's' brain with a large abscess in the left frontal lobe. Based on this case and on others he subsequently studied, Broca concluded that the two hemispheres of the brain were not identical in function and that the left hemisphere was the one involved in language. Loss of speech was localised in the left frontal lobe, more specifically in the posterior portion of the lower frontal lobe, the area now known as Broca's area. While Tan's language impairment appears to have been a very severe one, the language of patients with Broca's aphasia is usually described as being slow, laborious and nonfluent; speech is produced in short phrases with little variation in intonation and with frequent mispronunciations. People with this disorder often seem to grope for words but the words they do manage to come out with are usually meaningful. There follows an example of a brief exchange with a man with Broca's aphasia reported by Gardner (1977):

'What happened to make you lose your speech?'
'Head, fall, Jesus Christ, me no good, str . . . str . . . Oh Jesus . . . stroke.'
'I see. Could you tell me, Mr Ford, what you've been doing in the hospital?'
'Yes, sure. Me go, er, uh, P.T. nine o'cot, speech . . . two times . . . read . . . wr . . . ripe, er, write . . . practice . . . getting better.'
'And have you been going home on weekends?'
'Why yes . . . Thursday, er, er, er, no, er, Friday . . . Barbara . . . wife . . . and, oh, car . . . drive . . . purnpike . . . you know . . . rest and . . . tee-vee.'
'Are you able to understand everything on televsion?'
'Oh, yes, yes . . . well . . . almost.' [Ford grinned a bit.]

Within a few years Carl Wernicke had noticed that some forms of language disturbance present a different picture and not all involve Broca's area. He described a form of aphasia now known as Wernicke's aphasia in which the person's speech is fluent but has little informational value and in which there is poor comprehension of language. This form of aphasia is associated with damage in the upper part of the left temporal lobe. The following excerpt (again from Gardner, 1977) demonstrates why this form of language disorder is sometimes known as 'fluent aphasia':

'What brings you to the hospital?' I asked the 72-year-old retired butcher four weeks after his admission to the hospital.
'Boy, I'm sweating, I'm awful nervous, you know, once in a while I get caught up, I can't mention the tarripoi, a month ago, quite a little, I've done a lot well, I impose a lot, while, on the other hand, you know what I mean, I have to run around, look it over, trebbin and all that sort of stuff.'
I attempted several times to break in, but was unable to do so against this relentlessly steady and rapid outflow.

Difficulties with comprehension of language cannot be assumed just because questions are not answered meaningfully, but when comprehension is assessed on tasks which require nonverbal responses to verbal requests and instructions, people with Wernicke's aphasia do indeed show poor comprehension.

Wernicke (1874) also theorised about the neurological organisation for language, basing his ideas on a model in which Broca's area contained motor memories, memories of the sequences of motor movements needed to articulate words and thus was responsible for speech output. Wernicke suggested that the area that now bears his name recognises the sounds of words, being the location that holds memories of the sound patterns of words.

Wernicke also speculated about what might happen if the connecting pathways between Broca's area and Wernicke's area should be damaged, but the areas themselves remain intact. He suggested that comprehension of language and production of speech would not be impaired but there would be a difficulty in repeating back what had just been heard, because sound images received by Wernicke's area could not be transmitted forward to Broca's area to be produced. More recently it has been established that some people with aphasia do fit this picture, a pattern of aphasia which is referred to as **conduction aphasia** (Geschwind, 1965). When asked to repeat back a sentence these people often make phonological errors, leave out words, substitute other words or may have extreme difficulty in saying anything. A large tract of fibres, known as the arcuate fasciculus, does connect Broca's area with Wernicke's area and damage to this tract and surrounding tissues is indeed found in cases of conduction aphasia.

Wernicke's model was elaborated on by Lichtheim (1885), who argued that there was a third centre for language processing, a 'concept centre' which stores the mental representations of objects and associates them with words. Geschwind (1972) more recently postulated the location of such a centre in an area of the parietal lobe known as the angular gyrus. The three-centre Lichtheim–Geschwind model underlies the classic approach to the categorisation of the different types of aphasia. Because the model is based on ideas about connections between language centres it became known as the 'connectionist model of language' but it should be noted that this is not the same type of connectionist model as is now current in cognitive psychology (see Chapter 10).

Disruption could occur not only because of damage to Broca's area and Wernicke's area and to the fibres linking them, but also, it was thought, to the fibres linking the concept centre with Broca's and with Wernicke's areas. It was postulated that if there was disruption to the connections between the concept centre and Broca's area then the person's speech would be very disrupted. However, they should still be able to repeat back language they have heard if the connection from Wernicke's area to Broca's area is still intact. Such a pattern of language disorder has been found and is known as transcortical motor aphasia. The person has the same impairment of speech as in Broca's aphasia but is able to repeat what has just been said; in fact that person often seems to have a compulsion to repeat back what is heard, a characteristic known as **echolalia**. Using similar reasoning, if there was disruption to the links between Wernicke's area, where the sounds of words are processed, and the concept centre, but the links from Wernicke's area to Broca's area were intact, then the effect might be that the person could not interpret the meaning of words but could still repeat back what had been said. Again, such a pattern of language disorder has been observed and is known as transcortical sensory aphasia. The person with this type of disorder has a similar disruption to the ability to understand language as someone with Wernicke's aphasia, but is able to repeat back language and shows echolalia.

Another particularly striking pattern of language disruption in aphasia is one that has been found to occur in rare cases where Broca's area, Wernicke's area and the connection between them are intact, but they are essentially cut off from the rest of the brain. In these cases the 'ring' of tissue that surrounds those areas becomes starved of oxygen, being relatively far from the main artery which supplies it. Lung disease and some toxins, including carbon monoxide poisoning, can cause this loss of oxygen and of other nutrients causing the ring of tissue to become permanently damaged. The effect of such 'isolation of the language zone' (Geschwind et al., 1968; Caplan, 1992) is that the person loses the ability both to understand and to produce speech beyond a few stereotyped expressions but has some preservation of the ability to repeat sentences back verbatim. Some ability to recognise words must therefore be preserved but the person is unable to understand the meaning of what he or she hears and repeats.

It is sometimes overlooked in accounts of relatively rare aphasic syndromes that a common type of aphasia is where damage extends to a number of parts of the system and the ability to understand and to produce language is very disrupted. This global aphasia results from extensive damage to the language areas of the left hemisphere.

The various syndromes of aphasia, according to the classic syndrome approach, are shown in Figure 9.1. Other important types of language disorder are those of **acquired dyslexia** (also known as 'alexia') where the person experiences loss of the ability to read after brain injury, and **dysgraphia** (also known as 'agraphia') where the person loses the ability to write. According to the classic Lichtheim–Geschwind model, what occurs in these disorders is essentially that the visual areas of the brain become disconnected from the language areas because of damage to the angular gyrus, an association area in the brain that is important for the association of visual stimuli with linguistic symbols. Often dyslexia and dysgraphia co-occur but in some cases individuals have one without the other (Geschwind, 1965). A person with dyslexia without dysgraphia can write with little difficulty but is unable to read what he or she has written. Clearly the implication is that the neural systems for reading and writing are separable to some extent and do not critically rely on each other. We do not have one single module in the brain for both interpreting written language and producing it.

Alongside disturbances to language production and comprehension, many patients with aphasia have additional difficulties with reading. Patients with Wernicke's aphasia often have difficulties with both auditory and reading comprehension. Such a co-occurrence could be expected on the basis of the Lichtheim–Geschwind model since Wernicke's area is thought to control phonological access, a process important to most reading (see Chapter 8). However, difficulties with reading also occur in patients with Broca's aphasia, a finding less easy to explain in terms of the classic model according to which Broca's area is the speech centre.

Although the classic Lichtheim model, and its close relative the Lichtheim–Geschwind model, have been very influential in the study of aphasia, known as 'aphasiology', they have not been without their critics. The idea that there are language centres that function relatively independently of one another has been criticised, notably in an early commentary by Sigmund Freud in 1891. Freud wrote that many clinical cases did not neatly fit the pattern expected and argued that, despite Broca's and Wernicke's findings, language processes could be distributed widely throughout the cortex. Broca's and Wernicke's areas might not so much control certain functions but rather be areas where several cortical interconnections involved with language happen to cross. The English neurologist Henry Head (1926), who studied language disorders resulting from gunshot wounds to the head inflicted during the First World War also argued that similar injuries could lead to different types of aphasic symptoms. He, too, argued against a one-to-one correspondence between brain regions and language operations and proposed that the language system operated as an integrated whole.

Syndrome	Symptoms	Deficit	Lesion site
Broca's aphasia	Sparse halting speech misarticulations, understanding relatively intact, function words and inflections omitted	In speech planning and production	Posterior portion of left frontal lobe
Wernicke's aphasia	Poor auditory comprehension. Fluent speech but phonetic morphological and semantic errors	In representations of sound patterns of words	Posterior half of temporal cortex
Global aphasia	Major distrubance in all language functions	Disruption of all language processing components	Large portion of frontal and temporal lobes
Conduction aphasia	Disturbance of repetition and spontaneous speech	Disconnection: sound patterns of words from speech production mechanism	Arcuate fasciculus
Isolation of the language zone	Disturbance of speech production and comprehension with some preservation of repetition	Disconnection: concepts from word sounds and from speech production mechanism	Ring of cortical tissue around language areas

Figure 9.1 Major aphasic syndromes according to the classic view
Source: Adapted from Caplan (1992)

The main evidence in favour of the classic language circuit model is said to be that lesions in the language centres and to the connections between them do typically result in the occurrence of the classic aphasic syndromes described above (Benson and Geschwind, 1971; Geschwind, 1972). However, it has been pointed out by Caplan (1992) and others that groups of patients with the same syndrome, even those carefully selected for research purposes, may actually show considerable variation in the extent to which particular components of language are disrupted.

It is a major drawback to the classic view of brain–language relations that there is a considerable amount of variation in the brain lesion sites that produce a particular set of deficits. Lesions in Broca's area do not of necessity give rise to the classic symptoms of Broca's aphasia (Mohr *et al.*, 1978; Dronkers, 1996) and Broca's type aphasias can result from lesions outside Broca's area (Caplan and Hildebrandt, 1988). It has also been found that Wernicke's aphasia can result from a range of different lesions (Kertesz *et al.*, 1993). Data from PET scanning of patients with aphasia are broadly consistent with the classic syndromes so that patients with Broca's aphasia show abnormally low activity in the lower left frontal lobe and patients with Wernicke's aphasia show low activity in the temporal/ parietal area (Karbe *et al.*, 1990; Metter *et al.*, 1990; Metter, 1995). However, PET scanning in normal subjects has not always supported the classic language circuit model with the inferior parietal lobe, a crucial language area according to the theory, showing no activation on language tests (Peterson *et al.*, 1988; Posner *et al.*, 1988). Another type of neuroanatomical study involving electrocortical stimulation during neurosurgical operations has shown considerable individual variation in the localisation of language processes (Ojemann, 1983).

The language circuit approach provides information about the localisation of damage giving rise to the classic syndromes, not about the localisation of the individual language processing components. As research into the cognitive processes involved in language has developed, those working in the area of aphasiology have become very aware of the complexity of each of the components of the system that processes language. So, for example, Wernicke's area has been traditionally associated with processing speech input but, as described in the Chapter 8, such processing involves many components. These components include word identification and word recognition, parsing, and determining the structure of discourse. Questions arise as to whether all are disrupted or whether some may be disrupted and not others. It has also been recognised that it is important to approach aphasia with a detailed model of language and language processing in mind, rather than lumping together many different aspects. Such thinking has given rise to the psycholinguistic approach to the study of language disorders.

9.3 The psycholinguistic perspective

The psycholinguistic approach to aphasia attempts to identify for each patient which components of the language processing system are disrupted and to describe how those components are disrupted (Caplan, 1992). The approach is closely allied with the cognitive neuropsychological approach described elsewhere in this book and indeed language is one of the main areas in which cognitive neuropsychology has developed (Ellis and Young, 1988). In practice, the psycholinguistic approach involves setting a number of language-related tasks for the patient, tasks chosen on the basis of what is known of normal language functioning, to tap different aspects of the operation of the language processing system, and then to identify which tasks can be accomplished effectively and which cause difficulty. If it is found that a patient is able to accomplish one task but is impaired in performance of another task, then this pattern is taken to point towards that person having a selective deficit in one language processing operation and not in another. In addition, analysis of the types of errors made can provide evidence of the nature of a person's disorder. Insight into the particular pattern of disorder for that individual may help focus strategies for treatment or approaches to help the individual cope with or compensate for the impairment.

As well as providing insight for work with individual patients the psycholinguistic approach can provide insights into the workings of the language system, in particular about which components of the system can be selectively impaired, and therefore which components seem to operate as separate modules from one another. Instances are sought where performance on two language tasks is such that one patient performs relatively well on task 1 but poorly on task 2, whereas another patient performs relatively well on task 2 but poorly on task 1. This is known as the method of 'double dissociation' (see Chapter 1) (Shallice, 1988). The search for such dissociations has been a major focus of activity of psycholinguistic/cognitive neuropsychological approach to the study of language disorder (Ellis and Young, 1988) (see Parkin (1996) for a discussion of this approach).

It should be clear from this account of the psycholinguistic approach that its orientation is towards dealing with each patient with language disorder as a single case who may show an individual pattern of language impairment, rather than as a representative of a particular syndrome. In fact, some cognitive neuropsychologists with a particular interest in language suggest that very little can be gained from conducting research based on group studies of patients with aphasia, since syndrome-based groups often show marked individual variation in symptoms. In a series of papers debating the issue, Caramazza has argued that psycholinguists should abandon the syndrome approach and only consider data from single case studies (e.g. Caramazza, 1984; Caramazza and Badecker, 1991). Other psychologists have argued that single case studies raise problems of generalisation and replication and that, with strict criteria for subject inclusion, group studies can still be valuable. The ongoing nature of this debate can be seen in Caramazza's title for one of his articles: 'Clinical syndromes are not God's gift to cognitive neuropsychology: a reply to a rebuttal to an answer to a response to a case against syndrome-based research' (Caramazza and Badecker, 1991). Group studies continue to be published in journals alongside reports of single case studies.

In the following sections we will consider disruptions to three levels of language processing and the insights gained from the viewpoint of a psycholinguistic approach.

9.4 Disruption to language processing at word level

Processing spoken words

Just as there are many different aspects of language processing at word level (see Sections 8.4 and 8.5), detailed psycholinguistic analysis shows that there are many different ways in which word level processing may break down. Deficits may occur in recognising spoken words or in speaking words. They may occur in reading words or in spelling words. They may occur in repeating back a wordlike string of sounds or they may occur in grasping the meaning of a spoken word or in finding the appropriate word to name an object. Various combinations of such deficits may occur and some deficits may be even more specific and apply to only one type of word.

Cognitive neuropsychological models have been developed which help provide a systematic way of conceptualising such diverse patterns of impairments.

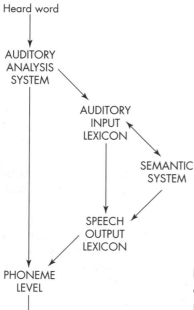

Heard word

AUDITORY
ANALYSIS
SYSTEM

AUDITORY
INPUT
LEXICON

SEMANTIC
SYSTEM

SPEECH
OUTPUT
LEXICON

PHONEME
LEVEL

Speech

Figure 9.2 Diagrammatic representation of a model for recognising, understanding, and repeating back spoken words.
Source: Ellis and Young (1996), reproduced with permission

Based, to a large extent, on psycholinguistic research on recognising and producing single words (as reviewed in Chapter 8), models of the component processes involved in recognising, understanding and repeating back spoken words and in reading and spelling words can help us understand in what ways processes can be impaired because of brain injury. Figures 9.2 and 9.3 present versions of these models based on those presented by Ellis and Young (1988).

In Figure 9.2 there are three routes between hearing a word and saying it. One route goes from the auditory analysis system, where the speech signal is converted into a phonemic code to the auditory input lexicon, where that code may be matched with one of the items in our store of how all the words we know sound, then through the semantic system, where its meaning may be identified, and then on through the speech output lexicon, to link up with the relevant item from our store of information about how to say all the words we know. From there it goes to the phonemic response buffer where the information about how to say the word is held until we are ready to say it. The second major route is directly from the auditory analysis system to the phonemic response buffer, allowing us to repeat back words we have never heard before and nonsense words. A third route, from the auditory input lexicon to the phonemic output lexicon, has also been hypothesised.

This model can be used to explicate the pattern of symptoms of patients and it is the basis for an approach to assessment of people with aphasia known as Psycholinguistic Assessments of Language Processing in Aphasia (PALPA: Kay *et al.*, 1992) which involves a systematic testing of one aspect of language functioning as against another so that an evaluation can be made of where in the processing model the individual's deficits might lie.

An example of the way the model can be applied is in understanding a pattern of symptoms that has come to be known as **pure word deafness**. Patients who show this pattern of symptoms can talk and read fluently but are unable to repeat back words they cannot understand and to understand speech addressed to them. This disability occurs despite relatively normal hearing. Ellis and Young (1988) cite the case of a Scottish sheep farmer who said he could 'hear everything, even a leaf falling', but when listening to speech, 'It sounds far away. You think you can catch it and it fades away . . . jumbled together like foreign folk speaking in the distance'.

The specific problem appears to be in the ability to perceive speech-like sounds and thus appears to lie in phonemic processing in the auditory analysis system of the language processing model.

Another pattern of symptoms related to word processing is known as **pure word meaning deafness**. The patient is unable to understand what words mean even though those words can be repeated and written accurately to dictation (Ellis, 1984; Schacter *et al.*, 1993). Franklin *et al.* (1994, cited by Parkin, 1996) describe an attempt to understand the word 'slow': 'Slow, slow, slow, I know what it is but I can't get it, slow, slow – you'll have to write it down for me. . . . [after word is written] Oh slow, well slow is the opposite of fast.' A person with pure word meaning deafness may be unimpaired on a lexical decision task (requiring discrimination between real words and non-words), suggesting that the representation of words in the auditory input lexicon is intact. Understanding of written material may be unimpaired, so that the semantic system may also be intact and the deficit may therefore lie in the connection between the auditory input lexicon and the semantic system. The case study below provides an example of the way psycholinguistic investigation of an individual's language processing may proceed.

The case of Derek B studied and described by Sue Franklin and David Howard (1992)

Over the years Derek B had been a joiner, a publican, a newsagent and a chauffeur. At the age of 54 he had a stroke which affected his speech so that at first he was completely unable to speak, but after a month he was speaking in sentences again and became aware that his biggest problem was in understanding speech. 'I thought I was deaf, couldn't hear it' (p. 119). Speech sounded like a 'mumble' to him. Eighteen months after his stroke he still had to concentrate hard on listening, on watching the speaker's face and on context in order to grasp what was being said to him.

As neuropsychologists who are also speech and language therapists, Sue Franklin and David Howard set out to investigate systematically what was going wrong with Derek's comprehension of speech, focusing on his understanding of single words. A cognitive neuropsychological model of single word comprehension, such as that of Ellis and Young (1988), suggests that it would be possible to have an impairment at any of three levels of processing: a problem in hearing the sounds of speech (word-sound deafness), a problem in accessing the word form in the auditory lexicon (word-form deafness) or a problem in deriving the word's meaning (word-meaning deafness).

Was Derek's problem one of hearing the sounds of speech (word-sound deafness)? It was certainly not just a simple hearing difficulty: his hearing when tested by pure tone audiometry was normal. But could he 'hear' sounds in words? To find out, Derek was asked to judge whether words in pairs like 'pack'/'pack' and 'pack'/'pad' were the same or different. He was able to do this, whether the words in the pairs were real words or non-words ('mip'/'mig').

The next question was to determine whether Derek could tell if the sequences of speech sounds he heard were words or not, thus testing for word-form deafness. This question could be answered with a lexical decision task where he heard a string of sounds (such as 'look' or 'loak') and had to decide whether or not they corresponded to a real word. Derek was able to do this even though the non-words differed from the words in only one sound and even when three syllable words were used. So Derek's difficulty was not in 'looking up' words in the auditory input lexicon. Intriguingly, sometimes he would say 'Yes, it's a word' yet add, 'but I can't hear it'!

It appeared, then, that Derek's problem must be in actually reaching or accessing word meanings (word-meaning deafness). Yet on a test of matching words to pictures, for example, choosing a picture to correspond to the word 'axe' from a set of pictures of an axe, a hammer and a pair of scissors, Derek had little problem.

Franklin and Howard's next line of thought was to wonder whether, like some people with impairments to reading following a stroke, Derek might have a problem only with words that are abstract in meaning. He was given a synonym test in which he heard two words and had to decide whether or not they had similar meanings. Half the word pairs were made up of concrete words (for example, 'flower/blossom' or 'flower/boat') and half were pairs of abstract words (for example, 'irony/sarcasm' or 'irony/kingdom'). Derek's performance on the abstract words was significantly worse than on the concrete words and did not differ significantly from chance. On a word definition task too, he had much more difficulty with abstract words.

Would Derek's difficulty in accessing the meaning of abstract words affect only his understanding of the words in spoken form or would it affect his written comprehension too? He was given the synonym test and the word definition test in written form and was found not to be impaired on either concrete or abstract words. His 'deafness' for word meanings affected auditory processing alone, a finding which supports the notion that the process for accessing meanings of heard words is not one and the same as the process for written words. Derek's difficulty with accessing the meanings of abstract words would have implications that would go beyond the understanding of single words. Since the grammatical function words such as 'the', 'would', 'of', 'for' and 'though' are abstract in meaning, problems in accessing their meaning would indeed have a wide and devastating impact on his ability to understand what was said to him.

A detailed account of Derek's pattern of abilities and impairments can be found in Franklin, S., Howard, D. and Patterson, K. (1994) Abstract word meaning deafness. *Cognitive Neuropsychology*, 11, 1–34.

Other patients have been described who can read aloud and write well but on closer investigation have difficulties with repetition of non-words. Their pattern of symptoms has been called 'auditory phonological agnosia'. Beauvois *et al.* (1980, cited by Parkin, 1996) report on a patient who could read and write but who had noticed difficulty with understanding place names and scientific terms which he had not encountered before. Subsequent testing revealed that words which he knew could be repeated correctly, indicating that the route via the auditory input lexicon was in order, but that non-words could not be repeated, suggesting that the direct route for repetition via the auditory analysis system and the phonemic response buffer was impaired. The problem was not simply in the pronunciation of non-words, since he was able to read them accurately.

Other patterns of symptoms in spoken word processing relate to aspects of semantic processing. Yamadori and Albert (1973) found that a patient whom they studied had more difficulties in understanding words from some semantic categories than from others. Particularly difficult for him were body parts and the names of objects in a room. For example, he could not identify a chair despite being able to understand the names of a range of tools, utensils and items of clothing. Warrington and McCarthy (1983) described a patient who had particular problems understanding the names of inanimate objects relative to understanding of names of items of food, flowers and animals. Contrasting with that pattern was the patient of Warrington and Shallice (1984) whose comprehension of words for living things was impaired relative to other categories. McCarthy and Warrington (1990) describe a number of other patients with 'category-specific access problems', as these are termed.

A very common symptom of patients with aphasia is a difficulty in finding the right word, a problem known as anomia. Mirroring our everyday experiences of difficulty in coming up with the names of people whom we feel we should know, some patients with anomia seem to have marked difficulty in producing people's names and other proper nouns (Hittmair-Delazer *et al.*, 1994). If proper nouns and common nouns are represented differently, it should be possible to find the opposite pattern and, indeed, McKenna and Warrington (1980) were able to identify a patient with a selective preservation of geographic names while other investigators have described the relative preservation of proper nouns (McNeil *et al.*, 1994; Semenza and Sgarmella, 1993).

A rare, but very interesting pattern of symptoms is that of **deep dysphasia**. In deep dysphasia the patient is unable to repeat back non-words and is likely to make semantic errors when repeating back real words, so that, for example, he or she might say 'yellow' for 'red' or 'kite' for 'balloon' (Morton, 1980). Abstract words are more difficult to repeat back than concrete words. In terms of the model of single word processing in Figure 9.2, Ellis and Young (1988) suggest that the most likely account of deep dysphasia is in terms of impaired access to semantics from the auditory input lexicon. Additionally, since non-words cannot be repeated, there is also impairment to both the route from the auditory analysis system to the phonemic response buffer and to the third route, the one going from the auditory input lexicon to the phonological output lexicon.

Processing words in reading and writing

Psycholinguistic investigations of disorders of reading and spelling have, to a large extent, been based on the sort of model of reading single words described in Chapter 8. A version of such a model, which was developed partly in the light of research on patients with reading and writing difficulties and which shows some of the ways in which reading can be disrupted, is shown in Figure 9.3.

Acquired dyslexia refers to the sudden loss of some aspect of reading ability due to a brain lesion and **acquired dysgraphia** refers to the sudden loss of the ability to spell words. Detailed psycholinguistic investigation of processes involved in reading and writing in such patients has revealed a number of different patterns of symptoms (Ellis and Young, 1988). The investigations centre around the patients' abilities to read and spell invented, but pronounceable, non-words, as compared with real words and to read and spell words that are regular in their

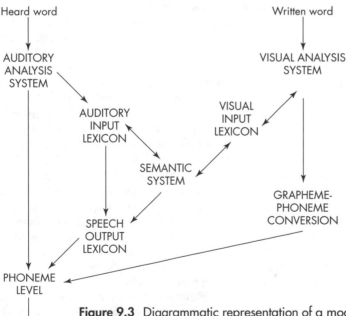

Figure 9.3 Diagrammatic representation of a model for recognising, understanding, and naming written words in reading.
Source: Ellis and Young (1996), reproduced with permission

253

reading and spelling patterns, such as 'hint' or 'toad', or irregular, such as 'pint' or 'broad'. Patients are also often tested on sets of words that vary in their frequency in the language, in their imageability and in whether they are content words (such as 'hound' or 'walk') or function words (such as 'and', 'that' or 'to').

Some patients can read many words correctly, provided those words are regular in their spelling, in the sense that they obey English grapheme-to-phoneme (or spelling-to-sound) correspondence rules. In addition, non-words can be read. However, words which are irregular and thus do not follow those rules (such as 'ache' and 'yacht') cause difficulty and a word like 'pint' may be pronounced as if it rhymed with 'hint'. This form of dyslexia, known as surface dyslexia, was first described by Marshall and Newcombe in 1973. Only when the patient has pronounced the word does he or she seem to know the word's meaning. This form of dyslexia seems to be associated with temporal lobe damage (Deloche *et al.*, 1982). The damage seems in some way to have interfered with the connections between the visual word forms and the semantic network so that the patient is not able to use the lexical-semantic route (sometimes known as the whole-word route) but has to work out the pronunciation of each word by using grapheme-to-phoneme correspondence rules.

Other patients are able to read real, familiar words but have difficulty with non-words (Shallice and Warrington, 1980; Ellis and Young, 1988). Patterson (1982) described a patient who in one testing session was able to read aloud 95 per cent of a list of content words including uncommon words such as 'decree' and 'phrase' but only 8 per cent of a list of non-words. He frequently read non-words as a visually similar real word; for example, he read 'soof' as 'soot'. This pattern suggests that patients with this pattern of reading difficulty, known as phonological dyslexia, cannot apply grapheme–phoneme conversion procedures but have retained the ability to pronounce words that are known to them because the lexical-semantic route is spared.

Sometimes the difficulty with reading non-words is very marked and is associated with a number of other features. The most striking of these is the **semantic error**, where a word is read aloud as another word which need not be similar in the way it looks or sounds to the target word but is similar in meaning. So, for example, 'cost' might be read as 'money', 'city' as 'town' and 'duel' as 'sword'. The presence of such errors alongside difficulty with non-words signals that the disorder may be a case of deep dyslexia (Marshall and Newcombe, 1973; Coltheart, 1980b). Other features commonly associated with deep dyslexia include a strong tendency for concrete imageable words to be easier to read than abstract words and for grammatical function words to be particularly problematic. As well as the occurrence of semantic errors, visual errors tend to occur, such as the misreading of 'signal' as 'single' and 'decree' as degree' and even what are known as 'visual-then-semantic' errors, where 'sympathy' may be read as 'orchestra', presumably because a visual error has led to it being interpreted as 'symphony' and then a semantic error has led to 'symphony' being read as 'orchestra'.

Deep dyslexia is associated with damage to the temporal lobe of the left hemisphere and one approach to explaining its pattern of features is to assume that there is impairment to the normal left hemisphere reading system. It has been argued (Morton and Patterson, 1987) that a number of components of the system become damaged in parallel. Not only has the grapheme-to-phoneme route been lost, as in phonological dyslexia, but there must also be some form of lexical deficit to explain why function words are so problematic and there must be impairment to the semantic system to explain semantic errors, not to mention impairments affecting visual analysis to explain visual errors. It is not easy to explain why such a range of deficits should occur together, yet deep dyslexia is a consistently recurring pattern of symptoms.

A quite different approach to explaining the pattern of features of deep dyslexia has been proposed by Coltheart (1980b, 1987) and by Saffran *et al.* (1987). It is argued that patients with deep dyslexia are reading with the right rather than the left hemisphere. According to this 'right hemisphere hypothesis', in deep dyslexia a lesion has disrupted visual access to the reading system in the left hemisphere but the right hemisphere is able to identify the word and assign semantics to it. This semantic information is then transferred to the intact left hemisphere speech output system which then allows the word to be spoken. The hypothesis explains the occurrence of semantic errors by arguing that the right hemisphere may generate a range of associates of the word and one of these other semantic representations may get transmitted to the left hemisphere. Abstract words and function words may be less well represented in the right hemisphere, where meaning is hypothesised to be more image-based, and therefore these words would be read less well by that hemisphere. Similarly non-words, not having meaning, could not be accessed by this postulated system.

The idea that word identification and semantic access can occur in the right hemisphere is a far cry from the classic language circuit of the left hemisphere as presented by Geschwind (1965). However, there has been growing evidence that the right hemisphere can read, even if it cannot speak. In split-brain studies (Sperry and Gazzaniga, 1975), when a word was flashed to the right hemisphere, some patients could pick out from an array of objects the one that the word represented. In studies of people with intact brains using the split-field method, there is evidence that words can be recognised in the right hemisphere and that, when presented to the right hemisphere, words high in imagery are reported better than those lower in imagery, but this difference does not apply when the words are presented to the left hemisphere (e.g. Ellis and Shepherd, 1974). This finding, though controversial (Patterson and Besner, 1984), is in line with the notion that the right hemisphere can process concrete, imageable words but is relatively poor at processing other types of words. Studies of semantic priming with normal subjects have also provided evidence which may suggest differences in semantic processing between the right and left hemispheres (Beeman *et al.*, 1994). They concluded that words presented to the right hemisphere result in weaker levels of activation of semantic associates over a wider range than those presented to the left hemisphere.

Deep dyslexia provides an excellent demonstration of a number of aspects of the psycholinguistic approach: it has been recognised through a detailed analysis of types of reading task that each patient can and cannot do and of the types of errors made. The pattern of symptoms has, however, been difficult to explain in a parsimonious way by the sorts of model based on a modular approach. One alternative model is based on the idea that one brain area may compensate for injury by taking over some of the function of a damaged area and this right hemisphere hypothesis may be confirmed by the results of functional scanning of the brains of people with deep dyslexia while they are reading different types of words. Alternatively, it may be that eventually a connectionist network account of language function in the brain may be able to simulate the impact of a brain lesion that will result in the pattern of deficits characteristic of deep dyslexia and indeed the other dyslexias (Hinton and Shallice, 1991; Plaut and Shallice, 1993) (see Chapter 10).

9.5 Disruption to processing of syntax

Impairments of syntactic aspects of language production have traditionally been associated with Broca's aphasia and the incidence of such impairments has been termed **agrammatism** by neuropsychologists.

For many years people with Broca's aphasia were described as having difficulties with producing language but having the ability to understand what is said to them essentially intact. Clinical observations and performance on language tests often backed up this view. However, since the 1970s when psycholinguists began to use more sophisticated tests of language comprehension, the traditional view has had to be reassessed.

In 1976 Carramazza and Zurif published a paper in which language comprehension of patients with aphasia was examined. Patients heard sentences that were either non-reversible such as (1) or reversible such as (2) and had to choose a picture to match the sentence (see Section 8.3 for discussion of reversible and non-reversible sentences).

(1) The bicycle that the boy is holding is broken.
(2) The man that the woman is hugging is happy.

In line with their known comprehension difficulties, patients with Wernicke's aphasia did poorly on both types of sentence. Patients with Broca's aphasia performed well on non-reversible sentences but their performance on reversible sentences fell to chance levels. These findings suggest that patients with Broca's aphasia make use of semantic cues when they are available, as they are in most everyday situations. When semantic cues are eliminated, as in the reversible sentences, patients with Broca's aphasia can be seen to have difficulties that suggest subtle deficits in parsing, the process of computing the syntactic structure of sentences (see Section 8.6). Backing up this proposal was the finding that simple reversible sentences such as (3) were liable to be be misinterpreted (Schwartz *et al.*, 1980).

(3) The policeman shot the robber.

It appeared that Broca's aphasia might result in virtually complete loss of syntactic ability, with agrammatism characterising comprehension as well as production of language (Berndt and Caramazza, 1980). Such a view might imply that the language module that controls syntax is located in Broca's area and is put out of commission when damage occurs in that area.

However, subsequent research has complicated such a picture. One such complication arises from research carried out by Linebarger et al. (1983), who investigated the ability of patients with Broca's aphasia to make judgements about whether or not sentences were grammatical. On the whole the patients performed surprisingly well. Their performance was particularly good on sentences in which the structure was distorted as in (4).

(4)   How many did you see birds in the park?

They were not so good at judging sentences where an inappropriate pronoun had been used such as (5).

(5)   The little boy fell down, didn't it?

It may be that patients with Broca's aphasia have knowledge of syntax that they can employ in the making of grammaticality judgements when sufficient time is available to them, but may not be able to access this knowledge quickly enough in comprehension of ongoing speech.

Further complications arise from growing evidence that individual patients may show some of the symptoms of agrammatism without showing others, and so any search for a single underlying deficit may be fruitless. For example, while many patients have difficulty both with ordering words into sentences and with using function words and inflections, Saffran et al. (1980) described a patient who used function words and inflections but had great difficulty in arranging words into grammatical sentences. Kolk et al. (1985) reported on two patients whose speech production was severely agrammatic but whose comprehension was at, or near, normal levels. Even the tendency to omit function words and inflections does not apply across the board to all such elements, with some elements more likely to be omitted than others. For instance, detailed analysis of speech output indicates that the '-s' ending on nouns is much more likely to be omitted when it is a possessive '-s' than when it is a plural '-s' (Goodglass and Berko, 1960; Kean, 1977; Caplan, 1992).

The complex picture that has emerged from recent research has led to debate about whether the terms Broca's aphasia and agrammatism should be abandoned as, it is argued, they no longer describe a meaningful syndrome. As has been indicated, single case studies have shown dissociations between the three main symptoms of agrammatism: sentence construction deficit, grammatical element loss and syntactic comprehension deficit (Saffran et al., 1980; Howard, 1985; Berndt, 1987). Other patients show a pattern of impairment similar to that of Broca's aphasia, even though their lesions are outside Broca's area (Caplan and Hildebrandt, 1988).

Caramazza's arguments about the nonviability of the syndrome approach have particular relevance to the concept of agrammatism. He proposes that, if there is no one syndrome of agrammatism, the methodological implication is that it is no longer meaningful to carry out research that involves groups of patients with this clinical diagnosis (Badecker and Caramazza, 1985). In a review of what Ellis and Young (1988) call 'the saga of agrammatism', Howard (1985) argued that a fundamental mistake was made in taking a cluster of symptoms and creating the notion of a 'syndrome' of agrammatism, a process of reification by which patients are seen as exemplars of the syndrome rather than as individuals with qualitatively different patterns of impairment. Such arguments led to a debate among aphasiologists, many of whom believe that, even if single case studies show dissociations among symptoms of a classic syndrome such as Broca's aphasia, it is still convenient to use the classic syndrome labels (Caplan, 1986, 1992) and that group studies should not be rejected entirely (Shallice, 1988).

Attempts to explain the nature of agrammatism continue to be pursued and recent approaches have attempted to explain it not as a loss of syntactic processing ability but as a disruption to it, because of an impairment in working memory. In this capacity approach, damage to Broca's area is thought to result in a lessening in processing capacity (Kolk and van Grunsven, 1985; Waters et al., 1991; Carpenter et al., 1994; Waters and Caplan, 1996). Carpenter et al. (1994) simulated agrammatism in normal speakers by reducing their working memory capacity. The lessening of processing capacity may come about either in a postulated separate working memory buffer dedicated to syntactic processes (Waters et al., 1991; Waters and Caplan, 1996), or in a general capacity, used by a range of language processes, not just syntax (Carpenter et al., 1994). According to the capacity approach, when the syntax of sentences becomes more complex, capacity limits are exceeded and syntactic parsing is impaired.

Research and theorising centred on the concept of agrammatism continues, despite Badecker and Caramazza's (1985) and Howard's (1985) arguments that the concept has long outlived its usefulness.

9.6 Disruption to processing of discourse

Can we find patients whose brain injury leads them to have particular difficulty at the level of processing of discourse, the level that is concerned with making inferences, going beyond literal meanings, drawing on knowledge of the listener and social conventions (see Section 8.7)?

In fact, many patients with aphasia perform surprisingly well on tasks that require comprehending and retaining aspects of discourse, relative to their problems at lexical and syntactic levels (Caplan, 1992). For example, Armus et al. (1989) found evidence that knowledge of scripts can be preserved in patients with aphasia. Scripts are abstract descriptions of events, for instance, eating a meal in a restaurant involves ordering, being served with food, eating and paying the bill. Subjects in their study performed as well as control subjects in discriminating events that that would occur in a script from those that would not be expected to occur and in ordering events in scripts.

However, some patients have difficulties affecting the comprehension of discourse but do not have other language impairments, and they are of particular interest from a neuropsychological point of view. These patients tend to have lesions in the right hemisphere (Joanette and Brownell, 1990). Although they may be able to tell coherent stories and to show a knowledge of scripts, some subtle disturbances of discourse processes can be found. One area that is affected is the ability to appreciate punchlines in jokes. In a study by Brownell *et al.* (1983), patients with right hemisphere lesions heard and read the start of a joke and then had to choose a humorous continuation of it from three possibilities: the real punchline, a *non sequitur* and a non humorous but coherent ending. One joke went as follows:

> The quack was selling a potion which he claimed would make men live to a great age. He claimed he himself was hale and hearty and over 300 years old. 'Is he really as old as that?' asked a listener of the youthful assistant. 'I can't say,' said the assistant:
> *Correct punchline*: 'I've only worked with him for 100 years.'
> *Non sequitur*: 'There are over 300 days in the year.'
> *Coherent non humorous ending*: 'I don't know how old he is.'

Patients with right hemisphere lesions made more errors than controls and were more likely to choose *non sequitur* endings, implying that they knew there should be an element of surprise in the ending but not how to make it coherent with the rest of the joke.

In a study by Hough (1990), two types of stories were read to patients with right hemisphere lesions and to a non-brain injured control group and questions about the stories asked. In one set of stories the theme of the story was stated at the outset and in the other the statement of the theme was delayed until the end. Patients with right hemisphere lesions performed very much worse when the theme was not stated till the end, suggesting they had particular difficulty in integrating the information in the sentences into a coherent theme.

In their own conversation too, patients with right hemisphere lesions show evidence of impairments at discourse level. They tend to mention specific information without giving the setting or theme for what they are talking about (Myers, 1993). They do not appear sensitive to other speakers' mood or intonation cues and their own intonation is very flat, leading sometimes to a misdiagnosis of depression (Brownell *et al.*, 1995). They have difficulties in picking up on ambiguities, metaphor and irony and may interpret familiar idioms such as 'pull your socks up' literally (Winner and Gardner, 1977). Such a pattern of symptoms has come to be termed the 'right hemisphere syndrome'. It remains to be seen whether this so-called syndrome will turn out to be caused by a single underlying deficit or whether, as with agrammatism, detailed single case studies will demonstrate dissociations between component processes.

Summary

- The way we view localisation of language functions has changed considerably from the earlier notion of the classic language circuit. Rather than classifying processes at the level of speech input and speech output, we now have considerably more sophisticated models of language processing which allow psycholinguists to investigate impairment of quite specific aspects of phonological, semantic, syntactic and discourse processes.

259

- Methods have also evolved, with increased focus on detailed analysis of single cases rather than group studies. Methods such as PET scans and fMRI scans are making a considerable impact on our understanding of language processing in both the intact brain and in people with disorders of language.
- There is substantial evidence that the components of the classic language circuitry are important in language functioning. However, the picture is considerably more complex than early theorists believed.
- The cognitive neuropsychological approach has provided useful models of the components and processes of language functioning, allowing systematic investigation of where in the system an individual's impairment in language functioning may lie.
- There is increasing indication from patterns of dissociation of language functions in people with brain injury that many components of the language processing system, though richly interconnected, are to some extent modular in their organisation.

Further reading

Caplan, D. (1992). *Language Structure, Processing and Disorders*. Cambridge, MA.: MIT Press. This book reviews psycholinguistic research and theory on processing of words, sentences and discourse, relating each to an understanding of language disorders in adults with neurological disorders and concluding with a chapter on diagnosis and treatment.

Ellis, A.W. and Young, A.W. (1996). *Human Cognitive Neuropsychology: A Textbook with Readings*. Hove: Psychology Press. The authors provide a very clear introduction to cognitive neuropsychology and a carefully argued rationale for a model of the processes involved in understanding and reading, saying and writing single words, a model that has been widely adopted in neuropsychological research and intervention. The revised edition includes a set of readings from books and journal articles which includes a paper on Derek B, described in Section 9.4.

Gardner, H. (1977). *The Shattered Mind*. Hove: Psychology Press. Although written some time ago the section on language in this book has yet to be equalled as a colourful and gripping introduction to patients with aphasia and the challenges they provide for an understanding of language function in the brain.

Parkin, A.J. (1996). *Explorations in Cognitive Psychology*. Oxford: Blackwell. The sections on disorders of language provide a clear overview of the cognitive neuropsychological approach.

Campbell, R. (ed.) (1992). *Mental Lives: Case Studies in Cognition*. Oxford: Blackwell. This is a collection of accounts by cognitive psychologists of individuals whose cognitive functioning poses questions for our understanding of mental processes. More detail about Derek B (described in Section 9.4) can be found in the chapter by Franklin and Howard.

Computational models of cognition

I T IS THE INTENTION in this chapter to outline some of the methods that have been used to model cognition. However, rather than simply give a disconnected list of techniques and recipes, we choose to emphasise some fundamental principles and high-level issues. Of course, we have to make any abstract ideas concrete with examples but the reader should not come away with the impression that, just because a model has not been given here for a particular cognitive process, no such model exists.

10.1 Theories of cognition: from metaphors to computational models

What constitutes a theory of cognition? What does it mean to build a model of a cognitive process? We will use the term 'theory' in a fairly liberal way; any body of concepts, ideas or hypothetical structures which enable us to understand, explain or predict some of the experimental data relating to an aspect of cognition will be deemed to be a theory. Newell (1990) also adopts such a stance and it seems better to start from such a catholic perspective than to become embroiled in the arguments about 'theory-chauvinism' that might ensue from being too specific in our requirements.

Why do we need theories of cognition? A collection of experimental data does not, of itself, constitute a science of cognition. Science proceeds by developing theories that explain a body of data and make predictions for the outcome of new experiments. If the predictions are wrong we may modify the theory or, if the results of this process are cumbersome and Byzantine, the theory may be dropped altogether. Experimental work does not operate in a vacuum; experiments should be designed to answer specific questions. These may be thought of as hypotheses to be tested *per se* but, more usually, they will only make sense within a wider theoretical framework that includes many tacit assumptions (Chapter 1, Section 1.1). Of course, the converse also applies; theories are prone to be irrelevant for explaining cognition unless they make contact with the relevant body of data.

Although we have allowed many candidates to be admitted to the status of theory, not all theories are of an equivalent form. Take, for example, the 'zoom-lens' theory of visual attention proposed by Erikson (1990). This claims that visual attention is restricted to a disc-like area much like that in the field of a camera lens. However, as in the case of a zoom-lens, the area of attention may be altered to encompass more or less of the visual field. The theory then predicts that, when a target (for example, in a letter recognition task) is placed within the attentional area, it will be recognised more rapidly than one which is placed outside this area. Although there is evidence both for and against this outcome, the point to emphasise here is that it is a perfectly good theory in that it posits a model of visual attention which has testable predictions. On the other hand, its status is really that of an analogy with, or metaphor for, visual attention as it makes no effort to make quantitative predictions (there are no numbers for us to measure) and further, it is a description of the empirical behaviour of attention rather than the underlying mechanisms. In spite of this, such metaphors can be useful in that they help direct an experimental programme by posing questions (e.g. is the visual attentional field like a variable spatial disc?).

Another type of theory goes one step further and hypothesises the existence of mechanisms that are supposed to be responsible for behaviour. Consider the multistore models of memory (e.g. Atkinson and Shiffrin, 1968) of which a typical example is shown in Figure 10.1. Three mechanisms are postulated together with their interrelationships. The arrows are supposed to indicate the flow of information and this example is typical of models which conform to this view of cognition as information processing.

Until now we have cavalierly used the terms 'model' and 'theory' in an interchangeable way. Although this is often the case in everyday parlance, it is timely at this stage to attempt to refine the use of these terms. A 'model' of cognitive process is a structure or system for which we believe it is useful to say that the process behaves 'as if' it were the model system. Thus, in the memory example given in Figure 10.1, it is proposed that memory behaves *as if* it were composed of three sequential stages of information processing. The corresponding theory looks at the wider picture as it were and has, additionally, to say something about how the cognitive process relates to or maps onto the model. In particular it must say how we are to relate experimental results to the model and how we are to interpret its output to obtain experimental predictions.

In spite of being more sophisticated than a simple analogy, the theory of memory given above is inadequate in one respect; it does not provide quantitative numerical or symbolic output *per se* and any predictions will be qualitative, addressing the nature of trends and ordering within data. For example, this model implies that more rehearsal will assist the laying down of long-term memories but we can say nothing about any mathematical laws relating the degree of rehearsal to memory. However, suppose we were to take this model and embody its behaviour in a computer program. We are now forced to articulate and make precise aspects of the theory which were previously unspecified. For example, how exactly would a visual scene be encoded as input and how would the information at each stage be represented in the model? Possible representations may make use of numbers, symbols or a mix of both; in any case we have to flesh out the details of how this is to be done. As we will see, the theme of representation is one which is central to the whole enterprise of model construction. Having instantiated a model as a computer program we can now simulate the process of storing memories and derive quantitative predictions which are testable in the laboratory and may be compared directly with the data. This process is not, however, risk-free; we must be sure that

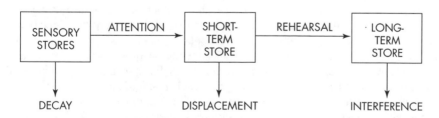

Figure 10.1 Typical multistore model of memory

we understand which low-level details are part of the cognitive model and which are by-products of having to implement it in a particular computer language.

In summary, theories of cognition come in several flavours ranging from high-level metaphors and analogies, to full simulation models in which low-level details are articulated and which generate quantitative prediction. One view would hold that the different types of model are quite unrelated to each other. Another view is to think of the transition from metaphor to simulation as a process of refinement. Thus, we might imagine endowing the zoom-lens model with systemic mechanism and, subsequently, implementing this in a full simulation. It is the intention of this chapter to focus primarily on models which have reached the maturity associated with low-level detail and computer simulation.

Paradigms and frameworks

Historically, there have been many general ways of thinking about the brain and the mind, although the earliest of these would now be regarded as pre-scientific. Descartes thought that it was controlled via the passage of fluid in the supposed 'nerve tubes' of some complex hydraulic system. Later, as new technologies emerged, the brain was likened to a telephone exchange. This might be considered to be the first model of the brain as an information processing system. A telephone exchange certainly processes information but does so in a rather passive way. More recently, the digital computer has offered more powerful ways of thinking about information processing and therefore more potential for models of the brain and mind.

At this point we wish to be sure about what we mean by information processing. In cognitive science this phrase has come to refer to a rather narrow definition which presupposes the manipulation of symbols according to a set of rules embodied in a program running on a conventional digital computer. This approach will be detailed later but it also goes under the name of classical cognitivism or simply **cognitivism** (Clark, 1990). In contrast to this we wish to broaden the definition of information processing to allow working with numbers, as performed by **neural networks** or **connectionist systems**. These are based on architectures that are supposed to more closely represent the circuits of neurons found in the brain, although the extent to which this is the case will warrant further discussion below. It is also possible to construct hybrids which make use of both symbolic and connectionist techniques.

The term **paradigm** was introduced by Kuhn (1970) to denote the general arena within which a branch of science operates. It does not necessarily refer to a specific theory in isolation (although one or more of these may be crucial) but rather to an overarching framework which contains a set of general assumptions and ideas. A characteristic hallmark of all information processing theories, and therefore of the information processing paradigm, is that they make use of internal **representations** of the outside world upon which manipulations are carried out that allow the cognitive system to draw conclusions about its environment. For example, suppose we are given two collections of objects and are asked how many objects there are altogether. One way would be to simply count serially through both sets and announce the answer. Another way would be to count the items in each set and then add them together. In this method, we internalise (encode) the numbers in each set, representing them in some way 'in our heads', and then perform a manipulation (the process of addition) on these representations. Finally, we decode the result by transforming the internal representation of the answer to a speech utterance or written token.

The nature of the information-processing paradigm will become clearer as each one of its variants alluded to above (symbols, networks, hybrids) is articulated in detail. However, there is one framework which is apparently at odds with even the wider remit of information processing outlined above. In the new field of **situated robotics** or behaviour-based robotics (Hallam and Malcolm, 1994), small autonomous machines interact directly with an environment to display simple 'intelligent', ecologically relevant behaviours such as wall avoidance, coping with movement on rough terrain, and seeking out the source of simple stimuli. The assumption here is that intelligence can only really be described in the context of a cognitive agent that is connected to its environment via sensory input and motor effector output. Intelligence is an emergent property of the intimate relation between the agent and the environment rather than something intrinsic to the agent itself. In pursuing this line, the workers in this field have abandoned any attempt to build a representational model of the world and rely on direct processing of the environmental stimuli. Although this framework circumvents many of the problems that are encountered in the process of building complex representations, it appears to echo some of the claims of the behaviourists in their emphasis on the study of stimulus–response associations at the expense of mental states. As in the case of behaviourism, it does not appear clear how this approach will scale up to capture the full richness and diversity of human cognition. Nevertheless, the agent–environment interaction stressed by the workers in situated robotics may prove to be a key aspect in understanding the nature of intelligence.

Whatever theoretical stance we take there is another question that is worthy of our attention here. Is it possible to build a general theory of cognition in which a uniform model architecture and set of operational principles can account for all cognitive processes? The alternative is that, within a given paradigm, we may have to construct several discrete models whose structures differ and which make use of different representations. This point is taken up by Newell (1990), who argues for unified models and two examples of these (Soar and ACT*) will be discussed later.

Studying cognition as computation

If, for the moment, we leave aside the stance of the situated roboticists, the information processing paradigm described so far views cognition and perception as processes of computation that solve problems about the world and the relation of the cognitive agent with its environment. How should we go about the business of building computational cognitive models?

In his book on vision David Marr (1982) set out a clarification of the methodology that he believed underpins an attempt to model *any* computational system. There are two ingredients to Marr's approach. The first concerns the nature of the internal representation of information used in the computation. The second (and major) strand to Marr's methodology is the setting of the problem in a hierarchical scheme which attempts to answer three different but related questions. The first and top-level of these asks: *What* is the goal of the computation and *why* is it being carried out? At the next level we ask: *How* is the computation to be performed? This will be specified by an algorithm or procedure of some kind and it is at this level that we normally invoke the knowledge representation to be used. Finally, we want to know: On what hardware is the computation to be *implemented*?

Marr illustrated his scheme using an example of computing a bill in a supermarket with a cash register. In answer to the top-level question of *what* is being computed here, it is the arithmetical operation of addition. As to *why* this is being done, it is simply that the laws of addition reflect or model the way we should accumulate prices from piles of goods in a trolley; it is incorrect, for example, to multiply the prices together. Next we wish to know how we do this arithmetic and the answer is that it is done by the normal procedure taught at school where we add individual digits in columns and carry over to the next column if required. Note that the question of representation rears its head here and we assume one in which numbers are denoted using the Arabic numerals $(0,1,2 \ldots 8,9)$.[1] As for the implementation, this occurs using logic gates made out of silicon, silicon-oxide and metal. Alternative implementations might make use of an older mechanical machine or pencil and paper. Notice that, as presented, the three levels are independent. In particular the type of algorithm used is quite independent of the particular implementation and, for any given computation, we may choose from a variety of algorithms to achieve the same final result.

The picture outlined by Marr with clearly defined boundaries between levels of the hierarchy is not always satisfied in practice. However, it is often useful to keep the scheme in mind when tackling a problem in cognitive science and to step back to look at the wood (computational level) rather than the trees (algorithm/implementation) that threaten to obscure the fundamental principles at work.

AI, psychology and cognitive science

Suppose we build a model of some cognitive process which performs almost perfectly according to the specification; for example, we might have a semantic memory system that never makes errors on recall. Is this likely to be an accurate model of the corresponding human processing used in this task? Almost certainly not since, if it was, it would have performance characteristics similar to humans, warts and all. If on the other hand, a model shows the same trends in behaviour as humans do in experimental situations, we have reason to believe that it might share

---

1 Machines for the manipulation of financial quantities often work with decimal representations rather than binary because of the possibility of incurring rounding errors when converting to and from binary.

similar internal structures and processes to those used in human cognition. Similarly, if the model shows a similar degradation of performance under damage to that of humans who have suffered from brain lesions, then this might also be taken as support for the model's biological integrity. As an analogy we might consider the problem of heavier than air flight; birds are the biological solution and aircraft the man-made equivalent, but do they achieve their common goal by the same methods? Thus it is useful to distinguish between a **computationally adequate** model of some aspect of cognition which adheres to some formal speci- fication, and a **cognitively faithful** model which may not meet the specification in full, but which is nevertheless closer to its human counterpart (for a discussion of this issue in connection with perception, see Gurney and Wright, 1996).

Under certain circumstances however, we may not be concerned with emulating human performance; our goal may be to construct a computationally adequate cognate agent to perform a certain task, irrespective of its internal struc- ture. This is nominally the agenda of workers in the field of Artificial Intelligence, or AI, who have sought to build intelligent systems (computer programs) using symbol-based approaches. This does not deny the fact that psychological modelling and AI enjoy a special relationship; indeed the two have been closely associated for many years, continually borrowing from each other's insights, and have tradi- tionally been the main ingredients in the interdisciplinary area of cognitive science. Workers in this area *are* concerned with the psychological plausibility of their models although they may make use of AI techniques. With the recent advent of connectionism, cognitive science now embraces a wider range of modelling techniques and the hegemony of classical AI no longer prevails. Cognitive scien- tists are also interested in high-level philosophical issues surrounding the subject and in the impact of neuroscientific knowledge; for an introduction to the role of each of these areas in cognitive science see the book by Gardner (1985).

Some see the AI-connectionist rivalry as a genuine schism in methodology. We will proceed by outlining both approaches followed by a 'compare and contrast' exercise, at the end of which it should be apparent that some synthesis is possible and both have a role to play.

10.2 Symbol-based systems

In this paradigm we attempt to capture knowledge as a set of irreducible objects – the symbols – and to model cognition as a series of processes that manipulate these symbols according to a set of well-defined rules which may be combined into a set of 'recipes' or **algorithms**. The symbols stand for or represent things, ideas or concepts which the cognitive process is supposed to deal with. The mapping between symbols and things in the world then defines a representation of the problem. The formal articulation of the symbolic paradigm has been made most vigorously by Newell and Simon (1976). They believe that symbol-based systems are necessary and sufficient for the instantiation of intelligence and, assuming that the symbols are brought into existence in a computer implementation, this stance becomes their so-called **physical symbol hypothesis**.

An example: playing chess

A simple example will serve to illustrate the main characteristics of the symbolic approach. The details of the example here have been chosen for pedagogical reasons rather than any relation to genuine chess programs. The first ingredient is a method for describing the state of the board at any time. This might easily be represented by assigning symbolic tokens to the pieces and using a grid system for the squares in which board columns are labelled (symbolised) by letters (a–h) and board rows by numbers (1–8). It then makes sense to say, for example, that 'white_pawn (2) is on square (d3)'. Any position or state of the game is then represented by a suitably ordered array of piece and grid symbols. Note that the symbolic token for 'white_pawn (2)' does not contain within it any knowledge of white pawns in relation to the game (such as legal moves, intrinsic value, etc.). Rather, the symbolic token is simply a marker which designates (or points to) the fact that this knowledge is pertinent and may then be accessed when needed. This illustrates the power of the symbolic approach which stems from the way in which symbols 'stand for' something else and their meaning is implicit in their interrelationships. Thus, the fact that white_pawn (2) is on square (d3) is encoded by some data structure in which both symbols are participants.

Next, the system must have knowledge of what constitutes a valid move. This might consist of a series of rules of the form '*if* there is a white pawn at square (d2) *and* square (d3) is empty *then* the pawn can move to square (d3)'. Of course, higher level abstractions of rules like this (which don't require specific square labels, etc.) will almost certainly be used. The use of legal moves should then guarantee that only legal board positions are obtained. Rules of the form '*if* C_1 *and* C_2 *and* . . . *then* R*' are known as **production rules** or simply productions, since they produce a result R if the conditions C_1, C, . . . prevail. They are one form of knowledge representation in symbolic systems – others will be described on p. 272.

So far we have laid the foundations, but how is the program to 'know' how to play chess? This is done by formalising the idea of the game as a sequence of board positions or states and that play consists of a series of moves or state transitions, each of which generates a new position. Thus, the game starts in an initial state and the goal is to arrive at some final state in which the machine's pieces have achieved checkmate. In between we need some controlling strategy which tells the system how to find goal states. This will take the form of a search through the set of board states (the *state-space*) for a path from the initial to a final, winning state. In fact, of course, this is not a realistic strategy as it stands since to each machine move there are a great many opponent moves, in reply to which there are an even greater number of machine responses, etc. We therefore have a so-called *combinatorial explosion* of possibilities and we need to be more cunning in our search strategy. To this end, we might allow the machine to look a fixed number of moves ahead, evaluate the board positions there and play to ensure that the new position is more advantageous to it than the one where it started. This will necessitate assigning a value to board states which measures the 'goodness' or utility of the position. For example, moves which result in loss of pieces will (usually) score poorly. The search may be guided by more rules or **heuristics** which embody further knowledge of the game, for example, '*if* your Queen is placed under attack *then* score poorly' or '*if* material loss is incurred *then* this should be done only if mate can be guaranteed in two moves'.

To summarise the main ingredients in our approach: symbolic descriptions are all-pervasive in helping to internalise the game of chess and its rules. The game is conceived of as a search through a state-space of board positions (starting with the conventional opening state) for final states that correspond to checkmate. In the case of chess this space is very large and the search must proceed piecemeal by using a utility function for each legal board state. Knowledge about the game is represented as a series of production rules; this includes knowledge to ensure legal moves, together with heuristics that aid the search. Symbols, production rules, searching in state-space and heuristics are all characteristic features of symbolic systems. Knowledge representations other than production rules are used but these will nevertheless be subject to manipulation by procedures or algorithms that are implemented in some high-level computer language.

Symbols and computers

The rise of the symbolic modelling approach was driven to a large extent by work in AI which, in turn, had many of its ideas channelled by the nature of general purpose computers. This section explores the intimate relation between the two.

Although the first computers were built to perform numerical calculations, it was apparent to the early workers that the machines they had built were also capable of manipulating symbols, since the machines themselves knew nothing of the semantics of the strings of binary digits (0s and 1s or bits) stored in their memories. Thus, Alan Turing, speaking in 1947 about the design for the proposed Automatic Computing Engine (ACE), saw the potential to deal with complex game-playing situations like chess: 'Given a position in chess the machine could be made to list all the "winning combinations" to a depth of about three moves' (cited in Hodges, 1985).

All general purpose, digital computers share the same underlying architecture which constitutes a natural way to implement symbolic, AI models of cognition. This architecture is named after John von Neumann who was instrumental in developing some of the early computers during the Second World War. The von Neumann machine consists of a Central Processing Unit (CPU) and a memory. The latter contains instructions and data while the CPU performs operations on the data according to a stored program also contained in the memory.

The von Neumann machine/computer repeatedly performs the following cycle of events:

1   Fetch an instruction from memory.
2   Fetch any data required by the instruction from memory.
3   Execute the instruction (process the data).
4   Store results in memory.
5   Go back to step 1.

The instructions available to the CPU constitute the machine instruction set and usually consist of very low-level (simple) operations. It is now possible to see how the this architecture lends itself naturally to instantiating symbolic AI systems. The symbols are represented as bit-patterns in memory locations which are accessed by the CPU. The algorithms (including search strategies and rules) are then articulated as computer programs by gradually breaking them down into successively smaller operations until these consist of members of the machine instruction set.

The machines on which the modern AI fraternity run their algorithms have not changed in any fundamental conceptual way from the pilot ACE, all of these being examples of the classic von Neumann architecture. Granted, there has been a speed increase of several orders of magnitude, and hardware parallelism is sometimes available, but contemporary 'AI engines' are still vehicles for the instantiation of the theoretic stance which claims that intelligent behaviour can be described completely as a process of formal, algorithmic symbol manipulation.

Knowledge representation

We have seen (in the chess example) how knowledge may be represented in a symbolic system as a set of production rules. This method will be fleshed out a little further below but, in the meantime, we will look at alternative ways of knowledge representation. The problem of representation is crucial to any cognitive model and its description must occur prior to elucidating any associated processing or dynamics.

Semantic nets

Semantic networks are a class of systems for representing knowledge that have been used for models of memory, concept storage and sentence understanding. They consist of a set of nodes, which represent objects or concepts, and links between nodes that indicate inter-node relationships. For example, the network shown in Figure 10.2 represents knowledge about a small subset of the bird family considered as a subclass of all animals. Thus, a canary is a bird because it is connected to the *bird* node via a link labelled with the relation 'is-a'; the bird named 'Canny' is an instance of the class of canaries because it is connected to the *canary* node via a link indicating this. It is apparent that the example network represents a hierarchy of ever more specific objects, from animals in general through birds and species to particular instances of birds. This is not necessarily the case but, where it applies, the implication is that knowledge about a general class is held at the node representing it and is not repeated at nodes which are more specific (but for which the knowledge applies). This property is known as inheritance and holds, say, for the *canary* node which inherits all the information supplied about birds (because it 'is-a' bird). Thus we infer that a canary's main locomotion is flying and that it is an animal. On the other hand, knowledge which is specific to a node overrides any contradictory inheritance so that, while an *ostrich* is a bird and, by inheritance, has flying as its main locomotion, it also has the node-specific main locomotion link to *running* which therefore prevails.

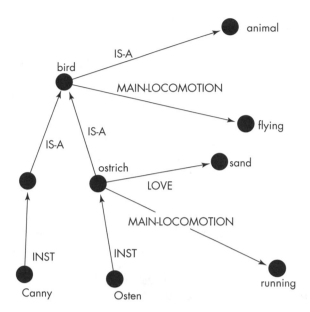

Figure 10.2 Semantic network

The example given above is similar to that of Collins and Quillian (1969) which attempted to model the way categories were stored and accessed in human memory. Accessing knowledge in the network is done by starting at the node we wish to enquire about and moving along links (applying inheritance) until we reach a node that supplies the required information. Thus, according to the model, if someone is asked if the bird named 'Canny' can fly they should take longer to answer than if they are asked if canaries (in general) can fly, since the former question requires traversing two links in the net whereas the latter only uses one. A similar argument would be made about asking if Canny is a bird. Collins and Quillian conducted experimental work based on this type of query and found their predictions were, indeed, borne out by their data.

A slightly different type of network was used by Collins and Loftus (1975) to model similarity relations in memory. These nets had no special relationships along their links but worked by spreading activity from the initial nodes and noting if the activity traces intersected at any time, thereby signifying a relationship. For example, in order to answer the previous query 'Can Canny fly?, the nodes for flying and Canny would be initialised and activity spread outwards along all links emanating from them. The resulting paths or traces of activity would intersect at the *canary* and *bird* nodes signifying a semantic link between the two nodes and indicating an affirmative response to the question.

Schemata, frames and scripts

Semantic nets with their item-attribute structure provide a limited framework for knowledge representation. This is particularly evident in respect of much of our so-called commonsense knowledge, each part of which consists of a complex mesh of ideas, objects, concepts and attributes which does not easily avail itself of a simple graphical (network) description with strict hierarchical inheritance. Two features of this type of knowledge supply clues as to how we might go about representing it. Firstly, it often refers to a stereotypical situation or schema (plural *schemata*) in which the constituent elements may change but their relations are constant and, secondly, there is the possibility for hierarchical *chunking* where a new schema may have elements consisting of entire schemata in themselves. As an example, consider the schema implied by a trip to eat out at a restaurant. Thus, a group of friends drive to a restaurant and wait to be seated. They are given menus, order drinks and each person chooses from the menu. The meal arrives, people eat, order sweets and coffee and pay the bill. Note that there are many variations on this theme which are provided by changing the values of variables in a number of *slots*. Thus, instead of a group of friends, we might have a family group; instead of driving to the restaurant they may take a taxi or use public transport; instead of waiting to be seated they may go straight to a table or have a drink at the bar first, etc. In spite of these variations the temporal sequence of events remains the same as does the relation between the slots. In this way schemata encode generic knowledge that may be applied to many situations. Further, each slot may consist of its own schema. For example, taking a taxi (to get to the restaurant) may be broken down into: wait at kerb, hail taxi, give directions, pay driver. Finally, in the absence of information to the contrary we assume that each slot is filled with some default value (group of friends, drive to restaurant, etc.).

There have been several similar theories that have refined the schemata representation in its form outlined above. Schank and Abelson (1977) coined the term **'script'** for their version of schema used to account for knowledge of everyday situations (indeed their famous restaurant script is the inspiration for the above example). Rumelhart (1975) introduced **story grammars** to help explain the comprehension of stories and Minsky (1975) invoked a structure called **frames** for visual perception.

Production systems

These embody the archetypal representation technique for symbolic systems introduced earlier. Recall that they consist of a set of conditional rules of the form '*if C_1 and C_2 and ... then R*' where C_1 and C_2 are conditions to be met and R is the result or consequence implied by these conditions. Psychologically we are supposed to think of a collection of items (the conditions C_i) existing in a working memory. Each production rule is supposed to be constantly looking out for a match between its pre-conditions and items in working memory and, if a match is obtained, the rule 'fires' and the result of the production is transferred into working memory. This new item may then be able to complete the pre-condition set for another production which is now allowed to fire and send its result into working memory. This iterative process is supposed to continue until no further production firings occur. This view of a production system makes it look like a pattern-matching, content-addressable memory whose operation is shown in Figure 10.3.

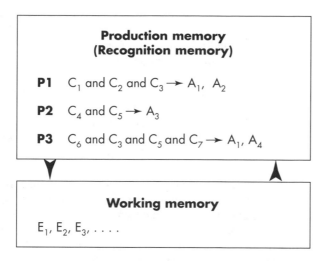

Figure 10.3 Production system as content addressable memory

Newell is the main champion of this view of production systems as models of human knowledge. It finds its fullest articulation in the system known as *Soar* (Laird *et al.*, 1984; Newell, 1990). This uses a working memory of the type outlined above with the productions constituting the long-term memory store. As with the chess example discussed on p. 268, solutions to problems take place in a state- or search-space, and goals (final states) are achieved by moving from state to state under a series of state transition inducing operators. Soar is, however, a large system and this simple scheme is supplemented by several additional features. The result is that Soar is supposed to be a unified theory of cognition; that is, it is to be thought of as a generic architecture (and accompanying computational processes) into which specific tasks can be mapped. As Newell (1990) notes, this allows for the possibility that existing cognitive theories may be taken and reframed in the language of Soar. In this way it should be possible to build on existing knowledge while embedding it within a common framework. Soar has been successfully applied to toy puzzles such as tic-tac-toe, Tower of Hanoi, etc., to problems in reasoning such as the Wason verification task, and to the implementation of large-scale expert systems, one of which (NEOMYCIN) is able to assist in the diagnosis of infectious diseases. For the most up-to-date review of its accomplishments readers should visit Soar's home page on the World Wide Web (Head, 1996).

Shortcomings of the symbolic approach

Mainstream AI (not necessarily psychologically motivated) has proved successful in many areas and indeed, with the advent of expert systems that can aid medical diagnosis or oil exploration, it has become big business. (For a brief history of its more noteworthy achievements see Raj, 1988.) However, AI has not fulfilled much of the early promise that was conjectured by the pioneers in the field. Dreyfus, in his book *What Computers Can't Do* (Dreyfus 1979), criticises the early extravagant claims of the AI practitioners and outlines the assumptions they made. Principal among these is the belief that all knowledge or information can be formalised, and that the mind can be viewed as a device that operates on information according to formal rules.

In game-playing, puzzle-solving, mathematics, etc. it is often clear how to formulate much of the knowledge representation, although the higher level heuristics may be less apparent. In less artificial domains even the 'ground rules' (as it were) may be less apparent as illustrated in the following example given by Minsky concerning the representation of the concept 'bird'.

> Let's take a very simple fact, such as all birds can fly. Well, that's true in a certain dictionary context but it's not true of all birds, so if you try to put this information in a rule-based system you'd have a little trouble. First you'd have to say if Tweetie is a bird it can fly, unless it is an ostrich or unless it's a penguin so now you're starting to get exceptions. Then somebody might say 'What if you clipped its feathers?' and you'd say 'If something is a bird and it has normal feathers and it is not an ostrich or a penguin, then it can fly'. Then someone might say 'Well what if it's dead?' so you'd reply 'If it's . . . and it's not dead then it can fly.' Someone else might say 'What if it's in a cage?', 'What if it got its feet stuck in concrete?' So you see it's almost impossible to think of any fact about the real world that's true.

This example characterises the kind of difficulty we typically get into using the symbol-based approach. It may be summarised in the notion that the rules appear 'brittle' and are easily broken. Thus, it has proved very difficult to formalise large areas of human perceptual and non-intellectual cognitive ability. These are principally the kinds of things that most of us take for granted and consist of natural language understanding, fine motor control (e.g. in sport and music) visual navigation and scene understanding, and some of the intuitive knowledge of experts in narrow domains that are non-technical in nature. Connectionist systems promise to offer an alternative that may be more suited to modelling these areas of human competence.

10.3 Connectionist systems

It is not the intention here to give a detailed description of the training and operation of connectionist systems or artificial neural networks. Several introductory accounts are readily available (Dayhoff, 1990; Gurney, 1997). Rather, the intention here is to sketch some basic principles, focus on the nature of knowledge representation and to give a flavour of the type of models that have been constructed to account for human cognition.

A connectionist system or neural network is an interconnected assembly of simple processing elements, **units** or **nodes**, whose functionality is loosely based on the animal neuron. The processing ability of the network is stored in the inter-unit connection strengths, or **weights**, usually obtained by a process of adaptation to, or learning from, a set of training patterns. The latter represent input from the external world and may range from digitised pictures, as in a visual recognition task, to phonological representations of speech for natural language understanding.

We may put some flesh on the bones of this definition by examining some of the key components of biological networks and comparing these with their artificial counterparts.

Real and artificial neurons

Real neurons communicate by stylised action potentials (voltage spikes). It is believed that different signal levels are encoded via the frequency or rate of spike production. In artificial nets, signals are often communicated simply by using a continuously variable output or activity value. Each real neuron combines the effect of incoming signals from other neurons by first passing each one of them through a synaptic contact. Synapses may be excitatory or inhibitory and have differing modulatory strengths. Thus, a strong excitatory synapse may make a significant contribution to the elicitation of action potentials in the neuron while weaker ones have little effect. Similarly, inhibitory synapses tend to prevent firing to an extent commensurate with their strength. The rate of firing of a real neuron depends, therefore, on the summed value of all its synapse-modulated inputs. This story is, of course, extremely simplified (so much so that some neuroscientists still balk at the appellation 'neural' in the context of connectionism). However, it is the version of events with which we wish to make contact.

Connectionist networks model the synapse as a single number that acts to multiply the incoming signal before sending the result to be summed with others. Thus a connectionist node or artificial neuron (see Figure 10.4) performs a linear weighted sum of its inputs with positive and negative weights corresponding

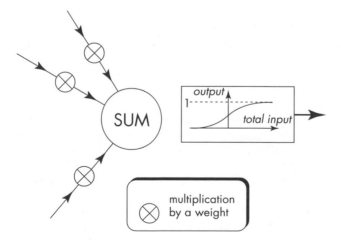

Figure 10.4 Artificial neuron

to excitatory and inhibitory synapses respectively. This total input is then often sent through a functional relation which compresses or squashes the range of the signal. We now move from individual nodes to consider networks as a whole.

Feed-forward networks

One type of arrangement of nodes in a network is shown in Figure 10.5. Here, information is presented from an external source at the bottom of the diagram and each node in the net evaluates its output. Conceptually, each node is supposed to be working independently of all the others in the net. That is, if we conceive of each node as a separate processor, they work in parallel so that the evaluation of the first layer output (say) takes only as long as the time required for a single node to produce its output. Of course, when a network is run in simulation on a conventional computer this parallelism is lost, but it should still be regarded as inherent in the connectionist architecture.

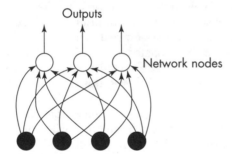

Outputs

Network nodes

External Inputs

Figure 10.5 Single layer feed-forward net

The task that the net is supposed to perform is encapsulated in a set of training examples. Each example consists of a pattern of inputs and a corresponding pattern of target outputs. In order for the net to implement the task, it must produce an output that is a close approximation, in each instance, to the target. To bring this situation about, the weights in the net must be adjusted to force each node to respond in the correct way across all exemplars. Thus, the net learns, or is trained, by a process of adaptation to the set of training patterns.

The use of target outputs means that the net undergoes **supervised learning**, since the targets are thought of in the context of a supervisory teacher supplying the desired network response to each input pattern. The general method in this case is to iteratively repeat the following sequence of steps: apply a training input pattern, find the net's output response, compare this with the target pattern, make small weight adjustments according to some **learning rule**. In contrast to this, it is possible to let the network discover regularities (clusters) in the training set for itself in which case it is said to undergo a process of **self-organisation**. We shall not be concerned a great deal with this type of learning here but there is a

Figure 10.6 Concept of pattern proximity in network generalisation

sense in which it is more biologically plausible. There are many supervised learning rules but they all work by making weight changes that depend on the size of the difference or error between the network output and the corresponding target.

What happens when a pattern is presented to a network like that in Figure 10.5 that it has not seen during training? The network must give some kind of output and we hope that this will be meaningful in the context of the task to be learned. One way in which this happens automatically occurs because a single artificial neuron will respond in a similar way to input patterns that are close to each other. What constitutes 'close' here is illustrated in Figure 10.6 with an example taken from the domain of visual pattern recognition.

Three versions of a letter 'X' are shown which are supposed to consist of a grid of small black and white squares or pixels. Suppose the 'X' on the left-hand side is the one presented during training and that a node has developed large positive weights on those inputs from the dark pixels in this pattern and negative weights to the rest. The result is that the total input to the node from this pattern will be large and positive and, given a suitable sigmoid output function, the final activity will be close to its maximum value of 1. Consider now the 'X' in the centre of the figure. Many of its pixels share a common value with the training pattern on the left and it is in this sense that the patterns are said to be close to each other. The total input to the node from the two patterns will then be approximately the same and so the final output will also be similar. The node is said to have **generalised** to give the correct output in response to the unseen 'X' in the centre.

Consider now the 'X' on the extreme right-hand side of the figure. There are no pixels in common between this and the training pattern on the left resulting in an output which is almost zero. The node has therefore failed to generalise to the 'X' on the right-hand side. The only way for a node to have similar outputs across all three patterns is for it to have large positive weights to any pixels that are dark in any of the patterns. However, this results in the node being very indiscriminate in its response, which is clearly not useful.

Psychologically, all the patterns in the figure are equivalent since they are all examples of the third from last letter in the Roman alphabet, and so we would normally require them all to elicit the same network response. The way to facilitate this is to re-represent the letters in such a way that, in the new representation, all the cognitively similar patterns (the 'X's, for example) have similar pattern representations. This requires (at least) another layer of nodes whose role is then

277

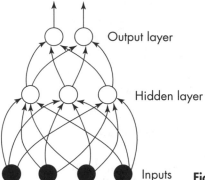

Output layer

Hidden layer

Inputs   **Figure 10.7** Multilayer feed-forward net

to transform the original input into a form suitable for a final output layer to act on (Figure 10.7; Rumelhart, 1993).

These intermediate layers are **hidden** because they take no part in the interaction of the net with the external environment. In particular, we do not directly influence their output during training via a set of target values. Instead, the hidden nodes have to learn their own internal representation of the input so as to help minimise the error at the output. However, unlike the output nodes, where there is a direct causal relationship between the error and the weight, it is not clear initially how we should assign 'blame' to the hidden nodes for any target output discrepancy. Thus, an error may be due to incorrect weight values on an output node or it may be due to the hidden nodes providing the outputs with poor information to work on. This is the so-called *credit assignment problem* and was a serious impediment to progress within connectionist modelling until the mid-1980s. Prior to this, training algorithms were known only for single-layer nets. This severely restricted the class of problems that could be solved, a point made forcibly by Minsky and Papert (1969) in their book *Perceptrons*. This work appeared to deal a serious blow to the field of neural networks but a renaissance of interest was assisted when it was shown that the credit assignment problem had an exact solution. The training algorithm that implements this is known as **back-propagation** and has claim to multiple authorship. Thus it was discovered by Werbos (1974), rediscovered by Parker (1982), but was discovered again and made popular by Rumelhart *et al.* (1986a).

Learning to read

We now describe a network which illustrates the kinds of issues that may be addressed by connectionist systems and shows the power of these models for explaining patterns of human cognitive behaviour.

Reading aloud is associated with two cognitive activities. One is concerned with translating the graphical structure or orthography of the written language into its spoken equivalent (the phonology). Another is concerned with interpreting the semantic content of the text. Evidence that there is considerable interaction between the two is provided by work with patients having acquired dyslexia in which one class of errors in reading aloud is centred around confusion of semantic relatedness. However, as a first simplification it is useful to consider the problem of going from orthography to phonology in isolation.

The problem may be characterised as quasi-regular since, although the pronunciation of many words follows some simple rules (e.g. the vowel sounds in *gave, mint*), there are often exceptions to the rules so that words with similar orthography to these like *have, pint* have quite a different sound. Indeed, there are some letter patterns which have no dominant pronunciation, as with the appearance of *-ough* in *cough, rough, bough, though, through*. This has led to the dual route theory of language processing in which two separate mechanisms are used: one rule-based system for the regular cases and another which takes the form of a look-up table for the exceptions.

Plaut *et al.* (1996), building on the earlier work of Seidenburg and McClelland (1989), have developed a series of connectionist models which can learn the pronunciation of a subset of English text with a single, unified network. The simplest of these is a feed-forward net containing a single hidden layer in which the input and output nodes represent orthographical and phonological primitives respectively. The network contained 105 inputs, sixty-one output nodes, a hundred hidden units, and the training data consisted of nearly 3000 monosyllabic words.

The net successfully learned the training set which contained both regular and rule-exception words. This appears to refute the dual route theories but Plaut *et al.* admitted the possibility that, in the process of training, the net may have divided itself into two sub-networks, one which processed the regular words and the other the exceptions. To test this out they cut away or 'lesioned' individual hidden nodes and measured the change in the error in the pronunciation of each type of word. It was found that hidden nodes were responsible for error in both word classes to roughly the same degree, although some nodes made a more significant overall change than others. They concluded that both regular and exception words were processed by the same mechanisms, thereby showing that it is not necessary to resort to a dual route theory.

There are two points to be made from the net lesioning exercise above. Firstly, we now know that a dual route structure is not a necessary prerequisite for human competence in reading aloud; the model demonstrates the existence of a solution to the problem which avoids this mechanism. Secondly, a more general point emerges from the way in which the net fails. Thus, it is not the case that the net suddenly fails to give the correct output in all instances. Rather, as the severity of the lesion increases, so does the number of errors made. This ability of the net to show a gradual change in performance as damage is incurred is known as **graceful degradation** and is a characteristic of all connectionist systems. It comes about because a node's output is a continuous function of its total input which is a sum of contributions from many other nodes, each of which can only have a limited effect. This effect is further enhanced by the nonlinear nature of the output function since, if the activity is very large (positive or negative) then the node is operating at a point on the function where the gradient is rather shallow and small changes in total input can have little influence on the output activity. This gradual decline in performance is analogous to the deterioration seen in dementias such as Alzheimer's and the late stages of Parkinson's disease. We might surmise, therefore, that similar mechanisms are at work as when we lesion individual nodes in a neural network.

Under some circumstances we may go further and use net lesioning to provided a direct way of testing the validity of a model, or a class of related models, against results from the neuropsychology of cognitive disorders. Thus, suppose a particular layer or group of nodes corresponds to an anatomically identified brain region and that this group of nodes is removed from the net. If the resulting performance of the net is similar to that observed when the brain has been damaged by a lesion to the area in question, then this may be interpreted as supporting evidence for the model. This type of study is exemplified in the network of Hinton and Shallice (1991) discussed on p. 283.

One of the key tests of a network is how well it generalises to input patterns which it has not seen during training. If it gives the correct output here it is a sign that the net has truly discovered the underlying regularities in the training set and has not merely established a complex look-up table for each input–output pair. One way of testing the reading network is to present it with non-words that are, nevertheless, pronounceable such as *hean, brane, frane*, etc. The network was able to accurately mimic human behaviour in this task as it correctly applied the rules of pronunciation where they are clear and often came up with exceptions where they were ambiguous. Finally, the net was able to emulate human performance in terms of the latency effects for naming various types of words; for example, when frequently encountered regular words are named rather more quickly than infrequent irregular words. The network of course, processes all words at the same speed but Plaut *et al.* (1996) interpreted the network error as an indication of duration to response in a full system that would have to take the output and articulate it in a speech motor system. This interpretation is somewhat unsatisfactory and is redundant in other so-called relaxation models to be discussed below, in which temporal effects arise naturally within the net.

The nature of representation in connectionist systems

At the end of training a network, any knowledge or long-term memory is stored in the weights or connection strengths – hence the term 'connectionism'. In one sense then, knowledge is stored in the weights of the net but there is an additional and more significant way in which knowledge representation occurs in networks. On applying an external input and allowing it to be processed, a characteristic pattern or profile of activity will be developed across the net that may be thought of as representing knowledge about the current input. For feed-forward nets the intermediate hidden layers provide the focus of interest here for it is across these nodes that an internal representation of the training set occurs. These are then operated on, or decoded by, the output layer into a form which is to be interpreted as the 'answer' or response to the input. As noted above, the role of the hidden layer(s) may be thought of as ensuring that cognitively similar inputs are re-represented so as to be close together in the pattern-matching sense. Another, related perspective conceives of hidden units as feature detectors that extract the underlying aspects of the training set while ignoring irrelevant clutter or noise.

In any event, there are two essentially different types of activity profile that can occur. In the **localist representation**, each semantically discrete item, concept or idea is associated with the activity of a single node. For example, in a letter recognition task, the occurrence of a particular letter may be signalled within a layer by a single node of that layer being active while all others are inactive. In contrast, in a **distributed representation**, each node within the layer plays a role in the activity profile representation of each semantic object. Thus, all nodes may be active to some extent for every pattern and so act as *micro-features* or *sub-symbolic* entities. In the letter recognition task, each node may encode small orthographic features such as line segments, curves or particular groupings of these. The emphasis on distributed representations and parallel processing has led to the acronym PDP (for Parallel Distributed Processing) to be applied sometimes to connectionist systems.

Rumelhart and Todd (1993) provide an example which explores the nature of connectionist representations. It is based on the idea of capturing the knowledge embedded in a semantic net. While the inputs are encoded using a localist representation of nodes in the semantic net, an intermediate layer learns a distributed representation of these inputs which gets passed to the hidden layer proper.

Networks with feedback

Consider the small network shown in Figure 10.8. Each node is connected to every other node by a weighted link in such a way that the weight values between two nodes in either direction are the same. There is no separate input and output in this net and so its operation is not governed by a simple flow of information from one end to another. Instead, we start the net in some state defined by a set of output values and then update the outputs gradually until the net 'relaxes' into a state of equilibrium. In this condition the output of each node is consistent with the input

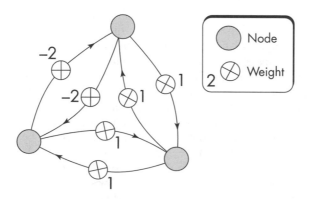

Figure 10.8 Small recurrent network

it receives from its neighbours. The dynamics of coming to equilibrium must be allowed to happen gradually because the effect of any node update has to be allowed to diffuse throughout the net. This flow of information includes feedback paths from each node, around the net and back to itself, leading to the description of these nets as **recurrent**.

A detailed description of the network dynamics, from an arbitrary initial state to one of equilibrium, is not usually available a priori and so we concern ourselves with the general behaviour and the nature of the stable states at equilibrium. Hopfield (1982, 1984) showed how nets such as these could be described in terms of an 'energy' function which always decreases as the net progresses through its state-space. Since the energy is bounded below by some minimum value this formulation demonstrates that a stable state is indeed always found. This perspective leads to nets of this type being thought of as associative memories in which the stable states correspond to the stored memories. In this framework, if the net is started in an initial state which is close to some stable state, then this state will be recalled as the associated pattern in memory. The set of initial states that produce recall of a particular memory is known as its **basin of attraction** or simply **attractor** since these states are all ultimately drawn to the given memory state. The entire state-space of the net is then divided into a series of mutually exclusive attractors.

At equilibrium, there will be an overall tendency for each weighted connection to support the current state. If a particular node has an output very close to 1 (implying a large total input) then this will most likely be due to a preponderance of positive weights with associated inputs which are also close to 1. In this way, each weight may be thought of as helping to constrain the network state by helping to force the activity across its link to take on a preferred value. This process is symmetrical because the weights between two nodes are the same in either direction and so the constraints take the form of node-pair activity correlation.

The constraint satisfaction perspective is demonstrated effectively in a network developed by Rumelhart *et al.* (1986b) which deals with knowledge about rooms in a domestic house. Each node stands for an item or attribute associated with one or more of the rooms envisaged: kitchen, bathroom, office, living room and bedroom. All nodes are connected to each other by symmetric weights which capture the degree of correlation to be expected in a typical room setting. Although the item-attribute representation is localist, higher level schema-like qualities which define the rooms are defined by the distributed pattern of activity across the network, both in terms of its weight encoding and its activity profiles.

Thinking of the weights in a recurrent net as capturing correlations or constraints between pattern components suggests a way that the net may be trained. Choose a training pattern and *clamp* it to the net; that is, force the outputs to take on the values implied by the pattern components. Next, if there is a correlation between the output on two nodes, increment the weight by a small amount, otherwise make a small weight decrement. If we were to allow only positive increments then this is essentially the learning mechanism postulated by Hebb in 1949 for the way that biological neurons learn and which may have similarities with what we now call long-term potentiation (LTP) at biological synaptic contacts.

A model of deep dyslexia

Previously we considered a model of reading aloud that addressed the process of transforming the orthographic (visual) appearance of a word directly into its acoustic or phonological representation. We consider below a model of reading due to Hinton and Shallice (1991) which is concerned with the translation of orthography into semantics.[2]

People with deep dyslexia make three types of error when reading aloud. The first consists of semantic errors where a word is confused with another which has a similar or related meaning (e.g. *cat* becomes *mice*). Another type consists of visual errors in which words are confused with others which appear to be similar (e.g. *patent* becomes *patient*). Finally, it is possible for errors to occur which mix both semantics and appearance (e.g. *last* becomes *late*).

Hinton and Shallice constructed a network which learned to encode semantics in a distributed fashion as a series of basins of attraction. They then proceeded to lesion the network by severing or corrupting groups of connections and to see what result this had on the network's performance. The network architecture is shown in Figure 10.9. It consists of two sub-networks. The first is a feed-forward net which contains the input layer of orthographic encoding *grapheme units* and a single hidden layer. The output of this net is then used to drive the input of a recurrent network capable of supporting stable state attractors. Conceptually this is broken down, in turn, into a set of *sememe* units, over which there is a

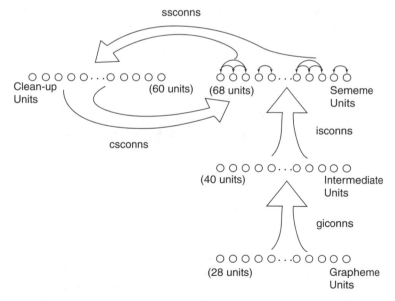

Figure 10.9 The semantic route network for reading and modelling dyslexia

---

2 A precis of this work has also appeared in *Scientific American* (Hinton *et al.*, 1993).

distributed representation of the word semantics, and a set of *clean-up* units. This division highlights an alternative view of the function of recurrent nets in which an approximately correct output pattern is passed on to another layer to be refined or 'cleaned up'. The improved pattern is then fed back to the original units for still further processing. This iterative refinement continues until no further change is possible at which point the net has reached equilibrium.

The training set consisted of forty short words divided into five categories: indoor objects, animals, body parts, foods and outdoor objects. The semantic representation occurs by activating the sememe units which have micro-features pertinent to the current word. For example, 'cat' (a member of the animal category) would activate units for 'mammal', 'has legs', 'soft', and 'fierce'. Of course, the recurrent net still operates as an associative memory store and, since the sememe units play an intimate role in its construction, the dynamics may be thought of as occurring in a semantic state-space in which words with similar meanings are encoded by nearby attractors.

The net was trained using a variant of backpropagation adapted for use with recurrent nets and it successfully learned the training set. The net was then lesioned in various ways, either by removing whole units, a random selection of connections, or by corrupting a group of weights with noise. No matter which inter-layer group of connections or method of lesioning was chosen, the effects were qualitatively similar in that both semantic and visual errors occurred. It is clear that, if connections in the recurrent sub-net are lesioned, then the attractor for some words may be diminished or removed entirely. Thus, a word whose semantic representation was previously closest to its correct attractor is now drawn into a neighbouring basin which, by virtue of its proximity in state-space, will most likely have related semantic content. However, damage in the feed-forward sub-net will have a similar effect since incorrect semantic encoding will now occur and be passed on to the recurrent net, where it proceeds to initiate the dynamics in the wrong (but nearby) attractor. This is in accordance with the experimental data that semantic errors are obtained in acquired dyslexia in spite of alternative lesion sites nominally associated with visual processing and semantic storage.

The origin of visual errors can be explained by the network's tendency to generalise over its input. Thus, although an undamaged net will be able to differentiate *cat* and *cot*, having managed to encode these in the intermediate units in such a way as to pull their representations apart, a damaged net may resort to the default behaviour of categorising orthographically similar inputs together. This explanation holds good for the feed-forward sub-net but is less convincing in the recurrent part. To see how damage here may play a part in visual errors, we need to consider the role of the clean-up units. These work to continually refine the representation delivered by the sememe units on a first pass through the feed-forward sub-net. Thus, the sememe units need not necessarily have to produce the optimal encodings that would be expected in a feed-forward-only net and so orthographically similar inputs may not be separated by as much as they might otherwise have to be. Damage to the attractors will then expose any shortcomings in the robustness of the initial encoding and produce erroneous results. In summary, the co-occurrence of semantic and visual errors over a wide range of lesion sites is accounted for by the network.

Another phenomenon in deep dyslexia occurs when a patient has a lesion so extensive that semantic identification is severely impaired. In this case, rather than make an incorrect identification of the word, all that can be done is to say which category the word is in, say, 'animal', rather than 'food'. If the network is made to suffer substantial damage, then the equilibrium patterns in the sememe units are no longer close to those of any of the words in the training set. However, the equilibria are close to the centres of the regions that were occupied by items in a particular group. Thus, it makes sense to say that the net is delivering a category rather than an individual item as output in accordance with the neurophysiological finding.

To what extent are the details of this particular network architecture responsible for the observed behaviour? Conversely, what are the key structural components in this respect? Hinton and Shallice (1991) tried variations in which there were connections within the sememe layer; in which there were sparse and fully interconnected layers; and in which the recurrent sub-net was placed closer to the input in the processing hierarchy. They also experimented with different orthographic representations at the input. The finding was that these features are all largely irrelevant; the behaviour appears to stem from the existence of a recurrent sub-net which can support basins of attraction.

The dyslexia network of Hinton and Shallice illustrates how several psychological phenomena (in this case types of error) can be considered to be emergent phenomena resulting from a single system model; it is not necessarily the case that multiple patterns of behaviour require multiple paths or sub-systems. The model accounts for many aspects of deep dyslexia and the experiments with structural modifications have managed to highlight the possibly key role played by attractor networks in processing semantic information.

Shortcomings of the connectionist approach

While neural network models appear to have many attractive explanatory features for modelling certain types of cognitive behaviour, attempts to use them to model tasks that are clearly algorithmically based can appear cumbersome and irrelevant. One of the test-beds for exhibiting the power of connectionist training algorithms in the late 1980s consisted of implementing the so-called Exclusive OR (XOR) problem. This consists simply of being able to classify the four inputs (00, 01, 10, 11) according to whether there is an even or odd number of 1s (set bits) in the pattern. It cannot be solved using a single-layer net and requires hidden units. The problem generalises quite easily to the n-bit parity problem which requires a similar process of bit counting, this time over a larger number of n binary digits. Now, it is quite possible to build a network to solve the parity problem but is it cognitively relevant? For two digits (the XOR case) it is clear that humans may solve this by some kind of pattern-matching process but consider the problem when $n=16$: does 1010111010010011 have an even or odd number of 1s? To find the answer we will probably start at one end and count the number of 1s in the pattern. The process of counting makes use of associative memory (3 follows 2, 4 follows 3, etc.) and a working memory store ('what was the last number we used?'). It is clearly not the case that we deal with this problem by forming a distributed internal representation and then decoding this to give an answer. Although the mechanisms used must eventually be represented in the neural network that is the brain, these will probably have nothing to do with connectionist models of parity. We are surely on safer ground here remaining at the higher level of a symbolic, algorithmic explanation in terms of counting.

Another criticism sometimes levelled against connectionism is that sensible explanations of cognition are obscured because the network is a 'black box' whose operation is difficult to understand. This attack is based on the nature of distributed representations which, by their very nature, are composed of micro-features which may not be semantically transparent. We have seen, however, that it is quite possible to understand the mechanisms at work in a network without having to have an intimate knowledge of the minutiae of each representation. General principles, such as the role of attractors, pattern space distance measures, graceful degradation and the like can be invoked that have high-level explanatory power.

Finally, as noted above, some workers are not happy to dispense with anatomical and physiological realism where there is the possibility that it might be incorporated into a model. Then, layers or modules within a network will be identified with specific cortical or sub-cortical areas, and connection schemes may be employed that are supposed to mirror those of the corresponding neural tissue inferred from electrophysiological and histochemical studies. The result is a brand of modelling which has recently emerged as a distinctive thread in cognitive science under the banner of **computational neuroscience**. It has found most relevance in models of early vision and motor control since these processes have benefited from a much closer scrutiny by neuroscientists than other areas of cognition, resulting in an enormous corpus of data. The reason for this is perhaps due to the comparative ease of interpreting signals appearing at the front end (pre-processing) and back end (post-processing) of the cognitive chain of information flow. Readers interested in a review of some of the work in computational neuroscience should consult the text by Churchland and Sejnowski (1994).

In Section 10.4 we continue with a critique of both the connectionist and symbolic paradigms, and examine their similarities and differences.

10.4 Symbols and neurons compared

As noted previously, the symbolic approach is good for modelling areas of cognition that can easily be formulated as a series of rule-based procedures, or which lend themselves to a fairly rigid knowledge representation. These areas include many high-level intellectual activities that require logical inference such as problem-solving, theorem-proving in mathematics, game-playing, and the enactment of some types of technical and scientific expertise; these are just the areas within which it is difficult to formulate connectionist models. On the other hand, symbolic systems often perform poorly at (for example) perceptual and motor tasks (including both low-level and high-level vision and visuomotor coordination) and some aspects of natural language understanding; these are just the areas at which connectionist models excel.

Apart from acknowledging this difference in the domain of applicability, it is instructive to draw up a series of points for comparison between the two approaches.

- **Learning**
  Connectionist: Learning is usually implicit – nets start with some random weight set and adapt these by repeatedly being shown examples from the problem to be solved or task to be done.
  Symbolic: Learning in these systems is possible but is not inherent. Further, what is learned is more rules and symbols, i.e. more of the same; if a problem does not lend itself to the symbolic approach then no amount of learning will help.
- **Knowledge representation**
  Connectionist: Knowledge is stored as a pattern of weighted connections. In one type of representation this knowledge then manifests itself in distributed patterns of activity. There is then no simple correspondence between nodes and high-level semantic objects. Rather, the representation of a 'concept' or 'idea' within the net is via the complete pattern of unit activities being distributed over the net as a whole. In this way, any given node may partake in many semantic representations. In contrast, localist representations imply a one-to-one mapping between nodes and features or ideas. However, even in this case, higher level structures may be implicitly distributed over the entire net (as in the room schema network model, for instance)
  Symbolic: There is a clear correspondence between the semantic objects being dealt with (numbers, words, concepts, etc.) and both the model structures (symbols) and the physical hardware of an implementation. Thus, each object can be 'pointed to' in a block of computer memory.
- **Style of processing**
  Connectionist: Is more akin to signal processing than computation *per se*; networks combine and process numerical signals rather than symbols. Further, they sometimes behave like physical, dynamical systems in that they relax to some equilibrium state.
  Symbolic: Executes a program stored in memory on a von Neuman machine. The program results in the processing of objects with symbolic value rather than simple numerical values.
- **Parallel/serial computation**
  Connectionist: is inherently parallel where many nodes may work at the same time.[3]
  Symbolic: Inherently serial in which each instruction or stage in the algorithm has to be executed before the next one can be performed.
- **Mode of failure under damage**
  Connectionist: Nets are robust under hardware failure; altering or even destroying a few connections may still allow the net to work and performance gradually declines rather than catastrophically collapsing.

---

3 In simulating networks on conventional computers we are limited by the serial computer architecture and not by the network itself.

Symbolic: Altering or destroying a few memory locations in a computer running a symbolic algorithm may prevent the machine from working altogether resulting in a so-called machine 'crash'.

Towards a synthesis

In spite of the differences outlined in the above list, we started our comparison by noting that the symbolic and connectionist paradigms can reasonably lay claim to non-overlapping domains of competence. It would therefore appear that there is room in the cognitive modeller's tool-box for both symbolic and connectionist systems. However, it is not satisfactory to simply ignore the fundamental difference in approach and try to live uneasily with two very different paradigms. If we are to embrace them both it is vital that we understand how they may be reconciled.

One important step in this direction was taken by Smolensky (1988), who attempted to clarify some of the issues surrounding the nature of connectionist and symbolic modelling. Smolensky advocated what he called the *Proper Treatment of Connectionism* (PTC) which embraced many aspects of the modelling problem in a lengthy argument which is, in places, rather subtle. One of the main aspects of PTC, however, is that it argues for the use of distributed (rather than localist) representations acting at what Smolensky calls the *sub-symbolic* level (the level of *micro-features*). He then claims that any rule-based description constitutes an emergent property of the sub-symbolic model. To illustrate what is meant here, consider the behaviour of the stock market. During a rapid rise in share prices, individual investors may be buying or selling according to their own predispositions. However, the overall (emergent) pattern is that of people buying the most significant shares. The investors or brokers are not 'obeying a law' that says they will buy to increase the market-index with a positive linear trend; rather the linear increase is an emergent property of many contributions from individuals acting independently. We can now see that, on occasion, symbolic models may be appropriate, although Smolensky conceives of these as secondary to an underlying sub-symbolic system from which it springs.

A rather different stance has been adopted by Clark (1990), who posits the ability of the brain (and hence connectionist architectures) to simulate or emulate a von Neumann machine directly. In this way the sub-symbolic description may be subservient in certain instances to the emulation of a serial, algorithmic processor. In defence of this stance, it would be appear to be almost a truism, for example, that when we perform mental arithmetic we are simulating a suite of well-defined algorithms. The point here is that, while processing within neural networks conforms to its own agenda, it is possible on occasion to liken the overall behaviour of the net to the manipulation of a high-level symbolic data structure.

A weaker version of this position arises in the context of a localist representation if we attempt to interpret the function of each node as a rule for combining its inputs. Thus, for example, suppose two inputs are associated with strong positive weights (while others are close to zero) and that both inputs have to be active to obtain a significant output. If *A* and *B* are the semantic labels attached to these inputs and *Y* is the label associated with the node output, then the node has developed the rule *if A and B then Y*.

In general, the presence of a small number of active inputs is not sufficient to guarantee full output activity on a particular node which is then contingent on the nature of the remaining inputs. Of course, this is the power of the connectionist approach – it is able to capture subtleties and nuances which are hard to encapsulate in the more brittle 'all-or-nothing' rules of conventional production systems. However, workers with rule-based systems have attempted to overcome this deficiency by introducing methods of **uncertain reasoning** such as Bayesian networks (Pearl, 1995) and Fuzzy sets (Kosko, 1992). There is a convergence of methodology here and localist networks clearly share many properties with uncertain reasoning systems. The other side of the 'networks-to-rules' coin of course is that rules may be instantiated in networks by suitable choice of weights. Ron Sun has recently championed the cause of hybrid models which integrate symbolic and connectionist ideas and has instantiated these ideas in the CLARION architecture (Sun and Peterson, 1995). However, prior to the resurgence of interest in connectionist systems and long before the serious development of hybrid models, J.R. Anderson (1983) discussed a unified model of cognition he called ACT*. This was to be the last in a series of architectures for the Adaptive Control of Thought (ACT) which had been developed during the 1970s and were supposed to be general theories in the same sense as Newell's Soar. Unlike Soar, ACT* has a declarative memory as well as working and procedural memories and, more radically, items of cognitive information are encoded in memory nodes, each of which is associated with a level of activity. Further, it is via its memory node becoming active that a cognitive unit becomes part of the working memory and the links between nodes themselves also have a strength. It is clear therefore that while it is not simply a neural network, there are several features of ACT* with a definite connectionist flavour so that it does constitute a hybrid system. Of course, it would have been difficult for Anderson to have made this case because the foundational work to make these links explicit had not been done when ACT* was being developed.

Summary

- Theories may vary in kind from metaphors, through structural descriptions, to fully implemented computational models that generate quantitative predictions. While generation of the latter is a desirable goal, earlier stages of model-building will necessarily be less well articulated.
- A paradigm is a general framework of (sometimes tacit) assumptions, ideas and theories that underpin an area of scientific investigation. The information processing paradigm in cognitive science views cognition as the effective manipulation and transformation of information about the environment which makes extensive use of internal representations of the world. Within this paradigm there are two sub-paradigms embodied in the symbolic (AI-based) and connectionist (neural network) approaches. The study of situated robotics is an attempt to break free from this representational stance.

- Computational models may be described using a three-level hierarchy proposed by Marr; the computational level describes what is being computed and why, the algorithmic level describes the way this is to be carried out in the abstract, and the implementation level describes the hardware that the algorithm runs on.

- Cognitive science has drawn heavily from the study of Artificial Intelligence (AI) but, while AI programs may perform a task well, they may not necessarily provide a good description of the corresponding human cognitive process.

- The symbolic paradigm assumes that knowledge can be captured in a set of elementary, semantically transparent objects (symbols) and that cognition may be described by supplying the rules according to which these objects are manipulated. There is a close parallel between models built in this paradigm and their implementation on von Neumann computing engines (conventional computers).

- One of the key features in a model is the way in which knowledge is represented. Within the symbolic paradigm several methods have been developed. In a semantic net, nodes in a graph represent concepts or objects and links between nodes denote inter-object/concept relationships. A schemata, frame or script describes a stereotypical situation whose specifics are fleshed out by assigning values to its slots or variables. A production system consists of a collection of rules and an information database to which the rules may be applied to obtain new rules or answers to queries.

- While the symbolic approach has proved very powerful, its dependence on semantically transparent, well-articulated rules and objects means that it can be rather 'brittle' when it is applied to perceptual problems or non-intellectual domains that make use of 'commonsense' reasoning.

- The main alternative to the symbolic approach – connectionism – is based on the belief that cognition may be represented more successfully by modelling more closely the underlying neural hardware of the brain. Networks of neurons are constructed using simplified artificial neurons whose interconnection strengths or weights are adapted under a training regime. The network learns by being exposed to a set of examples of the problem to be solved.

- Simple feed-forward networks tend to undergo supervised learning in which each input pattern is also supplied with a desired output. However, with some modifications a network may undergo self-organisation and learn to extract information about clusters of patterns.

- Neural networks can generalise their ability to classify information from training examples to patterns previously unseen.

- Multilayer nets contain one or more layers of hidden nodes which are not subject to intervention by supervision and instead, learn their own internal representation of the training data.

- The work of Plaut *et al.* (1996) uses a feed-forward net to model the process of reading aloud. The network processed regular and irregular words in the same way, thereby challenging the dual route theory of reading.

- Networks exhibit graceful degradation when lesioned. The precise way in which this occurs may correspond to the way in which certain cognitive deficits arise in the ability being modelled. This is sometimes used as evidence in support for a model but is more conservatively able to support a class of models which share some general architectural features.

- Information is represented in connectionist nets in the instantaneous pattern of activity over the node outputs and (long-term) knowledge via the weights. Patterns of activity may correspond to either a localist or distributed representation.
- Feedback or recurrent nets may be used as dynamic systems to store memories as foci within basins of attraction.
- The work of Hinton and Shallice used a combination of feed-forward and recurrent nets to encode word semantics as a series of basins of attraction. Lesioning the net led to behaviour comparable with that of deep dyslexia.
- While networks work well for modelling many types of cognitive behaviour, they are poor at tasks that are clearly governed by well-defined rules. A network's operation may be difficult to understand if it uses a distributed representation of node activity.
- Symbolic systems are fundamentally static (not adaptable), semantically transparent, serial models which have a natural implementation in von Neuman hardware leading to catastrophic failure under damage. Networks are fundamentally adaptable, semantically opaque (under a distributed representation), parallel models which exhibit graceful degradation under hardware failure.
- While the symbolic and connectionist approaches may appear quite different, points of contact and comparisons have been made by Smolensky ('the proper treatment of connectionism'), Clark (von Neuman emulation) and Sun (symbol–connectionist hybrid models).

Further reading

Copeland, J. (1993). *Artificial Intelligence – a Philosophical Introduction*, Oxford: Blackwell. A good introduction to (principally) the symbolic processing approach to the context of general philosophical questions about minds and machines.

Gardner, H. (1985). *The Mind's New Science*, New York: Basic Books Inc. An overview of cognitive science with sections devoted to each of the subdisciplines (psychology, AI, philosophy, linguistics, anthropology). While a little dated now, it does capture the vitality of the subject and the personal involvement of some of the main players from a historical perspective.

Green, D. W., *et al.* (eds) (1996). *Cognitive Science: An Introduction*, University College, London: Blackwell. A good introduction to many areas of cognitive science but with an emphasis on language. The first three chapters deal well with computational issues and the role of general architectures for cognition. Encourages critical thinking with devil's advocate scenarios.

Gurney, K. (1997). *An Introduction to Neural Networks*, London: UCL Press Ltd. An introduction to the technical aspects of connectionism with as little mathematics as possible.

Glossary

acquired dysgraphia A specific difficulty with writing words, caused by brain damage.

acquired dyslexia Impairment of the ability to read caused by brain damage.

agrammatism A pattern of aphasic symptoms characterised by a lack of grammatical structure in speech, with a tendency for grammatical function words and inflections to be omitted.

algorithm A well-defined procedure or recipe for processing information.

Alzheimer's disease (AD) A degenerative brain disorder usually (but not always) afflicting the elderly, which first appears as an impairment of memory but later develops into a more general dementia.

amnesia A pathological impairment of memory function.

anterograde amnesia (AA) Impaired memory for events which have occurred since the onset of the disorder (contrasts with retrograde amnesia).

aphasia Loss or impairment of one or more aspects of language abilities caused by brain damage.

apperceptive agnosia An inability to perceive objects accurately, caused by damage to the visual system.

associative agnosia An inability to associate a perceived object with the knowledge held about that object.

attractor *see* **basin of attraction**

automatic processing Processing that is not under conscious control, and which is rapid, inevitable, and does not suffer interference (contrasts with **controlled processing**).

availability heuristic Making judgements on the basis of how available relevant examples are in our memory store.

293

backpropagation A method for training feed-forward neural networks in which error information at the output is propagated back to the hidden nodes for use in adjusting their weights.

base rate fallacy Ignoring information about the base rate in light of other information.

basin of attraction In a recurrent net with stable states, the set of states which eventually lead to a particular stable state.

behaviourism An approach to psychology which constrained psychologists to the investigation of externally observable behaviour, and rejected any consideration of inner mental processes.

blindsight The ability of some functionally blind patients to detect visual stimuli at an unconscious level, despite having no conscious awareness of seeing them. Usually observed in patients with occipital lobe lesions.

bottom-up (or data-driven) processing Processing which is directed by information contained within the stimulus (contrasts with **top-down processing**).

Broca's area A region of the brain normally located in the left frontal region, which controls motor speech production.

canonical view The most typical and easily recognised view of an object.

cell assembly A group of cells which have become linked to one another to form a single functional network. Proposed by Hebb as a possible biological mechanism underlying the representation and storage of a memory trace.

central executive A hypothetical system which is assumed to have overall control of the working memory, and to control the allocation of conscious attention and the operation of the visuo-spatial and phonological storage loops.

cognitive interview An approach to interviewing eyewitnesses which makes use of the findings of cognitive psychology, such as context reinstatement.

cognitive neuropsychology The study of the brain activities underlying cognitive processes, often by investigating cognitive impairment.

cognitive psychology The study of the way in which the brain processes information. It includes the mental processes involved in perception, learning and memory storage, thinking, and language.

cognitivism A paradigm for cognitive science which holds that cognition may be adequately explained using symbol-based models.

cohesive devices Ways of indicating within a text that an item such as a word or sentence is linked with what has gone before.

competence The linguistic knowledge hypothesised to underlie the ability to use language.

computational neuroscience The study of models of cognition and perception which attempt to be faithful to anatomical and physiological data.

computationally adequate describes a model which may perform a cognitive task but which may not be in close correspondence with the underlying human cognitive processes.

computationally faithful describes a model which is believed to adequately describe some aspect of human cognition.

computer modelling The simulation of human cognitive processes by computer.

conduction aphasia An impairment of language in which the most obvious symptom is an inability to repeat back what was just heard.

confabulation The reporting of memories which are incorrect and apparently fabricated, but which the patient believes to be true.

configural processing Recognition by the configuration or arrangement of perceived features relative to one another (for example, the ratio of the length of the nose to the distance between the eyes).

conjunction fallacy The failure to acknowledge that everything that is both A and B must also be A.

connectionist system A neural network which attempts to model some aspect of perception or cognition.

constancy Ability to perceive constant objects in the world despite continual changes in viewing conditions.

content word A word such as a noun, verb or adjective that carries meaning beyond its grammatical role in the sentence.

contention scheduling A term used by Norman and Shallice to describe an operation which prevents two competing activated schemas from being selected on the basis of the strength of their initial activation.

controlled processing Processing that is under conscious control, and which is relatively slow, not inevitable, and suffers interference (contrasts with **automatic processing**).

declarative memory Memory which can be reported in a deliberate and conscious way (contrasts with **procedural memory**).

deductive reasoning task A problem that has a well-defined structure in a system of formal logic where the conclusion is certain.

deep dyslexia A specific pattern of dyslexic symptoms characterised by semantic errors, visual errors, difficulty reading non-words and function words.

deep dysphasia A specific pattern of aphasic symptoms in which the person is likely to make semantic errors when repeating back words, has more difficulty repeating back abstract words than concrete words and is unable to repeat back non-words.

diencephalon A brain structure which includes the thalamus and hypothalamus. Parts of the diencephalon are involved in processing and retrieving memories, and damage to these structures can cause amnesia.

discourse A set of sentences that are related to one another in a meaningful way.

disinhibition Impaired response inhibition, an inability to suppress previous incorrect responses observed in patients with frontal lobe epilepsy.

distributed representation A representation in connectionist models in which each node may partake in the encoding of many features, objects, or ideas.

dorsal route Projection from primary visual cortex to the posterior parietal cortex thought to underlie perception of spatial location.

double dissociation A method of distinguishing between two functions whereby each can be separately affected or impaired by some external factor without the other function being affected, thus providing particularly convincing evidence for the independence of the two functions.

dysexecutive syndrome A collection of deficits observed in frontal lobe patients which may include impaired concentration, impaired concept formation, disinhibition, inflexibility, perseveration, impaired cognitive estimation and impaired strategy formation.

echolalia A marked tendency to repeat back what has just been said.

ecological validity The extent to which the conditions of a research experiment resemble those encountered in real-life settings.

electroconvulsive therapy (ECT) A treatment used to alleviate depression which involves passing an electric current through the front of the patient's head.

encoding specificity principle (ESP) The theory that retrieval cues will only be successful in accessing a memory trace if they contain some of the same items of information which were stored with the original trace.

episodic memory Memory for specific episodes and events from personal experience, occurring in a particular context of time and place (contrasts with **semantic memory**).

experimental psychology The scientific testing of psychological processes in human and animal subjects.

explicit memory Memory which a subject is able to report consciously and deliberately (contrasts with **implicit memory**).

familiarity A feeling that an item has been encountered on some previous occasion.

feature detectors Mechanisms in an information processing device (such as a brain or a computer) which respond to specific features in a pattern of stimulation, such as lines or corners.

feature overlap The extent to which features of the memory trace stored at input match those available in the retrieval cues. According to the encoding specificity theory (qv) successful retrieval requires extensive feature overlap.

flashbulb memory A subject's recollection of details of what they were doing at the time of some major news event or dramatic incident.

frame A structural component of a schema.

frontal lobe syndrome A range of different behavioural deficits associated with frontal lobe damage pertaining to both cognitive processing and personality; however, no single pattern of deficits has emerged that would justify the use of the term.

functional fixedness The inability to use an object appropriately in a given situation because of prior experience of using the object in a different way.

garden path sentence A sentence that initially gives rise to an incorrect interpretation, necessitating backtracking and reinterpretation.

generalisation In a neural network occurs when a net correctly classifies examples it has not seen during training.

Gestalt psychology An approach to psychology which emphasised the way in which the components of perceptual input become grouped and integrated into patterns and whole figures.

global Information in a visual scene relating to gross outline or configuration (contrasts with **local** information).

glue (attentional) On Treisman's account focused attention has the effect of gluing together the perceived features of an object so as to form a complete internal representation of that object.

graceful degradation Describes the way in which a neural network gradually breaks down under lesion of its connections.

grammar In linguistics, a set of hypotheses about how language is organised.

grammatical function word A word such as an article, preposition or conjunction which serves a grammatical function in a sentence rather than in itself carrying meaning.

Herpes Simplex Encephalitis (HSE) A virus infection of the brain, which in some cases leaves the patient severely amnesic.

heuristic A loosely defined rule or strategy employed to help search for solutions to a problem.

hidden nodes Those units in a neural network which provide neither input nor output signals and whose activities may not be determined during training.

hippocampus A structure lying within the temporal lobes, which is involved in the creation of new memories. Hippocampal lesions usually cause impairment of memory, especially the storage of new memories.

holistic processing Processing which makes use of the properties of the whole object (for example, a face) rather than breaking it down into its component features.

implicit memory Memory whose influence can be detected by some indirect test of task performance, but which the subject is unable to report deliberately and consciously (contrasts with **explicit memory**).

individuation Recognising one specific item from other members of that class of item (for example, recognising the face of a particular individual).

inductive reasoning task A problem that has a well-defined structure in a system of formal logic where the conclusion is highly probable but not necessarily true.

inflectional endings An ending on a wordstem that expresses a grammatical relation such as the past tense '-ed' ending or the plural '-s' ending.

insight The reorganising or restructuring of the elements of the problem situation in such a way as to provide a solution. Also known as productive thinking.

interpolation Using computerised image processing systems to construct images that are intermediate between two other images.

Korsakoff's syndrome A brain disease which usually results from chronic alcoholism, and which is mainly characterised by a memory impairment.

learning rule The formula for changing the weights in a neural network.

lesions Injuries or damage of some kind.

lexical ambiguity Ambiguity caused by a word that has more than one meaning, for example, 'bank'.

lexical item A word.

Lexicalisation The process by which a thought that underlies a word is turned into the spoken form of that word.

local Information in a visual scene relating to fine detail (contrasts with **global** information).

localist representation A representation in connectionist models in which each node stands for a particular (semantically transparent) feature.

long-term memory Memory held in permanent storage, available for retrieval at some time in the future (contrasts with **short-term memory**).

long-term potentiation (LTP) A lasting change in synaptic resistance following the application of electrical stimulation to living brain tissue. Possibly one of the biological mechanisms underlying the learning process.

means–end analysis A general heuristic where a sub-problem is selected that will reduce the difference between the current state and the goal state.

mental lexicon The store in memory of information about words.

mental model A representation that we construct according to what is described in the premises of a reasoning problem, which will depend on how we interpret these premises.

mnemonic A technique or strategy used for improving the memorability of items (for example, adding meaningful associations).

modular system A system in which different types of processing are carried out by separate and relatively independent sub-systems.

morphemes The smallest meaningful units into which words can be divided. Some words such as 'cat' may consist of one morpheme while others may be analysed into units that recur in other words. For example, 'unthinkable' may be analysed into: un + think + able.

morphology The study of the internal structure of words.

negative priming Occurs when the processing of a target stimulus is inhibited if that stimulus or one similar to it had occurred on a previous trial as a distractor or as an unattended stimulus.

neural network A network of interconnected processing elements, loosely based on the networks of neurons found in the animal brain.

neurotransmitter A chemical substance which is secreted across the synapse between two neurons, enabling one neuron to stimulate another.

node A processing element in a neural network.

organic amnesia An impairment of memory function caused by physical damage to the brain.

orientation columns Columns of cells in the visual cortex sensitive to line stimuli having particular orientations.

orienting In the spotlight model of visual attention this refers to directing attention to regions of space that does not depend upon eye movements.

orienting task A set of instructions used to influence the type of cognitive processing employed.

paradigm An overarching framework of ideas, assumptions and theories that underpins an area of scientific investigation.

parallel processing Processing of multiple objects (or their attributes) simultaneously (contrasts with serial processing).

parsing The process of analysing a string of words into grammatical constituents.

performance The psychological processes involved in language use, as opposed to competence, the knowledge of language said to underlie that use.

perseveration An inability to shift response strategy characteristic of frontal lobe patients.

phoneme The smallest unit of sound that has an effect on meaning; for example, the initial phonemes differ between 'bin' and 'pin' and the two words differ in meaning.

phonetics The study of speech sounds, especially their articulation and acoustic properties.

phonology The study of the sound system of a language, especially the pattern of combinations of sounds in that language.

phrase structure rules Rules that describe the hierarchical organisation of sentences into grammatical elements.

physical symbol hypothesis The stance that holds that an intelligent (cognisant) agent must be equivalent to a symbol-based system capable of direct implementation on a von Neumann (conventional) computer architecture.

pragmatic reasoning schemata Clusters of rules that are highly generalised and abstracted but defined with respect to different types of relationships and goals.

prefixes A bound morpheme that is added to the beginning of a word, for example, '-pre', '-un' and '-dis'.

primal sketch First stage in Marr's model of vision. Results in computation of edges and other details from retinal images.

problem reduction An approach to problem-solving that converts the problem into a number of sub-problems, each of which can be solved separately.

problem space A term introduced by Newell and Simon to describe the first stage in problem-solving; represented in the problem space are the initial state, the goal state, the instructions, the constraints on the problem and all relevant information retrieved from long-term memory.

procedural memory Memory which can be demonstrated by performing some skilled procedure such as a motor task, but which the subject is not necessarily able to report consciously (contrasts with **declarative memory**).

production rule In a symbol-based system a conditional rule for combining data to produce a new result.

prototypes Representations of objects in terms of fairly abstract properties. More flexible than templates.

psychogenic amnesia An impairment of memory of psychological origin.

psycholinguistics The study of the comprehension, production and acquisition of language.

pure word deafness A type of aphasia in which the person is unable to understand spoken language, despite speaking and reading being relatively unaffected.

pure word meaning deafness A type of aphasia in which the person is unable to understand what words mean even though those words can be repeated and written accurately to dictation.

recollection Remembering a specific event or occasion on which an item was previously encountered.

recurrent Used to describe networks with feedback loops within their interconnections.

representation An internal coding of certain aspects of the information dealt with in a computational model of cognition.

representativeness heuristic Making judgements on the basis of the extent to which the salient features of an object or person are representative of the features thought to be characteristic of some category.

retrograde amnesia (RA) Impaired memory for events which occurred prior to the onset of amnesia (contrasts with **anterograde amnesia**).

saccadic eye movements Small eye movements which are automatic and involuntary.

schema A mental pattern derived from past experience which is used to assist with the interpretation of subsequent cognitions, for example, by identifying familiar shapes and sounds from new perceptual input.

scotoma A blind area within the visual field, resulting from damage to the visual system.

script A type of schema conveying the probable sequence of events in a certain situation.

self-organisation The process whereby a neural network may learn about the structure of the training examples without being shown target responses (contrasts with **supervised learning**).

semantic error A semantically related word is substituted for another word in speaking or in reading, for example, 'yellow' for 'red' or 'sleep' for 'night'.

semantic memory Memory for general knowledge, such as the meanings associated with particular words and shapes, without reference to any specific contextual episode (contrasts with **episodic memory**).

semantics The study of the meaning of words and sentences.

serial processing Processing of objects or attributes one at a time in sequence (contrasts with **parallel processing**).

short-term memory Memory held in conscious awareness, and which is currently receiving attention (contrasts with **long-term memory**).

situated robotics An area of cognitive modelling which claims not to make explicit use of internal representations.

slip of the tongue Errors people make when they talk.

spatial frequency analysis Analysis of contrasts in a visual scene enabling the discrimination of fine detail (high spatial frequencies) and gross outlines (low spatial frequencies).

state–action tree A diagram showing all the possible sequences of actions and intermediate states which can be constructed if the problem is well defined.

story grammar Schemas representing the structural components of the plot of a story.

structural ambiguity Ambiguity that arises from the possibility of parsing a phrase or sentence in more than one way.

suffix A bound morpheme that is added to the end of a word stem, for example, '-ing', '-ly' and '-s'.

supervised learning Learning in a neural network that proceeds by providing the network with a desired or target response to each input.

supervisory attentional system A term used by Norman and Shallice to describe a system that can heighten a schema's level of activation, allowing it to be in a better position to compete with other schemas for dominance and thus increasing its probability of being selected in contention scheduling.

synapse The gap between the axon of one neuron and the dendrite of another neuron.

syntax The study of the rules governing the combinations of words in sentences.

templates Stored representations of objects enabling object recognition.

three-dimensional (3-D) model Third stage in Marr's model of vision. This is a viewer-independent representation of the object which has achieved perceptual constancy or classification.

top-down (or conceptually driven) processing Processing which makes use of stored knowledge and schemas to interpret an incoming stimulus (contrasts with **bottom-up processing**).

two-and-a-half-dimensional (2.5-D) representation Second stage in Marr's theory of vision. Aligns details in primal sketch into a viewer-centred representation of the object.

uncertain reasoning Alternatives to the normally rigid application of rules in symbolic systems to incorporate more human-like flexibility.

unit *see* **node**

ventral route Projection from the primary visual cortex to the inferotemporal cortex thought to underlie object perception.

visual masking Experimental procedure of following a briefly presented stimulus by random visual noise or fragments of other stimuli. Interferes with or interrupts visual processing.

visual search Experimental procedure of searching through a field of objects ('distractors') for a desired object ('target').

weight The strength of a connection between two nodes in a **neural network**.

Wernicke's area A region of the brain normally located in the left temporal region, which is concerned with the perception and comprehension of speech.

References

Ackerly, S. (1937). Instinctive, emotional and mental changes following prefrontal lobe extirpation. *American Journal of Psychiatry*, 92, 717–729.

Adams, A. and Gathercole, S.E. (1996). Phonological working memory and spoken language development in young children. *Quarterly Journal of Experimental Psychology*, 49A, 216–233.

Adler, A. (1950). Course and outcome of visual agnosia. *Journal of Nervous and Mental Diseases*, 111, 41–51.

Adolphs, R. Tranel, D. Damasio, H. and Damasio, A. (1994). Impaired recognition of emotion in facial expressions following bilateral damage to the human amygdala. *Nature*, 372, 669–672.

Albert, M.S. Butters, N. and Levin, J. (1979). Temporal gradients in the retrograde amnesia of patients with alcoholic Korsakoff's disease. *Archives of Neurology*, 36, 211–216.

Allport, D.A. (1977). On knowing the meaning of words we are unable to report: The effects of visual masking. In S. Dornic (ed.) *Attention and Performance VI*, Hillsdale, NJ: LEA.

Alzheimer, A. (1907). Über eine eigenartige Erkrankung der Hirnrinde. *Allgemeine Zeitschrift fur Psychiatrie Psychoisch-Gerichliche Medicin*, 64, 146–148.

Anderson, J.R. (1980). *Cognitive Psychology and its Implications*. San Francisco, CA: W.H. Freeman.

Anderson, J.R. (1983). *The Architecture of Cognition*. Cambridge, MA: Harvard University Press.

Anderson, J.R. Bjork, R.A. and Bjork, E.L. (1994). Remembering can cause forgetting: Retrieval dynamics in long-term memory. *Journal of Experimental Psychology: Learning, Memory, and Cognition*, 20, 1063–1087.

Anderson, J.R. and Bower, G.H. (1972). *Human Associative Memory*. Washington DC: Winston.

Armus, S.R. Brookshire, R.H. and Nicholas, L.E. (1989). Aphasic and non-brain-damaged adults' knowledge of scripts for common situations. *Brain and Language*, 36, 518–528.

303

Assal, G. Favre, C. and Anders, J.P. (1984). Non-reconnaissance d'animaux familièrs chez un paysan: Zooagnosie ou prosopagnosie pour les animaux. Revue Neurologique, 140, 580–584.

Atkinson, R.C. and Shiffrin, R.M. (1968). Human memory: A proposed system and its control processes. In K.W. Spence and J.T. Spence (eds) *The Psychology of Learning and Motivation* (vol. 2). London: Academic Press.

Baddeley, A.D. (1978). The trouble with levels: A re-examination of Craik and Lockhart's framework for memory research. *Psychological Review*, 85, 139–152.

Baddeley, A.D. (1986). *Working Memory*. Oxford: Clarendon Press.

Baddeley, A.D. (1996). Exploring the central executive. *Quarterly Journal of Experimental Psychology*, 49A, 5–28.

Baddeley, A.D. (1997). *Human Memory: Theory and Practice*. Hove: Erlbaum.

Baddeley, A.D. and Hitch, G.J. (1974). Working memory. In G.H. Bower (ed.) *The Psychology of Learning and Motivation* (vol. 8). London: Academic Press.

Baddeley, A.D. and Lewis, V.J. (1981). Inner active processes in reading: The inner voice, the inner ear, and the inner eye. In A.M. Lesgold and C.A. Perfetti (eds) *Interactive Processes in Reading*. Hillsdale, NJ: Lawrence Erlbaum Associates Inc.

Baddeley, A.D, Papagno, C. and Vallar, G. (1988). When long-term learning depends on short-term storage. *Journal of Memory and Language*, 27, 586–595.

Baddeley, A.D., Thomson, N. and Buchanan, M. (1975). Word length and the structure of short-term memory. *Journal of Verbal Learning and Verbal Behaviour*, 14, 575–589.

Baddeley, A.D. and Warrington, E.K. (1970). Amnesia and the distinction between long- and short-term memory. *Journal of Verbal Learning and Verbal Behaviour*, 9, 176–189.

Baddeley, A.D. Wilson, B.A. and Watts, F.N. (1996). *Handbook of Memory Disorders*. Chichester: Wiley.

Badecker, W. and Caramazza, A. (1985). On considerations of method and theory governing the use of clinical categories in neurolinguistics and cognitive neuropsychology: the case against agrammatism. *Cognition*, 20, 97–125.

Balota, D.A. (1992). Visual word recognition: The journey from feature to meaning. In M. Gernsbacher (ed.) *Handbook of Psycholinguistics*. New York: Academic Press.

Barceló, F. Sanz, M. Molina, V. and Rubia, F.J. (1997). The Wisconsin Card Sorting Test and the assessment of frontal function: A validation study with event-related potentials. *Neuropsychologia*, 35, 399–408.

Baron-Cohen, S. (1992). The theory of mind hypothesis of autism: History and prospects of the idea. *The Psychologist*, 5, 9–12.

Bartlett, F.C. (1932). *Remembering*. Cambridge: Cambridge University Press.

Basso, A. Spinnler, H. Vallar, G. and Zanobio, M.E. (1982). Left hemisphere damage and selective impairment of auditory-verbal short-term memory. *Neuropsychologia*, 20, 263–274.

Bauer, R.M. (1984). Autonomic recognition of names and faces in prosopagnosia: a neuropsychological application of the Guilty Knowledge test. *Neuropsychologia*, 22, 457–469.

Bay, E. (1953). Disturbances of visual perception and their examination. *Brain*, 76, 515–551.

Baylis, G.C., Driver, J. and Rafal, R.D. (1993). Visual extinction and stimulus repetition. *Journal of Cognitive Neuroscience*, 5, 453–466.

Beeman, M. Friedman, R.B. Grafman, J. Perez, E. Diamond, S. and Beadle Lindsay, M.B. (1994). Summation priming and coarse semantic coding in the right hemisphere. *Journal of Cognitive Neuroscience*, 6, 26–45.

Bench, C.J. Frith, C.D. Grasby, P.M. Friston, K.J. Paulesu, E. Frackowiak, R.S.J. and Dolan, R.J. (1993). Investigations of the functional anatomy of attention using the stroop test. *Neuropsychologia*, 31, 907–922.

Bender, M.D. and Feldman, M. (1972). The so called 'visual agnosias'. *Brain*, 95, 173–186.

Benson, D.F. and Geschwind, N. (1971). Aphasia and related cortical disturbances. In A.B. Baker and L.H. Baker (eds) *Clinical Neurology*. New York: Harper & Row.

Benson, D.F. and Greenberg, J.P. (1969). Visual form agnosia: A specific defect in visual discrimination. *Archives of Neurology*, 20, 82–89.

Benton, A.L. (1991). The prefrontal region: Its early history. In H.S. Levin, H.M. Eisenberg and A.L. Benton (eds) *Frontal Lobe Function and Dysfunction*. Oxford: Oxford University Press.

Berndt, R.S. (1987). Symptom co-occurrence and dissociation in the interpretation of agrammatism. In M. Coltheart, G. Sartori and P. Job (eds.), *The Cognitive Neuropsychology of Language* (pp. 221–33), London: Erlbaum.

Berndt, R.S. and Caramazza, A. (1980). A redefinition of the syndrome of Broca's aphasia: Implications for a neuropsychological model of language. *Applied Psycholinguistics* 1, 225–278.

Bever, T.G. (1970). The cognitive basis for linguistic structures. In J.R. Hayes (ed.) *Cognition and the Development of Language*. New York: Wiley.

Bianchi, L. (1922). *The Mechanisms of the Brain and the Functions of the Frontal Lobes* (translation by J.H. Macdonald). Edinburgh: Livingstone.

Biedermann, I. (1977). On processing information from a glance at a scene: Implications for a syntax and semantics of visual processing. In S. Treu (ed.) *User-oriented Design of Interactive Graphics Systems*. New York: ACM.

Bisiach, E. and Luzzatti C. (1978) Unilateral neglect of representational space. *Cortex*, 14, 129–133.

Bjork, R.A. and Bjork, E.L. (1992). A new theory of disuse and an old theory of stimulus fluctuation. In A.F. Healy, S.M. Kosslyn and R.M. Shiffrin (eds) *From Learning Processes to Cognitive Processes: Essays in Honour of William K. Estes* (vol. 2, pp. 35–67). Hillsdale, NJ: Erlbaum.

Blakemore, C. and Nachmias, J. (1971). The orientation specificity of two visual after-effects. *Journal of Physiology*, 213: 157–174.

Bliss, T.V.P. and Lomo, T. (1973). Long-lasting potentiation of synaptic transmission in the dentate area of the anaesthetised rabbit following stimulation of the perforant path. *Journal of Physiology*, 232, 331–356.

Blumstein, S. Milberg, W. and Shrier, R. (1982). Semantic processing in aphasia: Evidence from an auditory lexical decision task. *Brain and Language*, 17, 301–315.

Bock, J.K. and Levelt, W.J.M. (1994). Language production: Grammatical encoding. In M.A. Gernsbacher (ed.) *Handbook of Psycholinguistics*. London: Academic Press.

Bodamer, J. (1947). Die Prosopa-Agnosie. *Archiv für Psychiatrie und Nervenkrankheiten*, 179, 6–53.

Bornstein, B. Sroka, M. and Munitz, H. (1969). Prosopagnosia with animal face agnosia. *Cortex*, 5, 164–169.

Boucart, M. and Humphreys, G.W. (1992). Global shape cannot be attended without object identification. *Journal of Experimental Psychology: Human Perception and Performance*, 18,3, 785–806.

Boucart, M. and Humphreys, G.W. (1994). Attention to orientation, size, luminance, and colour: attentional failure within the form domain. *Journal of Experimental Psychology: Human Perception and Performance*, 20,1, 61–80.

Boucart, M. Humphreys, G.W. and Lorenceau, J. (1995). Automatic access to object identity: Attention to global information not to particular physical dimensions, is important. *Journal of Experimental Psychology: Human Perception and Performance*, 21,3, 584–601.

Bower, G.H. (1981). Mood and Memory. *The American Psychologist*, 36, 129–220.

Bower, G.H. and Mayer, J.D. (1989). In search of mood-dependent memory: Theory, research, and applications. *Journal of Social Behaviour and Personality*, 4, 121–156.

Bower, G.H. Monteiro, K.P. and Gilligan, S.G. (1978). Emotional mood as a context for learning and recall. *Journal of Verbal Learning and Verbal Behaviour*, 17, 573–585.

Braine, M.D.S. (1978). On the relation between the natural logic of reasoning and standard logic. *Psychological Review*, 85, 1–21.

Braine, M.D.S. Reiser, B.J. and Rumain, B. (1984). Some empirical justification for a theory of natural propositional logic. In G.H. Bower (ed.) *The Psychology of Learning and Motivation* (Vol. 18, pp. 313–371). New York: Academic Press.

Bransford, J.D. and Johnson, M.K. (1972). Contextual prerequisites for understanding: Some investigations of comprehension and recall. *Journal of Verbal Learning and Verbal Behaviour*, 11, 717–726.

Brickner, R.M. (1936). *The Intellectual Functions of the Frontal Lobes*. New York: Macmillan.

Broadbent, D.E. (1958). *Perception and Communication*. Oxford: Pergammon.

Broadbent, D.E. (1966). The well-ordered mind. *American Education Research Journal*, 3, 281–295.

Broadbent, D.E. (1982). Task combination and the selective intake of information. *Acta Psychologica*, 50, 253–290.

Broca, P. (1861). Perte de la parole. Ramollissement chronique et destruction partielle du lobe anterieur gauche du cerveau. *Bulletin de la Société d'Anthropologie* (Paris), 2, 235–238.

Brown, J. (1958). Some tests of the decay theory of immediate memory. *Quarterly Journal of Experimental Psychology*, 10, 12–21.

Brown, R. and Kulik, J. (1977). Flashbulb memories. *Cognition*, 5, 73–99.

Brownell, H. Gardner, H. Prather, P. and Martino, G. (1995). Language, communication, and the right hemisphere. In H.S. Kirshner (ed.) *Handbook of Neurological Speech and Language Disorders: Neurological Disease and Therapy* (Vol. 33, pp. 325–350). New York: Marcel Dekker.

Brownell, H.H. Michel, D. Powelson, J.A. and Gardner, H. (1983). Surprise but not coherence: Sensitivity to verbal humor in right hemisphere patients. *Brain and Language*, 18, 20–27.

Bruce, V. and Humphreys, G. W. (1994). Recognizing objects and faces. *Visual Cognition*, 1, 141–180.

Bruce, V. and Young, A. (1986). Understanding face recognition. *British Journal of Psychology*, 77, 305–327.

Bruner, J.S. Goodnow, J.J. and Austin, G.A. (1956). *A Study of Thinking*. New York: Wiley.

Bruner, J.S. and Postman, L. (1947). Tension and tension-release as organising factors in perception. *Journal of Personality*, 15, 300–308.

Bruyer, R. Laterre, C. Seron, X. Feyereisen, P. Strypstein, E. Pierrard, E. and Rectem, D. (1983). A case of prosopagnosia with some preserved covert remembrance of familiar faces. *Brain and Cognition*, 2, 257–284.

Burgess, P.W. and Shallice, T. (1994). Fractionation of the frontal-lobe syndrome. *Revue de Neuropsychologie*, 4, 345–370.

Burgess, P.W. and Shallice, T. (1996a). Response suppression, initiation and strategy use following frontal lobe lesions. *Neuropsychologia*, 34, 263–273.

Burgess, P.W. and Shallice, T. (1996b). Bizarre responses, rule detection and frontal lobe lesions. *Cortex*, 32, 241–259.

Butters, N. and Cermak, L.S. (1986). A case study of the forgetting of autobiographical knowledge: Implications for the study of retrograde amnesia. In D.C. Rubin (ed.) *Autobiographical Memory*. Cambridge: Cambridge University Press.

Butterworth, B. Cipolotti, L. and Warrington, E.K. (1996). Short-term memory impairment and arithmetical ability. *Quarterly Journal of Experimental Psychology*, 49A, 251–262.

Calder, A.J. Young, A.W. Rowland, D. Perrett, D.I. Hodges, J.R. and Etcoff, N.L. (1996). Facial emotion recognition after bilateral amygdala damage: Differentially severe impairment of fear. *Cognitive Neuropsychology*, 13, 699–745.

Campbell, D. (1909). Störungen der Merkfähigkeit und fehlendes Krankheitsgefühl bei einem Fall von Stirnhirntumor. *Monatsschrift für Psychiatrie*, 26, 33–41.

Campbell, F.W. and Robson, J.G. (1968). Application of Fourier analysis to the visibility of gratings. *Journal of Physiology*, 197: 551–566.

Cambell, R. and Conway, M.A. (1995). *Broken Memories*. Oxford: Blackwell.

Campbell, R. Landis, T. and Regard, M. (1986). Face recognition and lip reading: A neurological dissociation. *Brain*, 109, 509–521.

Campion, J. and Latto, R. (1985). Apperceptive agnosia due to carbon monoxide poisoning. An interpretation based on critical band masking from disseminated lesions. *Behavioural Brain Research*, 15, 227–240.

Campion, J. Latto, R. and Smith, Y.M. (1983). Is blindsight an effect of scattered light, spared cortex, and near-threshold vision? *Behavioural and Brain Sciences*, 6, 423–428.

Caplan, D. (1986). In defense of agrammatism. *Cognition*, 24, 263–276.

Caplan, D. (1987). *Neurolinguistics and Linguistic Aphasiology*. Cambridge: Cambridge University Press.

Caplan, D. (1992). *Language: Structure, Processing and Disorders*. Cambridge, MA: MIT Press.

Caplan, D. and Hildebrandt, N. (1988). *Disorders of Syntactic Comprehension*. Cambridge, MA: MIT Press.

Caramazza, A. (1984). The logic of neuropsychological research and the problem of patient classification of aphasia. *Brain and Language*, 21, 9–20.

Caramazza, A. and Badecker, W. (1991). Clinical syndromes are not God's gift to cognitive neuropsychology: A reply to a rebuttal to an answer to a response to the case against syndrome-based research. *Brain and Cognition*, 16, 211–227.

Caramazza, A. and Zurif, E.B. (1976). Dissociation of algorithmic and heuristic processes in language comprehension. *Brain and Language*, 3, 572–582.

Carpenter, P.A. Miyake, A. and Just, M.A. (1994). Working memory constraints in comprehension: Evidence from individual differences, aphasia, and aging. In M.A. Gernsbacher (ed.) *Handbook of Psycholinguistics* (pp. 1075–1122). San Diego, CA: Academic Press.

Carroll, D.W. (1994). *Psychology of Language* (2nd edn). Belmont, CA: Brooks/Cole.

Cermak, L.S. and O'Connor, M. (1983). The anterograde and retrograde retrieval ability of a patient with amnesia due to encephalitis. *Neuropsychologia*, 21, 213–234.

Cermak, L.S. Talbot, N. Chandler, K. and Woolbarst, L.R. (1985). The perceptual priming phenomenon in amnesia. *Neuropsychologia*, 23, 615–622.

Chalmers, A.F. (1982). What is this Thing Called Science? Milton Keynes: Open University Press.

Chandler, C.C. and Gargano, G.J. (1998). Retrieval processes that produce interference in modified forced-choice recognition tests. *Memory and Cognition*, 26, 220–231.

Chase, W.G. and Simon, H.A. (1973a). The mind's eye in chess. In W.G. Chase (ed.) *Visual Information Processing*. New York: Academic Press.

Chase, W.G. and Simon, H.A. (1973b). Perception in chess. *Cognitive Psychology*, 4, 55–81.

Chater, N. (1997). Simplicity and the mind. *The Psychologist*, 10,11, 495–498.

Cheesman, J. and Merikle, P.M. (1986). Distinguishing conscious from unconscious perceptual processes. *Canadian Journal of Psychology*, 40, 343–367.

Cheng, P.W. and Holyoak, K.J. (1985). Pragmatic reasoning schemas. *Cognitive Psychology*, 17, 391–416.

Cheng, P.W. Holyoak, K.J. Nisbett, R.E. and Oliver, L.M. (1986). Pragmatic versus syntactic approaches to training deductive reasoning. *Cognitive Psychology*, 18, 293–328.

Cherry, E.C. (1953). Some experiments on the recognition of speech with one and two ears. *Journal of the Acoustical Society of America*, 25, 975–979.

Chi, M.T.H. Feltovich, P.J.and Glaser, R. (1981). Categorization and representation of physics problems by experts and novices. *Cognitive Science*, 5, 121–152.

Chiu, C.P. and Schacter, D.L. (1995). Auditory priming for non-verbal information: Implicit and explicit memory for environmental sounds. *Consciousness and Cognition*, 4, 440–458.

Chomsky, N. (1957). *Syntactic Structures*. The Hague: Mouton.

Chomsky, N. (1965). *Aspects of the Theory of Syntax*. Cambridge, MA: MIT Press.

Chomsky, N. (1968). *Language and Mind*. New York: Harcourt Brace.

Chomsky, N. (1981). *Lectures on Government and Binding*. Dordrecht: Foris.

Chomsky, N. (1986). *Knowledge of Language*. New York: Praeger Special Studies.

Churchland, P. and Sejnowski, T. (1994). *The Computational Brain*. Cambridge, MA: MIT Press (Bradford Books).

Cicerone, K. Lazar, R. and Shapiro, W. (1983). Effects of frontal lobe lesions on hypothesis sampling during concept formation. *Neuropsychologia*, 21, 513–524.

Claparede, E. (1911). Recognition et moité. *Archives Psychologiques Geneve*, 11, 79–90.

Clark, A. (1990). *Microcognition: Philosophy, Cognitive Science and Parallel Distributed Processing*. Cambridge, MA: MIT Press (Bradford Books).

Clark, H.H. (1994). Discourse in production. In M,A. Gernsbacher (ed.) *Handbook of Psycholinguistics*. London: Academic Press.

Clark, H.H. and Clark, E.V. (1977). *Psychology and Language: An Introduction to Psycholinguistics*. New York: Harcourt Brace Jovanovich.

Clark, H.H. and Haviland, S.E. (1977). Comprehension and the Given-New Contract. In R. Freedle (ed.) *Discourse Processes: Advances in Research and Theory*. Norwood, NJ: Ablex.

Clark, H.H. and Lucy, P. (1975). Understanding what is meant from what is said: A study in conversationally conveyed requests. *Journal of Verbal Learning and Verbal Behavior*, 14, 56–72.

Cohen, G. (1983). *The Psychology of Cognition* (2nd edn). London: Academic Press.

Cohen, N.J. (1984). Preserved learning capacity in amnesia: Evidence for multiple memory systems. In L.R. Squire and N. Butters (eds) *Neuropsychology of Memory*. New York: Guilford Press.

Cohen, N.J. (1997). Memory. In M.T. Banich, *Neuropsychology*. Boston, MA: Houghton Mifflin.

Cohen, N.J. and Eichenbaum, H.E. (1993). *Memory, Amnesia, and the Hippocampal System*. Cambridge, MA: MIT Press.

Cohen, N.J. Ramzy, C. Hu, Z. Tomaso, H. Strupp, J. Erhard, P. Anderson, P. and Ugurbil, K. (1994). Hippocampal activation in fMRI evoked by demand for declarative memory-based binding of multiple streams of information. *Society for Neuroscience Abstracts*, 20, 1290.

Cohen, N.J. and Squire, L.R. (1980). Preserved learning and retention of pattern-analysing skill in amnesia: Dissociation of knowing how and knowing that. *Science*, 210, 207–210.

Cohen, N.J. and Squire, L.R. (1981). Retrograde amnesia and remote memory impairment. *Neuropsychologia*, 19, 337–356.

Collins, A. and Loftus, E. (1975). A spreading activation theory of semantic processing. *Psychological Review*, 82, 407–428.

Collins, A. and Quillian, M. (1969). Retrieval time from semantic memory. *Journal of Verbal Learning and Verbal Behaviour*, 8, 240–248.

Coltheart, M. (1980a). Iconic memory and visible persistence. *Perception and Psychophysics*, 27, 183–228.

Coltheart, M. (1980b). Deep dyslexia: A review of the syndrome. In M. Coltheart, K.E. Patterson and J.C. Marshall (eds) *Deep Dyslexia* (pp. 22–47). London: Routledge & Kegan Paul.

Coltheart, M. (1987). Reading, phonological recoding and deep dyslexia. In M. Coltheart, K.E. Patterson and J.C. Marshall (eds) *Deep Dyslexia*. London: Routledge & Kegan Paul.

Connine, C.M. Mullennix, J. Shernoff, E. and Yelen, J. (1990). Word familiarity and frequency in visual and auditory word recognition. *Journal of Experimental Psychology: Learning, Memory and Cognition*, 16, 1084–1096.

Conway, M.A. (1990). *Autobiographical Memory: An Introduction*. Philadelphia, PA: Open University Press.

Conway, M.A. Anderson, S.J. Larsen, S.F. Donnelly, C.M. McDaniel, M.A. McLelland, A.G. and Rawles, R.E. (1994). The formation of flashbulb memories. *Memory and Cognition*, 22, 326–343.

Corkin, S. (1968). Acquisition of motor skill after bilateral medial temporal-lobe excision. *Neuropsychologia*, 6, 255–265.

Corkin, S. (1982). Some relationships between global amnesias and the memory impairments in Alzheimer's disease. In S. Corkin, K.L. Davis, J.H. Growden and E. Usdin (eds) *Alzheimer's Disease: A Report of Progress in Research*. New York: Raven Press.

Corkin, S. (1984). Lasting consequences of bilateral medial lobectomy: Clinical course and experimental findings in HM. *Seminars in Neurology*, 4, 249–259.

Cowey, A. Small, M. and Ellis, S. (1994). Left visuo-spatial neglect can be worse in far than in near space. *Neurospychologia*, 32, 1059–1066.

Craik, F.I.M. (1977). Depth of processing in recall and recognition. In S. Dornik (ed.) *Attention and Performance* (Vol. 6, pp. 679–698). New York: Raven Press.

Craik, F.I.M. and Lockhart, R.S. (1972). Levels of processing: A framework for memory research. *Journal of Verbal Learning and Verbal Behaviour*, 11, 671–684.

Craik, F.I.M. and Tulving, E. (1975). Depth of processing and the retention of words in episodic memory. *Journal of Experimental Psychology, General*, 104, 268–294.

Craik, F.I.M. and Watkins, M.J. (1973). The role of rehearsal in short-term memory. *Journal of Verbal Learning and Verbal Behaviour*, 12, 599–607.

Crick, F. (1994). *The Astonishing Hypothesis*. London: Simon & Schuster.

Crick, F. and Koch, C. (1990). Towards a neurobiological theory of consciousness. *Seminars in the Neurosciences*, 2, 263–275.

Damasio, A. Eslinger, P.J. Damasio, H. Van Hoesen, G.W. and Cornell, S. (1985). Multi-modal amnesic syndrome following bilateral temporal and basal forebrain lesions. *Archives of Neuropsychology*, 42, 252–259.

Davies, G.M. (1994). Children's testimony – research findings and policy implications. *Psychology, Crime, and Law*, 1, 175–180.

Davies, G.M. and Thomson, D.M. (1988). *Memory in Context: Context in Memory*. Chichester: Wiley.

Dayhoff, J. (1990). *Neural Network Architectures: An Introduction*. New York: Van Nostrand Reinhold.

De Haan, E.H.F. Young, A.W. and Newcombe, F. (1987). Face recognition without awareness. *Cognitive Neuropsychology*, 4, 385–415.

De Renzi, E. Faglioni, P. Grossi, D. and Nichelli, P. (1991). Apperceptive and associative forms of prosopagnosia. *Cortex*, 27, 213–221.

DeGroot, A.D. (1965). *Thought and Choice in Chess*. The Hague: Mouton.

Dekle, D.J. Beal, C.R. Elliott, R. and Huneycutt, D. (1996). Children as witnesses: A comparison of lineup versus showup identification methods. *Applied Cognitive Psychology*, 10, 1–12.

Delis, D.C. Squire, L.R., Bihrle, A. and Massman, P. (1992). Componential analysis of problem-solving ability: Performance of patients with frontal lobe damage and amnesic patients on a new sorting test. *Neuropsychologia*, 30, 683–697.

Dell, G.S. (1986). A spreading-activation theory of retrieval in sentence production. *Psychological Review*, 93, 283–321.

Dell, G.S. (1995). Speaking and misspeaking. In L.R. Gleitman and M. Liberman (eds) *Language: An Invitation to Cognitive Science* (Vol. 1, 2nd edn). Cambridge, MA: MIT Press.

Dell, G.S. and O'Seaghdha, P.G. (1991). Mediated and convergent lexical priming in language production: A comment on Levelt *et al.* (1991). *Psychological Review*, 98, 604–614.

Deloche, G. Andreewsky, E. and Desi, M. (1982). Surface dyslexia: A case report and some theoretical implications for reading models. *Brain and Language*, 15, 12–31.

Denes, G. and Semenza, C. (1975). Auditory modality-specific anomia: Evidence from a case of pure word deafness. *Cortex*, 11, 401–411.

Deschepper, B. and Treisman, A. (1996). Visual memory for novel shapes: Implicit coding without attention. *Journal of Experimental Psychology: Learning, Memory, and Cognition*, 22, 27–47.

Deutsch, J.A. and Deutsch, D. (1967). Comments on 'Selective attention: perception or response?' *Quarterly Journal of Experimental Psychology*, 19, 362–363.

Dixon, N.F. (1981). *Preconscious Processing*. Chichester: Wiley.

Dixon, N.F. (1990). Perceptual and other related defenses. *Polish Psychological Bulletin*, 21, 4, 319–330.

Dixon, N.F. and Henley, S.H.A. (1980). Without awareness. In M. Jeeves (ed.) *Psychology Survey No. 3*. London: George Allen & Unwin.

Drachman, D.A. and Arbit, J. (1966). Memory and hippocampal complex. II. Is memory a multiple process? *Archives of Neurology*, 15, 52–61.

Dreyfus, H. (1979). *What Computers Can't Do – The Limits of Artificial Intelligence*. New York: Harper & Row.

Driver, J. (1996). Attention and segmentation. *The Psychologist*, 9,3, 119–124.

Driver, J. and Baylis, G.C. (1989). Movement and visual attention: The spotlight metaphor breaks down. *Journal of Experimental Psychology: Human Perception and Performance*, 15, 448–456.

Driver, J. and McLeod, P. (1992). Reversing visual search asymmetries with conjunctions of movement and orientation. *Journal of Experimental Psychology: Human Perception and Performance* 18, 22–33.

Driver, J. and Tipper, S.P. (1989). On the non-selectivity of 'selective seeing': Contrast between interference and priming in selective attention. *Journal of Experimental Psychology: Human Perception and Performance*, 15, 304–314.

Dronkers, N. (1996). A new brain region for coordinating speech articulation. *Nature*, 384, 159–161.

Duncan, J. (1984). Selective attention and the organisation of visual information. *Journal of Experimental Psychology: General*, 113, 501–517.

Duncan, J. Emslie, H. and Williams, P. (1996). Intelligence and the frontal lobe: The organization of goal-directed behavior. *Cognitive Psychology*, 30, 257–303.

Duncan, J. and Humphreys, G.W. (1989). A resemblance theory of visual search. *Psychological Review*, 96, 433–458.

Duncan, J. and Humphreys, G.W. (1992). Beyond the search surface: Visual search and attentional engagement. *Journal of Experimental Psychology: Human Perception and Performance*, 18, 578–588.

Duncker, K. (1945). On problem solving. *Psychological Monographs*, 58 (Whole No. 270).

Ebbinghaus, H. (1885). *Über das Gedächtnis: Untersuchugen zur experimentellen Psychologie.* Leipzig: Dunker & Humbolt.

Efron, R. (1968). *What is Perception?* New York: Humanities Press.

Eich, E. (1985). Context memory, and integrated item/context imagery. *Journal of Experimental Psychology: Learning, Memory, and Cognition,* 11, 764–770.

Ekman, P. (1982). *Emotion in the Human Face* (2nd edn). Cambridge: Cambridge University Press.

Ekman, P. and Friesen, W.V. (1976). *Pictures of Facial Affect.* Palo Alto, CA: Consulting Psychologists Press.

Ellis, A.W. (1984). Introduction to Bramwell's (1887) case of word-meaning deafness. *Cognitive Neuropsychology,* 1, 245–248.

Ellis, A.W. and Young, A.W. (1988). *Human Cognitive Neuropsychology: A Textbook with Readings.* London: Lawrence Erlbaum Associates.

Ellis, A.W. and Young, A.W. (1996). *Human Cognitive Neuropsychology* (2nd edn). Hove: LEA.

Ellis, H.D. and Shepherd, J.W. (1974). Recognition of abstract and concrete words presented in left and right visual fields. *Journal of Experimental Psychology,* 103, 1035–1036.

Erdelyi, M.H. (1974). A new look at the New Look: Perceptual defense and vigilance. *Psychological Review,* 81, 1–25.

Eriksen, C.W. (1990). Attentional search of the visual field. In D. Brogan (ed.) *Visual Search.* London: Taylor & Francis.

Eslinger, P.J. and Damasio, A.R. (1985). Severe disturbance of higher cognition after bilateral frontal lobe ablation: Patient E.V.R. *Neurology, Cleveland,* 35, 1731–1741.

Evans, J. St B.T. (1989). *Bias in Human Reasoning: Causes and Consequences.* Hove: Erlbaum.

Evans, J. St B.T. (1996). Deciding before you think: Relevance and reasoning in the selection task. *British Journal of Psychology,* 87, 223–240.

Evans, J. St B.T. Barston, J.L. and Pollard, P. (1983). On the conflict between logic and belief in syllogistic reasoning. *Memory and Cognition,* 11, 295–306.

Evans, J. St B.T. and Lynch, J.S. (1973). Matching bias in the selection task. *British Journal of Psychology,* 64, 391–397.

Evans, J. St B.T. and Over, D.E. (1996). *Rationality and Reasoning.* Hove: Psychology Press.

Eysenck, M.W. (1978). Levels of processing: A critique. *British Journal of Psychology,* 69, 157–169.

Eysenck, M.W. (1979). Depth, elaboration, and distinctiveness. In L.S. Cermak and F.I.M. Craik (eds) *Levels of Processing in Human Memory.* Hillsdale, NJ: Lawrence Erlbaum Associates Inc.

Farah, M.J. (1990). *Visual Agnosia: Disorders of Object Recognition and What They Can Tell us about Normal Vision.* Cambridge, MA: MIT Press.

Farah, M.J. (1991) Patterns of co-occurrence among the associative agnosias: Implications for visual object representation. *Cognitive Neuropsychology,* 8, 1–19.

Farah, M.J. Hammond, K.M. Levine, D.N. and Calvanio, R. (1988). Visual and spatial mental imagery: Dissociable systems of representation. *Cognitive Psychology,* 20,439–462.

Farah, M. J. Hammond, K.M. Mehta, Z. and Ratcliff, G. (1989). Category-specificity and modality-specificity in semantic memory. *Neuropsychologia,* 27, 193–200.

Farah, M. J. McMullen, P. A. and Meyer, M.M. (1991). Can recognition of living things be selectively impaired? *Neuropsychologia,* 29, 185–193.

Ferrier, D. (1876). *The Functions of the Brain.* London: Smith, Elder.

Fisher, R.P. and Craik, F.I.M. (1977). Interaction between encoding and retrieval operations in cued recall. *Journal of Experimental Psychology: Human Learning and Memory,* 3, 701–711.

Fisher, R.P. and Geiselman, R.E. (1992). *Memory-enhancing Techniques for Investigative Interviewing: The Cognitive Interview.* Springfield, IL: Charles C. Thomas.

Flin, R. Boon, J. Knox, A. and Bull, R. (1992). The effect of a five-month delay on children's and adult's eyewitness memory. *British Journal of Psychology*, 83, 323–336.

Fodor, J.A. (1983). *Modularity of Mind*. Cambridge, MA: MIT Press.

Fodor, J.A. Bever, T.G. and Garrett, M.F. (1974). *The Psychology of Language*. New York: McGraw Hill.

Forster, K.I. (1976). Accessing the mental lexicon. In R.J. Wales and E.C.T. Walker (eds) *New Approaches to Language Mechanisms*. Amsterdam: North Holland.

Forster, K.I. (1979). Levels of processing and the structure of the language processor. In W.E. Cooper and E.C.T. Walker (eds.) *Sentence Processing: Psycholinguistic Studies Presented to Merrill Garrett*. Hillsdale, NJ: Lawrence Erlbaum Associates.

Forster, K.I. (1994). Computational modeling and elementary process analysis on visual word recognition. *Journal of Experimental Psychology: Human Perception and Performance*, 20, 1292–1310.

Foss, D.J. (1969). Decision processes during sentence comprehension: Effects of lexical item difficulty and position upon reaction times. *Journal of Verbal Learning and Verbal Behavior*, 8, 457–462.

Francolini, C.N. and Egeth, H.E. (1980). On the non-automaticity of automatic activation: Evidence of selective seeing. *Perception and Psychophysics*, 27, 331–342.

Frazier, L. (1987). Theories of sentence processing. In J.L. Garfield (ed.) *Modularity in Knowledge Representation and Natural Language Understanding*. Cambridge, MA: MIT Press.

Frazier, L. (1989). Against lexical generation of syntax. In W.D. Marslen-Wilson (ed.) *Lexical Representation and Process*. Cambridge, MA: MIT Press.

Frazier, L. (1990). Exploring the architecture of the language processing system. In G.T.M. Altmann (ed.) *Cognitive Models of Speech Processing*. Cambridge, MA: MIT Press.

Frazier, L. and Rayner, K. (1982). Making and correcting errors during sentence comprehension: Eye movements in the analysis of structurally ambiguous sentences. *Cognitive Psychology*, 14, 178–210.

Freeman, C.P.L. Weeks, D. and Kendell, R.E. (1980). ECT: Patients who complain. *British Journal of Psychiatry*, 137, 17–25.

Freud, S. (1891). *On Aphasia: A Critical Study*. New York: International Universities Press (trans. E. Stengel). (Reprinted in 1953.)

Freud, S. (1938). Psychopathology of everyday life. In A.A. Brill (ed.) *The Writings of Sigmund Freud*. New York: Modern Library.

Frisby, J. (1979). *Seeing*. Oxford: Oxford University Press.

Fromkin, V.A. (1971). The non-anomalous nature of anomalous utterances. *Language*, 47, 27–52.

Fromkin, V.A. (ed.) (1973). *Speech Errors as Linguistic Evidence*. The Hague: Mouton.

Fruzzetti, A.E. Toland, K. Teller, S.A. and Loftus, E.F. (1992). Memory and eyewitness testimony. In M. Gruneberg and P. Morris (eds) *Aspects of Memory: The Practical Aspects*. London: Routledge.

Funell, E. and Sheridan, J. (1992). Categories of knowledge? Unfamiliar aspects of living and nonliving things. *Cognitive Neuropsychology*, 9, 135–153.

Gabrieli, J.D.E. Cohen, N.J. and Corkin, S. (1988). The acquisition of lexical and semantic knowledge in amnesia. *Society for Neuroscience Abstracts*, 9, 328.

Gaffan, D. and Heywood, C. A. (1993). A spurious category specific visual agnosia for living things in normal human and non-human primates. *Journal of Cognitive Neuroscience*, 5, 118–128.

Gardiner, J.M. Gawlik, B. and Richardson-Klavehn, A. (1994). Maintenance rehearsal affects knowing, not remembering: Elaborative rehearsal affects remembering, not knowing. *Psychonomic Bulletin and Review*, 1, 107–110.

Gardiner, J.M. and Java, R.I. (1993) Recognising and remembering. In R.F. Collins, S.E. Gathercole, M.A. Conway and P.E. Morris (eds) *Theories of Memory*. Hove: Lawrence Erlbaum Associates Ltd.

Gardiner, J.M. and Parkin, A.J. (1990). Attention and recollective experience in recognition memory. *Memory and Cognition*, 18, 579–583.

Gardner, H. (1977). *The Shattered Mind*. Hove: Psychology Press.

Gardner, H. (1985). *The Mind's New Science*. New York: Basic Books Inc.

Garnham, A. and Oakhill, J. (1994). *Thinking and Reasoning*. Oxford: Blackwell.

Garrett, M.F. (1975). The analysis of sentence production. In G. Bower (ed.) *Psychology of Learning and Motivation* (Vol. 9). New York: Academic Press.

Garrett, M.F. (1976). Syntactic processes in sentence production. In R.J. Wales and E. Walker (eds.) *New Approaches to Language Mechanisms*. Amsterdam: North Holland.

Garrett, M.F. (1980). Levels of processing in sentence production. In B. Butterworth (ed.) *Language Production: Vol 1: Speech and Talk*. London: Academic Press.

Garrett, M.F. (1982). Production of speech: Observations from normal and pathological language use. In A.W. Ellis (ed.) *Normality and Pathology in Cognitive Functions*. London: Academic Press.

Garrett, M.F. (1984). The organisation of processing structure for language production: Applications to aphasic speech. In D. Caplan, A.R. Lecours and A. Smith (eds) *Biological Perspectives of language*. Cambridge, MA: MIT Press.

Gasquoine, P.J. (1991). Learning in post-traumatic amnesia following extremely severe closed-head injury. *Brain Injury*, 5, 169–175.

Gathercole, S.E. and Baddeley, A.D. (1990). Phonological memory deficits in language disordered children: Is there a causal connection? *Journal of Memory and Language*, 29, 336–360.

Gathercole, S.E. and Baddeley, A.D. (1993). *Working Memory and Language*. Hove: Lawrence Erlbaum Associates.

Gazzaniga, M.S. (1994). Blindsight reconsidered. *Current Directions in Psychological Science*, 3, 93–96.

Gazzaniga, M.S. (1998). *Cognitive Neuroscience: The Biology of the Mind*. New York: Norton.

Gazzaniga, M.S. Ivry, R.B. and Mangun, G.R. (1998). *Cognitive Neuroscience: The Biology of the Mind*. New York: Norton.

Geiselman, R.E. Fisher, R.P. MacKinnon, D.P. and Holland, H.L. (1985). Eyewitness memory enhancement in police interview: Cognitive retrieval mnemonics versus hypnosis. *Journal of Applied Psychology*, 70, 401–412.

Gentner, D. and Gentner, D.R. (1983). Flowing waters and teeming crowds: Mental models of electricity. In D. Genter and A.L. Stevens (eds) *Mental Models*. Hillsdale, NJ: Lawrence Erlbaum Associates.

Gentner, D. and Toupin, C. (1986). Systematicity and surface similarity in the development of analogy. *Cognitive Science*, 10, 227–300.

Geschwind, N. (1965). Disconnection syndromes in animals and man. *Brain*, 88, 237–294, 585–644.

Geschwind, N. (1972). Language and the brain. *Scientific American*, 226, 4, 76–83.

Geschwind, N. Quadfasel, F.A. and Segarra, J.M. (1968). Isolation of the speech area. *Neuropsychologia*, 6, 327–340.

Gibson, J.J. (1979). *The Ecological Approach to Visual Perception*. Boston, MA: Houghton Mifflin.

Gick, M.L. and Holyoak, K.J. (1980). Analogical problem solving. *Cognitive Psychology*, 12, 306–355.

Gick, M.L. and Holyoak, K.J. (1983). Schema induction and analogical transfer. *Cognitive Psychology*, 15, 1–38.

Gigerenzer, G. and Hoffrage, U. (1995). How to improve Bayesian reasoning without instruction: Frequency formats. *Psychological Review*, 102, 684–704.

Gilhooly, K.J. (1996). *Thinking: Directed, Undirected and Creative* (3rd edn). London: Academic Press.

Glanzer, M. and Cunitz, A.R. (1966). Two storage mechanisms in free recall. *Journal of Verbal Learning and Verbal Behaviour*, 5, 351–360.

Glisky, E.L. Schacter, D.L. and Tulving,E. (1986). Computer learning by memory-impaired patients: Acquisition and retention of complex knowledge. *Neuropsychologia*, 24, 313–328.

Godden, D.R. and Baddeley, A.D. (1975). Context-dependent memory in two natural environments: On land and under water. *British Journal of Psychology*, 66, 325–331.

Godden, D.R. and Baddeley, A.D. (1980). When does context influence recognition memory? *British Journal of Psychology*, 71, 99–104.

Goel, V. and Grafman, J. (1995). Are the frontal lobes implicated in 'planning' functions? Interpreting data from the Tower of Hanoi. *Neuropsychologia*, 33, 623–642.

Goldberg, E. Antin, S.P. Bilder, R.M. Gerstman, L.J. Hughes, J.E.O. and Mattis, S. (1981). Retrograde amnesia: Possible role of mesencephalic reticular activation in long-term memory. *Science*, 213, 1392–1394.

Goldman-Rakic, P.S. (1987). Circuitry of primate prefrontal cortex and regulation of behavior by representational knowledge. In F. Plum and V. Mountcastle (eds) *Handbook of Physiology* (Vol. 5, pp. 373–417). Bethesda, MD: American Physiological Society.

Goltz, F. (1892). Der Hund ohne Grosshirn: siebente Abteilung über die Verrichtungen des Grosshirns. *Pfuger's Archiv für die gesamte Physiologie*, 51, 570–614.

Goodale, M.A. Jakobson, L.S. Milner, A.D. Perrett, D.I., Benson, P.J. and Hietanen, J.K. (1994). The nature and limits of orientation and pattern processing supporting visuo-motor control in a visual form agnosic. *Journal of Cognitive Neuroscience*, 6, 46–56.

Goodale, M.A. and Milner, A.D. (1992). Separate visual pathways for perception and action. *Trends in Neurosciences*, 15, 20–25.

Goodale, M.A. Milner, A.D. Jakobson, L.S. and Carey, D.P. (1991). A neurological dissociation between perceiving objects and grasping them. *Nature*, 349, 154–156.

Goodale, M.A. Pelisson, D. and Prablanc, C. (1986). *Nature*, 320, 748–750.

Goodglass, H. and Berko, J. (1960). Agrammatism and inflectional morphology in English. *Journal of Speech and Hearing Research*, 3, 257–267.

Goodwin, D.W. Powell, B. Bremer, D. Hoine, H. and Stern, J. (1969). Alcohol and recall: State dependent effects in man. *Science*, 163, 1358.

Gordon, I.E. (1997). *Theories of Visual Perception* (2nd edn). Chichester: Wiley.

Gorman, M.E. and Gorman, M.E. (1984). A comparison of disconfirmation, confirmation and control strategy on Wason's 2–4–6 task. *Quarterly Journal of Experimental Psychology*, 36A, 629–648.

Govier, E. and Pitts, M. (1982). The contextual disambiguation of a polysemous word in an unattended message. *British Journal of Psychology*, 73, 537–545.

Graf, P. and Komatsu, S. (1994). Process dissociation procedure: Handle with caution. *European Journal of Cognitive Psychology*, 6, 113–129.

Graf, P. and Schacter, D.L. (1985). Implicit and explicit memory for novel associations in normal and amnesic subjects. *Journal of Experimental Psychology: Learning, Memory, and Cognition*, 11, 501–518.

Graf, P. Squire, L.R. and Mandler, G. (1984). The information that amnesic patients do not forget. *Journal of Experimental Psychology: Learning, Memory, and Cognition*, 9, 164–178.

Green, D.W. *et al.* (eds) (1996). *Cognitive Science: An Introduction*. University College, London: Blackwell.

Greene, R.L. (1987). Effects of maintenance rehearsal on human memory. *Psychological Bulletin*, 102, 403–413.

Greenough, W.T. (1987). Experience effects on the developing and the mature brain: Dendritic branching and synaptogenesis. In N.A. Krasnegor, E. Blass, M. Hofer, and W.P. Smotherman (eds) *Perinatal Development: A Psychobiological Perspective*. New York: Academic Press.

Greenspoon, J. and Ranyard, R. (1957). Stimulus conditions and retroactive inhibition. *Journal of Experimental Psychology*, 53, 55–59.

Greenwald, A.G. (1992). New Look 3: Unconscious cognition reclaimed. *American Psychologist*, 47,6, 766–779.

Gregory, R.L. (1970). *The Intelligent Eye*. London: Weidenfeld & Nicolson.

Gregory, R.L. (1980). Perceptions as hypotheses. *Philosophical Transactions of the Royal Society of London*, B290, 181–197.

Gregory, R.L. (1996). Twenty-five years after 'The intelligent eye'. *The Psychologist*, 9,10, 452–455.

Gregory, R.L. (1998). *Eye and Brain* (5th edn). New York: McGraw-Hill.

Grice, H.P. (1975). Logic and conversation. In P. Cole and J.L. Morgan (eds) *Syntax and Semantics* (Vol. 3. Speech Acts). New York: Seminar Press.

Griggs R.A. and Cox, J.R. (1982). The elusive thematic materials effect in the Wason selection task. *British Journal of Psychology*, 73, 407–420.

Griggs, R.A. and Cox, J.R. (1983). The effects of problem content and negation on Wason's selection task. *Quarterly Journal of Experimental Psychology*, 35A, 519–533.

Groeger, J.A. (1988). Qualitatively different effects of undetected and unidentified auditory primes. *Quarterly Journal of Experimental Psychology*, 40(A), 323–329.

Gruneberg, M.M. (1992). The practical application of memory aids: Knowing how, knowing when, and knowing when not. In M.M. Gruneberg and P. Morris (eds) *Aspects of Memory* (2nd edn). London: Routledge.

Gurney, K. (1997). *An Introduction to Neural Networks*. London: UCL Press Ltd.

Gurney, K. and Wright, M. (1996). A biologically plausible model of early visual motion processing I: Theory and implementation. *Biological Cybernetics*, 74, 339–348.

Hallam, J. and Malcolm, C. (1994). Behaviour: perception, action and intelligence – the view from situated robotics. *Philosophical Transactions of the Royal Society*, 349, 29–42.

Halliday, M.A.K. and Hasan, R. (1976). *Cohesion in English*. London: Longman.

Halligan, P.W. and Marshall, J.C. (1991). Left neglect for near but not far space in man. *Nature*, 350, 498–500.

Halligan, P.W. and Marshall, J.C. (1993). The history and clinical presentation of neglect. In I.H. Robertson and J.C. Marshall (Eds) *Unilateral Neglect: Clinical and Experimental Studies*. Hove UK: LEA.

Halligan, P.W. and Marshall, J.C. (1994). Towards a principled explanation of unilateral neglect. *Cognitive Neuropsychology*, 11, 543–578.

Halstead, W.C. (1940). Preliminary analysis of grouping behaviour in patients with cerebral injury by the method of equivalent and non-equivalent stimuli. *American Journal of Psychiatry*, 96, 1263–1294.

Hanley, J.R. Young, A.W. and Pearson, N.A. (1991). Impairment of the visuo-spatial sketch pad. *Quarterly Journal of Experimental Psychology*, 43A, 101–125.

Harley, T.A. (1995). *The Psychology of Language: From Data to Theory*. Hove: Psychology Press.

Harlow, J.M. (1848). Passage of an iron bar through the head. *Boston Medical and Surgical Journal*, 39, 389–393.

Harlow, J.M. (1868). Recovery from the passage of an iron bar through the head. *Publications of the Massachusetts Medical Society*, 2, 327–347.

Hartley, A.A. (1993). Evidence for the selective preservation of spatial selective attention in old age. *Psychology and Ageing*, 8, 371–379.

Haviland, S.E. and Clark, H.H. (1974). What's new? Acquiring new information as a process in comprehension. *Journal of Verbal Learning and Verbal Behavior*, 13, 512–521.

Hay, D.C. and Young, A.W. (1982). The human face. In A.W. Ellis (ed.) *Normality and Pathology in Cognitive Functions*. London: Academic Press.

Hayes, J.R. and Simon, H.A. (1974). Understanding written problem instructions. In L.W. Gregg (ed.) *Knowledge and Cognition*. Hillsdale, NJ: Lawrence Erlbaum Associates.

Hayman, C.A.G. and Tulving, E. (1989). Is priming in fragment completion based on a 'traceless' memory system? *Journal of Experimental Psychology: Learning, Memory, and Cognition*, 15, 941–956.

Head, H. (1926). *Aphasia and Kindred Disorders of Speech*. Cambridge: Cambridge University Press.

Head, T. (1996). Soar web page. WWW link. http://www.cs.cmu.edu/afs/cs.cmu.edu/project/soar/public/www/home-page.html.

Healy, A.F. and McNamara, D.S. (1996). Verbal learning and memory: Does the modal model still work? *Annual Review of Psychology*, 47, 143–172.

Hebb, D.O. (1949). *The Organisation of Behaviour*. New York: Wiley.

Helmstaedter, C. Kemper, B. and Elger, C.E. (1996). Neuropsychological aspects of frontal lobe epilepsy. *Neuropsychologia*, 34, 399–406.

Henle, M. (1962). On the relation between logic and thinking. *Psychological Review*, 69, 366–378.

Hertel, P.T. (1992). Improving memory and mood through automatic and controlled procedures of mind. In D.J. Herrmann, H. Weingartner, A. Searleman and C.L. McEvoy (eds) *Memory Improvement: Implications for Memory Theory*. New York: Springer-Verlag.

Hill, E. and Williamson, J. (1998). Choose six numbers, any numbers. *The Psychologist*, 11, 17–21.

Hinton, G. Plaut, D. and Shallice, T. (1993). Simulating brain damage. *Scientific American*, 269, 76–82.

Hinton, G. and Shallice, T. (1991). Lesioning an attractor network: Investigations of acquired dyslexia. *Psychological Review*, 98, 74–95.

Hittmair-Delazer, M. Denes, G. Semenza, C. and Mantovan, M.C. (1994). Anomia for people's names. *Neuropsychologia*, 32, 465–476.

Hodge, M.H. and Otani, H. (1996). Beyond category sorting and pleasantness rating: Inducing relational and item-specific processing. *Memory and Cognition*, 24, 110–115.

Hodges, A. (1985). Alan Turing – *The Enigma of Intelligence*. London: Counterpoint (Unwin).

Hodges, J.R. Salmon, D.P. and Butters, N. (1993). Recognition and naming of famous faces in Alzheimer's disease: A cognitive analysis. *Neuropsychologia*, 31, 775–788.

Hokkanen, L. Launes, R. and Vataja, L. (1995). Isolated retrograde amnesia for autobiographical memory associated with acute left temporal lobe encephalitis. *Psychological Medicine*, 25, 203–208.

Hopfield, J. (1982). Neural networks and physical systems with emergent collective computational properties. *Proceedings of the National Academy of Sciences of the USA*, 79, 2554–2588.

Hopfield, J. (1984). Neurons with graded response have collective computational properties like those of two-state neurons. *Proceedings of the National Academy of Sciences of the USA*, 81, 3088–3092.

Hough, M.S. (1990). Narrative comprehension in adults with right and left hemisphere brain-damage: Theme organisation. *Brain and Language*, 38, 253–277.

Howard, D. (1985). Introduction to 'On agrammatism' (Ueber Agrammatismus). *Cognitive Neuropsychology*, 2, 303–307. (Original work published in 1922 by M. Isserlin.)

Hubel, D.H. and Wiesel, T.N. (1962). Receptive fields, binocular interaction and functional architecture in the cat's visual cortex. *Journal of Physiology*, 166, 106–154.

Hubel, D.H. and Wiesel, T.N. (1968). Receptive fields and functional architecture of the monkey striate cortex. *Journal of Physiology*, 166, 215–243.

Hulme, C. Maughan, S. and Brown, G.D.A. (1991). Memory for familiar and unfamiliar words: Evidence for a long-term memory contribution to short-term memory span. *Journal of Memory and Language*, 30, 685–701.

Humphreys, G.W. (1981). Flexibility of attention between stimulus dimensions. *Perception and Psychophysics*, 30, 291–302.

Humphreys, G.W. and Bruce, V. (1989). *Visual Cognition: Computational, Experimental and Neuropsychological Perspectives*. Hove: LEA.

Humphreys, G.W. and Riddoch, M.J. (1984). Routes to object constancy: Implications for neurological impairments of object constancy. *Quarterly Journal of Experimental Psychology*, 36A, 385–415.

Humphreys, G.W. and Riddoch, M.J. (1985). Author's correction to 'Routes to object constancy'. *Quarterly Journal of Experimental Psychology*, 37A, 493–495.

Humphreys, G.W. and Riddoch, M.J. (1987). *To See but not to See: A Case study of Visual Agnosia*. Hove: LEA.

Humphreys, G.W. Riddoch, M.J. and Quinlan, P.T. (1985). Interactive processes in perceptual organisation: Evidence from visual agnosia. In M.I. Posner and O.S.M. Martin (eds.) *Attention and Performance XI*. Hillsdale, NJ: LEA.

Hunkin, N.M. Parkin, A.J. and Longmore, B.E. (1994). Aetiological variation in the amnesic syndrome: Comparisons using the temporal list discrimination task. *Neuropsychologia*, 32, 819–826.

Hunt, R.R. and McDaniel, M.A. (1993). The enigma of organisation and distinctiveness. *Journal of Memory and Language*, 32, 421–445.

Huppert, F.A. and Piercy, M. (1976) Recognition memory in amnesic patients: Effect of temporal context and familiarity of material. *Cortex*, 4, 3–20.

Huppert, F.A. and Piercy, M. (1978). The role of trace strength in recency and frequency judgements by amnesic and control subjects. *Quarterly Journal of Experimental Psychology*, 30, 346–354.

Hyde, T.S. and Jenkins, J.J. (1973) Recall for words as a function of semantic, graphic, and syntactic orienting tasks. *Journal of Verbal Learning and Verbal Behaviour*, 12, 471–480.

Jacobsen, C.F. Wolfe, J.B. and Jackson, T.A. (1935). An experimental analysis of the functions of the frontal association areas in primates. *Journal of Nervous and Mental Disease*, 82, 1–14.

Jacoby, L.L. (1991). A process dissociation framework: Separating automatic from intentional uses of memory. *Journal of Memory and Language*, 30, 513–541.

Jacoby, L.L. Toth, J.P. and Yonelinas, A.P. (1993). Separating conscious and unconscious influences of memory: Measuring recollection. *Journal of Experimental Psychology: General*, 122, 139–154.

James, W. (1890). *Principles of Psychology*. New York: Holt.

Jankowiak, J. and Albert, M.L. (1994) Lesion localization in visual agnosia. In A. Kertesz. (ed.) *Localization and Neuroimaging in Neuropsychology*. London: Academic Press.

Jankowiak, J. Kinsbourne, M. Shalev, R. and Bachman, D. (1992). Preserved visual imagery and categorization in a case of associative visual agnosia. *Journal of Cognitive Neuroscience*, 4, 119–131.

Janowsky, J.S. Shimamura, A.P. and Squire, L.R. (1989). Source memory impairment in patients with frontal lobe lesions. *Neuropsychologia*, 27, 1043–1056.

317

Jastrowitz, M. (1888). Beiträge zur Localisation im Grosshirn und über deren praktische Verwertung. *Deutsche Medizinische Wochenschrift*, 14, 81–83, 108–112, 125–128, 151–153, 172–175, 188–192, 209–211.

Jerabek, I. and Standing, L. (1992). Imagined test situations produce contextual memory enhancement. *Perceptual and Motor Skills*, 75, 400.

Joanette, Y. and Brownell, H. (eds) (1990). *Discourse Ability and Brain Damage*. New York: Springer-Verlag.

Johansson, G. (1973). Visual perception of biological motion and a model for its analysis. *Perception and Psychophysics*, 14, 201–211.

Johnson-Laird, P.N. (1983). *Mental Models*. Cambridge, MA: Harvard University Press.

Johnson-Laird, P.N. Byrne, R.M.J. and Schaeken, W. (1992). Propositional reasoning by model. *Psychological Review*, 99, 418–439.

Johnson-Laird, P.N. Legrenzi, P. and Legrenzi, M.S. (1972). Reasoning and a sense of reality. *British Journal of Psychology*, 63, 395–400.

Julesz, B. (1960). Binocular depth perception of computer generated patterns. *Bell System Technical Journal*, 39, 1125–1162.

Juola, J.F. Bowhuis, D.G. Cooper, E.E. and Warner, C.B. (1991). Control of attention around the fovea. *Journal of Experimental Psychology: Human Perception and Performance*, 15, 315–330.

Just, M.A. and Carpenter, P.A. (1980). A theory of reading: From eye fixations to comprehension. *Psychological Review*, 87, 329–354.

Just, M.A. and Carpenter, P.A. (1992). A capacity theory of comprehension: Individual differences in working memory. *Psychological Review*, 99, 122–149.

Kahan, T.L. and Johnson, M.K. (1992). Self effects in memory for person information. *Social Cognition*, 10, 30–50.

Kahneman, D. and Tversky, A. (1972). Subjective probability: A judgement of representativeness. *Cognitive Psychology*, 3, 430–454.

Kahneman, D. and Tversky, A. (1973). On the psychology of prediction. *Psychological Review*, 80, 237–251.

Kanwisher, N. and Driver, J. (1992). Objects, attributes and visual attention: Which, what and where. *Current Directions in Psychological Science*, 1, 26–31.

Kapur, N. Ellison, D. Smith, M. McLellan, D.L. and Burrows, E.H. (1992). Focal retrograde amnesia following bilateral temporal lobe pathology. *Brain*, 115, 73–85.

Karbe, H. Szelies, B. Herholz, K. and Heiss, W.D. (1990). Impairment of language is related to left parieto-temporal glucose metabolism in aphasic stroke patients. *Journal of Neurology*, 2327, 19–23.

Kay, J., Lesser, R. and Coltheart, M. (1992). *Psycholinguistic Assessments of Language Processing in Aphasia*. Hove: Lawrence Erlbaum Associates.

Kean, M.L. (1977). The linguistic interpretation of aphasic syndromes: Agrammatism in Broca's aphasia, an example. *Cognition*, 5, 9–46.

Keane, M.T.G. (1987). On retrieving analogues when solving problems. *Quarterly Journal of Experimental Psychology*, 39A, 29–41.

Keane, M.T.G. (1990). Incremental analogizing: Theory and model. In K.J. Gilhooly, M.T.G. Keane, R.H. Logie and G. Erdos (eds) *Lines of Thinking: Reflections on the Psychology of Thought* (Vol. 1: *Representation, Reasoning, Analogy and Decision Making*). Chichester: John Wiley.

Kemp, R. McManus, C. and Pigott, T. (1990). Sensitivity to the displacement of facial features in negative and inverted images. *Perception*, 19, 531–543.

Kemp, R. Pike, G. White, P. and Musselman, A. (1996). Perception and recognition of normal and negative faces: The role of shape from shading and pigmentation cues. *Perception*, 25, 37–52.

Kertesz, A. (1979) *Aphasia and Associated Disorders*. New York: Grune and Stratton.

Kertesz, A. Lau, W.K. and Polk, M. (1993). The structural determinants of recovery in Wernicke's aphasia. *Brain and Language*, 44, 153–164.

Kim, S.G. Ugurbil, K. and Strick, P.L. (1994). Activation of cerebellar output during cognitive processing. *Science*, 265, 949–951.

Kimball, J. (1973). Seven principles of surface structure parsing in natural language. *Cognition*, 2, 15–47.

Kimberg, D.Y. and Farah, M.J. (1993). A unified account of cognitive impairments following frontal lobe damage: The role of working memory in complex, organized behavior. *Journal of Experimental Psychology: General*. 122, 411–428.

Kintsch, W. (1968). Recognition and free recall of organised lists. *Journal of Experimental Psychology*, 78, 481–487.

Klein, S.B. Loftus, J.B. and Burton, H.A. (1989). Two self-reference effects: The importance of distinguishing between self-descriptive judgements and autobiographical retrieval in self-referent encoding. *Journal of Personality and Social Psychology*, 56, 853–865.

Koffka, K. (1935). *Principles of Gestalt Psychology*. New York: Harcourt Brace.

Kohler, W. (1925). *The Mentality of Apes*. New York: Harcourt Brace.

Kolb, B. and Whishaw, I.Q. (1996). *Fundamentals of Human Neuropsychology* (4th edn). New York: W.H. Freeman.

Kolk, H.H.J. and Van Grunsven, M.J.F. (1985). Agrammatism as a variable phenomenon. *Cognitive Neuropsychology*, 2, 347–384.

Kolk, H.H.J. van Grunsven, M.J.F. and Keyser, A. (1985). On parallelism between production and comprehension in agrammatism. In M.L. Kean (ed.) *Agrammatism*. New York: Academic Press.

Kopelman, M.D. (1989). Remote and autobiographical memory, temporal context memory and frontal atrophy in Korsakoff and Alzheimer patients. *Neuropsychologia*, 27, 437–460.

Kopelman, M.D. Wilson, B.A. and Baddeley, A.D. (1990). *The Autobiographical Memory Interview*. Bury St Edmunds: Thames Valley Test Company.

Korsakoff, S.S. (1887). Troubles de l'activité psychique dans la paralysie alcoolique et leurs rapports avec les troubles de la sphère psychique dans la vérité multiple d'origine non alcoolique. *Vestnik Psychiatrii*, 4, 2.

Kosko, B. (1992). *Neural Networks and Fuzzy Systems*. Princeton, NJ: Prentice Hall.

Kramer, A.F. Tham, M. and Yeh, Y. (1991). Movement and focused attention: A failure to replicate. *Perception and Psychophysics*, 50, 537–546.

Kucera, H. and Francis, W.N. (1967). *Computational Analysis of Present-day American English*. Providence, RI: Brown University Press.

Kuffler, S.W. (1953). Discharge patterns and functional organisation of mammalian retina. *Journal of Neurophysiology*, 16: 37–56.

Kuhn, D. (1991). *The Skills of Argument*. Cambridge: Cambridge University Press.

Kuhn, T. (1970). *The Structure of Scientific Revolutions*. Chicago, IL: Chicago University Press.

Kurucz, J. Feldmar, G. and Werner, W. (1979). Prosopo-affective agnosia associated with chronic organic brain syndrome. *Journal of the American Geriatrics Society*, 27, 91–95.

Laberge, D. (1983). Spatial extent of attention to letters and words. *Journal of Experimental Psychology: Human Perception and Performance*, 9, 371–379.

Laird, J. Newell, A. and Rosenbloom, P. (1987). SOAR: An architecture for general intelligence. *Artificial Intelligence*, 33, 1–64.

Laird, J. Rosenbloom, P. and Newell, A. (1984). Towards chunking as a general learning mechanism. In *Proceedings of the AAAI '84: National Conference on Artificial Intelligence*, Menlo Park, California. American Association for Artificial Intelligence.

Larkin, J.H. McDermott, J. Simon, D. and Simon, H.A. (1980). Expert and novice performance in solving physics problems. *Science*, 208, 1335–1342.

Larrabee, G.J. Levin, H.S. Huff, F.J. Kay, M.C. and Guinto, F.C. (1985) Visual agnosia contrasted with visual-verbal disconnection. *Neuropsychologia*, 23, 1–12.

Lefford, A. (1946). The influence of emotional subject matter on logical reasoning. *Journal of General Psychology*, 34, 127–151.

Levelt, W.J.M. (1989). *Speaking: From Intention to Articulation*. Cambridge, MA: MIT Press.

Levelt, W.J.M. (1992). Accessing words in speech production: Stages, processes and representations. *Cognition*, 42, 1–22.

Levelt, W.J.M. Schriefers, H. Vorberg, D. Meyer, A.S. Pechmann, T. and Havinga, J. (1991). The time course of lexical access in speech production: A study of picture naming. *Psychological Review*, 98, 122–142.

Levin, H.S. Eisenberg, H.M. and Benton, A.L. (eds) (1991). *Frontal Lobe Function and Dysfunction*. Oxford: Oxford University Press.

Levine, D.N. (1978). Prosopagnosia and visual object agnosia: A behavioral study. *Brain and Language*, 5, 341–365.

Lhermitte, F. (1983). 'Utilization behaviour' and its relation to lesions of the frontal lobes. *Brain*, 106, 237–255.

Lichtheim, L. (1885). On aphasia. *Brain*, 7, 433–484.

Linebarger, M.C. and Schwarz, M.F. and Saffran, E.M. (1983). Sensitivity to grammatical structure in so-called agrammatic aphasics. *Cognition*, 13, 361–392.

Linton, M. (1975). Memory for real-world events. In D.A. Norman and D.E. Rumelhart (eds) *Explorations in Cognition*. San Francisco, CA: W.H. Freeman.

Lisman, J.E. and Harris, K.M. (1993). Quantal analysis and synaptic anatomy – integrating two views of hippocampal plasticity. *Trends in Neurosciences*, 16, 141–146.

Lissauer, H. (1890) Ein fall von seelenblinheit nebst einem beitrage zur theorie derselben. *Archiv für Psychiatrie und Nervenkrankheiten*, 21, 222–270.

Liu, H. Bates, E. Powell, T. and Wulfeck, B. (1997). Single-word shadowing and the study of lexical access. *Applied Psycholinguistics*, 18, 157–180.

Lockhart, R.S. and Craik, F.I.M. (1990). Levels of processing: A retrospective commentary on a framework for memory research. *Canadian Journal of Psychology*, 44, 87–112.

Loeb, J. (1902). *Comparative Physiology of the Brain and Comparative Psychology*. New York: Putnam.

Loftus, E.L. and Burns, H.J. (1982). Mental shock can produce retrograde amnesia. *Memory and Cognition*, 10, 318–323.

Loftus, E.L. Levidow, B. and Duensing, S. (1992). Who remembers best? Individual differences in memory for events that occurred in a science museum. *Applied Cognitive Psychology*, 6, 93–107.

Loftus, E.F. and Klinger, M.R. (1992). Is the unconscious smart or dumb? *American Psychologist*, 47,6, 761–765.

Loftus, E.L. and Palmer, J.C. (1974). Reconstruction of automobile destruction: An example of the interaction between language and memory. *Journal of Verbal Learning and Verbal Behaviour*, 13, 585–589.

Loftus, E.L. and Zanni, G. (1975). Eyewitness testimony: The influence of the wording of a question. *Bulletin of the Psychonomic Society*, 5, 866–888.

Logie, R.H. (1986). Visuo-spatial processes in working memory. *Quarterly Journal of Experimental Psychology*, 38A, 229–247.

Logie, R.H. (1995). *Visuo-spatial Working Memory*. Hove: Erlbaum.

Lorayne, H. and Lucas, J. (1974). *The Memory Book*. London: W.H. Allen.

Lowe, G. (1981). State-dependent recall decrements with moderate doses of alcohol. *Current Psychological Research*, 1, 3–8.

Luchins, A.S. (1942). Mechanization in problem solving. *Psychological Monographs*, 54,6, Whole No. 248.

Luria, A.R. (1966). *Higher Cortical Functions in Man*. London: Tavistock.

Lynch, G. (1986). *Synapses, Circuits, and the Beginnings of Memory*. Cambridge, MA: MIT Press.

McCarthy, R.A. and Warrington, E.K. (1987). The double dissociation of short-term memory for lists and sentences. *Brain*, 110, 1545–1563.

McCarthy, R.A. and Warrington, E.K. (1990). *Cognitive Neuropsychology: A Clinical Introduction*. London: Academic Press.

McClelland, J.L. (1979). On the time relations of mental processes: An examination of systems of processes in cascade. *Psychological Review*, 86, 287–330.

McClelland, J.L. and Rumelhart, D.E. (1981). An interactive activation model of context effects in letter perception. Part 1: An account of basic findings. *Psychological Review*, 88, 375–407.

McClelland, J.L. and Rumelhart, D.E. (1986). *Parallel distributed processing: Explorations in the microstructure of cognition* (Vols 1 and 2). Cambridge, MA: MIT Press.

McCloskey, M. Wible, C.G. and Cohen, N.J. (1988). Is there a special flashbulb-memory mechanism? *Journal of Experimental Psychology: General*, 117, 171–181.

McGeoch, J.A. (1932). Forgetting and the law of disuse. *Psychological Review*, 39, 352–370.

McGurk, H. and MacDonald, J. (1976). Hearing lips and seeing voices. *Nature*, 264, 746–748.

McIntyre, J.S. and Craik, F.I.M. (1987). Age differences in memory for item and source information. *Canadian Journal of Psychology*, 41, 175–192.

Mack, A. Tang, B. Tuma, R. Kahn, S. and Rock, I. (1992). Perceptual organisation and attention. *Cognitive Psychology*, 24, 475–501.

McKenna, P. and Warrington E.K. (1980). Testing for nominal dysphasia. *Journal of Neurology, Neurosurgery and Psychiatry*, 43, 781–788.

MacLeod, C.M. (1998). Training on integrated versus separated stroop tasks: The progression of interference and facilitation. *Memory and Cognition*, 26, 201–211.

McLeod, P. Driver, J. Dienes, Z. and Crisp, J. (1991). Filtering by movement in visual search. *Journal of Experimental Psychology: Human Perception and Performance*, 17, 55–64.

Macmillan, M.B. (1986). A wonderful journey through the skull and brains: The travels of Mr Gage's tamping iron. *Brain and Cognition*, 5, 67–107.

McNeil, J.E. Cipolotti, L. and Warrington, E.K. (1994). The accessibility of proper names. *Neuropsychologia*, 32, 193–208.

McNeil, J.E. and Warrington, E.K. (1993). Prosopagnosia: A face-specific disorder. *Quarterly Journal of Experimental Psychology*, 46A, 1–10.

Maier, N.R.F. (1930). Reasoning in humans I: On direction. *Journal of Comparative Psychology*, 10, 115–143.

Maier, N.R.F. (1931). Reasoning in humans II: The solution of a problem and its appearance in consciousness. *Journal of Comparative Psychology*, 12, 181–194.

Mair, W.G.P. Warrington, E.K. and Weiskrantz, L. (1979). Memory disorders in Korsakoff's psychosis: A neuropathological and neuropsychological investigation of two cases. *Brain*, 102, 749–783.

Mandler, G. (1980). Recognising: The judgement of a previous occurrence. *Psychological Review*, 27, 252–271.

Mandler, G. (1989). Memory: Conscious and unconscious. In P.R. Soloman, G.R. Goethals, C.M. Kelley and B.R. Stephens (eds) *Memory: Interdisciplinary Approaches*. New York: Springer-Verlag.

Mandler, G. Pearlstone, Z. and Koopmans, H.S. (1969). Effects of organisation and semantic similarity on a recall and recognition task. *Journal of Verbal Learning and Verbal Behaviour*, 8, 410–423.

Marcel, A.J. (1983). Conscious and unconscious perception: An approach to the relations between phenomenal experience and perceptual processes. *Cognitive Psychology*, 15, 238–300.

Marr, D. (1982). *Vision: A Computational Investigation into the Human Representation and Processing of Visual Information*. San Francisco: W.H. Freeman.

Marshall, J.C. and Halligan, P.W. (1988) Blindsight and insight in visuo-spatial neglect. *Nature*, 336, 766–767.

Marshall, J.C. and Halligan, P.W. (1993) Visuo-spatial neglect: A new copying test to assess perceptual parsing. *Journal of Neurology*, 240, 37–40.

Marshall, J.C. and Newcombe, F. (1973). Patterns of paralexia: A psycholinguistic approach. *Journal of Psycholinguistic Research*, 2, 175–199.

Marslen-Wilson, W. (1973). Linguistic structure and speech shadowing at very short latencies. *Nature*, 244, 522–523.

Marslen-Wilson, W. (1975). Sentence perception as an interactive parallel process. *Science*, 189, 226–228.

Marslen-Wilson, W. (1987). Functional parallelism in spoken word recognition. *Cognition*, 25, 71–102.

Marslen-Wilson, W. (ed.) (1989). *Lexical Representation and Process*. Cambridge, MA: MIT Press.

Marslen-Wilson, W.D. and Teuber, H.L. (1975). Memory for remote events in anterograde amnesia: Recognition of public figures from news photographs. *Neuropsychologia*, 13, 353–364.

Marslen-Wilson, W. and Tyler, L. (1980). The temporal structure of spoken language understanding. *Cognition*, 8, 1–71.

Martin, A. Wiggs, C.L. Ungerleider, G. and Haxby, J.V. (1996). Neural correlates of category specific knowledge. *Nature*, 379, 649–652.

Martin, G.N. (1998). *Human Neuropsychology*. New York: Prentice Hall.

Mehler, J. (1963). Some effects of grammatical transformations on the recall of English sentences. *Journal of Verbal Learning and Verbal Behavior*, 2, 346–351.

Memon, A. Wark, L. Bull, R. and Koehnken, G. (1997). Isolating the effects of the cognitive interview techniques. *British Journal of Psychology*, 88, 179–197.

Mendez, M.F. (1988). Visuoperceptual function in visual agnosia. *Neurology*, 38, 1754–1759.

Mendez, M.F. Tomsak, R.L. and Remler, B. (1990) Disorders of the visual system in Alzheimer's disease. *Journal of Clinical Neuro-Ophthalmology*, 10, 62–69.

Metter, E.J. (1995). PET in aphasia and language. In H.S. Kirsner (ed.) *Handbook of Neurological Speech and Language Disorders: Neurological Disease and Therapy* (Vol. 33). New York: Marcel Dekker.

Metter, E.J. Hanson, W.R. Jackson, C.A. Kempler, D. Van Lancker, D. Mazziotta, J.C. and Phelps, M.E. (1990). Temporoparietal cortex in aphasia: Evidence from positron emission tomography. *Archives of Neurology*, 47, 1235–1238.

Meyer, D.E. and Schvaneveldt, R.W. (1971). Facilitation in recognising pairs of words: Evidence of a dependence between retrieval operations. *Journal of Experimental Psychology*, 90, 227–234.

Miller, E. (1977). *Abnormal Ageing: The Psychology of Senile and Presenile Dementia*. Chichester: Wiley.

Miller, G.A. (1956). The magic number seven, plus or minus two: Some limits on our capacity for processing information. *Psychological Review*, 63, 81–93.

Miller, G.A. and McKean, K.E. (1964). A chronometric study of some relations between sentences. *Quarterly Journal of Experimental Psychology*, 16, 297–308.

Miller, L.A. and Tippett, L.J. (1996). Effects of focal brain lesions on visual problem-solving. *Neuropsychologia*, 34, 387–398.

Milner, B. (1964). Some effects of frontal lobectomy in man. In J.M. Warren and K. Akert (eds) *The Frontal Granular Cortex and Behavior*. New York: McGraw-Hill.

Milner, B. (1966). Amnesia following operation on the temporal lobes. In C.W.M. Whitty and O.L. Zangwill (eds) *Amnesia*. London: Butterworth.

Milner, B. Corkin, S. and Teuber, H.L. (1968). Further analysis of hippocampal amnesia – 14-year follow-up of H.M. *Neuropsychologia*, 6, 215–234.

Milner, B. Corsi, P. and Leonard, G. (1991). Frontal-lobe contribution to recency judgements. *Neuropsychologia*, 29, 601–618.

Minsky, M. (1975). A framework for representing knowledge. In P. Winston (ed.) *The Psychology of Computer Vision*. New York: McGraw-Hill.

Minsky, M. and Papert, S. (1969). *Perceptrons*. Cambridge, MA: MIT Press.

Mitchell, D. (1994). Sentence parsing. In M.A. Gernsbacher (ed.) *Handbook of Psycho-linguistics*. London: Academic Press.

Mohr, J.P. Pessin, M.S. Finkelstein, S. Funkenstein, H.H. Duncan, G.W. and Davis, K.R. (1978). Broca's aphasia: Pathologic and clinical. *Neurology*, 28, 311–324.

Moray, N. (1959). *Attention: Selective Processes in Vision and Hearing*. London: Hutchinson.

Morris, C.D. Bransford, J.D. and Franks, J.J. (1977). Levels of processing versus transfer appropriate processing. *Journal of Verbal Learning and Verbal Behaviour*, 16, 519–533.

Morris, J.S. Frith, C.D. Perrett, D.I. Rowland, D. Young, A.W. Calder, A.J. and Dolan, R.J. (1996). A differential neural response in the human amygdala to fearful and happy facial expressions. *Nature*, 383, 821–815.

Morris, P.E. Gruneberg, M.M. Sykes, R.M. and Merrick, A. (1981). Football knowledge and the acquisition of new results. *British Journal of Psychology*, 72, 479–484.

Morris, R.G. Ahmed, S. Syed, G.M. and Toone, B.K. (1993). Neural correlates of planning ability: Frontal lobe activation during the Tower of London test. *Neuropsychologia*, 31, 1367–1378.

Morton, J. (1969). The interaction of information in word recognition. *Psychological Review*, 76, 165–178.

Morton, J. (1970). A functional model of memory. In D.A. Norman (ed.) *Models of Human Memory*. New York: Academic Press.

Morton, J. (1979). Word recognition. In J. Morton and J.C. Marshall (eds) *Psycholinguistics (Series 2)*. London: Elek.

Morton, J. (1980). Two auditory parallels to deep dyslexia. In M. Coltheart, K.E. Patterson and J.C. Marshall (eds) *Deep Dyslexia* (2nd edn). London: Routledge.

Morton, J. and Patterson, K.E. (1987). A new attempt at an interpretation, or, an attempt at a new interpretation. In M. Coltheart, K.E. Patterson and J.C. Marshall (eds) *Deep Dyslexia* (2nd edn). London: Routledge.

Moscovitch, M. (1989). Confabulation and the frontal system: Strategic versus associative retrieval in neuropsychological theories of memory. In H.L. Roediger and F.I.M. Craik (eds) *Variety of Memory and Consciousness: Essays in Honour of Endel Tulving*. Hillsdale, NJ: Lawrence Erlbaum Associates.

Munk, H. (1881). *Über die Funktionen der Grosshirnrinde*. Gesammelte Mitteilungen aus den Jahren 1877–1880. Berlin: Hirschwald.

Muter, P. (1980). Very rapid forgetting. *Memory and Cognition*, 8, 174–179.

Muter, P. (1995). Very rapid forgetting: Reply to Cunningham, Healy, Till, Fendrich, and Dimitry. *Memory and Cognition*, 23, 383–386.

Myers, P.S. (1993). Narrative expressive deficits associated with right-hemisphere damage. In H.H. Brownell and Y. Joanette (eds) *Narrative Discourse in Neurologically Impaired and Normal Aging Adults*. San Diego, CA: Singular Publishing.

Naveh-Benjamin, M. (1990). Coding of temporal order information: An automatic process? *Journal of Experimental Psychology: Learning, Memory, and Cognition*, 16, 117–126.

REFERENCES

Navon, D. (1977). Forest before trees: The precedence of global features in visual perception. *Cognitive Psychology*, 9, 353–383.

Neely, J.H. (1977). Semantic priming and retrieval from lexical memory: Roles of inhibition-less spreading activation and limited-capacity attention. *Journal of Experimental Psychology: General*, 106, 226–254.

Neisser, U. (1964). Visual search. *Scientific American*, 210, 94–102.

Neisser, U. (1967). *Cognitive Psychology*. New York: Appleton-Century-Crofts.

Neisser, U. (1976). *Cognition and Reality*. San Francisco, CA: W.H. Freeman.

Neisser, U. (1982). *Memory Observed*. San Francisco, CA: W.H. Freeman.

Neisser, U. and Becklin, P. (1975). Selective looking: Attending to visually superimposed events. *Cognitive Psychology*, 7, 480–494.

Neisser, U. and Harsch, N. (1992). Phantom flashbulbs: False connections of hearing the news about Challenger. In E. Winograd and U. Neisser (eds) *Affect and Accuracy in Recall: Studies of 'Flashbulb' Memories*. New York: Cambridge University Press.

Nelson, H.E. (1976). A modified card sorting test sensitive to frontal lobe defects. *Cortex*, 12, 313–324.

Newell, A. (1990). *Unified Theories of Cognition*. Cambridge, MA: Harvard University Press.

Newell, A. Shaw, J.C. and Simon, H.A. (1958). Elements of a theory of human problem solving. *Psychological Review*, 65, 151–166.

Newell, A. and Simon, H.A. (1972). *Human Problem Solving*. Englewood Cliffs, NJ: Prentice-Hall.

Newell, A. and Simon, H. (1976). Computer science as empirical enquiry: Symbols and search. *Communications of the ACM*, 19, 113–126.

Nickerson, R.S. and Adams, M.J. (1979). Long-term memory for a common object. *Cognitive Psychology*, 11, 287–307.

Nilsson, L.G. and Gardiner, J.M. (1993). Identifying exceptions in a database of recognition failure studies from 1973 to 1992. *Memory and Cognition*, 21, 397–410.

Norman, D.A. (1988). *The Psychology of Everyday Things*. New York: Basic Books, a member of the Perseus Group.

Norman, D.A. and Shallice, T. (1986). Attention to action: Willed and automatic control of behaviour. In R.J. Davidson, G.E. Schwartz and D.E. Shapiro (eds) *Consciousness and Self-regulation* (Vol. 4). New York: Plenum Press.

O'Connor, M. Butters, N. Miliotis, P. Eslinger, P. and Cermak, L.S. (1992). The dissociation of retrograde and anterograde amnesia in a patient with Herpes Encephalitis. *Journal of Clinical and Experimental Neuropsychology*, 14, 159–178.

Oaksford, M. (1997). Thinking and the rational analysis of human reasoning. *The Psychologist*, 10, 257–260.

Ogden, J.A. and Corkin, S. (1991). Memories of H.M. In W.C. Abraham, M.C. Corballis and K.G. White (eds) *Memory Mechanisms: A tribute to G.V. Goddard*. Hillsdale, NJ: Erlbaum.

Ojemann, G.A. (1983). Brain organisation for language from the perspective of electrical stimulation mapping. *Behavioral and Brain Sciences*, 6, 189–230.

Owen, A.M. Downes, J.J. Sahakian, B.J. Polkey, C.E. and Robbins, T.W. (1990). Planning and spatial working memory following frontal lobe lesions in man. *Neuropsychologia*, 28, 1021–1034.

Owen, A.M. Roberts, A.C. Polkey, C.E. Sahakian, B.J. and Robbins, T.W. (1991). Extra-dimension versus intra-dimensional shifting performance following frontal lobe excisions, temporal lobe excisions or amygdalo-hippocampectomy in man. *Neuropsychologia*, 29, 993–1006.

Papagno, C. (1998). Transient retrograde amnesia associated with impaired naming of living categories. *Cortex*, 34, 111–121.

Parker, D. (1982). Learning-logic. Technical Report 581–64, Office of Technology Licensing, Stanford University.

Parkin, A.J. (1983). The relationship between orienting tasks and the structure of memory traces – evidence from false recognition. *British Journal of Psychology*, 74, 61–69.

Parkin, A.J. (1996). *Explorations in Cognitive Neuropsychology*. Oxford: Blackwell.

Parkin, A.J. (1997). *Memory and Amnesia*. Oxford: Blackwell.

Parkin, A.J. Gardiner, J.M. and Rosser, R. (1995). Functional aspects of recollective experience in face recognition. *Consciousness and Cognition*, 4, 387–398.

Parkin, A.J. Leng, N.R.C. and Hunkin, N.M. (1990a). Differential sensitivity to contextual information in diencephalic and temporal lobe amnesia. *Cortex*, 26, 373–380.

Parkin, A.J. Reid, T. and Russo, R. (1990b). On the differential nature of implicit and explicit memory. *Memory and Cognition*, 18, 507–514.

Parkin, A.J. and Walter, B. (1992). Ageing, conscious recollection, and frontal lobe dysfunction. *Psychology and Ageing*, 7, 290–298.

Patterson, K.E. (1982). The relation between reading and phonological coding: Further neuropsychological observations. In A.W. Ellis (ed.) *Normality and Pathology in Cognitive Functions*. London: Academic Press.

Patterson, K.E. and Besner, D. (1984). Is the right hemisphere literate? *Cognitive Neuropsychology*, 1, 315–341.

Payne, D.G. and Wenger, M.J. (1998). *Cognitive Psychology*. Houghton Mifflin.

Pearl, J. (1995). Bayesian networks. In M. Arbib, (ed.) *The Handbook of Brain Theory and Neural Networks* (pp. 149–153). Cambridge, MA: MIT Press.

Perkins, D.N. Farady, M. and Bushey, B. (1991). Everyday reasoning and the roots of intelligence. In J.F. Voss, D.N. Perkins and J.W. Segal (eds) *Informal Reasoning and Education* (pp. 83–105). Hillsdale, NJ: Lawrence Erlbaum Associates; Ann Arbor: University of Michigan Press.

Perret, E. (1974). The left frontal lobe of man and the suppression of habitual responses in verbal categorical behavior. *Neuropsychologica*, 12, 323–330.

Peterson, L.R. and Peterson, M.J. (1959). Short-term retention of individual items. *Journal of Experimental Psychology*, 58, 193–198.

Peterson, S.E. Fox, P.T. Posner, M.I. Mintun, M. and Raichle, M.E. (1988). Positron emission tomographic studies of the cortical anatomy of single-word processing. *Nature*, 331, 585–589.

Piercy, M.F. (1977). Experimental studies of the organic amnesic syndrome. In C.W.M. Whitty and O.L. Zangwill (eds) *Amnesia*. London: Butterworth.

Pinker, S. (1994). *The Language Instinct: The New Science of Language and Mind*. Harmondsworth: Penguin.

Plaut, D.C. McClelland, J. Seidenburg, M. and Patterson, K. (1996). Understanding normal and impaired word reading: computational principles in quasi-regular domains. *Psychological Review*, 103, 56–115.

Plaut, D.C. and Shallice, T. (1993). Deep dyslexia: A case study of connectionist neuropsychology. *Cognitive Neuropsychology*, 10, 377–500.

Poppel, E. Held, R. and Frost, D. (1973). Residual visual function after brain wounds involving the central visual pathways in man. *Nature*, 243, 295–296.

Posner, M.I. (1978). *Chronometric Explorations of Mind*. Hillsdale, NJ: LEA.

Posner, M.I. (1980). Orienting of attention. *Quarterly Journal of Experimental Psychology*, 32, 3–25.

Posner, M.I. and Cohen, Y. (1984). Components of visual orienting. In H. Bouma and D.G. Bouwhuis (eds) *Attention and Performance X*. Hove: LEA.

Posner, M.I. and Petersen, S.E. (1990). The attention system of the human brain. *Annual Review of Neuroscience*, 13, 25–42.

Posner, M.I. Peterson, S.E. Fox, P.T. and Raichle, M.E. (1988). Localization of cognitive operations in the human brain. *Science*, 240, 1627–1632.

Posner, M.I. Rafal, R.D. Choate, L.S. and Vaughan J. (1985). Inhibition of return: Neural bias and function. *Cognitive Neuropsychology*, 2, 211–228.

Posner, M.I. Walker, J.A. Friedrich, F.J. and Rafal, R.D. (1984). Effects of parietal lobe injury on covert orienting of visual attention. *Journal of Neuroscience*, 4, 1863–1874.

Rafal, R.D. and Posner, M.I. (1987). Deficits in human visual spatial attention following thalamic lesions. *Proceedings of the National Academy of Science*, 84, 7349–7353.

Raine, A. Hulme, C. Chadderton, H. and Bailey, P. (1992). Verbal short-term memory span in speech-disordered children: Implications for articulatory coding in short-term memory. *Child Development*, 62, 415–423.

Raj, R. (1988). Foundations and grand challenges of artificial intelligence. *AI Magazine*, 9, 9–21.

Rayner, K. Carlson, M. and Frazier, L. (1983). The interaction of syntax and semantics during sentence processing: Eye movements in the analysis of semantically biased sentences. *Journal of Verbal Learning and Verbal Behavior*, 22, 358–374.

Rayner, K. and Duffy, S.A. (1986). Lexical complexity and fixation times in reading: Effects of word frequency, verb complexity, and lexical ambiguity. *Memory and Cognition*, 14, 191–201.

Rayner, K. and Pollatsek, A. (1989). *The Psychology of Reading*. Hove: Psychology Press.

Reason, J.T. (1979). Actions not as planned: The price of automatisation. In G. Underwood and R. Stevens (eds) *Aspects of Consciousness: Vol. 1. Psychological Issues*. London: Academic Press.

Reeve, D.K. and Aggleton, J.P. (1998). On the specificity of expert knowledge about a soap opera: An everyday story of farming folk. *Applied Cognitive Psychology*, 12, 35–42.

Regard, M. and Landis, T. (1984). Transient global amnesia: Neuropsychological dysfunction during attack and recovery of two 'pure' cases. *Journal of Neurology, Neurosurgery, and Psychiatry*, 47, 668–672.

Reicher, G.M. (1969). Perceptual recognition as a function of meaningfulness of stimulus material. *Journal of Experimental Psychology*, 81, 274–280.

Ribot, T. (1882). *Diseases of Memory*. New York: Appleton.

Richardson-Klavehn, A. and Gardiner, J.M. (1995). Retrieval volition and memorial awareness in stem completion: An empirical analysis. *Psychological Research*, 57, 166–178.

Robbins, T.W. Anderson, E.J. Barker, D.R. Bradley, A.C. Fearnyhough, C. Henson, R. Hudson, S.R. and Baddeley, A.D. (1996). Working memory in chess. *Memory and Cognition*, 24, 83–93.

Robertson, I.H. and Marshall, J.C. (eds) (1993). *Unilateral Neglect: Clinical and Experimental Studies*. Hove: LEA.

Rogers, T.B. Kuiper, N.A. and Kirker, W.S. (1977). Self-reference and the encoding of personal information. *Journal of Personality and Social Psychology*, 35, 677–688.

Rosch, E. and Mervis, C.B. (1975). Family resemblances: Studies in the internal structure of categories. *Cognitive Psychology*, 7, 573–605.

Roy, D.F. (1991). Improving recall by eyewitnesses through the cognitive interview: Practical applications and implications for the police service. *The Psychologist: Bulletin of the British Psychological Society*, 4, 398–400.

Rubin, D.C. Rahhal, T.A. and Poon, L.W. (1998). Things learned in early adulthood are remembered best. *Memory and Cognition*, 26, 3–19.

Rubin, D.C. Wetzler, S.E. and Nebes, R.D. (1986). Autobiographical memory across the life span. In D.C. Rubin (ed.) *Autobiographical Memory*. Cambridge: Cambridge University Press.

Rubin, E. (1915). *Visuell wahrgenommene figuren*. Copenhagen: Gyldendalske.

Rueckert, L. and Grafman, J. (1996). Sustained attention deficits in patients with right frontal lesions. *Neuropsychologia*, 34, 953–963.

Rumelhart, D. (1975). Notes on schema for stories. In D. Bobrow and A. Collins (eds) *Representation and Understanding: Studies in Cognitive Science*. London: Academic Press.

Rumelhart, D. Hinton, G. and Williams, R. (1986a). Learning representations by back-propagating errors. *Nature*, 323, 533–536.

Rumelhart, D. Smolensky, P. McClelland, J. and Hinton, G. (1986b). Schemata and sequential thought processes in PDP models. In *Parallel Distributed Processing* (Vol. 2, pp. 7–57). Cambridge, MA: MIT Press.

Rumelhart, D. and Todd, P. (1993). Learning and connectionist representations. In D. Meyer and S. Kornblum (eds) *Attention and Performance* (Vol. XIV, pp. 3–31). Cambridge, MA: MIT Press.

Rumiati, R.I. Humphreys, G.W. Riddoch, M.J. and Bateman, A. (1994). Visual object agnosia without prosopagnosia or alexia: Evidence for hierarchial theories of visual recognition. *Visual Cognition*, 1, 181–225.

Rumiati, R.I. Humphreys, G.W. Riddoch, J.M. and Bateman, A. (1994). Visual object agnosia without prosopagnosia or alexia: Evidence for hierarchical theories of visual recognition. In V. Bruce and G.W. Humphreys (Eds) *Object and Face Recognition*, special issue of *Visual Cognition*, vol. 1, No. 2/3. Hove UK: LEA.

Russell, W.R. (1971). *The Traumatic Amnesias*. London: Oxford University Press.

Sacco, W.P. and Beck, A.T. (1985). Cognitive therapy of depression. In E.E. Beckham and W.R. Leber (eds) *Handbook of Depression*. Homewood, IL: Dorsey.

Sachs, J.S. (1967). Recognition memory for syntactic and semantic aspects of connected discourse. *Perception and Psychophysics*, 2, 437–442.

Saffran, E.M. Bogyo, L.C. Schwartz, M.F. and Marin, O.S.M. (1987). Does deep dyslexia reflect right hemisphere reading? In M. Coltheart, K.E. Patterson and J.C. Marshall (eds) *Deep Dyslexia* (2nd edn). London: Routledge & Kegan Paul.

Saffran, E.M. Schwartz, M.F. and Marin, O.S.M. (1980). Evidence from aphasia: Isolating the components of a production model. In B. Butterworth (ed.) *Language Production: Speech and Talk* (Vol. 1). London: Academic Press.

Salmaso, D. and Denes, G. (1982). The frontal lobes on an attention task: A signal detection analysis. *Perceptual and Motor Skills*, 45, 1147–1152.

Salthouse, T.A. (1994). Ageing associations: Influence of speed on adult age differences in associative learning. *Journal of Experimental Psychology: Learning, Memory, and Cognition*, 20, 1486–1503.

Sanders, H.I. and Warrington, E.K. (1971). Memory for remote events in amnesia patients. *Brain*, 94, 661–668.

Savin, H.B. and Perchonock, E. (1965). Grammatical structure and the immediate recall of English sentences. *Journal of Verbal Learning and Verbal Behavior*, 4, 348–353.

Schacter, D.L. (1987). Implicit memory: History and current status. *Journal of Experimental Psychology: Learning, Memory, and Cognition*, 13, 501–518.

Schacter, D.L. Cooper, L.A. and Delaney, S.M. (1990). Implicit memory for unfamiliar objects depends on access to structural descriptions. *Journal of Experimental Psychology: General*, 119, 5–24.

Schacter, D.L. Harbluk, J.L. and McLachlan, D.R. (1984). Retrieval without recollection: An experimental analysis of source amnesia. *Journal of Verbal Learning and Verbal Behaviour*, 23, 593–611.

Schacter, D.L. McGlynn, S.M. Milberg, W.P. and Church, B.A. (1993). Spared priming despite impaired comprehension: Implicit memory in a case of word-meaning deafness. *Neuropsychology*, 7, 107–118.

Schank, R.C. (1982). *Dynamic Memory*. Cambridge: Cambridge University Press.

Schank, R.C. and Abelson, R.P. (1977). *Scripts, Plans, Goals, and Understanding.* Hillsdale, NJ: Lawrence Erlbaum Associates Inc.

Scheerer, M. (1963). Problem solving. *Scientific American*, 208, 118–128.

Schindler, B.A. Ramchandani, D. Matthews, M.K. and Podell, K. (1995). Competency and the frontal lobe. *Psychosomatics*, 36, 400–404.

Schneider, G.E. (1969). Two visual systems. *Science*, 163, 895–902.

Schneider, W. and Shiffrin, R.M. (1977). Controlled and automatic human information processing: 1. Detection, search, and attention. *Psychological Review*, 84, 1–66.

Schwartz, M.F. Saffran, E. and Marin, O. (1980). The word order problem in agrammatism I: Comprehension. *Brain and Language*, 10, 249–262.

Scoville, W.B. and Milner, B. (1957). Loss of recent memory after bilateral hippocampal lesions. *Journal of Neurology, Neurosurgery, and Psychiatry*, 20, 11–21.

Searleman, A. and Herrmann, D. (1994). *Memory from a Broader Perspective.* New York: McGraw-Hill.

Seidenberg, M.S. and McClelland, J.L. (1989). A distributed developmental model of word recognition. *Psychological Review*, 96, 523–568.

Selfridge, O.G. (1959). Pandemonium: A paradigm for learning. In *Mechanisms of Thought Processes.* London: HMSO.

Selfridge, O.G. and Neisser, U. (1960). Pattern recognition by machine. *Scientific American*, 203, 60–68.

Semenza, C. and Sgarmella, T. (1993). Proper names production: A clinical case study of the effects of phonemic cueing. *Memory*, 1, 265–80.

Sergent, J. and Signoret, J.L. (1992) Varieties of functional deficits in prosopagnosia. *Cerebral Cortex*, 2, 375–388.

Shallice, T. (1982). Specific impairments of planning. *Philosophical Transactions of the Royal Society of London*, B298, 199–209.

Shallice, T. (1988). *From Neuropsychology to Mental Structure.* Cambridge: Cambridge University Press.

Shallice, T. and Burgess, P.W. (1991a). Deficits in strategy application following frontal lobe damage in man. *Brain*, 114, 727–741.

Shallice, T. and Burgess, P.W. (1991b). Higher-order cognitive impairments and frontal lobe lesions. In H.S. Levin, H.M. Eisenberg and A.L. Benton (eds) *Frontal Lobe Function and Dysfunction.* Oxford: Oxford University Press.

Shallice, T. Burgess, P.W. Schon, F. and Baxter, D.M. (1989). The origins of utilization behaviour. *Brain*, 112, 1587–1598.

Shallice, T. and Evans, M.E. (1978). The involvement of frontal lobes in cognitive estimation. *Cortex*, 13, 294–303.

Shallice, T. Fletcher, P. Grasby, P. Frackowiak, R.S. and Dolan, R.J. (1994). Brain regions associated with acquisition and retrieval of verbal episodic memory. *Nature*, 368, 633–635.

Shallice, T. and Warrington, E.K. (1980). Single and multiple component central dyslexic syndromes. In M. Coltheart, K.E. Patterson and J.C. Marshall (eds) *Deep Dyslexia.* London: Routledge & Kegan Paul.

Shankweiler, D. and Studdert-Kennedy, M. (1967). Identification of consonants and vowels presented to the left and right ears. *Quarterly Journal of Experimental Psychology*, 19, 59–63.

Shiffrin, R.M. and Schneider, W. (1977). Controlled and automatic human information processing: II. Perceptual learning, automatic attending, and a general theory. *Psychological Review*, 84, 127–190.

Shimamura, A.P. Janowsky, J. and Squire, L.R. (1990). Memory for temporal order of events in patients with frontal lobe lesions and amnesic patients. *Neuropsychologia*, 28, 803–813.

Shimamura, A.P. Jernigan, T.L. and Squire, L.R. (1988). Korsakoff's syndrome: Radiological (CT) findings and neuropsychological correlates. *Journal of Neuroscience*, 8, 4400–4410.

Simon, H.A. (1957). *Models of Man: Social and Rational*. New York: Wiley.

Simon, H.A. and Reed, S.K. (1976). Modelling strategy shifts on a problem solving task. *Cognitive Psychology*, 8, 86–97.

Skinner, B.F. (1938). *The Behaviour of Organisms*. New York: Appleton-Century-Crofts.

Slamecka, N.J. and Graf, P. (1978). The generation effect: Delineation of a phenomenon. *Journal of Experimental Psychology: Human Learning and Memory*, 4, 592–604.

Slamecka, N.J. and McElree, B. (1983). Normal forgetting of verbal lists as a function of their degree of learning. *Journal of Experimental Psychology: Learning, Memory, and Cognition*, 9, 384–397.

Slobin, D. (1966). Grammatical transformations and sentence comprehension in childhood and adulthood. *Journal of Verbal Learning and Verbal Behavior*, 5, 219–227.

Smith, M.L. and Milner, B. (1984). Differential effects of frontal-lobe lesions on cognitive estimation and spatial memory. *Neuropsychologia*, 19, 781–793.

Smith, M.L. and Milner, B. (1988). Estimation of frequency of occurrence of abstract designs after frontal or temporal lobectomy. *Neuropsychologia*, 26, 297–306.

Smith, R.W. and Healy, A.F. (1998). The time-course of the generation effect. *Memory and Cognition*, 26, 135–142.

Smith, S.M. Glenberg, A. and Bjork, R.A. (1978). Environmental context and human memory. *Memory and Cognition*, 6, 342–353.

Smolensky, P. (1988). On the proper treatment of connectionism. *Behavioural and Brain Sciences*, 11, 1–74.

Spar, S.A. Jay, M. Drislane, F.W. and Venna, N. (1991). A historic case of visual agnosia revisited after 40 years. *Brain*, 114, 789–800.

Sperling, G. (1960). The information available in brief visual presentations. *Psychological Monographs*, 74, 1–29.

Sperry, R.W. and Gazzaniga, M.S. (1975). Dichotic testing of partial and complete split-brain subjects. *Neuropsychologia*, 13, 341–346.

Sprengelmeyer, R. Young, A.W. Calder, A.J. Karnat, A. Lange, H.W. Hömberg, V. Perrett, D.I. and Rowland, D. (1996). Loss of disgust: Perception of faces and emotions in Huntington's disease. *Brain*, 119, 1647–1665.

Squire, L.R. and Chace, P.M. (1975). Memory functions six to nine months after electroconvulsive therapy. *Archives of General Psychiatry*, 32, 1557–1564.

Squire, L.R. Cohen, N.J. and Nadel, L. (1984). The medial temporal region and memory consolidation: A new hypothesis. In H. Weingartner and E. Parker (eds) *Memory Consolidation*. Hillsdale, NJ: Erlbaum.

Squire, L.R. and Slater, P.C. (1975). Forgetting in very long-term memory as assessed by an improved questionnaire technique. *Journal of Experimental Psychology*, 104, 50–54.

Squire, L.R. Slater, P.C. and Miller, P.L. (1981). Retrograde amnesia and bilateral electro-convulsive therapy. *Archives of General Psychiatry*, 38, 89–95.

Squire, L.R. Wetzel, C.D. and Slater, P.C. (1979). Memory complaint after electroconvulsive therapy: Assessment with a new self-rating instrument. *Biological Psychiatry*, 14, 791–801.

Starr, A. and Phillips, L. (1970). Verbal and motor memory in the amnestic syndrome. *Neuropsychologia*, 8, 75–88.

Stevenson, R. (1993). *Language, Thought and Representation*. Chichester: John Wiley.

Stewart, F. Parkin, A.J. and Hunkin, N.M. (1992). Naming impairments following recovery from Herpes Simplex Encephalitis: Category specific? *The Quarterly Journal of Experimental Psychology*, 44A, 261–284.

Stroop, J.R. (1935). Studies of interference in serial verbal reactions. *Journal of Experimental Psychology*, 18, 643–662.

Stuss, D.T. and Benson, D.F. (1987). The frontal lobes and control of cognition and memory. In *The Frontal Lobes Revisited* (pp. 141–158). New York: IRBN Press.

Styles, E.A. (1997). *The Psychology of Attention*. Hove: Psychology Press.

Sun, R. and Peterson, T. (1995). A hybrid learning model for reactive sequential decision making. In *Proceedings of IJCAI Workshop on Connectionist-Symbolic Integration*.

Sutherland, N.S. (1973). Object recognition. In E.D. Carterette and M.P. Friedman (eds) *Handbook of Perception Vol. 3: Biology of Perceptual Systems*. London: Academic Press.

Sutherland, S. (1989). *The International Dictionary of Psychology*. London: Macmillan.

Swain, S.A. Polkey, C.E. Bullock, P. and Morris, R.B. (1998). Recognition memory and memory for order in script-based stories following frontal lobe excisions. *Cortex*, 34, 25–45.

Swinney, D. (1979). Lexical access during sentence comprehension: (Re)consideration of context effects. *Journal of Verbal Learning and Verbal Behavior*, 18, 645–712.

Talland, G.A. (1965). *Deranged Memory*. New York: Academic Press.

Taraban, R. and McClelland, J.L. (1988). Constituent attachment and thematic role assignment in sentence processing: Influences of content-based expectations. *Journal of Memory and Language*, 27, 597–632.

Teuber, H.L. (1968) Alteration of perception and memory in man. In L. Weiskrantz (ed.) *Analysis of Behavioural Change*. New York: Harper & Row.

Thomas, J.C. (1974). An analysis of behaviour in the hobbits-orcs problems. *Cognitive Psychology*, 6, 257–269.

Thorndike, E.L. (1898). Animal intelligence: An experimental study of the associative processes in animals. *Psychological Monographs*, 2, No. 8.

Thorndyke, E.L. (1914). *The Psychology of Learning*. New York: Teachers College.

Thorndike, E.L. and Lorge, I. (1944). *The Teacher's Word Book of 30,000 Words*. New York: Teachers College, Columbia University.

Tipper, S.P. and Driver, J. (1988). Negative priming between pictures and words: Evidence for semantic analysis of ignored stimuli. *Memory and Cognition*, 16, 64–70.

Tipper, S.P. Weaver, B. and Houghton, G. (1994). Behavioural goals determine inhibitory mechanisms of selective attention. *Quarterly Journal of Experimental Psychology*, 47(A), 809–840.

Tipper, S.P. Weaver, B. Jerreat, L.M. and Burak, A.L. (1994). Object-based and environment-based inhibition of return of visual attention. *Journal of Experimental Psychology: Human Perception and Performance*, 20(3), 478–499.

Toth, J.P. Reingold, E.M. and Jacoby, L.L. (1995). A response to Graf and Komatsu's critique of the process dissociation procedure: When is caution necessary? *European Journal of Cognitive Psychology*, 7, 113–130.

Treisman, A.M. (1964). Verbal cues, language and meaning in selective attention. *American Journal of Psychology*, 77, 206–219.

Treisman, A.M. (1988). Features and objects: The fourteenth Bartlett Memorial Lecture. *Quarterly Journal of Experimental Psychology*, 40A, 201–237.

Treisman, A.M. (1993). The perception of features and objects. In A.D. Baddeley and L. Weiskrantz (eds) *Attention: Awareness, Selection, and Control*. Oxford: Oxford University Press.

Treisman, A.M. and Geffen, G. (1967). Selective attention: Perception or response? *Quarterly Journal of Experimental Psychology*, 12, 1–18.

Treisman, A.M. and Gelade, G. (1980). A feature integration theory of attention. *Cognitive Psychology*, 12, 97–136.

Treisman, A.M. and Schmidt, H. (1982). Illusory conjunctions in the perception of objects. *Cognitive Psychology*, 14, 107–141.

Trueswell, J.C. Tanenhaus, M. and Garnsey, S. (1994). Semantic influences on parsing: Use of thematic role information on syntactic ambiguity resolution. *Journal of Memory and Language*, 33, 285–318.

Tulving, E. (1972). Episodic and semantic memory. In E. Tulving and W. Donaldson (eds) *The Organisation of Memory*. New York: Academic Press.

Tulving, E. (1976). Ecphoric processes in recall and recognition. In J.Brown (ed.) *Recall and Recognition*. New York: Wiley.

Tulving, E. (1985). How many memory systems are there? *American Psychologist*, 40, 385–398.

Tulving, E. (1987). Multiple memory systems and consciousness. *Human Neurobiology*, 6, 67–80.

Tulving, E. (1989). Memory: Performance, knowledge, and experience. *The European Journal of Cognitive Psychology*, 1, 3–26.

Tulving, E. Hayman, C.A.G. and MacDonald, C.A. (1991). Long-lasting perceptual priming and semantic learning in amnesia: A case experiment. *Journal of Experimental Psychology: Learning, Memory, and Cognition*, 17, 595–617.

Tulving, E. Schacter, D.L. and Stark, H.A. (1982). Priming effects in word fragment completion are independent of recognition memory. *Journal of Experimental Psychology: Learning, Memory, and Cognition*, 17, 595–617.

Tulving, E. and Thomson, D.M. (1973). Encoding specificity and retrieval processes in episodic memory. *Psychological Review*, 80, 352–373.

Turvey, M.T. (1973). On peripheral and central processes in vision: Inferences from information processing analysis of masking with patterned stimuli. *Psychological Review*, 80, 1–52.

Tversky, A. (1977). Features of similarity. *Psychological Review*, 84, 327–352.

Tversky, A. and Kahneman, D. (1973). Availability: A heuristic for judging frequency and probability. *Cognitive Psychology*, 5, 207–232.

Tversky, A. and Kahneman, D. (1980). Causal schemas in judgements under uncertainty. In M. Fishbein (ed.) *Progress in Social Psychology*. Hillsdale, NJ: Erlbaum Inc.

Tversky, A. and Kahneman, D. (1982). Judgements of and by representativeness. In D. Kahneman, P. Slovic and A. Tversky (eds) *Judgement under Uncertainty: Heuristics and Biases* (pp. 84–98). Cambridge: Cambridge University Press.

Underwood, G. (1974). Moray vs. the rest: The effects of extended shadowing practice. *Quarterly Journal of Experimental Psychology*, 67, 73–95.

Underwood, B.J. and Postman, L. (1960). Extra-experimental sources of interference in forgetting. *Psychological Review*, 67, 73–95.

Ungar, G. Galvan, L. and Clark, R.H. (1968). Chemical transfer of learned fear. *Nature*, 217, 1259–1261.

Ungerleider, L. and Mishkin, M. (1982). Two cortical visual systems. In D.J. Ingle, M.A. Goodale and R.J.W. Mansfield (eds) *Analysis of Visual Behaviour*. Cambridge, MA: MIT Press.

Vaidya, C.J. Gabrieli, J.D.E. Keane, M.M. Monti, L.A. (1995). Perceptual and conceptual processes in global amnesia. *Neuropsychology*, 9, 580–591.

Valentine, T. (1988). Upside-down faces: A review of the effect of inversion upon face recognition. *British Journal of Psychology*, 79, 471–491.

Vallar, G. and Baddeley, A.D. (1982). Short-term forgetting and the articulatory loop. *Quarterly Journal of Experimental Psychology*, 34A, 53–60.

Vallar, G. and Baddeley, A.D. (1984) Fractionation of working memory: Neuropsychological evidence for a phonological short-term store. *Journal of Verbal Learning and Verbal Behaviour*, 23, 151–161.

Verfaellie, M. and Roth, H.L. (1995). Knowledge of English vocabulary in amnesia: an examination of premorbidly acquired semantic memory. *Journal of the International Neuropsychology Society*, 5, 443–453.

REFERENCES

Verfaellie, M. and Treadwell, J.R. (1993). Studies of recognition memory in amnesia. *Neuropsychology*, 7, 5–13.

Victor, M. Adams, R.D. and Collings, G.H. (1989). *The Wernicke–Korsakoff Syndrome and Related Neurologic Disorders due to Alcoholism and Malnutrition* (2nd edn). Philadelphia, PA: Davis.

Von Wright, J.M. Anderson, K. and Stenman, U. (1985). Generalisation of conditioned GSRs in dichotic listening. In P.M.A. Rabbitt and S. Dornic (eds) *Attention and Performance V*. London: Academic Press.

Wagenaar, W.A. (1986). My memory: A study of autobiographical memory over six years. *Cognitive Psychology*, 18, 225–252.

Wagenaar, W.A. (1994). The subjective probability of guilt. In G. Wright and P. Ayton (eds) *Subjective Probability* (pp. 529–547). Chichester: John Wiley & Sons Ltd.

Warren, E.W. and Groome, D.H. (1984). Memory test performance under three different waveforms of ECT for depression. *British Journal of Psychiatry*, 144, 370–375.

Warrington, E.K. (1979). Neuropsychological evidence for multiple memory systems. *Brain and Mind: CIBA Foundation Symposium 69*. Amsterdam: Excerpta Medica.

Warrington, E.K. (1982) Neuropsychological studies of object recognition. *Philosophical Transactions of the Royal Society of London Series B*, 298, 15–33.

Warrington, E.K. (1985) Agnosia: The impairment of object recognition. In P.J. Vinken, G.W. Gruyen and H.L. Klawans (eds) *Handbook of Clinical Neurology*. Amsterdam: Elsevier.

Warrington, E.K. (1986) Memory for facts and memory for events. *British Journal of Clinical Psychology*, 25, 1–12.

Warrington, E.K. and McCarthy, R.A. (1983). Category specific access dysphasia. *Brain*, 106, 859–878.

Warrington, E.K. and Shallice, T. (1969). The selective impairment of auditory-visual short-term memory. *Brain*, 92, 885–896.

Warrington, E.K. and Shallice, T. (1984) Category specific semantic impairments. *Brain*, 107, 829–853.

Warrington, E.K. and Taylor, A.M. (1973) Contribution of the right parietal lobe to object recognition. *Cortex*, 9, 152–164.

Warrington, E.K. and Taylor, A.M. (1978) Two categorical stages of object recognition. *Perception*, 7, 695–705.

Warrington, E.K. and Weiskrantz, L. (1968). A new method of testing long-term retention with special reference to amnesic patients. *Nature*, 217, 972–974.

Warrington, E.K. and Weiskrantz, L. (1970). Amnesic syndrome: Consolidation or retrieval? *Nature*, 228, 628–630.

Wason, P.C. (1960). On the failure to eliminate hypotheses in a conceptual task. *Quarterly Journal of Experimental Psychology*, 12, 129–140.

Wason, P.C. (1968). Reasoning about a rule. *Quarterly Journal of Experimental Psychology*, 23, 63–71.

Wason, P.C. and Shapiro, D. (1971). Natural and contrived experience in a reasoning problem. *Quarterly Journal of Experimental Psychology*, 23, 63–71.

Waters, G. and Caplan, D. (1996). The capacity theory of sentence comprehension: Critique of Just and Carpenter (1992). *Psychological Review*, 103, 761–772.

Waters, G. Caplan, D. and Hildebrandt, N. (1991). On the structure of verbal short-term memory and its functional role in sentence comprehension: Evidence from neuropsychology. *Cognitive Neuropsychology*, 9, 81–126.

Watson, J.B. (1913). Psychology as the behaviourist views it. *Psychological Review*, 20, 158–177.

Weeks, D. Freeman, C.P.L. and Kendell, R.E. (1980). ECT: II. Enduring cognitive deficits? *British Journal of Psychiatry*, 137, 26–37.

Weiskrantz, L. (1980) Varieties of residual experience. *Quarterly Journal of Experimental Psychology*, 32, 365–386.

Weiskrantz, L. (1986). *Blindsight: A Case Study and Implications*. Oxford: Oxford University Press.

Weiskrantz, L. Warrington, E.K. Sanders, M.D. and Marshall, J. (1974) Visual capacity of the hemianopic field following a restricted occipital ablation. *Brain*, 97, 709–728.

Welt, L. (1888). Über Charakterveränderungen des Menschen infolge von Läsionen des Stirnhirns. *Deutsche Archiv für Klinische Medizin*, 42, 339–390.

Werbos, P. (1974). *Beyond Regression: New Tools for Prediction and Analysis in the Behavioural Sciences*. Ph.D. thesis, Harvard University, Cambridge, MA.

Wernicke, C. (1874). Der Aphasische Symptomen Komplex. Breslau: Cohn & Weigert. Reprinted in G. Eggert (ed.) *Wernicke's Works on Aphasia: A Source Book and Review*, Vol. 1. The Hague: Mouton, 1977.

Wertheimer, M. (1912). Experimentelle Studien über das Sehen von Bewegung. *Zeitschrift fur Psychologie*, 61, 161–265.

Wertheimer, M. (1923). Untersuchungen zur Lehre von der Gestalt. *Psychologische Forschung*, 4, 301–350.

West, M.J. Coleman, P.D. Flood, D.G. and Troncoso, J.C. (1994). Differences in the pattern of hippocampal neuronal loss in normal ageing and Alzheimer's disease. *The Lancet*, 344, 769–772.

Wheeldon, L.R. and Monsell, S. (1992). The locus of repetition priming of spoken word production. *Quarterly Journal of Experimental Psychology*, 44A, 723–761.

Wheeler, D.D. (1970). Processes in word recognition. *Cognitive Psychology*, 1, 59–85.

White, N. and Cunningham, W.R. (1982). What is the evidence for retrieval problems in the elderly? *Experimental Ageing Research*, 8, 169–171.

Whitney, P. (1998). *The Psychology of Language*. Boston, MA: Houghton Mifflin.

Wickelgren, W.A. (1968). Sparing of short-term memory in an amnesic patient: Implications for strength theory of memory. *Neuropsychologia*, 6, 235–244.

Wilding, J.M. (1994). Pattern perception. In M.W. Eysenck (ed.) *The Blackwell Dictionary of Cognitive Psychology*. Oxford: Blackwell.

Wilkins, A.J. Shallice, T. and McCarthy, R. (1987). Frontal lesions and sustained attention. *Neuropsychologia*, 25, 259–365.

Williams, J.M.G. Watts, F.N. MacLeod, C. and Mathews, A. (1988). *Cognitive Psychology and Emotional Disorders*. New York: Wiley.

Wilson, B.A. Baddeley, A.D. and Kapur, N. (1995). Dense amnesia in a professional musician following herpes simplex virus encephalitis. *Journal of Clinical and Experimental Neuropsychology*, 17, 668–681.

Wilson, B.A. Kazniak, A.W. and Fox, J.H. (1981). Remote memory in senile dementia. *Cortex*, 17, 41–48.

Wilson, B.A. and Wearing, D. (1995). Amnesia in a musician. In R. Campbell and M. Conway (eds) *Broken Memories*. Oxford: Blackwell.

Winner, E. and Gardner, H. (1977). The comprehension of metaphor in brain damaged patients. *Brain*, 100, 717–729.

Winograd, E. (1976) Recognition memory for faces following nine different judgements. *Bulletin of the Psychonomic Society*, 8, 419–421.

Wright, D.B. Gaskell, G. and O'Muircheartaigh, C.A. (1998). Flashbulb memory assumptions: Using national surveys to explore cognitive phenomena. *British Journal of Psychology*, 89, 103–121.

Yamadori, A. and Albert, M.L. (1973). Word category aphasia. *Cortex*, 9, 112–125.

Yin, R.K. (1969) Looking at upside-down faces. *Journal of Experimental Psychology*, 81, 141–145.

Young, A.W. (ed.) (1998). *Face and Mind*. Oxford: Oxford University Press.

Young, A.W. Newcombe, F. de Haan, E.H.F. Small, M. and Hay, D.C. (1993). Face perception after brain injury: Selective impairments affecting identity and expression. *Brain*, 116, 941–959.

Zacher, W. (1901). Über ein Fall von doppelseitigem, symmetrisch gelegenem Erweichungsherd im Stirnhirn und Neuritis optica. *Neurologisches Zentralblatt*, 20, 1074–1083.

Zola, D. (1984). Redundancy and word perception during reading. *Perception and Psychophysics*, 36, 277–284.

Zola-Morgan, S. Squire, L.R. and Amaral, D.G. (1986). Human amnesia and the medial temporal region: Enduring memory impairment following a bilateral lesion limited to field CA1 of the hippocampus. *Journal of Neuroscience*, 6, 2950–2967.

Author index

Subject index